Less managing. More teaching. Greater learning.

 # INSTRUCTORS...

Would you like your **students** to show up for class more **prepared**? *(Let's face it, class is much more fun if everyone is engaged and prepared...)*

Want ready-made application-level **interactive assignments,** student progress reporting, and auto-assignment grading? *(Less time grading means more time teaching...)*

Want an **instant view of student or class performance** relative to learning objectives? *(No more wondering if students understand...)*

Need to **collect data and generate reports** required for administration or accreditation? *(Say goodbye to manually tracking student learning outcomes...)*

Want to **record and post your lectures** for students to view online?

 With **McGraw-Hill's** *Connect*™ *Plus Business Communication,*

INSTRUCTORS GET:

- Interactive Applications – **book-specific interactive assignments** that require students to APPLY what they've learned.

- Simple **assignment management,** allowing you to spend more time teaching.

- **Auto-graded** assignments, quizzes, and tests.

- **Detailed Visual Reporting** where student and section results can be viewed and analyzed.

- Sophisticated **online testing** capability.

- A **filtering and reporting** function that allows you to easily assign and report on materials that are correlated to accreditation standards, learning outcomes, and Bloom's taxonomy.

- An easy-to-use **lecture capture** tool.

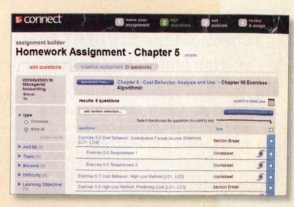

Want an online, searchable version of your textbook?

Wish your textbook could be **available online** while you're doing your assignments?

 ### Connect™ *Plus Business Communication* eBook

If you choose to use *Connect™ Plus Business Communication*, you have an affordable and searchable online version of your book integrated with your other online tools.

Connect™ *Plus Business Communication* eBook offers features like:

- Topic search
- Direct links from assignments
- Adjustable text size
- Jump to page number
- Print by section

 Want to get more value from your textbook purchase?

Think learning business communication should be a bit more **interesting**?

 ### Check out the STUDENT RESOURCES section under the *Connect™* Library tab.

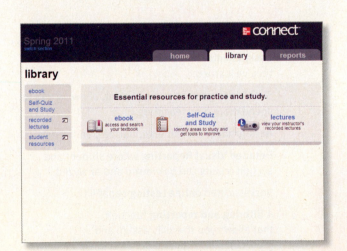

Here you'll find a wealth of resources designed to help you achieve your goals in the course. You'll find things like **quizzes, PowerPoints, and Internet activities** to help you study. Every student has different needs, so explore the STUDENT RESOURCES to find the materials best suited to you.

business communication

Marie Flatley
San Diego State University

Kathryn Rentz
University of Cincinnati

Paula Lentz
University of Wisconsin—Eau Claire

business communication

VICE PRESIDENT AND EDITOR-IN-CHIEF	**BRENT GORDON**
EDITORIAL DIRECTOR	**PAUL DUCHAM**
EXECUTIVE EDITOR	**JOHN WEIMEISTER**
EXECUTIVE DIRECTOR OF DEVELOPMENT	**ANN TORBERT**
DEVELOPMENT EDITOR	**KELLY I. PEKELDER**
EDITORIAL ASSISTANT	**HEATHER DARR**
VICE PRESIDENT AND DIRECTOR OF MARKETING	**ROBIN J. ZWETTLER**
MARKETING DIRECTOR	**AMEE MOSLEY**
MARKETING MANAGER	**DONIELLE XU**
VICE PRESIDENT OF EDITING, DESIGN, AND PRODUCTION	**SESHA BOLISETTY**
LEAD PROJECT MANAGER	**CHRISTINE A. VAUGHAN**
SENIOR BUYER	**CAROL A. BIELSKI**
SENIOR DESIGNER	**MARY KAZAK SANDER**
PHOTO RESEARCH COORDINATOR	**JOANNE MENNEMEIER**
PHOTO RESEARCHER	**POYEE OSTER**
SENIOR MEDIA PROJECT MANAGER	**GREG BATES**
MEDIA PROJECT MANAGER	**CATHY L. TEPPER**
COVER IMAGE	**© PAUL CHINN/SAN FRANCISCO CHRONICLE/CORBIS**
BACK COVER IMAGE	**© JOHN CUMMING/GETTY**
TYPEFACE	**10/12 MINION PRO REGULAR**
COMPOSITOR	**MPS LIMITED, A MACMILLAN COMPANY**
PRINTER	**QUAD/GRAPHICS**

M: BUSINESS COMMUNICATION, SECOND EDITION

Published by McGraw-Hill, a business unit of The McGraw-Hill Companies, Inc., 1221 Avenue of the Americas, New York, NY 10020.
Copyright © 2012 by The McGraw-Hill Companies, Inc. All rights reserved. Previous editions © 2010 No part of this publication may be reproduced or distributed in any form or by any means, or stored in a database or retrieval system, without the prior written consent of The McGraw-Hill Companies, Inc., including, but not limited to, in any network or other electronic storage or transmission, or broadcast for distance learning.

Some ancillaries, including electronic and print components, may not be available to customers outside the United States.
Printed in the United States of America.
4 5 6 7 8 9 0 QVS/QVS 1 0 9 8 7 6 5 4 3

ISBN 978-0-07-340316-8
MHID 0-07-340316-4

All credits appearing on page or at the end of the book are considered to be an extension of the copyright page.

Library of Congress Control Number: 2010938655

www.mhhe.com

brief contents

contents

part three   Writing Effective Messages 94

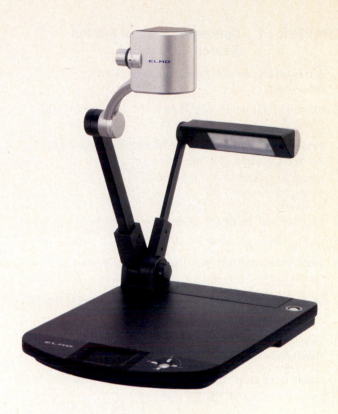

supplementary chapters (online)

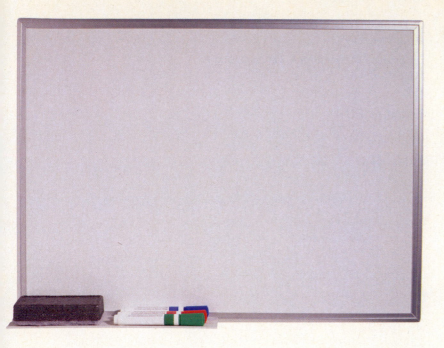

business
communication

communicating in
the workplace

chapter one

Norm Fjeldheim, Senior Vice President and CIO of Qualcomm, credits much of the success in his career to learning and developing his business writing and reporting skills. As an executive in a leading company in the digital wireless communications industry, he relies heavily on these well-honed skills.

When asked about the most important class to take, he definitively answers "Business Communication." He says, "Even if you have great technical skills, your career will get stalled without good communication skills. In fact, the better your communication skills, the further you will go. While technology changes over time, being able to communicate well will always be valuable."

This chapter will explain why communication skills are critical and introduce you to business communication in the 21st century. ■

LEARNING OBJECTIVES

LO1 Explain the importance of communication to you and to business.

LO2 Describe the main challenges facing business communicators today.

LO3 Describe the three main categories of business communication.

LO4 Describe the formal and informal communication networks of the business organization.

LO5 Describe factors that affect the types and amount of communicating that a business does.

LO6 Explain why business communication is a form of problem solving.

LO7 Describe the contexts for each act of business communication.

LO8 Describe the business communication process.

THE ROLE OF COMMUNICATION IN BUSINESS

Your work in business will involve communication—a lot of it—because communication is an essential part of the work of business.

LO 1 Explain the importance of communication to you and to business.

The Importance of Communication Skills to You

Because communication is so important in business, businesses want and need people with good communication skills. Evidence of the importance of communication in business is even the college trained, do not communicate well. Accounting recruiters, for example, have complained about graduates' "weak writing and speaking skills."[5] Surveys show that, in the opinion of their employees, even managers and executives who think they communicate well actually fall short.[6] Effective communicators are, therefore, in high demand. In fact, if you search for "communication skills" in the U.S. government's *Occupational Outlook Handbook* (<www.bls.gov/OCO/>), virtually every type of professional job will come up on the results list.

The communication shortcomings of employees and the importance of communication in business explain why you should work to improve your communication skills. Whatever position you have in business, your performance will be judged largely on the basis of your communication ability. And that ability will be on display in today's media-rich business environment. A study by Office Team revealed that technology magnifies the exposure of one's communications

> " Your work in business will involve communication—a lot of it—because communication is a major and essential part of the work of business. "

found in numerous surveys of executives, recruiters, and academics. Without exception, communication (especially written communication) ranks at or near the top of the business skills needed for success.

For example, NFI Research, a private organization that regularly surveys over 2,000 executives and senior managers, found that 94 percent of the members "rank 'communicating well' as the most important skill for them to succeed today and tomorrow."[1] This skill is needed for entry-level jobs, too. The companies included in *BusinessWeek*'s 2009 list of "best places to launch a career" cited communication skills as the "most desirable trait" in a job candidate—more desirable than any other trait besides "college major."[2] Employers surveyed for the National Association of Colleges and Employers' *Job Outlook 2009* also cited communication skills and the related traits of "a strong work ethic, ability to work in a team, and initiative" as highly prized qualities in job applicants.[3] Recruiters who participated in *The Wall Street Journal*'s latest ranking of MBA programs agreed. They rated "interpersonal and communication skills, a teamwork orientation, personal ethics and integrity, analytical and problem-solving abilities, and a strong work ethic" as most important.[4]

Unfortunately, business's need for employees with good communication skills is all too often not fulfilled. Many employees,

skills. Email often results in a sender's writing ability being displayed to many placed in front of different people simultaneously, while audio and video will reveal the caliber of one's communication strengths as well.[7]

If you perform and communicate well, you are likely to be rewarded with advancement. And the higher you advance, the more you will need your communication ability. The evidence is clear: Improving your communication skills improves your chances for success in business.

Why Business Depends upon Communication

Every business, even a one-person business, is actually an economic and social system. To produce and sell goods and services, any business must coordinate the activities of many groups of people: employees, suppliers, customers, legal advisors, community representatives, government agencies that might be involved, and others. These connections are achieved through communication.

Consider, for example, the communications of a pharmaceutical manufacturer. Throughout the company, employees send and receive information about all aspects of the company's business, from sales to business strategy to manufacturing.

Communication is the most-used skill in almost every job. How you communicate your accomplishments to others is a reflection of the quality of your work. Sure, you must know how to do your tasks to accomplish great results, but that is only a portion of professional success. Good communication skills are required to report your results to others, persuade colleagues to take action, and (most importantly at review time) sell your successes to management.

Don Zatyko, Lead Project Manager
Kaiser Permanente

Communication is essential to building trust and teamwork among employees. To become a successful leader, you must have a great team. Just look at Michelangelo. He didn't paint the Sistine Chapel by himself, but with the help of his team. It is considered one of the best works in history. It's all about the team.

Mark Federighi,
Director of Retail—Northern California
Pepsi Bottling Group

Your message will get lost if it's not clear, concise, and high impact! Get to the point quickly, let the recipient know exactly what you want, and use attention-grabbing techniques whenever possible.

Amy Betterton, Director of Information Technology
San Diego Hospice and Palliative Care

Communicating is key to any successful relationship, both professional and personal.

Without proper communication skills, it is difficult not only to meet your goals but also to explain your progress on meeting them. In my experience, those who are the most successful at any level are those who can articulate well and communicate effectively.

Katie McPhee, Marketing Manager
Intuit Inc.

The ability to communicate effectively in today's business environment is essential across all industries and is required through a diverse number of communication channels. Ultimately, it is the sole distinguishing characteristic in the formation of professional perceptions.

David M. Seaton, Managing Broker
Realty Consulting Group

They process information with computers, write messages, complete forms, give and receive orders, talk over the phone, and meet face to face.

Salespeople receive instructions and information from the home office and submit orders and regular reports of their contact with customers. Executives use written and oral messages to conduct business with customers and other specialists receive or propose problems to investigate, make detailed records of their research, monitor lab operations for compliance with government regulations, and communicate their findings to management. Public relations professionals use various media to maintain the public's trust. Numerous communication-related activities occur in every other niche of the company as well: finance and accounting, human

Whatever your position in business, your performance will be judged largely on the basis of your communication ability.

companies, manage company operations, and perform strategic planning. Production supervisors receive work orders, issue instructions, receive status reports, and submit production summaries. Shop floor supervisors deliver orders to the employees on the production line, communicate and enforce guidelines for safety and efficiency, troubleshoot problems that arise, and bring any concerns or suggestions to management. Marketing professionals gather market information, propose new directions for company production and sales efforts, coordinate with the research and development staff, and receive direction from the company's executives. Research resources, legal, information systems, and others. Everywhere workers receive and send information as they conduct their work, and they may be doing so across or between continents as well as between buildings or offices.

Oral communication is a major part of this information flow. So, too, are various types of forms and records, as well as the storage and retrieval facilities provided by computers. Yet another major part consists of various forms of written communication—instant messaging, text messaging, online postings and comments, email, letters, and reports.

> ## WHAT KINDS OF ABILITIES DOES KNOWLEDGE WORK REQUIRE? "ABSTRACT REASONING, PROBLEM-SOLVING, COMMUNICATION, AND COLLABORATION."

All of this communicating goes on in business because communication is essential to the organized effort involved in business. Simply put, communication enables human beings to work together.

LO 2 Describe the main challenges facing business communicators today.

Current Challenges for Business Communicators

While communication has always been central to business, the nature of work in the 21st century presents particular communication challenges. A recent study prepared for the U.S. Department of Labor by the RAND Corporation, a nonprofit research group, discusses trends that are likely to have a huge impact on your communication practices and purposes.[8] Here we highlight three of them.

the ongoing development of new information technologies
You have probably heard that we live in "the information age." What does this mean exactly, and how might it affect your future work? According to sociologists and business experts, it means that information has become the hottest commodity there is. Those who can generate, harness, and share information the most quickly and effectively are those who will create the most profitable innovations (think Amazon and Google), tap the best markets, provide the best service, and take advantage of the next great opportunity.

Information technologies—from microchips, nanotechnologies, and the Internet to software, personal computers, and hand-held communication devices—are fueling this competition. And as more means of acquiring, storing, retrieving, transmitting, and using information develop, people's jobs become increasingly information related. To use the term coined by renowned management thinker Peter Drucker, "knowledge workers" are the employees who are now most in demand. What kinds of abilities does knowledge work require? According to the RAND study, the answer is "strong nonroutine cognitive skills, such as abstract reasoning, problem-solving, communication, and collaboration."[9]

As Exhibit 1.1 says, you will also need several kinds of literacy to do knowledge work. Of course you will need *verbal literacy*—the ability to use words to get things done. But you will also

need *information literacy*—the ability to find, evaluate, select, and use information. You will need *technological literacy*—the ability to learn and use computer applications, as well as to understand their strengths and limitations. And frequently you will need *visual literacy*—the ability to interpret and assess visuals and to create visual components for your messages that convey information meaningfully, accurately, and efficiently. There has never been a more demanding—or exciting—time for business communication.

the increasingly global nature of business
With the information revolution has come rapid globalization. E-commerce, communication technologies, and the expansion of business-based economies throughout the world have forged new connections among countries. A purchase at a U.S. store, for example, can trigger an electronic message to a supplier in China who is meeting the demand for that product. The outsourcing of core business functions, such as manufacturing and customer service, to other countries is on the rise, and customers can come from all over the world. No doubt about it—working with those from other cultures is likely to be in your future.

For this reason, you will need to be keenly aware that your assumptions about business and communication are not shared by everyone everywhere. Businesspeople from other countries may have distinctly different attitudes about *punctuality* and *efficiency*. They can also differ from you in their preference—or lack thereof—for *directness* and the *show of emotion*. And, of course, the core features of their culture, such as their preference for *individualism* or *collectivism*, their *religious beliefs*, their *political environment*, their ideas about *social hierarchy*, and their *attitudes toward work itself* can make their view of how to do business quite different from yours.

▼ **EXHIBIT 1.1** The Types of Literacy Needed for the 21st Century

According to educators, librarians, and businesspeople, today's students need to develop

- Verbal literacy
- Information literacy
- Technological literacy
- Visual literacy

Communication in brief

The Benefits of Cross-Cultural Diversity

Ratna Omidvar, president of a Toronto-based firm that accelerates the settlement of immigrants in Canada, recently commented on today's "increasing globalization and the worldwide movement of people with skills and talent." Her job is to help immigrants and companies benefit from these trends.

Can a business case be made for diversity? She says "yes."

Research has shown that a diverse group of people from different parts of the world with different life experiences create prosperous organizations.

That said, we know that friction between ethnic groups can be very strong and possibly carry over into the workplace. Where there is potential for intercultural conflict, it can be mitigated by diversity training, as well as by clear communication from leadership that the company will be more innovative, creative—and ultimately successful—when diverse teams work together.

Source: "Diversity: Thinking Globally, Recruiting Locally," with Dave Michaels, *globeandmail.com*, CTVglobemedia Publishing Inc., 20 May 2009, Web, 3 Mar. 2010.

▼ **EXHIBIT 1.2** The Different Goals of Different Generations

Authors Lynne C. Lancaster and David Stillman propose that the different generations now working together in the United States have the following different motivational goals:

Traditionalists: "The satisfaction of a job well done."

Baby Boomers: "Money, title, recognition, the corner office."

Generation Xers: "Freedom is the ultimate reward."

Millenials: "Work that has meaning for me."

Source: Lynne C. Lancaster and David Stillman, *When Generations Collide: Who They Are. Why They Clash. How to Solve the Generational Puzzle at Work* (New York: HarperCollins, 2002) 77, print.

growing diversity in the workplace and in types of workplaces An awareness of others' preferences and values is crucial not just for cross-cultural communication but also for communication within one's own country and one's own organization. According to the RAND study, we will continue to see more diverse workplaces, with employees of both sexes, various cultures, and all ages (see Exhibit 1.2) working together. The globalization of business, immigration, the aging of the so-called "Baby Boomers," the growing number of women into the workforce, and better access to education are all fueling this trend.

In addition, the 20th century model of the vertical organization is giving way to myriad organizational structures. Because they need to be nimble enough to respond to new information quickly, companies are less hierarchical, with front-line employees having a level of authority and problem-solving responsibility once afforded only to managers. In addition, the breakdown of the old hierarchical model is generating new

> [Because they need to be nimble enough to respond to new information quickly, companies are less hierarchical, with front-line employees having a level of authority and problem-solving responsibility once afforded only to managers.]
>
> —RAND Corporation

On the other hand, global business is possible because businesspeople, from whatever country, generally do share certain goals and values. Your job as a cross-cultural communicator will be to learn about and honor others' cultural orientations in such a way that you and your communication partners can work together for mutual benefit. (For additional concepts and advice, see the online chapter "Cross-Cultural Communication" and the BC Resources links.)

kinds of employment relationships, such as self-employment, contract work, and temporary help. The challenge for the business communicator is to be able to adapt to quickly changing responsibilities and work relationships.

One more widespread trend underway in business will likely affect the goals of the organization you work for. It is an *increased focus on ethics and social responsibility.*

While ethical scandals have plagued businesses throughout history, the Enron and WorldCom scandals of 2002, in which false reports of financial health cheated employees and shareholders alike, seemed to usher in a new era of concern. That concern was well founded: With 2008 came unprecedented discoveries of mismanagement and fraud on the part of some of the United States' largest financial institutions. And accounts of predatory lending, business espionage, and exploitative labor practices continue to shake the public's confidence in business. On a moral level, doing business in a way that harms others is wrong. On a practical level, doing so undermines trust, which is critical to the success of business. The more an organization builds trust among its employees, its shareholders, its business partners, and its community, the better for the business and for economic prosperity overall. A key way to build trust is through respectful, honest communication, backed up by quality goods and services.

Lately, another important dimension of business ethics has developed: corporate social responsibility. The Internet has brought a new transparency to companies' business practices, with negative information traveling quickly and widely. And nongovernmental organizations (NGOs) such as Corporate Watch, Consumer Federation of America, and Greenpeace can exert a powerful influence on public opinion and even on governments. Businesses now operate in an age of social accountability, and their response has been the development of corporate social responsibility (CSR) departments and initiatives. While the business benefits of CSR have been questioned,[10] the public demand for such programs is strong.[11] You may well find that social issues will influence how you do business and communicate in business.

www.corpwatch.org

LO 3 Describe the three main categories of business communication.

Main Categories of Business Communication

As you prepare yourself for all the communicating you will do on the job, it can help to think about business communication as falling into three main categories, as summarized in Exhibit 1.3: internal operational, external operational, and personal.

internal-operational communication All the communication that occurs in conducting work within a business is internal operational. This is the communication among the business's employees that is done to create, implement, and track the success of the business's operating plan. By *operating plan* we mean the procedure that the business has developed to do whatever it was formed to do—for example, to manufacture products, provide a service, or sell goods.

Internal-operational communication takes many forms. It includes the ongoing discussions that senior management undertakes to determine the goals and processes of the business. It includes the orders and instructions that supervisors give employees, as well as oral exchanges among employees about work matters. It includes reports that employees prepare concerning sales, production, inventories, finance, maintenance, and so on. It includes the email messages that employees write in carrying out their assignments and contributing their ideas to the business.

Much of this internal-operational communication is performed on computer networks. Employees send email, use

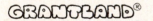

Source: GRANTLAND® Copyright Grantland Enterprises, www.grantland.net

instant-messaging, and post information on company portals, blogs, and wikis for others throughout the business, whether located down the hall, across the street, or around the world. As you will see in later chapters, technology assists the business writer and speaker in many other aspects of communication as well.

external-operational communication

The work-related communicating that a business does with people and groups outside the business is external-operational communication. This is the business's communication with its publics—suppliers, service companies, customers, government agencies, the general public, and others.

External-operational communication includes all of the business's efforts at direct selling: salespeople's "spiels," descriptive brochures, telephone callbacks, follow-up service calls, and the like. It also includes the advertising the business does to generate and retain customers. Radio and television messages, newspaper and magazine advertising, Web advertising, social networking, microblogging, viral videos, product placement, and point-of-purchase display material obviously play a role in the business's plan to achieve its work objective. Also in this category is all that a business does to improve its public relations, whether through planned publicity or formal and informal contacts between company representatives and the outside world. In fact, every act of communication with an external audience can be regarded as a public-relations message, conveying a certain image of the company. For this reason, all such acts should be undertaken with careful attention to both content and tone.

The importance of external-operational communication to a business is obvious. Because the success of a business depends on its ability to satisfy customers' needs, it must communicate

Companies often use portals or intranets, such as this one at John Deere, to communicate with employees.

effectively with those customers. But businesses also depend on one another in the production and distribution of goods and services. Coordinating with contractors, consultants, and suppliers requires skillful communication. In addition, every business must communicate to some extent with a variety of other external parties, such as government agencies and public-interest groups. Some external audiences for today's businesses are illustrated in Exhibit 1.4. Like internal communication, external communication is vital to business success.

▼ **EXHIBIT 1.4** Likely External Audiences for Today's Businesses

Core Business Partners
(suppliers, contract workers, manufacturers, shippers, distributors ...)

Customers
(consumers, business customers, the government ...)

Your company

Public Groups
(community groups, citizen groups, nongovernmental organizations, schools and foundations ...)

Industry Partners
(competitors, similar businesses, lobbyists ...)

Regulatory Agents
(the government, trade alliances, union officials, national and international legal experts ...)

personal communication Not all the communication that occurs in business is operational. In fact, much of it is without apparent purpose as far as the operating plan of the business is concerned. This type of communication is personal. Do not underestimate its importance. Personal communication helps make and sustain the relationships upon which business depends.

Personal communication is the exchange of information and feelings in which we human beings engage whenever we come together. We are social animals. We have a need to communicate, and we will communicate even when we have little or nothing to say. Although not an obvious part of the business's plan of operation, personal communication can have a significant effect on the success of that plan. This effect is a result of the influence that personal communication can have on the attitudes of the employees and those with whom they communicate.

The employees' attitudes toward the business, each other, and their assignments directly affect their productivity. And the nature of conversation in a work situation affects attitudes. In an environment where heated words and flaming tempers are often present, the employees are not likely to give their best efforts to their jobs. Likewise, a workplace that is too rollicking or jovial can undermine business goals. Wise managers cultivate the optimum balance between employees' focus on job-related tasks and their freedom to bring their personal selves to work. They also know that chat around the water cooler or in the break room encourages a team attitude and can often be the medium in which important business issues get discussed.

Even communication that is largely internal-operational will often include personal elements that relieve the tedium of daily routine and enable employees to build personal relationships. Similarly, communication with external parties will naturally include personal remarks at some point. Sometimes you may find yourself writing a wholly personal message to a client, as when he or she has won a major award or experienced a loss of some kind. Other times, you may compose an external-operational message that also includes a brief personal note, perhaps thanking a client for a pleasant lunch or referring to a personal matter that came up in the course of a business meeting. Personal communication on the job is inevitable. When wisely undertaken, it makes business more successful, pleasant, and fulfilling.

LO 4 Describe the formal and informal communication networks of the business organization.

Communication Networks of the Organization

When viewing all the communication in a business (internal, external, and personal), we see an extremely complex system of information flow and human interaction, with dozens,

Organizations actually have two communication networks:
- The formal network
- The informal network

hundreds, or even thousands of individuals engaging in untold numbers of communication events throughout each workday.

As Exhibit 1.5 shows, there are two complex networks of information in virtually any organization—one formal and one informal. Both are critical to the success of the business.

the formal network In simplified form, information pathways in a modern business are much like the network of arteries and veins in the body. Just as the body has blood vessels, a business has major, well-established channels for information exchange. These are the formal channels—the main lines of operational communication. Through these channels flows the bulk of the communication that the business needs to operate. The flow includes the upward, lateral, and downward movement of information in reports, memos, email, and other formats; the downward movement of policies, instructions, advisories, and announcements; and the broad dissemination of company information through the organization's newsletter, bulletin boards, email, intranet, blogs, or wikis. As we have seen, information routinely flows outward as well. Order acknowledgements, invoices, receipts, correspondence with suppliers and consultants, and other standard external-operational communications can make external audiences part of the formal communication network.

These officially sanctioned lines of communication cause certain forms of communication to develop within the organization. For example, it may be customary in one company for project leaders to require a weekly report from team members. Or the executives in another company may hold monthly staff meetings. Whatever the established form, it will bring with it certain expectations about what can and cannot be said, who may and may not say it, and how the messages should be structured and worded. This means that the favored forms, or *genres,* will advance certain practices in the organization and discourage others. It is, therefore, important that the main channels in the formal communication network be carefully thought out and changed as the needs of the business change.

the informal network Operating alongside the formal network is the informal network (see Exhibit 1.6). It comprises the thousands upon thousands of personal communications that may or may not support the formal communication network of a business. Such communications follow no set pattern; they form an ever-changing and infinitely complex structure linking the members of the organization.

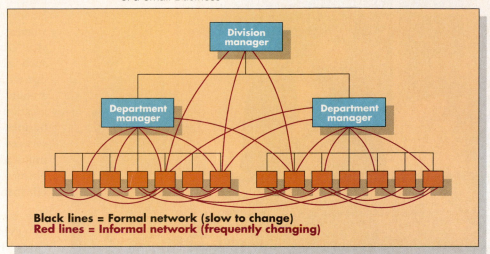

Black lines = Formal network (slow to change)
Red lines = Informal network (frequently changing)

The complexity of this informal network, especially in larger organizations, cannot be overemphasized. Typically, it is really not a single network but a complex relationship of smaller networks consisting of certain groups of people. The relationship is made even more complex by the fact that these people may belong to more than one group and that group memberships and the links between and among groups are continually changing. The department you belong to, the other employees you see in the course of your workday, and even random personal connections, such as having the same home town or having children the same age, can cause links in this network to form.

Internally, the communication network is known as the *grapevine,* and it is more valuable to the company's operations than a first impression might indicate. Certainly, it carries much gossip and rumor. Even so, the grapevine usually carries far more information than the formal communication system, and on many matters it is more effective in determining the course of an organization. Skillful managers recognize the presence of the grapevine,

and they know that the powerful people in this network are often not those at the top of the formal organizational hierarchy. They find out who the talk leaders are and give them the information that will do the most good for the organization. They also make management decisions that will cultivate positive talk.

In large businesses, much of the work done involves internal-operational communication.

Personal communication in business is inevitable and important.

communicate with their customers, especially through letters and mailing pieces, whereas housecleaning service companies have little such need. The business's operating plan affects the amount of internal communication. Relatively simple businesses, such as repair services, require far less communication than complex businesses, such as automobile manufacturers.

The business's relation to its environment also influences its communication practices. Businesses in a comparatively stable environment, such as textile manufacturing or commercial food processing, will tend to depend on established types of formal communication in a set organizational hierarchy. Those in a dynamic environment, such as software development or telecommunications, will tend to improvise more in terms of their communications and company structure.

Employees' personal relations with external audiences add another dimension to a company's informal network. To give just one example, someone who leaves a company will be likely to maintain personal relations with at least a few employees in that company. As with the grapevine, such relations can either help or hurt the company. Here again, wise managers will be sensitive to the informal network and manage in such a way as to encourage talk that is beneficial to the company.

Yet another factor is the geographic dispersion of the operations of a business. Obviously, internal communication in a business with multiple locations differs from that of a one-location business.

How much and what kind of communicating a business does depends on several factors.

LO 5 Describe factors that affect the types and amount of communicating that a business does.

Also, the people who make up a business affect its volume of communication. Every human being is unique in his or her communication needs and abilities. Thus, varying combinations of people will produce varying needs for communication.

Variation in Communication Activity by Business

Just how much and what kind of communicating a business does depends on several factors. The nature of the business is one. For example, insurance companies have a great need to

Each business can also be said to possess a certain organizational *culture*, which has a strong effect upon and is strongly affected by the company's communication. The concept of organizational or corporate culture was popularized in the early 1980s, and it continues to be a central focus of management consultants and theorists.[12] You can think of a given company's culture as its customary, often unexpressed, ways of perceiving and doing things. It is the medium of preferred values and practices in which the company's members do their work.

Recall places you've worked or businesses you've patronized. In some, the employees' demeanor suggests a coherent, healthy culture in which people seem to know what to do and to be happy doing it. At the other extreme are companies where employees exhibit little affiliation with the business and may even be sabotaging it through poor customer service or lack of knowledge about their jobs. The content and quality of the company's communication has a great deal to do with employees' attitudes and behavior.

Take care to note that the official culture and the actual culture in a company are not necessarily the same. Officially, the company management may announce and try to promote a certain culture through formal communications such as mission

LO 6 Explain why business communication is a form of problem solving.

Business Communication as Problem Solving

Virtually every significant communication task you will face will involve analyzing a unique configuration of factors that requires at least a somewhat unique solution. For this reason, it makes sense to think of business communication as a problem-solving activity.

Researchers in many fields—management, medicine, writing, psychology, and others—have studied problem solving. In general, they define *problem* as simply "a gap between where you are now and where you want to be."[13] Within this framework, a problem isn't always something negative;

> ## "Each business can also be said to possess a certain organizational *culture*, which has a strong effect upon and is strongly affected by the company's communication."

statements and mottos. But the actual culture of a company is an organic, living realm of meaning constructed daily through infinite behaviors and communications at all levels of the company. Being sensitive to the assumptions that actually drive people's conduct in your or your client's workplace will help you become a more effective communicator.

THE BUSINESS COMMUNICATION PROCESS

Although we may view the communication of a business as a network of information flow, we must keep in mind that a business organization consists of people and that communication with those inside and outside the organization occurs between people. It is also helpful to bear in mind that, by and large, each act of business communication is designed to achieve particular goals. The following discussion explains our approach to interpersonal business communication and highlights the main steps in tackling business communication problems.

it can also be an opportunity to improve a situation or do things in a better way. As a goal-focused enterprise, business is all about solving problems, and so, therefore, is business communication.

The problem-solving literature divides problems into two main types: well defined and ill defined. The former can be solved by following a formula, such as when you are computing how much money is left in your department's budget. But most real-world problems, including business communication problems, cannot be solved this way. They do not come to us in neat packages with the path to the best solution clearly implied. Instead, they require research, analysis, creativity, and judgment.

One reason why this is the case in business communication is that, as in any communication situation, people are involved—and people are both complex and unique. But the business context itself is often complex, presenting you with multiple options for handling any given situation. For example, if a customer has complained, what will you do about it? Nothing? Apologize? Imply that the customer was at fault? Give a conciliatory discount? Refuse to adjust the bill? Even a "simple" problem like this one requires thinking through the likely short- and long-term effects of several possible solutions.

Solving ill-defined problems involves combining existing resources with innovation and good judgment. Although this book presents basic plans for several common types of business communication messages, you will not be able to solve particular communication problems by just filling in the blanks of these plans. The plans can be thought of as *heuristics*—"rules of thumb" that keep you from reinventing the wheel with each new problem. But the plans do not tell you all you need to do to solve each unique communication problem. You must decide how to adapt each plan to the given situation.

What this means is that successful business communication is both more challenging and more exciting than you may have thought. You will need to draw on your own powers of interpretation and decision making to succeed with your human communication partners.

Of course, people will handle cases somewhat differently depending on who they are, how they interpret the situation, and who they imagine their recipients to be. Does this mean that all communication solutions are equally valid? Not at all. While no one perfect solution exists, many bad ones can result from insufficient analysis and effort. Focused thinking, research, and planning will not guarantee success in the shifting, complex world of human communication, but they will make your chances of success as high as possible. The next section will help you perform this kind of analysis.

A Model of Business Communication

Exhibit 1.7 shows the basic elements of the business communication process. Even though people can, and often do, communicate without forethought, this communication model focuses on what happens when someone deliberately attempts to communicate with someone else to achieve particular business-related goals.

You'll notice that the two communicators in the figure are labeled simply "Communicator 1" and "Communicator 2," instead of "Sender" and "Receiver" or "Communicator" and "Audience." Certainly any communication event begins with someone deciding that communication is needed and initiating that communication, with an intended "receiver" (a popular term in speech communication) or "audience" (the preferred term in composition) on the other end. But in many situations, especially those involving real-time conversation, the two parties work together to reach a mutual understanding. Even in situations where a communicator is attempting to deliver a complete, carefully prepared message—as in an email message, report, or oral presentation—the intended recipients have in a sense already participated in the construction of the message via the memory or imagination of the writer or presenter, who has kept them in mind when composing and designing the message. The labels in this model are thus intended to convey the cooperative effort behind every successful communication event.

LO 7 Describe the contexts for each act of business communication.

the contexts for business communication Certain features of the communication situation are already in place as the communicators in our model begin to communicate.

The *larger context* includes the general business-economic climate; the language, values, and customs in the surrounding culture; and the historical moment in which the communication

▼ **EXHIBIT 1.7** The Business Communication Process

Communicator 1 ...

1. senses a communication need

2. defines the problem

3. searches for possible solutions

4. selects a course of action (message type, contents, style, format, channel)

5. composes the message

6. delivers the message

The Larger Context
Business-Economic, Sociocultural, Historical

Communicator 1's World
Organizational
Professional
Personal

The Communicators' Relationship

Communicator 2's World
Organizational
Professional
Personal

initial message chosen channel

1–6

7-10

chosen channel responding message

Communicator 2 ...

7. receives the message

8. interprets the message

9. decides on a response

10. may send a responding message

is taking place. Think about how these contexts might influence communication. For example, if the country's economy or a particular industry is flourishing, a communicator's message and the recipient's response may well be different from what they would be in an economic slump. The sociocultural context also affects how they communicate. Whether they are communicating in the context of U.S. urban culture, for instance, or the culture of a particular region or another country, or whether they are communicating across cultures, their communication choices will be affected.

communication in the workplace. The skillful communicator is alert to these larger contexts, which always exert an influence and, to some extent, are always changing.

The *relationship of the communicators* also forms an important context for communication. Certainly, communication is about moving information from point A to point B, but it is also about interaction between human beings. Your first contact with someone begins a relationship between the two of you, whether as individuals, people in certain roles, or both. All

> " The *relationship of the communicators* also forms an important context for communication. "

The particular historical context of their communication can also be a factor. Consider two popular themes in business today, "employee engagement" and "work/life balance." These concepts were unheard of before the 1960s and 1970s, when the U.S. government passed legislation to assist female employees, especially working mothers. Since then, many additional domestic and personal issues have surfaced, fueled by increasing caregiver responsibilities, stress from overwork, and exposure to other cultures with shorter work hours. Such issues affect high-level corporate conversations as well as daily acts of

future communication between you will need to take this relationship into account.

The communicators' *particular contexts* exert perhaps the strongest influence on the act of communication. These interrelated contexts can be

- *Organizational contexts.* As we've discussed, the type and culture of the organization you represent will shape your communication choices in many ways, and the organizational contexts of your audiences will, in turn, shape their

TO CREATE A SUCCESSFUL MESSAGE OR PLAN A COMMUNICATION EVENT, YOU NEED TO HAVE A WELL-INFORMED SENSE OF THE SITUATION. "

responses. In fact, in every act of business communication, at least one of the parties involved is likely to be representing an organization. What you communicate and how you do so will be strongly shaped by the organization you represent. In turn, the organization to which your audience belongs—its

Communication in brief

Channel Choice Affects Message Success

"Its [sic] official, you no longer work for JNI Traffic Control and u [sic] have forfided (sic) any arrangements made." Can you imagine getting such a text message? The Sydney employer was sued over this inappropriate choice of a communication channel for firing an employee. In settling the matter the commissioner went further in stating that email, text messages, and even answering machines were inappropriate for official business communication. Or what about being notified by text message of an overdue bill? While some might think of that as a service, others regard it as invasive and inappropriate.

Historically, the importance of channel choice has been disputed, with some arguing that it is simply a means for transmitting words and others arguing that the chosen channel is, in itself, a message. However, today most people realize that the appropriate choice of communication channel contributes significantly, along with the words, to the success of the message.

In selecting a channel, a communicator needs to weigh several factors. Some of these include the message content, the communicators' levels of competency with the channel, the recipient's access to the channel, and the recipient's environment. Appropriate choice of a communication channel helps people improve both their productivity and their personal relationships.

priorities, its current circumstances, even how fast or slow its pace of work—can strongly influence the way your message is received.

- *Professional contexts*. You know from school and experience that different professionals—whether physicians, social workers, managers, accountants, or those involved in other fields—possess different kinds of expertise, speak differently, and tend to focus on different things. What gets communicated and how can be heavily influenced by the communicators' professional roles. Be aware that internal audiences as well as external ones can occupy different professional roles and, therefore, favor different kinds of content and language. Employees in management and engineering, for example, have been demonstrated to have quite different priorities, with the former focusing on financial benefit and the latter on technological achievement.[14] Part of successful communication is being alert to your audiences' different professional contexts.

- *Personal contexts*. Who you are as a person comes from many sources: the genes you inherited, your family and upbringing, your life experiences, your schooling, the many people with whom you've come in contact, the culture in which you were reared. Who you are as a person also, to some extent, depends on your current circumstances. Successes and failures, current relationships, financial ups and downs, the state of your health, your physical environment—all can affect a particular communicative act. Since much business communication is between individuals occupying organizational roles, personal matters are usually not disclosed. But it is important to keep in mind what you do know about the communicators' personal worlds.

LO 8 Describe the business communication process.

---

the process of business communication No one can know exactly what occurs inside the minds of communicators when they undertake to create a message, but researchers generally agree that the process includes the following activities, generally in this order:

1. *Sensing a communication need*. A problem has come to your attention, or you have an idea about how to achieve a certain goal. Perhaps someone has sent an email of complaint and you must answer it, or perhaps you've noticed that the company could benefit from computerizing a certain procedure. Whatever the case, you find that an action is in order, and

> ## "THE GOAL OF BUSINESS COMMUNICATION IS TO CREATE A SHARED UNDERSTANDING OF BUSINESS SITUATIONS THAT WILL ENABLE PEOPLE TO WORK TOGETHER SUCCESSFULLY."

you believe that some form of communication will help you achieve the desired state.

2. *Defining the situation*. To create a successful message or plan a communication event, you need to have a well-informed sense of the situation. For example, if you have received a complaint from a customer, what exactly is the problem here? Does the customer have a legitimate point? What further information might you need to understand the situation? In what ways is this problem like or unlike others you have solved? How might you or your organization's goals be hindered or helped depending on your communication choices?

3. *Considering possible communication strategies*. As your definition of the situation takes shape, you will start considering different options for solving it. What kind of communication event will you initiate, and what will you want to achieve with it? What image of yourself, your company, and your communication partners might you project in your message? To generate a good solution, you will need to think about and research your potential audiences and their contexts, your own goals and contexts, your relationship with each audience, and any relevant larger contexts.

4. *Selecting a course of action*. Considering the situation as you've defined it and looking at your communication options, you will consider the potential costs and benefits of each option and select the optimum one. Your decision will include preliminary choices about the message type, contents, structure, verbal style, and visual format, and about the channel you will use to deliver the message.

5. *Composing the message*. Here is where you craft your written message, carefully working out its contents, structure, verbal style, and visual format, or plan your strategy for orally communicating with your audience. If you have decided to present or initiate your message orally, you will make careful notes or perhaps even write out your whole message or presentation and design any visuals you may need. If you have decided to write your message, you will use your favorite strategies for composing effectively. See the section on "The Process of Writing" in Chapter 2 for the strategies that writing researchers recommend.

6. *Sending the message*. When your message is prepared or carefully planned, you are ready to deliver it to your intended recipients in the channel you have chosen. You choose a good time to deliver it, realizing, for example, that Monday morning may not be the best time to make an important phone call to a busy executive. You also consider sending auxiliary messages, such as a "heads-up" phone call or email, that could increase your main message's chances of success. You want to do all you can to ensure that your message doesn't get lost amid all the other stimuli competing for your intended audience's attention.

While these activities tend to occur in this order, the communicator often needs to revisit earlier steps while moving through the different activities. In other words, solving a communication problem can be a *recursive* process. This is particularly true for situations that invite many different solutions or heavily involve the audience in the communication process. A communicator may begin a communication event with a certain conception of the situation and then discover, upon further analysis or the discovery of additional facts, that this conception needs to be revised in order to take into account all the involved parties and their goals.

If all goes as planned, here is what will happen on the recipient's end:

7. *Receiving the message*. Your chosen channel has delivered your message to each intended recipient, who perceives and decides to read or listen to the message.

8. *Interpreting the message*. Just as you had to interpret the situation that prompted your communication, your recipient now has to interpret the message you sent. This activity will involve not only extracting information from the message but also identifying your communication purpose, forming judgments about you and those you represent, and picking up on cues about the relationship you want to promote between the communicators. If you have anticipated your recipient's particular contexts and interests successfully, you have a good chance of being interpreted correctly. The recipient may prompt the initiating communicator for help with this interpretive act, especially if the communication is a live conversation.

9. *Deciding on a response*. Any time you send a message, your goal is a certain response from your audiences, whether it be increased goodwill, increased knowledge, a specific responding action, or a combination of these. If your message has been carefully adapted to the recipient, its odds of achieving the desired response will be high.

10. *Replying to the message*. The recipient's response to your message will often take the form, at least in part, of replying to your message. When this is the case, the receiver is acting as the initiating communicator, following the process that you followed to generate your message.

Carefully thinking through the elements of each situation will give you the best odds of communicating successfully.

What is the situation?

- What has happened to make you think you need to communicate?
- What background and prior knowledge can you apply to this situation? How is this situation like or unlike others you have encountered?
- What do you need to find out in order to understand every facet of this situation? Where can you get this information?

What are some possible communication strategies?

- To whom might you communicate? Who might be your primary and secondary audiences? What are their different organizational, professional, and personal contexts? What would each care about or want to know? What, if any, is your prior relationship with them?
- What purpose might you want to achieve with each recipient? What are your organizational, professional, and personal contexts?
- What are some communication strategies that might help you achieve your goals?
- How might the larger business-economic, sociocultural, and historical contexts affect the success of different strategies?

Which is the best course of action?

- Which strategies are impractical, incomplete, or potentially dangerous? Why?
- Which of the remaining strategies looks like the optimum one? Why?
- What will be the best message type, contents, structure, style, and format for your message?
- What channel will you use to deliver it?

What is the best way to design the chosen message?

- Given your goals for each recipient, what information should your message include?
- What logical structure (ordering and grouping of information) should you use?
- What kind of style should you use? How formal or informal should you be? What kinds of associations should your language have? What image of yourself and your audience should you try to convey? What kind of relationship with each recipient should your message promote?
- How can you use text formatting, graphics, and/or supporting media to make your message easier to comprehend?
- What are your recipients' expectations for the channel you've chosen?

What is the best way to deliver the message?

- Are there any timing considerations related to delivering your message?
- Should you combine the main message with any other messages?
- How can you best ensure that each intended recipient receives and reads or hears your message?

Exhibit 1.8 lists the main questions to consider when developing a communication strategy. Taking this analytical approach will help you think consciously about each stage of the process and give you the best chance of achieving the desired results with your messages.

BUSINESS COMMUNICATION: THE BOTTOM LINE

The theme of this chapter might be summed up this way: The goal of business communication is to create a shared understanding of business situations that will enable people to work together successfully.

Timely and clear transfer of information is critical to business, now more than ever. But figuring out what kind of information to send, whom to send it to, how to send it, and in what form to send it requires good decision making. Since every person has his or her own unique contexts and mental "filters"—preconceptions, frames of reference, and verbal worlds—wording the information so that it will be understood can be a challenge. You and your audience may even ascribe completely different meanings to the same words (a problem that the communication literature calls "bypassing").

Complicating this picture is the fact that communication is not just about information transfer. The creation and maintenance of positive human relations is also essential to business and thus to business communication. Every act of communication conveys an image of you and of the way you regard those to whom you're speaking or writing. Successful business communicators pay careful attention to the human-relations dimension of their messages.

Yes, business communication can be challenging. It can also be extremely rewarding because of the results you achieve and the relationships you build. The advice, examples, and exercises in this book will jump-start you toward success. But it will be your ability to analyze and solve specific communication problems that will take you the rest of the way there. ■

Get Online

mhhe.com/FlatleyM2e

for study materials including quizzes and Internet resources.

understanding the writing process and
the main forms of business messages

LEARNING OBJECTIVES

LO1 Describe the writing process and effective writing strategies.

LO2 Describe the current usage of the business letter.

LO3 Describe the purpose and forms of memorandums.

LO4 Understand the appropriate use of email.

LO5 Understand the nature and business use of text messaging.

LO6 Understand how instant messaging works.

LO7 Understand the nature and business use of social networking.

Much of this book focuses on writing in business. Is skillful oral communication important? Absolutely. How about skillful use of visuals? It's critical. Then why the extra emphasis on writing?

Experienced businesspeople themselves tend to place writing skills ahead of other communication skills when asked what they seek in job applicants. And they seek strong writing skills in particular when considering whom to promote. For example, in one study, a majority of the 305 executives surveyed commented that fewer than half their job applicants were well-versed enough in "global knowledge, self-direction, and writing skills" to be able to advance in their companies.[1] As people move up, they do more and more knowledge work, and this work often requires expertise in the written forms of communication. ◼

workplace scenario

Managing Your Writing Process and Choosing the Right Form

Place yourself in a hypothetical situation. You are the owner of a struggling small business, and you work very hard to make certain that all aspects of your business function effectively and efficiently. At the moment, your attention is focused on the communicating done by Max Elliott, your new assistant manager. Specifically, you are concerned about the writing skills— or lack of them—that you see displayed in his emails.

Clearly, he doesn't know when and when not to use email as his communication channel. Some of the more formal situations he writes about would be better handled with letter format, while some of the sensitive material he discusses shouldn't be included in his emails at all. Plus, he doesn't think enough before he writes or reviews his emails carefully before sending them. Sometimes an email will start with one point and then end on another, creating an ambiguous message. Sometimes important information is left out. Sometimes texting shortcuts such as *b4* and *ur* are used. And the slang and grammatical problems in his writing create an unprofessional effect.

Max obviously needs instruction on his writing process and on the appropriate use of the main forms of business communication. This chapter provides such instruction.

One reason for our strong focus on writing is that writing is in some ways more difficult to do well than other kinds of communication. Writing is what researchers call a "lean medium," which means that it does not offer the multiple information cues, feedback, and intense personal focus that face-to-face or even phone conversations offer.[2] Writers essentially have no safety net; they can't rely on their facial expressions, body language, or tone of voice to make up for wording that isn't quite what they mean. The symbols on the page or screen must do the whole communication job. Plus, the symbols used in writing— the alphabet, words, punctuation, and so forth—share no characteristics with the thing they represent (unless you count words that sound like the sounds they name, such as "buzz"). Representing something with a photograph is relatively easy.

LO 1 Describe the writing process and effective writing strategies.

THE PROCESS OF WRITING

Writing researchers have been studying the composing process since the 1970s. They have found, not surprisingly, that each person's way of developing a piece of writing for a given situation is unique. On the other hand, they have also drawn some general conclusions about the nature of the process and about strategies that can help it along. Familiarizing yourself with these findings will help make you a more deliberate, effective writer.

> [As people move up, they do more and more knowledge work, and this work often requires expertise in the written forms of communication.]

Representing that same thing in words is much harder. Capturing a complex reality by putting one word after another requires ingenuity, discipline, and the ability to anticipate how readers will be likely to react as they read.

The first major section of this chapter helps you achieve this impressive but commonplace feat in the workplace by showing you how to break the writing process down into parts and skillfully manage each part. The remainder of the chapter introduces you to the main forms of business messages, which bring with them certain features and conventions of use. These discussions provide the foundation for subsequent chapters on writing different kinds of messages.

As Exhibit 2.1 shows, there are essentially three stages in preparing any piece of writing: planning, drafting, and revising. These stages can be defined, roughly, as figuring out what you want to say, saying it, and then saying it better. Each of these stages can be broken down into more specific activities, which the next section describes. As the arrows in the figure suggest, however, it is important not to think of the three stages as strictly chronological or separate. In practice, the stages are interrelated—that is, like the steps described in Chapter 1 for solving business communication problems, they are *recursive*. For example, a writer in the planning stage may start writing pieces of the draft. Or, he or she may find when drafting that

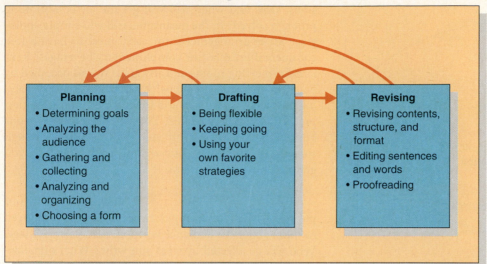

define the problem that you are trying to address. To find a solution, you will need an informed sense of your audiences and their individual contexts—organizational, professional, and personal. You will also need to think about your own organizational, professional, and personal contexts and their possible impact on your communication goal. And you will need to think about the larger contexts in which your act of communication will be taking place, including the context of your relationship with your reader. All these deliberations will help you figure out what you want your message to achieve.

gathering more information is necessary. Or, he or she may decide that it's necessary to revise a piece of the document carefully before continuing with the drafting. An undue emphasis on keeping the stages separate and chronological may hinder the success of your messages. Allow yourself to blend these stages as necessary.

A good rule of thumb for inexperienced writers is to spend roughly a third of their writing time in each of the three stages. A common mistake is to spend too much time on drafting and too little on the other two stages, planning and revising. Preparing to write and improving what you have written are as critical to success as the drafting stage, and careful attention to all three stages can actually make your writing process

Once you have chosen your message's purpose, you'll need to figure out the best way to achieve it. You'll consider the different kinds of content you could include and choose what will best serve your purpose. You will develop a rough idea of how to organize and format that content, decide on the channel you will use, and settle on a general sense of the style you will use. Most people, before drafting, have at least some sense of how they want to handle these elements.

For simplicity's sake, we might group all these planning activities into five categories: determining goals; analyzing your audience; gathering and collecting information; analyzing and organizing the information; and choosing the form, channel, and format it will take (Exhibit 2.2).

> ## "A good rule of thumb for inexperienced writers is to spend roughly a third of their writing time in each of the three stages."

more efficient. When you have become an experienced business writer, you will be able to write many routine messages without as much planning and revising. Even so, some planning and revising will still be essential to getting the best results with your messages.

Planning the Message

The guide for solving business problems presented in Exhibit 1.8 of Chapter 1 is also a good guide for the planning stage of writing. As the questions indicate, you will need to

▼ **EXHIBIT 2.2** The Five Stages of Planning

Planning consists of five general activities:

- Determining goals.
- Analyzing the audience.
- Gathering and collecting information.
- Analyzing and organizing information.
- Choosing the form, channel, and format for the message.

Bear in mind that these are not strictly chronological—you can revisit earlier stages as needed.

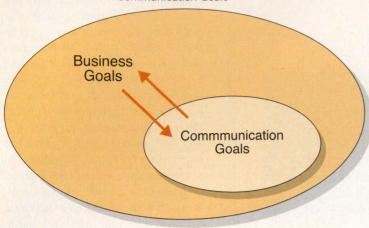

determining goals Because business writing is largely performed in response to a certain situation, one of your main planning tasks is to figure out what you want to do about that situation. Bear in mind that in business communication "what to do" means not only what you want your communication to achieve but also any action related to the larger business problem. For example, if you manage a hotel where the air conditioning has stopped functioning, you will need to decide what, if anything, to communicate to your guests about

this problem. But this decision is related to other decisions. How and when will you get the air conditioning problem solved? In the meantime, will you simply apologize? Make arrangements for each guest to have a free continental breakfast or complimentary beverages? Rent fans for meeting rooms and any guest rooms occupied by people with health problems? As Exhibit 2.3 shows, solving the business problem and solving the communication problem are closely related. You will need to bring your business goals to bear on your writing goals—though sometimes, clarifying your writing goals will help you generate business solutions.

analyzing your audience Once you know your purpose—what you want your message to do—you need to think about the audience who will read your message. Who will be affected by what you write? What organizational, professional, and personal issues or qualities will affect the audience's response to your message? What organizational, professional, and personal issues or qualities do you have that affect how you will write your message? What is your relationship with your reader? Are you writing to your superior? Your colleagues? Your subordinates? Clients? Answers to these questions and others will influence your channel of communication, tone, style, content, organization, and format.

In the hotel manager scenario, for instance, how might your approach in an announcement to guests who are currently at the hotel differ from your approach in a response to a guest's complaint letter a week after the incident? Though you should take time to analyze your audience early in the planning process, you should continue to think of your audience as you proceed through the rest of the planning stage and through the drafting and revising stages, too. Always be thinking about what kind of information will matter most to your audience and adapt your message accordingly. If you fail to meet your audience's needs, your message fails as well, and your professional image is compromised.

gathering and collecting information Gathering and collecting information means doing some research. In many cases this research can be informal—finding past correspondence; consulting with other employees or with outside advisors; getting sales records, warranties, and product descriptions; and so forth. In other cases you will do such formal research as conducting surveys or reviewing the literature on a certain subject. Chapter 8 discusses various methods and sources at your disposal for this kind of research. In general, you will collect any information that can help you decide what to do and what to say in your message.

But collecting information by using your memory, imagination, and creativity is also important. Visualizing your readers and bearing their interests in mind is an excellent planning technique. Making a list of pertinent facts is helpful. Brainstorming, or generating possible solutions without censoring them, will

Communication in brief

Do I Need to Write It?

When you have a substantial message to convey—that is, one not suitable for a quick text or instant message—is it better to write it or speak it? You'll probably want to write it if one or more of the following applies:

- You want a written record of the communication.
- You want the communication to be perceived as at least somewhat formal.
- You think you can explain better in writing, and you don't want the recipient to interrupt you until you're done.
- Your reader will want to be able to go back over what you said.
- You have to reach a lot of people at once with the same message.
- The situation isn't so sensitive that it requires a richer, more personal communication channel.

allow you to come up with creative solutions. Drawing a diagram of your ideas can also enable you to collect your thoughts. Let yourself use any strategy that shows promise of contributing to a solution.

analyzing and organizing information Once you have a good number of ideas, you will start to assess them. If your data are numerical, you will do the calculations that will enable you to see patterns and meaning in the numbers. You will put other kinds of data together as well to see what course of action they might indicate, weighing what the parties involved stand to gain or lose from each possible solution.

As you ponder what to do and say with your message, you will, of course, keep your readers in mind. What kind of information will most matter to them? In the scenario described above, will the hotel guests more likely want information about what caused the air conditioning problem or about when it will be fixed and what they can do to stay comfortable in the meantime? As always, your intended readers are your best guide to what information to include.

prepares the reader to receive the news as positively as possible. As you will see in Chapter 6, such a message usually requires a more skillful use of organization and word choice than one written in direct order. Regardless of the situation, all readers appreciate a logical pattern for the information.

choosing a form, channel, and format Writers in school typically produce writing of two types: essays or research papers. But on the job you have a wide range of established forms of communication (genres) to choose from. Which one you think you will use has a huge impact on your planning. For instance, if you want to advertise your company's services, how will you do it? Write potential customers a letter? Email them? Include a brochure? Create a website? Use some combination of these? Each form has its own formatting and stylistic conventions and even conventions about content. Business writers do not launch into writing a document without some sense of what kind of document it will be. On the job, choosing the type of document to be written is an important part of planning.

> ## [Whatever order will draw the most positive reaction from your readers is the best order to use.]

They are also your guide for organizing the information. Whatever order will draw the most positive reaction from your readers is the best order to use. If you have information that your readers will want, put it first. This plan, called the *direct order,* is discussed in Chapter 5. On the other hand, if you think your information could run the risk of evoking a negative response, you will use an *indirect order,* in which your message's opening

Closely related to genre is the communication channel or medium. How will you deliver your message? Mail it? Send it electronically? Post it to a blog or wiki? Text it? Thinking about the means of transmission will help you decide on form and content.

Because formatting devices have a large impact on readers' reactions, you should also think about them in the planning stage.

What kind and size of type will you use? What kind of headings? Will you use any means of typographical emphasis? How about numbered or bulleted lists? Should the document include such visual elements as logos, textboxes, pictures, or diagrams? Smart decisions on such matters not only increase your readers' motivation to read but also enable them quickly to comprehend the main points of the message (see Exhibit 2.4). Including formatting questions in your planning will help you achieve a reader-friendly result.

Drafting

Writing experts' main advice about drafting boils down to these words: "Be flexible." Writers often hinder themselves by thinking that they have to write a finished document all at once, with the parts in their correct order and in a perfect style. Writing is such a cognitively difficult task that it is better to concentrate only on certain things at a time. The following suggestions can help you draft your messages as painlessly and effectively as possible.

▼ **EXHIBIT 2.4** What a Difference Formatting Makes!

Here is the starting text of a memo (sent by email) from a university registrar to the faculty regarding two new grades about to go into effect. How inviting do you find the format of the following message, and how easy is it to extract the information about the two new grades?

At its October 20, 2011, meeting, the Faculty Senate, having received a favorable recommendation from the Academic Affairs Committee, voted to approve the creation and Autumn Quarter implementation of two new grades: "X" and "WX." Instructors will record an "X" on the final grade roster for students who never attended any classes and did not submit any assigned work. The "X" will appear on the transcript and will carry zero (0.00) quality points, thus computed into the GPA like the grades of "F" and "UW." Instructors will record a "WX" for those students who officially withdrew from the class (as denoted on the grade roster by either EW or W) but who never attended any classes and did not submit any assigned work. The "WX" may be entered to overwrite a "W" appearing on the grade roster. An assignment of "WX" has no impact on the student's GPA. A "W" will appear on the student's online grade report and on the transcript. The "WX" recognizes the student's official withdrawal from the class and only records the fact of nonparticipation. The need to record nonparticipation is defined in "Rationale" below. With the introduction of the "X" and "WX" grades to denote nonparticipation, by definition all other grades can only be awarded to students who had participated in the class in some way. Instructors will record a "UW" (unofficial withdrawal) only for students who cease to attend a class following some participation. Previously, instructors utilized the "UW" both for those students who had never attended classes and for those who had attended and participated initially but had ceased to attend at some point during the term. In cases of official withdrawal, instructors have three options available at the time of grading: "W," "WX," and "F." If the student has officially withdrawn from the class, a "W" (withdrawal) or "EW" (electronic withdrawal) will appear on the grade roster. If the student participated in the class and the withdrawal was in accordance with the instructor's withdrawal policy as communicated by the syllabus, the instructor may retain the student's "W" grade by making no alteration to the grade roster. . . .

Now look at the first part of the actual message that was sent out. What formatting decisions on the part of the writer made this document much more readable?

At its October 20, 2011, meeting, the Faculty Senate, having received a favorable recommendation from the Academic Affairs Committee, voted to approve the creation and Autumn Quarter implementation of two new grades: "X" and "WX."

Definition of "X" and "WX" Grades, Effective Autumn Quarter 2011

- "X" (nonattendance):

  Instructors will record an "X" on the final grade roster for students who never attended any classes and did not submit any assigned work.

  The "X" will appear on the transcript and will carry zero (0.00) quality points, thus computed into the GPA like the grades of "F" and "UW."

- "WX" (official withdrawal, nonattending):

  Instructors will record a "WX" for those students who officially withdrew from the class (as denoted on the grade roster by either EW or W) but who never attended any classes and did not submit any assigned work.

  The "WX" may be entered to overwrite a "W" appearing on the grade roster. An assignment of "WX" has no impact on the student's GPA. A "W" will appear on the student's online grade report and on the transcript. The "WX" recognizes the student's official withdrawal from the class and only records the fact of nonparticipation. The need to record nonparticipation is defined in "Rationale" below.

Participation and Nonparticipation Grades

With the introduction of the "X" and "WX" grades to denote nonparticipation, by definition all other grades can only be awarded to students who had participated in the class in some way.

Instructors will record a "UW" (unofficial withdrawal) only for students who cease to attend a class following some participation. Previously, instructors utilized the "UW" both for those students who had never attended classes and for those who had attended and participated initially but had ceased to attend at some point during the term.

Official Withdrawals

In cases of official withdrawal, instructors have three options available at the time of grading: "W," "WX," and "F."

1. *If the student has officially withdrawn from the class,* a "W" (withdrawal) or "EW" (electronic withdrawal) will appear on the grade roster. If the student participated in the class and the withdrawal was in accordance with the instructor's withdrawal policy as communicated by the syllabus, the instructor may retain the student's "W" grade by making no alteration to the grade roster. . . .

Source: Reprinted with permission of Dr. Douglas K. Burgess, University Registrar, University of Cincinnati.

WHEN REVISING TURN INTO YOUR OWN TOUGHEST CRITIC. "

avoid perfectionism when drafting Trying to make your first draft a perfect draft causes two problems. First, spending too much energy perfecting the early parts can make you forget important pieces and purposes of the later parts. Second, premature perfectionism can make drafting frustrating and slow, thus keeping you from wanting to revise your message when you're done. You will be much more inclined to go back over your message and improve it if you have not agonized over the draft.

keep going When turning your planning into a draft, don't let minor problems with wording or grammar distract you from your main goal—to generate your first version of the document. Have an understanding with yourself that you will draft relatively quickly to get the ideas down on paper or onto the screen, and then go back and carefully revise. Expressing your points in a somewhat coherent, complete, and orderly fashion is hard enough. Allow yourself to save close reexamination and evaluation of what you've written for the revision stage.

use any other strategies that will keep you working productively The idea with drafting is to keep moving forward at a reasonably steady pace with as little stalling as possible. Do anything you can think of that will make your drafting relatively free and easy. For example, write at your most productive time of day, write in chunks, start with a favorite part, talk aloud or write to yourself to clarify your thoughts, take breaks, let the project sit for a while, create a setting conducive to writing—even promise yourself a little reward for getting a certain amount accomplished. Your goal is to get the first orderly expression of your planned contents written out just well enough so that you can go back and work with it.

Revising

Getting your draft ready for your reader requires going back over it carefully, again and again. Did you say what you mean? Could someone misunderstand or take offense at what you wrote? Is your organizational pattern best for the situation? Is each word the right one for your goals? Are there better, more concise ways of structuring your sentences? Can you move the reader more smoothly from point to point? Does each element of

Successful writers often seek out others' perspectives on important documents.

format enhance readability and highlight the structure of the contents? When revising, you turn into your own toughest critic. You challenge what you have written and look for better alternatives.

Any message has so many facets that it can help to use what professional writers call "levels of edit." There are three main levels of edit, commonly referred to as *revision, editing,* and *proofreading.*

With *revision*, you look at top-level concerns: whether or not you included all necessary information, if the pattern of organization is logical and as effective as possible, if the overall meaning of the message comes through, and if the formatting is appropriate and helpful.

You then move to the *editing* level, focusing on your style. You examine your sentences to see if they pace the information in such a way that the reader can easily follow it, if they emphasize the right things, and if they combine pieces of information coherently. You also look at your word choices to see if they best serve your purpose.

Finally, you *proofread*, looking at particular mechanical and grammatical elements—spelling, typography, punctuation, and any particular grammar problems that tend to give you trouble. Editing functions in your word-processing applications can help you with this task. Careful attention to each level will result in a polished, effective message.

One last word about revising: Get feedback from others. As you may well know, it is difficult to find weaknesses or errors in your own work. Seek out assistance from willing colleagues, and if they give you criticism, receive it with an open mind. Better to hear it from them than from your intended readers when costly mistakes may have already been made.

The remaining sections of this chapter describe specific purposes and traits of different message media. In-depth advice about their physical design can be found in Supplementary Chapter B. No matter what you're writing, a thorough, methodical writing process will significantly enhance your chances of achieving your communication goals.

LETTERS

Letters are the oldest form of business messages. The ancient Chinese wrote letters, as did the early Egyptians, Romans, and Greeks. Although many of these early letters pertained to military and personal matters, some clearly concerned business.

Today, letters are used mostly in relatively formal circumstances and primarily for corresponding with people outside your organization. When you write to internal readers, they are often familiar to you—and even if they are not, you all share the connection of being in the same company. Your messages to such audiences tend to use less formal media. But when you write to customers, to suppliers, to citizens and community leaders, and to other external audiences, you will often want to choose the letter format, complete with an attractive company letterhead and the elements of courtesy built into this traditional format. And your readers will expect this gesture of respect. Once you have established friendly relations with them, you may also conduct your business through emails and phone calls. But especially when corresponding with an external party whom you do not know well, a letter is an appropriate form to use.

You may already know the format of the business letter, illustrated in Exhibit 2.5. Although some variations in format are generally acceptable, typically these information items are included: date, inside address, salutation (Dear Ms. Smith), body, and complimentary close (Sincerely). Other items sometimes needed are attention line, subject line, return address (when letterhead paper is not used), and enclosure information. Placement of these items as well as guidelines for processing the text of the letter are presented online.

A century ago and even as recently as the 1950s, the writing in business letters was excessively formal, which resulted in a stiff, awkward tone and style. Today, though business letters are formal, their tone and style are more conversational. Like other forms of business writing, letters should be viewed as exchanges between real people. And as with other forms, they should use any formatting devices and organizational strategies that will help you achieve your purpose. You can write engaging, easy-to-read letters, even with their heightened formality.

▼ **EXHIBIT 2.5**   Illustration of a Letter in Full Block Format (Mixed Punctuation)

*Doing it right . . .
the first time*

Ralston's Plumbing and Heating
2424 Medville Road
Urbana, OH 45702
(515) 555-5555
Fax: (515) 555-5544

February 28, 2011

Ms. Diane Taylor
747 Gateway Avenue
Urbana, OH 45702

Dear Ms. Taylor:

Thank you for allowing one of our certified technicians to serve you recently.

Enclosed is a coupon for $25 toward your next purchase or service call from Ralston. It's just our way of saying that we appreciate your business.

Sincerely yours,

Jack Ralston

Jack Ralston
Owner and President

Enclosure

MEMORANDUMS

Memorandums (memos) are a form of letter written inside the business. While in rare cases they may be used to communicate with those outside the business, they are typically written messages exchanged by employees as they conduct of their work. They may be distinguished from other messages primarily by their form. Originally, they were used only in hard copy, but with the advent of computers, many were processed electronically as faxes. Nowadays, their function of communicating

Businesses with multiple locations send many of their documents by email, instant messages, or even fax.

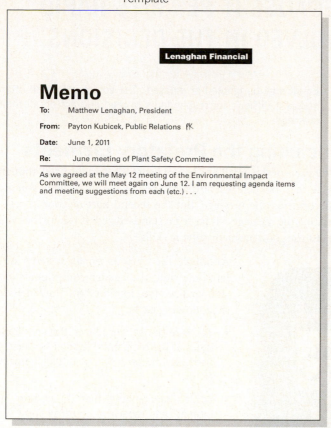

Lenaghan Financial

Memo

To: Matthew Lenaghan, President

From: Payton Kubicek, Public Relations *PK*

Date: June 1, 2011

Re: June meeting of Plant Safety Committee

As we agreed at the May 12 meeting of the Environmental Impact Committee, we will meet again on June 12. I am requesting agenda items and meeting suggestions from each (etc.) . . .

PENNY-WISE STORES, INC.

MEMORANDUM

To:		Date:
		From:
Store:		Store:
At:		At:
Territory:		Territory:
Copies to:		

Subject: Form for in-house memos

This is an illustration of our memorandum stationery. It should be used for written communications within the organization.

Notice that the memorandum uses no form of salutation. Neither does it have any form of complimentary close. The writer does not need to sign the message. He or she needs only to initial after the typed name in the heading.

Notice also that the message is single-spaced with double-spacing between paragraphs.

within the business has been largely taken over by email. Even so, they still are a part of most company communication. They are especially useful in communicating with employees who do not use computers in their work.

Some companies have stationery printed especially for memorandums, while many use standard or customized templates in word processors. Sometimes the word *memorandum* appears at the top in large, heavy type. But some companies prefer other titles, such as *Interoffice Memorandum* or *Interoffice Communication*. Below this main heading come the specific headings common to all memorandums: *Date, To, From,* and *Subject* (though not necessarily in this order). This simple arrangement is displayed in Exhibit 2.6. Because memorandums are often short, some companies use 5 × 8½-inch stationery for them instead of the conventional 8½ × 11-inch size. Hardcopy memorandums are usually initialed by the writer rather than signed.

Large organizations, especially those with a number of locations and departments, often include additional information on their memorandum stationery. *Department, Plant, Location, Territory, Store Number*, and *Copies to* are examples (see Exhibit 2.7). Since in some companies memorandums are often addressed to more than one reader, the

heading *To* may be followed by enough space to list a number of names.

Because memorandums usually are sent and received by people who work with and know one another, they tend to use casual or informal language. Even so, their degree of formality ranges from one extreme to the other. At one end are the casual notes that workers exchange. At the other are the formal messages written by lower-ranking employees to their top administrators and vice versa. The typical memorandum falls somewhere between these extremes.

The techniques for writing memorandums are much like those for writing the other business messages (letters and email). Short, simple memos are often written in casual or informal language, much like short, simple email messages. Longer, more formal memorandums are appropriately organized in the patterns appropriate for longer, more formal messages, such as those discussed in Chapters 5 through 7. Even a short or medium-length report can use memo format. Like most other business messages, most memorandums are appropriately written in a direct pattern, beginning with the main point and then providing details. Still, memorandums conveying sensitive or negative information are best written in an indirect order. Direct and indirect patterns are discussed in detail in following chapters.

EMAIL CAN SPEED THE PROCESS OF MAKING BUSINESS DECISIONS BECAUSE IT PERMITS RAPID EXCHANGES FROM ALL INVOLVED IN THE DECISIONS. "

EMAIL

The rapid growth of email has been one of the most exciting developments in the history of business communication. In just a short time, email has emerged as a mainstream form of business communication. Its volume surpasses that of the U.S. Postal Service. According to one authority, there are more emails sent every day than telephone calls made. It has become widely used in both small and large organizations, and its explosive growth continues.

Evaluating Email's Pros and Cons

The reasons for this rapid growth are the advantages email has over other communication forms, especially over its principal competitor, the phone. Among these advantages, the following are most significant:

- Email eliminates "phone tag"—the problem of trying to contact busy people who are not always available for phone calls. Messages sent to them can be stored in their digital mailboxes until they are ready to read them.

- Conversely, email saves the time of these busy people. They are spared the interruptions of phone calls.

- Email can speed the process of making business decisions because it permits rapid exchanges from all involved in the decisions.

- Email is cheap. It permits unlimited use for no more than the cost of an Internet connection.

- Email provides a written record.

Email also has its disadvantages:

- Email is not confidential. "You might as well spray paint your gripes on the wall of your cubicle."[3]

- Email doesn't communicate the sender's emotions well. Voice intonations, facial expressions, body movements, and other such elements are not a part of the message as they are in phone, video, and face-to-face communication.

Many business people use their phones to send and receive emails and text messages. With such a small display screen, conciseness is especially important.

- Email may be ignored or delayed. The volume of email often makes it difficult for respondents to read and act on all their messages.

Including the Prefatory Elements

The parts of the email header are generally standardized, though what they look like will be determined by the email client you use to construct the message. But the second part of your effort—writing the message—is far from standardized. It is here that you must use good problem-solving skills.

Although the various email systems differ somewhat, the header components are standardized (see Exhibit 2.8). They include the following parts:

- **To:** Here the sender places the email address of the recipients. It must be perfect because any error will result in delivery failure.

- **Cc:** If someone other than the primary recipient is to receive a *courtesy copy*, his or her address goes here.

- **Bcc:** This line stands for *blind courtesy copy*. The recipient's message will not show this information; that is, he or she will not know who else is receiving a copy of the message.

- **Subject:** This line describes the message as precisely as the situation permits. The reader should get from it a clear idea of what the message is about and feel motivated to read the rest of the message.

- **Attachments:** This area identifies file names that you send with the message. As will be emphasized later, you should make certain that what you attach is really needed.

- **The message:** The information you are sending goes here. How to write it is the subject of much of the following discussion.

Beginning the Message

Typically, email messages begin with the recipient's name. If the writer and reader are acquainted, first name only is the rule (e.g., "Bob," or "Hi, Bob"). If you would normally address the reader as Ms., Dr., or Mr., address him or her this way in an initial email. But you can change the salutation in subsequent messages if the

EXHIBIT 2.8 Typical Electronic Mail Clients

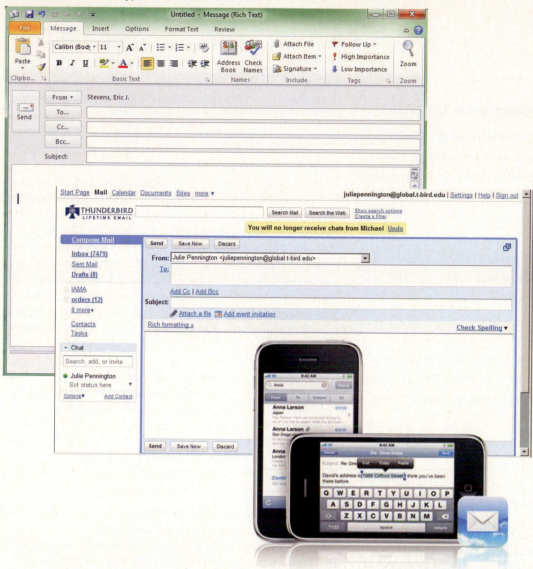

accessing email on a smart-phone or other small screen can get the essential facts more easily.

As with letters and memos, longer, more complex, and formal email messages frequently follow more involved and strategic organization patterns. As you will see, these patterns vary depending on how the reader will likely perceive the writer's objective. In general, those messages that are likely to be received positively or neutrally are written in a direct pattern, while those messages that are likely to be received negatively are appropriately written in an indirect pattern, with their negative content preceded by conditioning and explanatory words.

Some long email messages may resemble business reports. With these messages, you may well follow the organization and writing instructions for business reports (Chapters 8 and 9). In fact, almost any kind of message can be communicated by email as long as your reader will expect this choice of medium.

person indicates that informality is desired. A friendly generic greeting such as "Dear Quality Team" is appropriate for a group of people with whom you communicate. Use of the recipient's full name also is acceptable. When writing to someone or a group you do not know, it is appropriate to identify yourself early in the message. This identification may include your purpose and your company. Your title and position also may be helpful.

Organizing the Contents

Even though email messages often are written under time pressure, you should organize them carefully. For most short, informative messages, a "top-down" order is appropriate. This plan, used in newspaper writing, involves presenting the most important material first. The remaining information follows in descending order of importance. Such an arrangement permits a busy reader to get the essential facts first, and the reader

> PS. Dear Boss. I know you are reading this
> email as I type so I am writing to you to say
> STOP SPYING ON ME AND GET BACK
> TO WORK THIS MINUTE!

Communication in brief

Should I Use Shortcuts in My Email?

Probably because email began as an informal medium with space and character limitations, certain shortcuts have become widely used. Here are some of the more popular ones:

ASAP	as soon as possible
BTW	by the way
FYI	for your information
IMHO	in my humble opinion
LOL	laughing out loud
THX or TX	thanks
UR	you are

Be cautious in your use of such shortcuts. If your readers know them and expect them, they can be appropriate. For now, they tend to be suitable only when the situation is casual or where message-length limitations exist.

Writing the Email Message

The characteristics of effective email messages are much the same as those described in Chapter 4 for messages in general. For the purpose of email writing, we may group the more important of these under four heads: formality, conciseness, clarity, and etiquette. A fifth, correctness (covered in the "Correctness of Communication" chapter available online), is equally vital. These important dimensions of email writing are briefly reviewed in the following paragraphs.

formality Emails run the range from highly informal to formal. Some sound like chitchat among friends, while others convey important policy statements from the highest executive officers in the company. How formal should your business emails be? When deciding, consider three general classifications: casual, informal, and formal.[4]

Sometimes, *casual* language can be appropriate. It uses contractions and personal pronouns freely and may use slang, colloquialisms, and text-messaging initialisms. It may even lack complete sentences. While such writing is not always out of bounds in business, it should be used sparingly and only with readers who you know prefer such language. A better style for business email is usually

▼ **EXHIBIT 2.9** Be Careful with "Reply All"

The "Reply All" button may not your friend.
    According to management consultant Tracy Peterson Turner, hitting "Reply All" to email messages contributes to information overload at work. It can also be destructive if used to show off or to show up previous commenters. Her advice? "Use 'Reply All' only when all those people on the recipient list need the information. . . . Otherwise, respond only to the initiator of the message and let the others do their jobs better."

Source: "Use the 'Reply All' Function in Email Judiciously," *SEO Copywriting,* SEO Copywriting, 2009, Web, 8 Oct. 2009.

informal language, which may retain the use of contractions and personal pronouns but which is carefully structured and grammatically correct. It is the writing that you will find in most of the positive examples in this book and in the text of the book itself. Occasionally, you will use a *formal* style in your emails. Formal writing tends to avoid contractions and may contain no personal pronouns. Because it creates a greater distance between writer and reader than the informal style, it is appropriate to use in email messages resembling formal reports, in messages to people of higher status, and to people not known to the writer.

conciseness As we have mentioned, email often is written by busy people for busy people. In the best interests of all concerned, email messages should be as short as complete coverage of the subject matter will permit. This means culling the extra information and using only that which is essential. It means also that the information remaining should be worded concisely. (See Exhibit 2.9 for a related point: sending the message only to those who actually need it.)

Frequently in email communication, you may need to refer to previous email messages. The easiest way, of course, is to tell your mailer to include the entire message. Unless the entire message is needed, however, this practice adds length. It is better either to paraphrase the essentials from the original or to quote the selected parts that cover the essentials. All quoted material should be distinguished from your own words. Symbols (<>), color, and font can be used to indicate whose words are whose. If you know your reader uses an email client such as Outlook 2010 that will sort email by threads, you may be able to leave out references or links to the original message.

> "Clarity is especially important in email writing."

clarity Clarity is especially important in email writing. As you will see in Chapter 4, several techniques help make your writing easy to read. You should select words that quickly create clear meanings. Typically, these are the short, familiar ones. You should strive for concreteness, vigor, and precision. Your sentences should be short, and so should your paragraphs. In fact, all of the advice about clear writing in Chapter 4 is applicable to email messages.

etiquette Of course, courtesy should be practiced in all business relations. Even so, the current literature has much to say about anger among email participants. "Flaming," as the practice of sending abusive or offensive language is called, has no place in business. Good email etiquette should prevail. This includes using all of the practices discussed in Chapter 4 for building goodwill.

correctness Because email messages are frequently written quickly and because their tone is frequently (though not always) informal, writers may be tempted to let speed affect their level of professionalism in terms of proofreading and editing. However, "email is a serious business communications tool, and you should treat it with the same respect as any other business document you write."[5] In other words, though the tone of your writing may be informal, the style of your writing must still be professional, which means you must proofread and edit carefully for grammar, mechanics, spelling, and punctuation.

How one communicates is very much a part of the message. In commenting on the importance of correctness to a writer's professional image, one expert says, "The email you write says a lot about you. It tells the readers that you are thorough, accurate, and attentive—or not. It indicates that your message is to be taken seriously—or not. It implies that you know what you're talking about—or not."[6] Bad spelling, illogical punctuation, and awkward wording stand out. Such errors reflect poorly on

the writer, and they can compromise the credibility of the message. You do not want to make yourself or your company appear incompetent.

To avoid any such problems, you should follow the grammatical and punctuation principles presented in the online chapter Correctness of Communication. And you should follow the basic instructions for using words, constructing sentences, and designing paragraphs presented in Chapter 4. Before pressing the Send button, proofread your message carefully.

Closing the Email Message

Most email messages end with just the writer's name—the first name alone if the recipient knows the writer well. But in some messages, especially the more formal ones, a closing statement may be appropriate. "Thank you" and "Best" are popular. In casual messages, shortcuts, such as THX (thanks), are often used. The conventional complimentary closes used in traditional letters (sincerely, cordially) are appropriate in messages that involve formal business relationships. In messages to other businesses, it is important that your signature include your company name and position title.

Today most email applications have a signature feature that will automatically attach a signature file to a message. Most programs even allow the writer to set up an alternative signature, giving users the flexibility to choose between a standard signature, an alternate, or none at all. Writers sometimes set up both a formal

> "Flaming," as the practice of sending abusive or offensive language is called, has no place in business.

technology in brief
Using Good Email Etiquette Helps You Convey Your Message

Using proper email etiquette is as easy as applying a bit of empathy—sending only what you would want to receive. The following questions will help you consider specific etiquette issues when using email.

- Does the recipient really need your message?

- Is your message routine rather than sensitive?

- Are you sure your message is not spam (an annoying message) or a chain message?

- Have you carefully checked that your message is going where you want it to go?

- Has your wording avoided defamatory or libelous language?

- Have you complied with copyright laws and attributed sources accurately?

- Have you avoided humor and sarcasm that your reader may not understand as intended?

- Have you proofread your message carefully?

- Is this a message you would not mind having distributed widely?

- Does your signature avoid offensive quotes or illustrations, especially those that are religious, political, or sexual?

- Is your recipient willing or able to accept attached files?

- Are attached files a size and format that your recipient's system can handle?

- Are the files you are attaching virus free?

full signature and an informal signature. The important point to remember is to close with a signature that gives the reader the information he or she needs to know.

Avoiding Inappropriate Use of Email

In spite of its popularity and ease of use, email is not always a good medium for your communications. As summarized by two authorities, "it should not be used when

- The message is long, complicated, or requires negotiation.

- Questions or information need clarification and discussion.

- The information is confidential or sensitive, requires security, or could be misinterpreted.

- The message is emotionally charged and really requires tone of voice or conversational feedback to soften the words or negotiate meaning.

- The message is sent to *avoid* direct contact with a person, especially if the message is unpleasant and uncomfortable or seems too difficult to say face-to-face.

- The message contains sensitive issues, relays feelings, or attempts to resolve conflict. Email can make conflict worse."[7]

LO 5 Understand the nature and business use of text messaging.

TEXT MESSAGING

Text messaging, also called short message service (SMS), is, as its name suggests, used for sending short messages generally from a mobile phone. Because the purpose of a text message is to convey a quick message, the writing of text messages is quite different from that of other messages. Because the message generally is limited to 160 characters, the emphasis is on brevity. You include only the essentials (Exhibit 2.10).

▼ **EXHIBIT 2.10** An Illustration of Text Messaging

The need for brevity has led to the use of many abbreviations. So many of these abbreviations have developed that one might say a new language has developed. In fact, a dictionary of over 1,100 text messaging abbreviations has been compiled at Webopedia, an online computer technology encyclopedia (<http://www.webopedia.com/quick_ref/textmessageabbreviations.asp>). Some examples are the following:

b4 (before)	**u** (you)
gr8 (great)	**BTW** (by the way)
CU (see you)	**NP** (no problem)
FBM (fine by me)	**HRY** (how are you)
TC (take care)	**TYT** (take your time)

In addition to abbreviations, writers use typed symbols to convey emotions (emoticons), which can also be found at Webopedia:

:-) standard smiley	**:-!** foot in mouth
;) winking smile	**:-(** sad or frown
:-O yell	**(((H)))** hugs

Whether and when these abbreviations and emoticons are used depends on the writer's relationship with the audience.

Good business writers will compose text messages that not only convey the writer's message but also allow for brief responses from the receiver. Let's say, for example, that you've learned that an important visiting customer is a vegetarian and you have reservations for lunch at Ruth's Chris Steakhouse. You might need to let your boss know—before the lunch meeting. However, the boss is leading an important meeting in which a phone call would be disruptive and inappropriate, so you decide to send a text message.

"...and I'm proficient in two languages — English and text messaging."

Your immediate thought might be to send the following: *Marina Smith is a vegetarian. Where should we take her for lunch today? Zeke.*

Although your message does convey the major fact and is only 77 characters counting spaces, it forces the recipient to enter a long response—the name of another place. It might also result in more message exchanges about availability and time.

A better version might be this: *Marina Smith is a vegetarian. Shall we go to (1) Fish House, (2) Souplantation, (3) Mandarin House? All are available at noon. Zeke*

This version conveys the major fact in 130 characters and allows the recipient to respond simply with 1, 2, or 3. As the writer, you took the initiative to anticipate your reader's needs, identify appropriate alternatives, and then gather information—steps that are as important with text messaging as they are with other messages. If your text messages are clear, complete, and concise and have a professional and pleasant tone, you will find them a valuable tool for business use.

LO 6   Understand how instant messaging works.

INSTANT MESSAGING

Instant messaging, commonly referred to as IM-ing or online chatting, is much like phone conversation in that parties communicate in real time (instantly) (Exhibit 2.11). It differs

Communication in brief

Text Messaging: Another Language?

A dictionary of over 1200 text-messaging abbreviations and over 40 kinds of smiley faces has been compiled at Webopedia.com, an online computer technology encyclopedia. If you don't know what WYGAM or %-(mean, you can find out at <http://www.webopedia.com/quick_ref/textmessageabbreviations.asp>.

As with shortcuts in emails, be careful when using such abbreviations and emoticons. It's true they can save on typing, but they can also derail your communication if your reader doesn't speak the same text-messaging language. Predictive technology—the capability of some devices to finish typing a word or phrase for you—helps solve this problem while also spelling correctly.

primarily in that it is text-based (typed) rather than voice-based communication, though recent developments have made voice-based instant messaging possible. Many writers will use the same abbreviations and emoticons in instant messages that they use in text messages. Here again the use of these devices depends on your audience and purpose.

Because instant messages are similar to phone conversations, you should write instant messages much as you would talk in conversation with another person. If the person is a personal friend, your language should reflect this friendship. If the person is the president of your company, a business associate, or fellow worker, the relationship should guide your language. The message bits presented in instant messaging are determined largely by the exchange of information. Responses often are impromptu. Even so, in business situations you should consciously direct the flow toward your objective and maintain a professional tone and style.

> " If your text messages are clear, complete, and concise and have a professional and pleasant tone, you will find them a valuable tool for business use. "

LO 7 Understand the nature and business use of social networking.

SOCIAL NETWORKING

You may already be familiar with such social networking sites as Facebook, MySpace, Twitter, or LinkedIn. Perhaps you have a blog (a "Web log") where you keep an online diary or journal that you share publicly. Or maybe you have used or contributed to a wiki. These social networking sites are increasingly popular—so much so, says *The New York Times*, that in February 2009 people actually spent more time on social networks than they did on their email. The author suggests that this represents "a paradigm shift in consumer engagement with the Internet."[8]

Although you may use these sites to connect with friends, family, or classmates, many business writers also use them to connect with clients, customers, colleagues, and supervisors as they answer questions, promote products, network with other professionals, or interact briefly with co-workers. Many companies have found that these networks promote personal and corporate success. One survey of 1,600 executives "found that firms that rely heavily on external social networks scored 24 percent higher on a measure of radical innovation than companies that don't."[9] Business professionals, then, are using social networking sites for purposes that are likely very different from your personal purposes in using them (see the corporate blog in Exhibit 2.12, for example).

Generally, the messages on social networking sites are brief, with some sites, such as Twitter, restricting messages to 140 characters. Therefore, as with text messaging, messages must not only be brief but concise and clear. In addition, because the messages on these sites are public, you would never want to use language or a tone or writing style that you would be embarrassed to have your boss see, that may have legal implications, or that might get you fired.

In fact, if you currently have a page on a social networking site where family and friends are your audience, you will want to remove any pictures or language that you wouldn't want a prospective employer, current employer, co-worker, customer, or client to see. No matter how private you believe your page to be, you can never know what your friends and family are sharing with other people. One expert advises that even though employers may not be within their rights to use information on social networking sites in their hiring decisions (e.g., age, race, or health history), 40 percent of employers indicate that they check social networking sites when hiring new employees,

While we've covered the most common forms of business messages here, new ones will continue to develop as communication technologies and business needs change. Staying abreast of these changes and analyzing each situation carefully will help you choose the right form at the right time. ■

Get Online

mhhe.com/FlatleyM2e

for study materials including quizzes and Internet resources.

and 80 percent of these employers say the content of these sites influences their hiring decisions.[10]

Even on the job, companies may monitor employees' social networking and other computer activity. In doing this, companies can detect excessive use, inappropriate or unethical behavior, disclosure of proprietary information, sexually explicit content, and attachments with viruses. Companies' monitoring systems also have features that protect the company from legal liabilities. As a business professional, you must know your company's computer use policy and avoid writing anything that would reflect poorly on you or your company or put you or your company at risk.

In addition, you will want to be familiar with privacy policies on social networking sites such as Facebook and LinkedIn that indicate how your information is collected, managed, and shared.

using visuals in
written and oral
communication

UNDERSTANDING THE VISUAL COMMUNICATION PROCESS

Visuals are pervasive in today's media-rich society in both our work and leisure activities. We read and write documents and reports that include images; we hear and give presentations where the audience expects graphs and other visuals. In fact, each day millions of people are clicking on websites such as Flickr.com and YouTube.com where they view and post photos and videos. Additionally, other specialty sites, such as SlideShare.net, are becoming increasingly popular. Visuals are even being used as search expressions with smartphone apps, such as Google Goggles, for finding information. This growing use of images for conveying information confirms that being visually literate is extremely important in order to communicate effectively today.

Some credit (or blame) technology for this expanding growth. They say that the computer has given us the ability to collect, store, and access an abundance of information. The blamers accuse the technology of leading to information overload, overwhelming and paralyzing businesspeople. In reality, this problem can happen, but Stephen Few, an expert in business intelligence and information design, believes that technology presents a wealth of opportunity. While it has in some cases allowed us to become lazy and rely on the software to report the information in its default formats,

continued on p. 40

LEARNING OBJECTIVES

LO1 Describe the process for effective visual communication: planning, gathering and collecting, analyzing and organizing, choosing a form, placing and interpreting, and evaluating.

LO2 Choose the appropriate type of visual for the communication task.

LO3 Construct text-based visuals such as tables, pull quotes, flowcharts, and process charts.

LO4 Construct data-generated visuals such as bar, pie, line, area, and x-y (scatter) charts as well as combinations and mashups.

LO5 Appropriately use visuals such as maps, photos, videos, drawings, diagrams, and three-dimensional visuals.

LO6 Apply visual literacy concepts at the document and presentation level.

continued from p. 39

it has also given us a rich arsenal of analytic tools that help us understand and present the data, tools that need the human mind to exploit their power.[1]

One recent experimental study of business executives examined the impact of using visuals in group work. Its results clearly showed that groups who were using visuals in their work had higher productivity, higher quality of outcomes, and greater knowledge gains for the individuals in the group.[2]

Whether working individually or with a group, it is clear that to be an effective communicator today, one needs to be able to interpret, create, and select visuals to convey clear meanings.[3] ▪

In this chapter you will learn the principles needed to help you convey information visually so that your audience can extract it quickly and accurately. Specifically, the following sections will help you (1) understand the visual communication process, (2) choose the appropriate visual for the situation, (3) skillfully manage the mechanics of visuals, and (4) design layouts that effectively integrate the visuals.

LO 1 Describe the process for effective visual communication: planning, gathering and collecting, analyzing and organizing, choosing a form, placing and interpreting, and evaluating.

UNDERSTANDING THE VISUAL COMMUNICATION PROCESS

The stages of the visual communication process are very similar to the stages of the writing process you learned about in Chapter 2. These steps—planning, gathering and collecting, analyzing and organizing, choosing a form, placing and interpreting, and evaluating—are steps writers can follow to improve the effectiveness of their visuals.

Planning

You should plan visuals for a document or presentation soon after you organize your facts. Visuals serve one main purpose—to communicate—and you should use them primarily for that purpose. Your planning of visuals should be based on determining what to communicate and how to do it. Visuals can help clarify complex or difficult information; illustrate relations; reveal trends, patterns, and outliers; emphasize facts; add coherence; overview and summarize data; and provide and keep interest. Of course, well-constructed visuals also enhance the appearance of a document or presentation, lending credibility to the writer or presenter.

As you plan the visuals, remember that, unlike infographics that stand alone (such as those you often see in *USA Today*), yours will supplement the writing or speaking—not take its place. They should help the words by covering the more difficult parts, emphasizing the important points, and presenting the details. But the words should carry the main message.

workplace scenario

Using Visuals to Help Convey Ideas

Prepare for this chapter by playing the role of owner at Pinnacle, where you often proofread documents and presentations prepared by your co-workers. Because Pinnacle uses chemicals in its products, many of the documents are highly technical and complex. Many others, especially those coming from finance and sales, are filled with facts and figures. In your judgment, most of the documents you proofread are hard to understand.

The one you are looking at now is packed with page after page of sales statistics. Your mind quickly gets lost in the mass of details. Why didn't the writer take the time to summarize the more important figures in a visual? And why didn't the writer put some of the details in tables? Many of the other documents and presentations you have been reading, especially the technical ones, are in equal need of visuals. Bar charts, pie charts, and maps would certainly

help explain some of the data included. If only the writers would understand that words alone sometimes cannot communicate clearly—that words sometimes need to be supplemented with visuals. If the writers of these documents studied the following review of visual literacy principles, your job would be easier and more enjoyable. So would the jobs of the documents' readers and listeners.

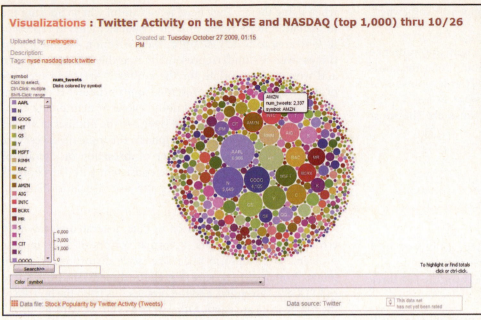

Visualizations : Twitter Activity on the NYSE and NASDAQ (top 1,000) thru 10/26

Today's data-mining tools, such as IBM's ManyEyes web-based application shown here, give writers and readers many options for presenting and viewing data.

Gathering and Collecting

The information represented in visuals should be what you want your audience to remember after reading or listening to your presentation. You may need to mine data you already have on hand in order to create your visuals, or you may need to gather new data for examples relevant to your audience. Your new data may be internal data your company already collects, or it may be external data collected from public and private sources. The time and money you spend on gathering information or creating a visual should be balanced in terms of the importance of the message you want to convey. You can find more specific information on gathering data in Chapter 8 on conducting research.

Analyzing and Organizing

Once you have your data or facts, you need to analyze the information you want to present and determine how best to organize it for your audience. Today's text analytics, data mining, and visualization tools help writers filter the vast amounts of data that are collected and stored regularly. But which data will you emphasize? What colors will convey the information best? When should it be presented? Will the visual be appropriate for the audience? All these are matters that you will decide using a problem-solving approach.

Choosing a Form

You will choose visuals appropriate to both the content and the context where they will be presented. And you will include any kind of visuals that will help the reader understand the document or presentation quickly, easily, and completely.

In selecting visuals, you should review the information that your document or presentation will contain, looking for any possibility of improving communication of the information through the use of visuals. Specifically, you should look for complex information that visual presentation can make clear, for information too detailed to be covered solely in words, and for information that deserves special emphasis.

Once you have identified the information you need to communicate, let the wording of your points about that information guide your choice of visuals. If your words reveal that you are comparing, revealing a trend, or showing parts of a whole, you will likely choose one of the data-generated forms. If your words indicate that you are describing a process, illustrating a concept, or even portraying an emotion, you will likely choose other visuals such as flowcharts, diagrams, drawings, and even photos. Later in this chapter you will learn what kind of information is best conveyed by different types of visuals. By looking carefully at the words in your document or presentation, you should be able to determine what form of visual expression is best for your audience.

Placing and Interpreting

For the best communication effect, you should place each visual near the place where it will be discussed. Exactly where on the page or in the presentation you should place it, however, should be determined by its size. If the visual is small, you should place it with the text that discusses it. If it is a full page or screen, you should place it following the first reference to the information it covers.

Some writers like to place all visuals at the end of documents, usually in the appendix. This arrangement may save preparation time, but it does not help the readers. They have to flip or click through the document every time they want to see a visual. Common sense requires that you place visuals in such a way as to help readers understand the words.

Sometimes you may need to include visuals that do not fit a specific part of the document or presentation. For example, you may have a visual that is necessary for completeness but is not discussed in the document. Or you may have summary charts or tables that apply to the entire document but to no specific place in it. You may even have visuals you plan to use in a Q&A if your audience asks for them. When such visuals are appropriate, you should place them in the appendix or at the end of a presentation. And you should refer to the appendix somewhere in the document.

Visuals communicate most effectively when the audience sees them at the right place. Thus, you should refer the audience to them at the right place and time. That is, you should tell them when to look at a visual and what to see. Of the many wordings used for this purpose, these are the most common:

. . . . as shown in Figure 4. . . . .

. . . . indicated in Figure 4. . . . .

. . . . as a glance at Figure 4 reveals. . . .

. . . (see Figure 4). . . .

If your visual is carrying the primary message, as in a detailed table, you can just make an incidental reference to the information in the visual, as in "Our increased sales over the last three years. . . . "

However, if the words are carrying the primary message such as in the area chart in Exhibit 3.14 (page 52), you might start with a reference to the chart followed closely by a thorough interpretation. One good mnemonic to use is GEE, standing for *generalization, example*, and *exception*.[4] You'll start with a summary statement that reveals the big picture. In the case of Exhibit 3.14, you might say, "As Chart 14 shows, both optimists' and pessimists' projections show we will have plenty of oil through 2050." After presenting the figure, you'll give one or more supporting examples that call your audience's attention to key findings. Then you will give the exception to the general trend, if there is one—for example, "While the optimists' projections are nearly twice the pessimists' using conventional modes, the optimists' projections using unconventional modes are almost four times greater."

Your readers will appreciate well-chosen, well-designed, and well-explained visuals, and you will achieve powerful communication results.

Evaluating

The success your visuals will achieve in fulfilling your purpose—to communicate effectively—needs to be evaluated or assessed on several fronts. Visuals must be evaluated for their integrity, their accuracy, their clarity, and their audience appeal.

You are ethically bound to present data and visuals in ways that enable readers and listeners to interpret them easily and accurately. By being aware of some of the common errors made in presenting visuals, you learn how to avoid them as well as how to spot them in other documents. Even when errors are not deliberately created to deceive a reader, they cause loss of credibility—casting doubt on the document as well as on other work you have completed.

All visuals can misrepresent information. Writers and speakers need to be diligent in applying high quality standards when using them.[5] They need to be careful when choosing the information to represent and the visual elements to represent it. One area to watch is appropriate selection. Are people or things over- or underrepresented? Are the numbers of men and women appropriate for the context? Are their ages appropriate? Is ethnicity represented appropriately? Have colors been used appropriately and not to evoke or manipulate emotions? What about volume and size? Are the number of visuals and size appropriate for the emphasis the topic deserves? Are visuals presented accurately, free of distortion or alteration? Have photos been cropped to be consistent with the context? Writers need to carefully select and use visuals to maintain high integrity.

Accuracy can be compromised in data-generated visuals with errors of scale and errors of format. Errors of scale include problems with uniform scale size, scale distortion, and zero points. You need to be sure that all the dimensions from left to right (X axis) are equal, and the dimensions from the bottom to the top (Y axis) are equal. Otherwise, as you see here, an incorrect picture would be shown.

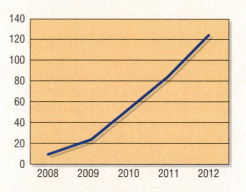

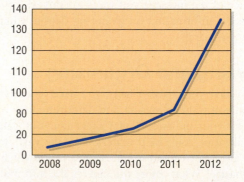

Scale distortion occurs when a graph is stretched excessively horizontally or vertically to change the meaning it conveys. Expanding a scale can change the appearance of the line. For example if the values on a chart are plotted one-half unit apart, changes appear much more suddenly. Determining the distances that present the most accurate picture is a matter of judgment. Notice the different looks of the graph shown here when stretched horizontally.

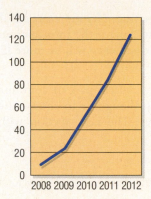

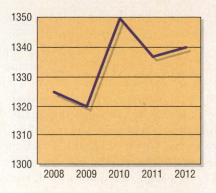

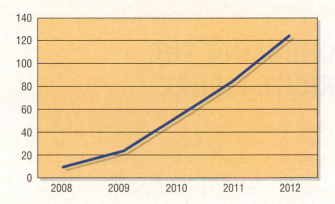

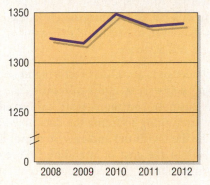

Finally, another type of scale error is violating the zero beginning of the series. For accuracy, you should begin the scale at zero. But when all the information shown in the chart has high values, it is awkward to show the entire scale from zero to the highest value. For example, if the quantities compared range from 1320 to 1350 and the chart shows the entire area from zero to 1350, the line showing these quantities would be almost straight and very high on the chart. Your solution in this case is not to begin the scale at a high number (say 1300), which would still distort the information, but to begin at zero and show a scale break. Realize, however, that while this makes the differences easier to see, it does exaggerate the differences. You can see this here.

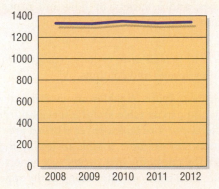

Communication in brief

Practicing Visual Ethics

As you have learned in this chapter, visuals can serve several useful purposes for the business writer. However, the writer needs to be accountable in using visuals to present images that in the eye and mind of the reader communicate accurately and completely. To do this, the careful writer pays attention to both the design and content of the visual. These are particularly important, for readers often skim text but read the visuals. Research shows that people remember images much better and longer than text.

The following guides will help you in evaluating the visuals you use:
- Does the visual's design create accurate expectations?
- Does the story told match the data?
- Is the implied message congruent with the actual message?
- Will the impact of the visual on your audience be appropriate?
- Does the visual convey all critical information free of distortion?
- Are the data depicted accurately?

Source: Adapted from Donna S. Kienzler, "Visual Ethics," *Journal of Business Communication* 34 (1997): 171–87, print.

Clarity can be compromised with errors of format. Some of the more common ones include choice of wrong chart type; distracting use of grids, shading, and background; misuse of typeface; and problems with labels. If a company used pie charts to compare expenses from one year to the next, the audience might be tempted to draw conclusions that would be inappropriate because, although the pies both represent 100 percent of the expenses, the size of the business and the expenses may have grown or shrunk drastically in a year's time. If one piece of the pie had been colored or shaded in such a way as to make it stand out from the others, readers could be mislead. And, of course, small type or unlabeled, inconsistently labeled, or inappropriately labeled visuals confuse readers. You need to be careful to present visuals that are both complete and accurate.

An ethical challenge is accurately factoring in context. Politicians are often deliberately guilty of framing the issue to suit their cause. Business communicators can avoid this problem both by attempting to frame the data objectively and by presenting the data with the audience in mind. For example, one might look at the cost of attending college for the past 16 years. A line chart of the actual dollar cost over the years would show a clear upward trend. However, to present the costs without factoring in inflation during that 16-year period would distort the results. In Exhibit 3.1,[6] you can see that the actual cost of college tuition and fees in dollars adjusted for inflation would show costs that are actually a little lower or equal to today's costs.

Finally, the visuals need to be assessed for their ability to hold the readers' or listeners' attention and to help them retain the information. If your visuals hold attention, you have the ability to convey the information. And if they are well executed, the audience will be more likely to retain the information.

Perhaps the most critical part of communicating successfully with visuals, though, is to choose the right visual for the circumstances. The next section will help with such choices.

LO 2 Choose the appropriate type of visual for the communication task.

CHOOSING THE RIGHT VISUAL

One is often tempted to jump right in and create a visual for a document. Sometimes it is the technological tools that lure us, and sometimes it is an innate desire to be creative. But you would be wise to resist this temptation. The most effective visuals are those that are right for the circumstances. To choose the right type, you will need to think carefully about the kind of information you have and the purpose you want to achieve.

Visuals for communicating information fall into three general categories: (1) those that communicate primarily through their textual content (words and numerals), (2) those that communicate primarily through some form of data-generated chart, and (3) those that communicate primarily by some form of picture. As the following descriptions and examples show, each type has its own advantages.

LO 3 Construct text-based visuals such as tables, pull quotes, flowcharts, and process charts.

Text-based Visuals

Included in the text-based group are tables, pull quotes, and a variety of flow and process charts (Gantt, flow, organization).

tables A *table* is an orderly arrangement of information in rows and columns.

Two basic types of tables are available to you: the general-purpose table and the special-purpose table. General-purpose tables cover a broad area of information. For example, a table reviewing the answers to all the questions in a survey is a general-purpose table. Such tables usually belong in the appendix.

▼ **EXHIBIT 3.1** Illustration of Accuracy of Content

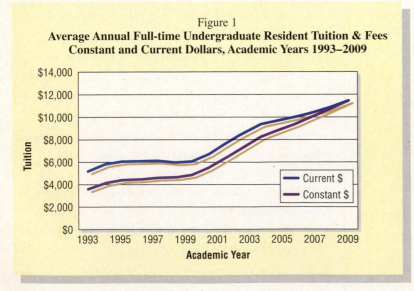

Figure 1
**Average Annual Full-time Undergraduate Resident Tuition & Fees
Constant and Current Dollars, Academic Years 1993–2009**

Source: Michigan Office of Higher Education, 2010.

Special-purpose tables are prepared for one special purpose: to illustrate a particular part of a document or presentation. They contain information that could be included with related information in a general-purpose table. For example, a table presenting the answer to one of the questions in a survey is a special-purpose table. Such tables belong in the text near the discussion of their contents.

Aside from the title, footnotes, and source designations that it might include, a table contains heads, columns, and rows of data, as shown in Exhibit 3.2.[7] Row heads are the title of single rows of data; column heads are heads of single columns of data. Spanner heads cover two or more column or row heads.

The construction of text tables is largely influenced by their purpose. Nevertheless, a few general rules apply:

- If rows are long, the row heads may be repeated at the right.

- The em dash (—) or the abbreviation *n.a.* (or *N.A.* or *NA*), but not the zero, is used to indicate data not available.

- Footnote references to numbers in the table should be keyed with asterisks, daggers, double daggers, and similar symbols. Numbers followed by footnote reference numbers may cause confusion. Lowercase of the alphabet can be used when many references are made.

- Totals and subtotals should appear whenever they help achieve the purpose of the table. The totals may be for each column and sometimes for each row. Row totals are usually placed at the right; but when they need emphasis, they may be placed at the left. Likewise, column totals are generally placed at the bottom of the column, but they may be placed at the top when the writer wants to emphasize them. A ruled line (usually a double one) separates the totals from their components.

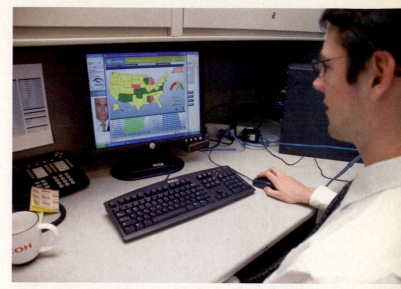

Software enables writers to create a wide variety of graphics from small to huge data sets.

- The units in which the data are recorded must be clear. Unit descriptions (bushels, acres, pounds, and the like) appropriately appear above the columns, as part of the headings or subheadings. If the data are in dollars, however, placing the dollar mark ($) before the first entry in each column is sufficient.

Tabular information need not always be presented in formal tables. In fact, short arrangements of data may be presented more effectively as parts of the text. Such arrangements are generally made as either leaderwork or text tabulations.

Leaderwork is the presentation of tabular material in the text without titles or rules. (*Leaders* are the repeated dots with

▼ **EXHIBIT 3.2** Good Arrangement of the Parts of a Typical Table

		Actual			Projected			
Table I—U.S. Internet User Penetration by Race/Ethnicity 2008–2014 (% of population in each group)								
		2008	2009	2010	2011	2012	2013	2014
Non-Hispanic								
White alone		72.0%	74.0%	76.1%	77.5%	79.0%	80.1%	81.2%
Black alone		58.2%	60.5%	63.8%	66.9%	69.6%	71.7%	72.3%
Asian alone		70.0%	71.2%	73.4%	75.5%	77.5%	79.5%	81.0%
Other*		46.4%	50.0%	52.5%	55.0%	58.0%	62.0%	65.5%
Hispanic**		53.5%	56.5%	59.5%	62.9%	65.0%	67.6%	70.0%

Table number and title → Table I—U.S. Internet User Penetration by Race/Ethnicity 2008–2014 (% of population in each group)

Spanner heads →

Column heads →

Row heads →

Footnote → *Includes native Americans, Alaska natives, Hawaiian and Pacific Islanders, and bi- and multiracial individuals.

**Could be of any race.

Source acknowledgment → SOURCE: Reprinted with permission of eMarketer.

intervening spaces.) Typically, a complete main clause ending in a colon precedes the tabulation, as in this illustration:

The August sales of the representatives in the Western Region were as follows:

Kate McPhee $53,517

Donald Zatyko............................49,703

Bill Riedy.....................................48,198

Text tabulations are simple tables, usually with column heads and some rules. But they are not numbered, and they have no titles. They are made to read with the text, as in this example:

In August the sales of the representatives in the Western Region increased sharply from those for the preceding month, as these figures show:

Representative	July Sales	August Sales	Increase
Kate McPhee	$52,819	$53,517	$ 698
Donald Zatyko	47,225	49,703	2,478
Bill Riedy	46,838	48,198	1,360

▼ **EXHIBIT 3.3** Illustration of a Pull Quote

Smart Ideas Dyan Machan ▬▬▬▬

Business By Avatar

"Virtual worlds" were supposed to be a new frontier for small businesses. That's finally happening–after a few plot twists.

AFTER SEEING *AVATAR*, THE MOVIE, I wondered whether the record-breaking intake at the box office might spur more entrepreneurial activity in places populated by, er, "real" avatars—like Second Life, the best-known and largest of the 3-D virtual-world platforms. Could *Avatar* do for avatars what *Titanic* did for Leonardo DiCaprio?

An avatar is a digital, simulated representation of a person. On sites like Second Life, There and ActiveWorlds, you can engage your avatar alter ego in all sorts of escapist fantasies, like designing and dancing in your own underwater disco. When Second Life and its peers came out in 2003, companies rushed in to build outposts and sell products to the hoards of consumers rushing in to play. Attire companies like American Apparel and Giorgio Armani and tech giants like IBM and Dell set up virtual stores, using the build-it-and-they-will-come approach. Problem is, nobody came. The supposed consumers used the site to attend concerts or become unicorns, not to buy a computer. And what did they want to buy? White hair and goth outfits for their avatars. Which is not to say entrepreneurs should dismiss the immersive reality trip. In the past few years, much has changed, and many companies are doing virtual business—just not the kind they originally envisioned.

Two years ago Second Life, the largest of the virtual sites, with 1 million monthly visitors, created an enterprise group, to better cater to businesses. Companies like Dell shut storefronts and

retooled their virtual-world platforms for meetings and training. A whole flock of specialized sites now provide business services, such as hosting conventions. "Companies learned they didn't need to have a shop on Main Street," says Gartner analyst Jeff Mann.

It turns out, these virtual worlds may be especially well suited to new companies. In these simulated realities, one's avatar can attend a trade show, keep up with technology, show off a new product and network with a very global reach. The sites cut costs—both to budgets and the planet—by reducing travel, and they lend companies an undeniable cool factor. Software engineering firm Agile Dimensions had 35 avatars attending its recent conference on Second Life; the firm says the conference cost $8,567, mostly in software expenses, as opposed to the $35,695 it would have cost to host a face-to-face meeting. It saved 27 tons of CO_2, to say nothing of the ham sandwiches.

With many new technologies, there's a period of hype-fueled growth, followed by disillusionment. Only later does stable growth arrive. Virtual worlds have reached a stage where new users continue to build, even though the media has moved

On Second Life, conventional retail never took off. But you can pay real money for a virtual suit for your next big virtual meeting.

on to fan the fires of Facebook and Twitter, says Douglas Thompson, CEO of Remedy Communications, a Toronto marketing firm. Second Life says the time spent on the site by users increased 21 percent in 2009. Most paying customers on Second Life are purely social, but it still boasts 1,400 business-related organizations as users. Thompson says traffic on Metanomics, his company's Second Life video presence, has picked up in the past year, with 50 percent of new users coming from small or medium-size companies. "People no longer ask what an avatar is," says Thompson. "We can thank Jim Cameron for that."

There is a learning curve, however, especially if you didn't spend your youth on video games. When I first visited Second Life, my avatar walked into a drunk, bumping into other avatars who were kind enough to show me around. I also noted something

36 SMARTMONEY   APRIL 2010

pull quotes The pull quote is an often-overlooked textual visual that can be extremely useful in emphasizing key points. It is also useful when the content of a document does not lend itself naturally or easily to other visuals. By selecting a key sentence, copying it to a text box, enlarging it, and perhaps even enhancing it with a new font, style, or color, a writer can break up the visual boredom of a full page or screen of text. Word processors let users easily wrap text around shapes as well as along curves and irregular lines. Exhibit 3.3[8] shows an example that is simple yet effective in both drawing the reader's attention to a key point and adding visual interest to a page.

bullet lists *Bullet lists* are listings of points arranged with bullets (•) to set them off. These lists can have a title that covers all the points, or they can appear without titles, as they appear at various places in this book. When you use this arrangement, make the points grammatically parallel. If the points have subparts, use sub-bullets for them. Make the sub-bullets different by color, size, shape, or weight. Darts, check marks, squares, or triangles can be used for the secondary bullets.

text-based charts If you have studied business management, you know that administrators use a variety of specialized charts in their work. Often these charts are a part of the information presented in reports. Perhaps the most common of these is the *organization chart* (see Exhibit 3.4). These charts show hierarchical information or reporting relationships in an organization. As the word implies, a *flowchart* (see Exhibit 3.5) shows the sequence of activities in a process. Traditionally, flowcharts use specific designs and symbols to show process distinctions. Variations of the organization chart and flowchart are the *decision tree* and the *concept* or *mind map*. A *decision tree* helps one follow a path to an appropriate decision. A *concept or mind map* shows relationships between ideas, helping writers plan and organize their documents. A *Gantt chart* is a visual representation that identifies tasks and their scheduling. Using one can help writers get their projects done on time. You can easily construct these charts with presentation and drawing applications.

LO 4 Construct data-generated visuals such as bar, pie, line, area, and x-y (scatter) charts as well as combinations and mashups.

Data-generated Graphs and Mashups

Charts are visuals built with raw data and include bar, pie, and line charts and all their variations and combinations. Mashups are visuals that combine separate data files to provide a single visual.

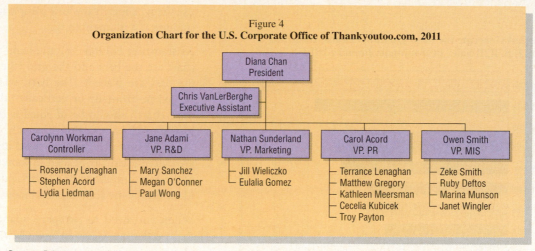

Figure 4
Organization Chart for the U.S. Corporate Office of Thankyoutoo.com, 2011

Source: Primary.

▼ **EXHIBIT 3.5**   Illustration of a Flowchart

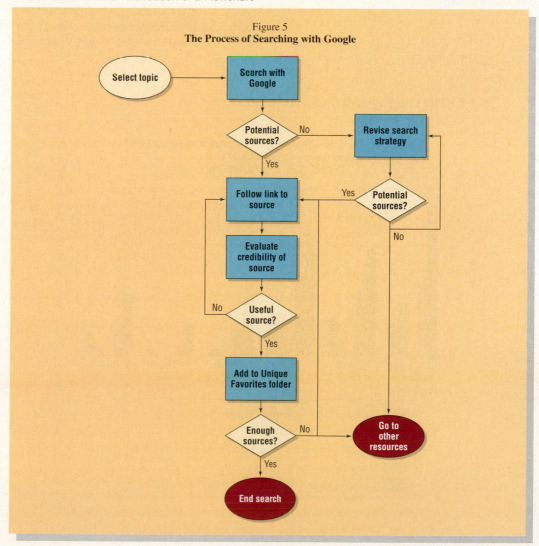

Figure 5
The Process of Searching with Google

Source: Primary.

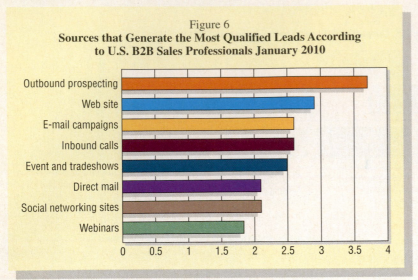

Figure 6
**Sources that Generate the Most Qualified Leads According
to U.S. B2B Sales Professionals January 2010**

Note: n = 136, 1 = least leads, and 5-most leads
Source: Reprinted with permission of eMarketer.

bar and column charts *Simple bar* and *column charts* compare differences in quantities by differences in the lengths of the bars representing those quantities. You should use them primarily to show comparisons of quantity changes at a moment in time.

As shown in Exhibit 3.6,[9] the main parts of the bar chart are the bars and the grid (the field on which the bars are placed). The bars, which may be arranged horizontally or vertically (also called a column chart), should be of equal width. You should identify each bar or column, usually with a caption at the left or bottom. The grid (field) on which the bars are placed is usually needed to show the magnitudes of the bars, and the units (dollars, pounds, miles) are identified by the scale caption below.

When you need to compare quantities of two or three different values in one chart, you can use a *clustered* (or *multiple*) *bar* or *column chart*. Crosshatching, colors, or the like on the bars distinguish the different kinds of information (see Exhibit 3.7).[10] Somewhere within the chart, a legend (explanation) gives a key to the differences in the bars. Because clustered bar charts can become cluttered, usually you should limit comparisons to three to five kinds of information in one of them.

▼ **EXHIBIT 3.7** Illustration of a Clustered Column Chart

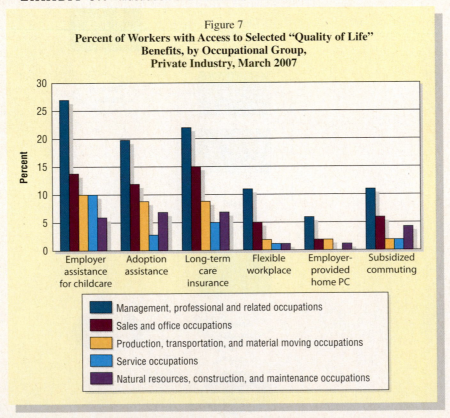

Figure 7
**Percent of Workers with Access to Selected "Quality of Life"
Benefits, by Occupational Group,
Private Industry, March 2007**

Source: George I. Long, "Employer Provided 'Quality-of-Life' Benefits for Workers in Private Industry," *Compensation and Working Conditions*, Bureau of labor Statistics, October 24, 2007, web 19 August 2009.

Figure 8
**Annual Change in the Number of Restaurants
Operating in the U.S.**

Source: From *The Wall Street Journal,* February 8, 2010. Copyright © Dow Jones & Company, Inc.
Reproduced with permission of Dow Jones & Company, Inc. via Copyright Clearance Center.

When you need to show plus and minus differences, you can use *bilateral column charts*. The columns of these charts begin at a central point of reference and may go either up or down, as illustrated in Exhibit 3.8.[11] Column titles appear either within, above, or below the columns, depending on which placement fits best. Bilateral column charts are especially good for showing percentage changes, but you may use them for any series in which plus and minus quantities are present.

If you need to compare subdivisions of columns, you can use *a stacked column chart*. As shown in Exhibit 3.9,[12] such a chart divides each column into its parts. It distinguishes these parts by color, cross-hatching, or the like; and it explains these differences in a legend. Stacked columns may be difficult for your reader to interpret since both the beginning and ending points need to be found. Then the reader has to subtract to find the size of the column component. Clustered column charts or pie charts do not introduce this possibility for error.

Another feature that can lead to reader error in interpreting bar and column chart data is the use of three dimensions when only two variables are being compared. PowerPoint and other applications contribute to the problem by allowing users to create graphs with the option to apply a 3-D effect to data with only two variables. One study evaluated the speed and accuracy of readers' interpretation of (1) two-dimensional columns on two-dimensional axes with (2) both three-dimensional columns on two-dimensional axes and (3) three-dimensional columns on three-dimensional axes. The results showed that readers were able to

extract information from the column chart fastest and most accurately when it was presented in the simple two-dimensional column on the two-dimensional axis.[13] Therefore, unless more than two variables are used, choosing the two-dimensional form over the two-dimensional with a 3-D effect is usually better.

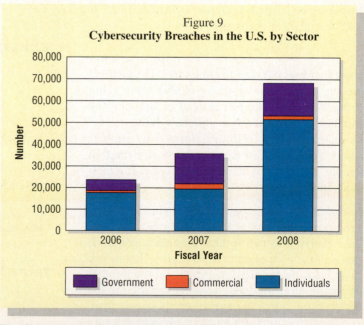

Figure 9
Cybersecurity Breaches in the U.S. by Sector

Note: Fiscal year ends September 30.
Source: From *The Wall Street Journal,* April 9, 2009. Copyright © Dow Jones & Company, Inc. Reproduced with permission of Dow Jones & Company, Inc. via Copyright Clearance Center.

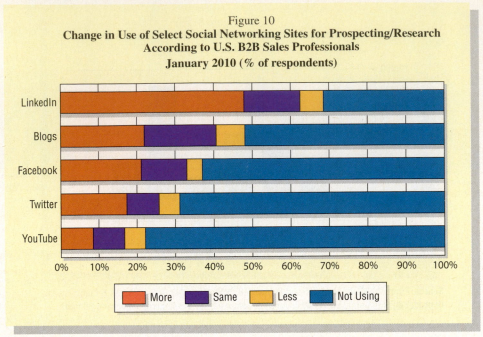

Figure 10
Change in Use of Select Social Networking Sites for Prospecting/Research According to U.S. B2B Sales Professionals January 2010 (% of respondents)

Note: n = 136.
Source: Reprinted with permission of eMarketer.

A special form of stacked column chart is used to compare the percentages of subdivisions. In this form, all the bars are equal in length, for each represents 100 percent. Only the subdivisions within the bars vary. The objective of this form is to compare differences in how wholes are divided. The component parts may be labeled, as shown in Exhibit 3.10,[14] but they also may be explained in a legend.

pictographs A *pictograph* is a bar or column chart that uses bars made of pictures. The pictures are typically representations of the items being compared. For example, instead of showing the number of executives at different bonus levels by using ordinary columns (formed by straight lines), you could use columns with drawings of people. This type of column chart is a pictograph (see Exhibit 3.11).[15]

In constructing a pictograph, you should follow the procedures you use in constructing bar and column charts, plus two special rules. First, you must make all the picture units equal in size. That is, you must base the comparisons wholly on the number of picture units used and never on variation in the areas of the units. The human eye is grossly inaccurate when comparing geometric designs that vary in more than one dimension, so show differences by varying the number, not the size, of the picture units to ensure accurate interpretation. Second, you

should select pictures or symbols that fit the information to be illustrated. In comparing the cruise lines of the world, for example, you might use ships. In comparing computers used in the world's major countries, you might use computers. The meaning of the drawings you use must be immediately clear to the readers.

▼ **EXHIBIT 3.11** Illustration of a Pictograph

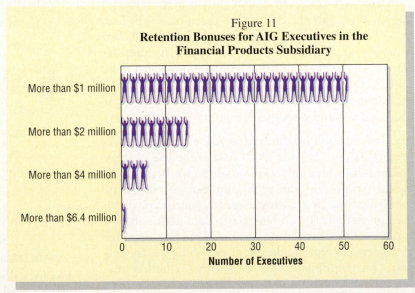

Figure 11
Retention Bonuses for AIG Executives in the Financial Products Subsidiary

Source: From *Wall Street Journal,* March 18, 2009. Copyright © Dow Jones & Company, Inc. Reproduced with permission of Dow Jones & Company, Inc. via Copyright Clearance Center.

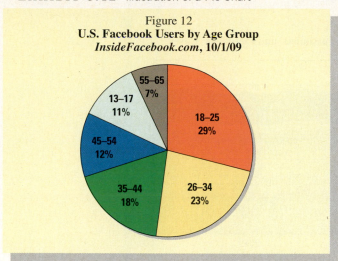

Figure 12
U.S. Facebook Users by Age Group
InsideFacebook.com, 10/1/09

Source: From Justin Smith, "December Data on Facebook's US Growth by Age and Gender: Beyond 100 Million," January 4, 2010, *Inside Facebook Gold.* Reprinted with permission.

pie charts

The most frequently used chart for comparing the subdivisions of wholes is the *pie chart* (see Exhibit 3.12).[16] As the name implies, pie charts show the whole of the information being studied as a pie (circle), and the parts of this whole as slices of the pie. The slices may be differentiated by labeling and color or cross-hatching. A single slice can be emphasized by exploding it (pulling it out). Because it is hard to judge the values of the slices with the naked eye, it is good to include the percentage values within or near each slice. Also, placing a label near each slice ensures quicker understanding than using a legend to identify components. A good rule to follow is to begin slicing the pie at the 12 o' clock position and then to move around clockwise. It is also good to arrange the slices in descending order from largest to smallest.

line charts

Line charts are useful in showing trends—changes of information over time. For example, changes in prices, sales totals, employment, or production over a period of years can be shown well in a line chart.

In constructing a line chart, you draw the information to be illustrated as a continuous line on a grid. The grid is the area in which the line is displayed. It is scaled to show time changes from left to right across the chart (X-axis) and quantity changes from bottom to top (Y-axis). You should mark clearly the scale values and the time periods. They should be in equal increments.

You also may compare two or more series on the same line chart (see Exhibit 3.13).[17] In such a comparison, you should clearly differentiate the lines by color or form (dots, dashes, dots and dashes, and the like). You should clearly label them on the chart or with a legend somewhere in the chart. But the number of series that you may compare on one line chart is limited. The maximum number is usually five to eight.

It is also possible to show parts of a series by use of an *area* chart. Such a chart, however, can show only one series. You should construct this type of chart, as shown in Exhibit 3.14,[18] with a top line representing the total of the series. Then, starting from the base, you should cumulate the parts, beginning with the largest and ending with the smallest. You may use cross-hatching or coloring to distinguish the parts.

Line charts that show a range of data for particular times are called *variance* or high-low charts. Some variance charts show high and low points as well as the mean, median, or mode. When used to chart daily stock prices, they typically include closing price in addition to the high and low. When you use points other than high and low, be sure to make it clear what these points are.

X-Y (scatter) charts

X-Y (scatter) charts are often considered another variation of the line chart. Although they do use X and Y axes to plot paired values, the points stand alone without a line drawn through them. For example, a writer might use a scatter diagram in a report on digital cameras to plot values for price and resolution of several cameras. While clustering the points allows users to validate hunches about cause and effect, they can only be interpreted for correlation—the direction and strength relationships.

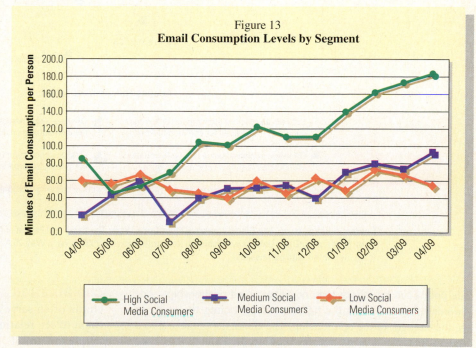

Figure 13
Email Consumption Levels by Segment

Legend:
- High Social Media Consumers
- Medium Social Media Consumers
- Low Social Media Consumers

Source: Reprinted with permission of The Nielsen Company.

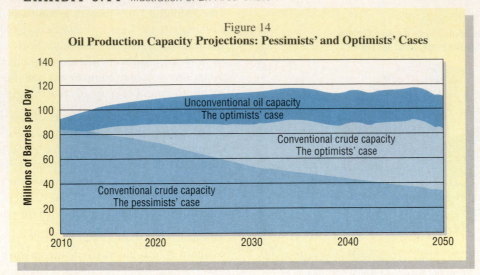

Figure 14
Oil Production Capacity Projections: Pessimists' and Optimists' Cases

Source: Adapted with special permission from "The Argument for and Against Oil Abundance," *Bloomberg BusinessWeek,* 18 January 2010, p. 48.

▼ **EXHIBIT 3.15** Illustration of a XY (Scatter) Chart

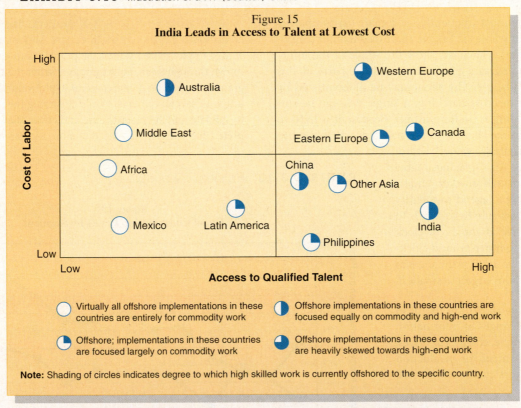

Figure 15
India Leads in Access to Talent at Lowest Cost

Note: Shading of circles indicates degree to which high skilled work is currently offshored to the specific country.

Source: Adapted from "The Globalization of White-Color Work: The Facts and Fallout of Next Generation Offshoring," Booz & Company/Duke University Offshoring Research Network 2006 Survey, Web 20 August 2009, http://www.booz .com. Reprinted with permission.

The points can reveal positive, negative, or no relationships. Additionally, by examining the tightness of the points, the user can see the strength of the relationship. The closer the points are to a straight line, the stronger the relationship. In Exhibit 3.15,[19] the paired values are *the cost of labor* and *the access to qualified talent.*

combination charts and mashups Combination charts often serve your audience extremely well by allowing them to see relationships of different kinds of data. The example in Exhibit 3.16[20] shows the reader or listener the price of the stock over time (the trend) as well as the volume of

Source: Reproduced with permission of Yahoo! Inc. © 2010 Yahoo! Inc. YAHOO! and the YAHOO! logo are registered trademarks of Yahoo! Inc.

sales over time (comparisons). It allows the reader to detect whether the change in volume affects the price of the stock. This kind of information would be difficult to get from raw data. *The Wall Street Journal* often uses this type of visual, allowing its readers to get more depth of information from a single visual.

Mashups are visuals created from separate data files to form a new visual. You may have used a mashup if you've looked for the nearest pizza restaurant on a map. Exhibit 3.17[21] gives an illustration of this type of mashup, showing location, picture, type of ship, and more around the coast of Florida. And at Forbes.com, users might click on a data point on a map to pull up a table of facts related to that one particular data point—such as names of the rich who live there.

LO 5 Appropriately use visuals such as maps, photos, videos, drawings, diagrams, and three-dimensional visuals.

Other Visuals

Some visuals do not fall clearly into the previous categories, but they nevertheless, are visuals that help writers communicate. These include maps, three-dimensional visuals, photos, diagrams, drawings, and more.

maps You may use *maps* to communicate quantitative (statistical) as well as physical (or geographic)

information. Statistical maps are useful primarily when quantitative information is to be compared by geographic areas. On such maps, the geographic areas are clearly outlined, and some graphic technique is used to show the differences between areas (see Exhibit 3.18).[22] Quantitative maps are particularly useful in illustrating and analyzing complex data. Traffic patterns on a Web site could be mapped as well as patterns in a retail store. Physical or geographic maps can show distributions as well as specific locations. Of the numerous techniques available to you, these are the most common:

- Showing different areas by color, shading, or cross-hatching is perhaps the most popular technique. Of course, maps using this technique must have a legend to explain the quantitative meanings of the various colors, cross-hatchings, and so forth.

- Graphics, symbols, or clip art may be placed within each geographic area to depict the quantity for that area or geographic location.

- Placing the quantities in numerical form within each geographic area is another widely used technique.

three-dimensional visuals Until now you have learned that three-dimensional graphs are generally undesirable when the three-dimensional effect is applied to graphs with two variables. But when you actually have three or more variables, presenting them in three dimensions is an option. It is

▼ **EXHIBIT 3.17** Illustration of a Mashup

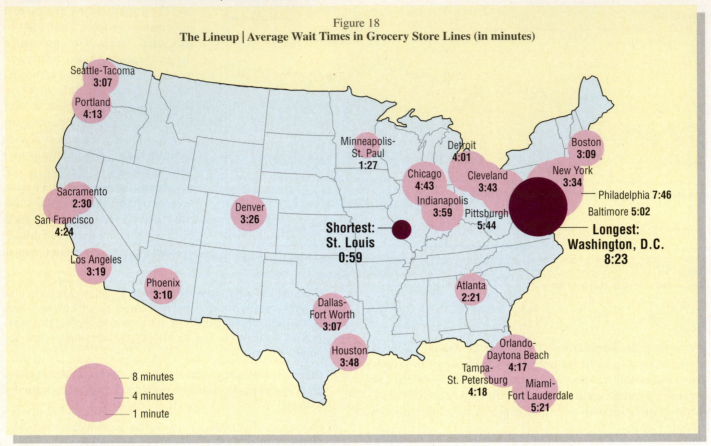

Figure 18
The Lineup | Average Wait Times in Grocery Store Lines (in minutes)

Note: Time spent waiting in line prior to checkout in 2007, as reported by 1,200 shoppers contracted to measure and report their time in line.
Source: From Carl Bialik, "Justice—Wait for it—On the Checkout Line," *Wall Street Journal*, August 19, 2009. Copyright © Dow Jones & Company, Inc. Reproduced with permission of Dow Jones & Company, Inc. via Copyright Clearance Center.

the difference between the raised pie chart versus a ball. Adding a third dimension to a pie chart by "raising" it (including a shadow) will not enhance its information value, but if you actually have three-dimensional data, putting it in the form of a ball will enable your readers to see it from multiple perspectives and gain additional information. In fact, Francis Crick, who won a Nobel prize for discovering the structure of DNA, once revealed that it was not until he and his collaborators took a sheet of paper, cut it, and twisted it that they understood the configuration of DNA. Today we have sophisticated statistics, visualization, and data-mining tools to help us filter and see our data from multiple perspectives.

These three-dimensional tools are beginning to make their way from science labs into business settings. Several factors seem to be driving the trend. Businesses large and small are collecting and attempting to analyze extremely large amounts of detailed data. They are analyzing not only their own data but also data on their competitors. And advances in hardware, software, and Web-based applications are making it easier to graphically represent both quantitative and qualitative data.

Although 3-D graphics help writers display the results of their data analysis, they change how readers look at information and

may take some time getting used to. These tools enable users both to see data from new perspectives and to interact with it. They allow users to free themselves from two dimensions and give them ways to stretch their insights and see new possibilities. These graphics can help businesses make timely decisions through leveraging their corporate information assets.

Exhibit 3.19 shows a three-dimensional visual plot factors identified as the major ones consumers use when deciding which slate (or pad) computer to purchase. Five products are plotted on three variables: cost, battery life, and slate weight. This visual could help a company identify its major competitors and help consumers identify those products that are the best fit for their needs. The more products (or the larger the data set) that are plotted, the more valuable the graph is at helping one extract meaning and understanding.

Using 3-D visualization tools clearly has a place. They are especially good for helping readers analyze large data sets with multiple variables, query them, and interpret them. In deciding whether to use a three-dimensional representation such as this one or a two-dimensional one, you need to consider your audience, the context, and the goal of your communication. Overall, multidimensional presentation on paper is

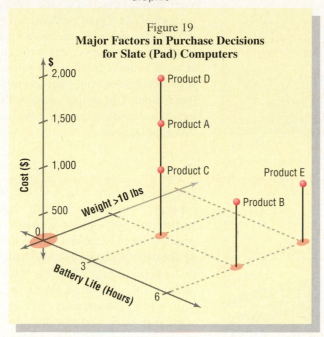

Figure 19
**Major Factors in Purchase Decisions
for Slate (Pad) Computers**

Source: Primary.

difficult; multiple representations can be made from separate two-dimensional views, but not always effectively. If the document is being presented online or digitally where the reader can rotate it to see perspectives, it is likely to be much more effective with a larger number of readers. Writers should take care to use three-dimensional graphics appropriately.

photographs Cameras are everywhere today. If we do not have them in our phones, we might have them in a credit card size or even smaller. And free and for-fee photos are readily available on the Internet, too. In documents, photos can serve useful communication purposes. They can be used to document things and events as well as show products, processes, or services. You could use the photo in Exhibit 3.20 as a metaphor for the concept of a hole in a company's computer security (someone getting in) or the loss of corporate intelligence (something getting out). Today photos, like data-generated graphs, can easily be manipulated. A writer's job is to use them ethically, including getting permission when needed and presenting them objectively.

diagrams, drawings, and more The types of visuals discussed thus far are the ones most commonly used. Other types also may be helpful. *Diagrams* (see Exhibit 3.21) and drawings (see Exhibit 3.22) may help simplify a complicated explanation or description. *Icons* are another useful type of graphic. You can create new icons and use them consistently, or you can draw from an existing body of icons with easily recognized meanings, such as ⊘. Even carefully selected *cartoons* can be used effectively. *Animation* and *video clips* are now used in digital documents and presentations.

For all practical purposes, any visual is acceptable as long as it helps communicate the intended story. The possibilities are almost unlimited.

MANAGING VISUAL MECHANICS

Once you have chosen the right visual for the job, you will need to think about its specific design and placement. How big will the visual be? How will you label it? What colors and type should you choose? The following pargraphs address such design issues.

▼ **EXHIBIT 3.20** Illustration of a Photo

Blind Spot:
Don't linger

Blind Spot: No visibility for 30 feet behind truck.
Stay back 20–25 car lengths.

Blind Spot: Leave 4 car
lengths between vehicles

Blind Spot: Pass
through, don't linger

Source: U.S. Department of Transportation, *Share the Road Safely Program.*

Layout Arrangement

You should determine the layout (shape) of the visual by considering its size and content. Sometimes a tall, narrow rectangle (portrait) is the answer; sometimes the answer is a short, wide rectangle or a full-page rectangle (landscape). You simply consider the logical possibilities and select the one that appears best.

Type

The type used in visuals should be generally consistent in both style and font throughout a document or presentation. Style refers to the look of the type such as bold or italics; font refers to the look of the letters such as with or without feet (*serif* or *sans serif*). Occasionally you may want to vary the type, but do so for a reason. Be aware that even the design of the font you choose will convey a message, a message that should work with the text content.

▼ **EXHIBIT 3.22** Illustration of a Drawing

Source: Reprinted with permission of Zeke Smith © 2003.

If your reader will be viewing the document or presentation on screen in Office 2007 or on a Vista or later computer with ClearType, be sure to use one of the fonts optimized for use with ClearType such as Cambria or Calibri. They were designed to render well on the screen, and Microsoft's research has confirmed that they enable people to read faster and more accurately, leading to a 7 percent average increase in productivity.[23]

Size is another variable to watch. The size you choose should look appropriate in the context in which it is used. Your top priority in choosing type style, font, and size should be readability.

Size

One of the first decisions you must make in constructing a visual is determining its size. This decision should not be arbitrary, and it should not be based on convenience. You should give the visual the size that its contents and importance justify. If a visual is simple (with only two or three quantities), a quarter page might be enough and a full page would be too much. But if a visual must display complex or detailed information, a full page might be justified.

With extremely complex, involved information, you may need to use more than a full page. When you do, make certain that this large page is inserted and folded so that the readers can open it easily. The fold you select will be determined by the size of the page. You simply have to experiment until you find a convenient fold.

Rules and Borders

You should use rules and borders when they help the appearance of the visual. Rules help distinguish one section or visual from another, while borders help separate visuals from the text. In general, you should place borders around visuals that occupy less than a full page. You also can place borders around full-page visuals, but such borders have little practical value. Except in cases in which visuals simply will not fit into the normal page layout, you should not extend the borders of visuals beyond the normal page margins.

"THIS HELPS ME KEEP TRACK OF WHO'S AFTER MY JOB."

Color and Cross-Hatching

Color and cross-hatching, appropriately used, help readers see comparisons and distinctions (see Exhibit 3.23). In fact, research has found that color in graphics improves the comprehension, retention, and ease of extracting information. Also, both color and cross-hatching add to the attractiveness of the report. Because color is especially effective for this purpose, you should use it whenever practical and appropriate.

Clip Art

Today you can get good-looking clip art easily—so easily in fact that some writers often overuse it. Although clip art can add interest and bring the reader or listener into a visual effectively, it also can overpower and distract. The general rule is to keep in mind the purpose your clip art is serving: to help the reader

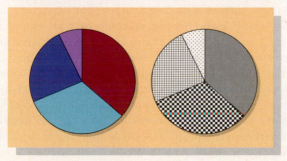

▼ **EXHIBIT 3.23** Color versus Cross-hatched Pie

understand the content. It should be appropriate in both its nature and size. It also should be appropriate in its representation of gender, race, and age. Also, if it is copyrighted, you need permission to use it.

Background

Background colors, photos, and art for your visuals should be chosen carefully. The color should provide high contrast with the data and not distract from the main message. Photos, especially faded photos, that are well chosen can add interest and draw the reader in. However, be aware that photos as well as other background art can evoke meanings or emotions not appropriate or desirable given your intended message. Additionally, when visuals are used cross-culturally, you will want to be sure the message your background sends is the one you intended by testing or reviewing it with the receivers.

Numbering

Pull quotes, clip art, and other decorative visuals do not need to be numbered. Neither does a lone table or figure in a document. Otherwise, you should number all the visuals in documents and presentations. Many schemes of numbering are available to you, depending on the types of visuals you are using.

If you have many visuals that fall into two or more categories, you may number each of the categories consecutively. For example, if your document is illustrated by six tables, five charts, and six maps, you may number these graphics Table I, Table II, . . . Table VI; Chart 1, Chart 2, . . . Chart 5; and Map 1, Map 2, . . . Map 6.

But if your visuals comprise a wide mixture of types, you may number them in two groups: tables and figures. Figures, a miscellaneous grouping, may include all types other than tables. To illustrate, consider a document containing three tables, two maps, three charts, one diagram, and one photograph. You could number these visuals Table I, Table II, and Table III and Figure 1, Figure 2, . . . Figure 7. By convention, tables are not grouped with other types of visuals. But it would not be wrong to group and number as figures all visuals other than tables even if the group contained sufficient subgroups (charts, maps, and the like) to permit separate numbering of each of them.

Construction of Titles and Captions

Every graph or table should have a title or caption that adequately describes its contents. A title is often used with visuals displayed in oral presentations; a caption is more often used with visuals included in documents. Like the headings used in other parts of documents, the title or caption of the visual has the objective of concisely covering the contents. As a check of content coverage, you might well use the journalist's five Ws: *who, what, where, when,* and *why,* and sometimes you also might use *how.* But because conciseness also is desired, it is not always necessary to include all the Ws in the title. The title or caption of a chart comparing the annual sales volume of the Texas and California territories of the Dell Company for the years 2010–11 might be constructed as follows:

Who: **Dell Company**

What: **Annual sales**

Where: **Texas and California**

When: **2010–11**

Why: **For comparison**

The title or caption might read, "Comparative Annual Sales of Texas and California Territories of the Dell Company, 2010–11." For even more conciseness, you could use a major title and subtitle. The major title might read, "A Texas and California Sales Comparison"; the subtitle might read, "Dell Company 2010–11." Similarly, the caption might read "A Texas and California Sales Comparison: Dell Company 2010–11."

An alternative to this kind of topic heading is a talking heading. The talking heading, or headline, makes the claim in the form of a sentence. In this case a talking heading might read, "Texas Leads California in Total Annual Sales for 2010." In a sense, it gives the audience the main message of the visual. You saw another example of a talking heading in Exhibit 3.15, an Illustration of an X-Y (scatter) chart, which reads, "India Leads in Access to Talent at the Lowest Cost."

Placement of Titles and Captions

In documents, titles of tables conventionally appear above the tabular display; captions of all other types of visuals conventionally appear below it. In presentations, titles of both tables and other charts and illustrations are usually placed above the visual. There has been a trend toward using title case type for all illustration titles and placing the titles of both tables and figures at the top. In fact, most presentation applications default to the top. These practices are simple and logical; however, you should follow the conventional practices for more formal documents and presentations.

Footnotes and Acknowledgments

Parts of a visual sometimes require special explanation or elaboration. When this happens, as when similar situations arise in connection with the text, you should use footnotes. Such footnotes are concise explanations placed below the illustration and keyed to the part explained by means of a superscript (raised) number or symbol (asterisk, dagger, double dagger, and so on). Footnotes for tables are best placed immediately below the visual. Footnotes for other visual forms follow the illustration when the title or caption is placed at the bottom of the visual.

Usually, a source acknowledgment is the bottommost component of a visual. By *source acknowledgment* we mean a reference to the body or authority that deserves the credit for gathering the data used in the illustration. The entry consists simply of the word *Source* followed by a colon and the source name. A

Sparklines are intended to communicate quickly and to stand separately from text in a document, usually running with the text or within a table. You can now create them in Excel 2010.

	Q1	Q2	Q3	Q4	Trends
Rep 1	8,552	1,800	8,857	9,133	
Rep 2	9,458	7,594	6,930	3,920	
Rep 3	8,839	1,929	8,476	8,474	
Rep 4	5,766	2,877	9,586	10,989	
Rep 5	8,345	954	8,574	6,453	
Rep 6	7,564	8,692	11,992	8,574	
Rep 7	8,489	8,485	4,903	8,746	

Line   Column   Win/Loss

Sparklines

source note for data based on information gathered by the U.S. Department of Commerce might read like this:

Source: U.S. Department of Commerce.

If you or your staff collected the data, you may either omit the source note or give the source as "Primary," in which case the note would read like this:

Source: Primary

LO 6 Apply visual literacy concepts at the document and presentation level.

MAKING DOCUMENT DESIGN DECISIONS

To work well, visuals need to be part of the document or presentation—not to compete with it. One way to achieve this goal is to follow guidelines for good document design. Following such guidelines not only enhances the appearance of a document or presentation but also contributes to its readability, usefulness, and ultimate value.

Three basic elements of design are layout, type, and art. A fourth element, color, has more recently become an important element, too, as its cost and ease of use in digital documents and presentations moves to print. Today laser printers are capable of printing high-quality documents in color with the same cost and speed as black and white printers. While no one set of rules or even guidelines exist for applying design principles in all situations, creators of documents and presentations need to be aware of them so they can consciously apply the ones that work best for their purpose, content, context, and audience.

Communication in brief

Getting Help to Select the Right Visual

While this chapter presents some of the common options for visuals you can use to present your text and data, one online tool, a Table of Visualization Methods, can give you even more ideas. By running your cursor over the Periodic Table of Visualization Methods at its Web site (http://www.visual-literacy.org/periodic_table/periodic_table.html), you will find more ways to show data, information, concepts, strategies, metaphors, and compound visuals.

A pop-up screen shows what each kind of visual looks like. In the pop-up shown here, you can see an illustration of a mind map. By keeping your purpose in mind, you will be able to choose wisely and be confident that your visual not only looks good but is the most appropriate one for your message.

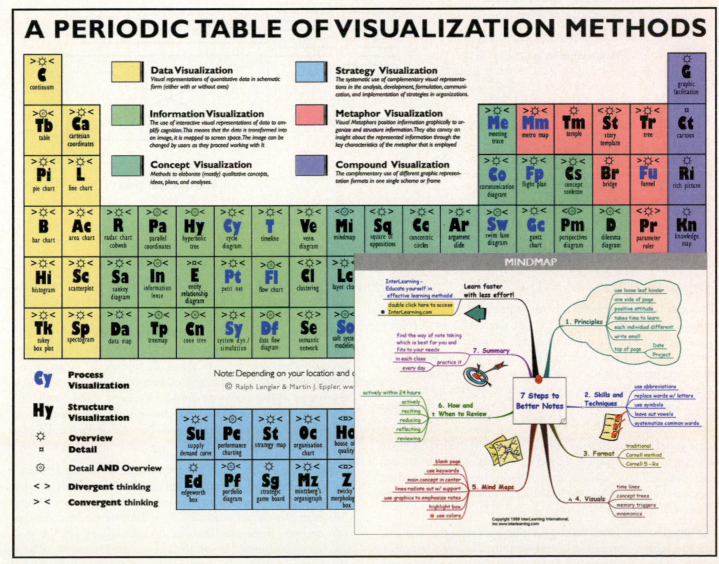

Source: Ralph Lengler and Martin J. Eppler, Visual-literacy.org, University of Lugarno (and three other Swiss university partners), n.d., Web, 20 April 2010. Reprinted with permission.

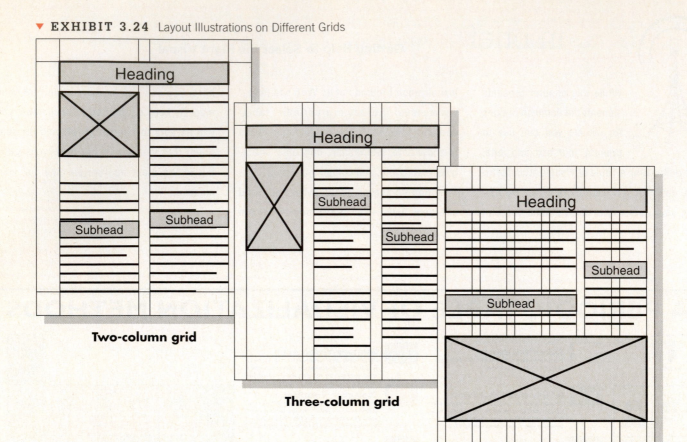

Two-column grid

Three-column grid

Six-column grid

Layout

The orientation of the document or presentation is the most basic decision. The defaults are portrait (vertical) for print documents and landscape (horizontal) for presentations. However, both forms are flexible. Documents can be printed for landscape presentation, and they can be viewed on screens that way as well. Presentations can be viewed vertically, too. And some devices—tablet PCs and smartphones—allow the viewer to choose the orientation.

One good rule of thumb is to stay with the defaults since most readers or listeners expect it. However, if the content will look better or if the context the receiver will be reading in seems to require it, you can and probably should change the orientation.

For decades we have used prescribed layouts for business memos, letters, and reports. Presentations are less prescribed; many companies use standard templates for both print documents and digital presentations. Following the prescribed formats and using the templates that most large companies have developed offer advantages for both the employee and the company. The employee has clear direction about what the company wants the document to include, and the template helps the employee to remember to include it. Using the prescribed formats makes it easier and more efficient for the user of the information as well. Consistency across documents helps promote their effective use. Also, oftentimes the company incorporates its logo, slogan, and other images in order to control the image of its name—its brand. However, some companies give employees more leeway to create documents for special uses or special clients or customers. So fully understanding the layout element is necessary.

Other common layout decisions involve grids, spacing, and margins. Grids are the nonprinting horizontal and vertical lines that help you place your text and visuals precisely and consistently. The examples shown in Exhibit 3.24 illustrate the placement of text on two-, three-, and six-column grids. The grids also provide an opportunity for you to plan for the placement of your headings and subheads. Headings are organizing elements that provide your reader not only with improved navigation help but also with content and quick retrieval of information. You can readily see how important it is to plan their placement.

▼ EXHIBIT 3.25 Different Forms of Justification

Left-justified **Right-justified** **Fully justified**

To make the document or presentation look its best, you must consider both external and internal spacing. External spacing is the white space—the space some never think about carefully. Just as volume gives emphasis to writing, white space gives importance. Surrounding text or a visual with white space sets it apart, emphasizing it to the reader. Used effectively, white space also has been shown to increase the readability of documents and presentations, giving your reader's eyes a rest. And no one wants to read densely packed text. Ideally, white space should be a careful part of the design of your document or presentation.

Internal spacing refers to both vertical and horizontal spacing. The spacing between letters on a line is called *kerning*. With word processing applications, you can adjust how close the letters are to each other. These applications also allow you to adjust how close the lines are to each other vertically, called *leading*. Currently, many still refer to spacing in business documents as single or double spacing. However, this is a carryover from the typewriter era when a vertical line space was always ⅙ inch or when six lines equaled an inch. Today's software and hardware allow you to control this aspect of your document much more exactly. In fact, Word 2007 sets its default spacing to 1.15 lines, which seems to contribute to the readability of the default font, Calibri. The best spacing to use depends on the typeface you decide to use and the length of the lines. In any case, you need to make a conscious decision about the spacing aspect of the layout of your documents.

Another aspect of layout is your margin settings. Ideally, you should want your document or presentation should look like a framed picture. This arrangement calls for all margins to be equal. However, some businesses use fixed left and right margins on all documents regardless of their length. Some do this to line up with design features on their letterhead; others believe it increases productivity. In either case, the side margins will be equal. And with today's word processors you easily make your top and bottom margins equal by telling the application to center the document vertically on the page. Although all margins will not be exactly equal, the page will still have horizontal and vertical balance. And some software applications have "shrink to fit" tools. With this feature, the writer tells the application the number of pages, allowing it to select such aspects as margins, font size, and spacing to fit the message to the desired space.

Today's programs also have the capability to align your type at the margins or in the center. This is called *justification*. Left justification aligns every line at the left, right justification aligns every line at the right, and full justification aligns every line at both the left and the right (see Exhibit 3.25). Full justification takes the extra spaces between the last word and the right margin and distributes them across the line. This adds extra white spaces across the line, stopping most readers' eyes a bit. Therefore, it is usually best to set a left-justified margin and keep the resulting ragged right margin. However, if your document's ragged margin is distracting, you may want to turn on the hyphenation feature. Your program will then hyphenate words at the end of lines, smoothing the raggedness of the right margin.

Type

Type is purported to influence the appearance of your document more than any other aspect. You need to decide on the typeface, the type style, and the type size. Typeface refers to the font or shape of the characters. Although thousands of fonts are

Fonts optimized for display:

Calibri is a sans serif typeface.

Cambria is a serif typeface.

Fonts optimized for print:

Times New Roman is a serif typeface.
Arial is a sans serif typeface.

available, they are generally classified as *serif* or *sans serif*. Serif typefaces have feet; sans serif do not. You can see the difference clearly in the examples in Exhibit 3.26.

Since readers use the visual cues they get from the feet to form the words in their minds, they find the text of these documents easier to read if a serif typeface is used. Sans serif typefaces are particularly good for headings where clear, distinct letters are important. With online documents, which have poorer resolution than printed ones, sans serif type is usually better overall because it makes the outline of the letters cleaner.

Type style refers to the way the typeface can be modified. The most basic styles include normal, **bold**, *italic,* and ***bold italic***. Depending on your software and printer, you may have other options such as outline or shadow. You usually will decide to use modifications for specific reasons. For example, you may present all actions you want the reader to take in boldface type. Or you may decide to apply different styles to different levels of headings. In any case, use of type styles should be planned.

Finally, you will need to decide on size of type. Type is measured in points. Characters one inch high are 72 points. While this is a standard measure, different typefaces in the same size often appear to be a different size. You will need to consider your typeface in choosing the size for your documents. Generally, in print documents body text is between 9 and 14 points, and headings are 15 points and larger. In presentations, the size of the type should be governed by the context. But the body type should usually be at least 24 points and the headings 30 points. Every viewer should be able to read the screen no matter how far back or to the side one is located.

Art

Art as used here in its broadest sense refers to visuals such as drawings, graphs, photos, and other illustrations. As a writer,

you primarily need to remember that art should always serve a message's purpose. Both its look and placement must be carefully planned.

While older versions of Office let writers import a variety of art formats, Microsoft made it even easier beginning with Office 2007 for writers to insert both tables and illustrations. And its SmartArt feature adds the ability to include lists, processes, cycles, matrices, and more by clicking looks, selecting a color, and filling in a text. Two art elements especially valuable in presentations are the arrow or pointer and the callout. Arrows allow presenters to point to a particular item, directing the readers' attention and interpreting for them. Not only does this help the reader follow the presentation, but it also focuses the attention where the presenter wants it. A callout (found under Shapes in PowerPoint) is similar. It focuses the attention and spells out the interpretation for the viewers, reinforcing the idea the presenter wants the viewers to take away with them. But the fact that it's easy doesn't mean it should be overused either. Careful selection and placement of art are still the responsibility of the designer.

Color

Color is a design element that is growing in importance—more and more business communicators are using it due to its lower costs and ready availability. We have already touched on color in the discussion of different types of visuals and of backgrounds. But color serves other purposes when used in the design of the whole document or presentation.

One of the most basic decisions is the color of the paper or the background of slides in presentations. Color communicates. Bright bold colors announce one's presence, while soft colors tend to fade into the background. Colors often convey meanings, meanings that vary from culture to culture. Color can draw attention and it can distract. Many, many studies have been done on the use of color and its effectiveness in various settings. Do you feel cooler in rooms painted light blue or green? Do you eat more and faster in restaurants decorated in red and yellow? Are résumés more apt to be reviewed when printed on lime green paper? Do dark backgrounds in presentations put viewers to sleep? As you have probably figured out, different people come to different conclusions about how best to use color. Probably sticking to the default paper color (white) and default PowerPoint background (white) is a good starting place. Then add and choose color to serve the purpose, content, context, and audience.

But one significant ability of color is its ability to help organize your contents and guide your readers. For example, you could use different colors in document headings and subheadings to help your reader navigate the document or presentation. You might use one specific color to highlight key points, another to highlight new items, and a third to highlight cost. By using it consistently for a planned purpose, you convey meaning to the reader and attract attention. One feature in PowerPoint that can be used this way is the dimming tool. It allows the presenter to dim points already reviewed, forcing the viewers' attention to the next item.

One word of caution—be careful not to overdo it. If the reader does not know or cannot easily figure out how you have used color, it could be distracting. Not only would you be defeating your purpose, but, even worse, you might confuse your readers. But do consider its use in organizing documents so your reader can follow them easily and grasp your meaning quickly and accurately.

In conclusion, by understanding these basic principles of visual literacy, you will develop skills that will enable you both to understand documents and presentations and to create and select images to communicate ideas to your readers and listeners. ■

LEARNING OBJECTIVES

LO1 Simplify writing by selecting familiar and short words.

LO2 Use technical words and acronyms with caution.

LO3 Write concretely and use active verbs.

LO4 Write with clarity and precision by selecting the right words and by using idioms correctly.

LO5 Use words that do not discriminate against others.

LO6 Write short, clear sentences by limiting sentence content and economizing on words.

LO7 Design sentences that give the right emphasis to content.

LO8 Employ unity and logical wording to make sentences clear.

LO9 Compose paragraphs that are short and unified, use topic sentences effectively, and communicate coherently.

LO10 Use a conversational style that eliminates rubber stamps.

LO11 Use the you-viewpoint to build goodwill.

LO12 Accent the positive through word choice and positioning to achieve goodwill and other desired effects.

four

using an
appropriate
style

Once you have analyzed your communication task, decided what kind of message you need to write, and planned your verbal and visual contents you're ready to get down to the challenge of writing—putting one word, sentence, and paragraph after another to communicate what you want to say.

While each document you write will need to respond to the unique features of the situation, keeping in mind certain guidelines can help you make good writing choices. This chapter offers advice on selecting appropriate words, writing clear sentences and paragraphs, and achieving the desired effect with your readers. The goal is documents that communicate clearly, completely, efficiently, and engagingly. ■

THE IMPORTANCE OF ADAPTATION

Clear, effective writing begins with adapting your message to your specific readers. As Chapter 1 explains, readers occupy particular organizational, professional, and personal contexts. They do not all have the same vocabulary, knowledge, or values. And you do not have the same relationship with all of them.

To communicate clearly and with the appropriate tone, you should learn everything possible about those with whom you wish to communicate and consider any prior correspondence with them. Then you should word and organize your message so that it is easy for them to understand it and respond favorably. Tailoring your message to your readers is not only strategically necessary; it is also a sign of consideration for their time and energy. Everyone benefits when your writing is reader focused.

SELECTING APPROPRIATE WORDS

Consider the following excerpts from two companies' reports to shareholders:

Company A: Last year your company's total sales were $117,400,000, which was slightly higher than the $109,800,000 total for the year before. After deducting for all expenses, we had $4,593,000 in profits, compared with $2,830,000 for 2010. Because of these increased profits, we were able to increase your annual dividend payments per share from the 50 cents paid over the last 10 years.

Company B: The corporation's investments and advances in three unconsolidated subsidiaries (all in the development stage) and in 50 percent–owned companies was $42,200,000 on December 31, 2011, and the excess of the investments in certain companies over net asset value at dates of acquisition was $1,760,000. The corporation's equity in the net assets as of December 31, 2011, was $41,800,000 and in the results of operations for the years ended December 31, 2010 and 2011, was $1,350,000 and $887,500, respectively. Dividend income was $750,000 and $388,000 for the years 2010 and 2011, respectively.

> "Choosing the best words for any document requires thinking about what you want to achieve and with whom."

Which paragraph is better written? If you answered "it depends on the targeted readers," you're right. The wording in the first version would be appropriate for an audience without a background in finance, while that in the second is directed more toward finance professionals. Obviously, the lesson of the exercise is this: Choosing the best words for any document requires thinking about what you want to achieve and with whom.

Still, we can identify several stylistic principles that will apply to most of your documents. Whoever your readers, your selection of words is likely to be more effective if you keep the following suggestions in mind.

LO 1 Simplify writing by selecting familiar and short words.

Use Familiar Words

No matter who your readers are, a practice to avoid is using a complex word where an everyday word will do. Do you really need *ascertain* instead of *find out*? *Initiate* instead of *begin*? To convey your meaning as efficiently as possible, try to use the simplest words that will carry the meaning without insulting your readers' intelligence or being too informal.

A great resource for business writers—and a great model of the advice it gives—is the U.S. Securities and Exchange Commission's *A Plain English Handbook: How to Create Clear SEC Disclosure Documents* (available at http:www.sec.gov/pdf/handbook.pdf).

Here's what the handbook says about using familiar words:

> Surround complex ideas with short, common words. For example, use *end* instead of *terminate*, *explain* rather than *elucidate*, and *use* instead of *utilize*. When a shorter, simpler synonym exists, use it.

Use Slang and Popular Clichés with Caution

At any given time in any society, some slang words and clichés are in vogue. In the United States, for example, you might currently hear "voted off the island," "Are you smarter than a 5th grader?," or "Come on down!"—all of which come from U.S. television shows. But other expressions from U.S. television, such as "Where's the beef?" and "That's the $64,000 question," have faded into the past. Business clichés come and go as well. One 2008 television commercial had employees playing business-cliché bingo, listening to a speech and checking off such phrases as "think outside the box" and "push the envelope" as the speaker said them. These once-popular expressions seem to be on their way out.

Slang and clichés may achieve a desired effect in a certain context, but they run the risk of sounding stale and out of date. They can also create problems in cross-cultural communication. Use such expressions sparingly and only in informal communication with people who will understand and appreciate them.

Prefer Short Words

According to studies of readability, short words generally communicate better than long words. Of course, part of the explanation is that short words tend to be familiar words. But there is another explanation: Heavy use of long words—even long words that are understood—leaves an impression of difficulty that hinders communication.

Communication in brief

Managing Formality in Your Writing

Though today's workplaces are much less formal than they used to be, a degree of formality is still expected when you are

- communicating with someone you don't know.
- communicating with someone at a higher level than you.
- using a conventionally formal medium, such as a letter, long report, or external proposal.
- writing a ceremonial message, such as a commendation or inspirational announcement.
- writing an extremely serious message, such as a crisis response or official reprimand.

In such situations, you can often achieve the desired level of formality by making substitutions like the following:

Informal Wording	More Formal Substitute
Looked into	Studied, investigated, analyzed
Juggled	Rearranged
Make sure	Ensure
Great	Exceptional, award-winning
So (as a conjunction)	As a result, therefore
Double check	Confirm
Check with	Consult with
Right	Correct, accurate, appropriate
Won't	Will not

As you can see, being more formal sometimes requires using more words or syllables. When your readers expect formality, the exta length is justified. Just keep your writing as clear and efficient as you can while meeting the formality requirements of the situation.

The suggestion that short words be chosen does not mean that all short words are easy and all long words are hard. Many exceptions exist. Not everyone knows such one-syllable words as *gybe, verd,* and *id,* whereas even children know such long words as *hippopotamus, automobile,* and *bicycle.* Generally, however, word length and word difficulty are related. Thus, you should rely mostly on short words and use long ones with caution.

The point is illustrated by the following examples (the long words and their short replacements are in italics).

Long Words	Short Words
During the *preceding year* the company *operated* at a *financial deficit.*	*Last year* the company *lost money.*
Prior to *accelerating productive operation,* the supervisor inspected the machinery.	Before *speeding up production,* the supervisor inspected the machinery.
The *unanimity* of current forecasts is not *incontrovertible evidence* of an *impending business acceleration.*	*Agreement* of the forecasts is not *proof* that *business will improve.*
This *antiquated merchandising* strategy *is ineffectual* in *contemporary business operations.*	This *old sales* strategy *will not work* in *today's business.*

LO 2 Use technical words and acronyms with caution.

Use Technical Words and Acronyms with Caution

Every field of business—accounting, information systems, finance, marketing, and management—has its technical language. This language can be so complex that in some cases specialized dictionaries have been compiled. Such dictionaries exist for technology, law, finance, and other business specialties. There are even dictionaries for subareas such as databases, ecommerce, and real estate.

As you work in your chosen field, you will learn its technical words and acronyms. In time you will use these terms freely in communicating with people in your field. Frequently, one such word will communicate a concept that would otherwise take dozens of words to describe. Moreover, specialized language can signal to other specialists that you are qualified to communicate on their level.

Problems can arise, however, when you use technical terms with people outside your field. If you forget that not everyone knows them, the result will be miscommunication. You can avoid such miscommunication by using technical words only when you're sure your readers know them.

Examples of misuse of technical wording are easy to find. To a worker in the Social Security Administration, the words *covered employment* commonly mean employment covered by social security. To some outsiders, however, they could mean working under a roof. *Annuity* has a clear meaning to someone in insurance. A *contract that guarantees an income for a specified period* would have more meaning to uninformed outsiders. Computer specialists know C++ and Java to be popular programming languages, but these words may have different meanings for others.

Initials (including acronyms) should be used with caution, too. While some initials, such as IBM, are widely recognized, others, such as SEO (search engine optimization), are not. If you have any doubt that your reader is familiar with the initials, the best practice is to spell out the words the first time you use them and follow them with the initials. You may also need to go one step further and define what they mean.

Whatever your field of expertise, you will need to be careful not to use technical language when you write to people who do not understand it.

Alphabet Soup

Do you know what the following business abbreviations stand for?

B2B	CRM	EPS	FIFO	SWOT
GAAP	ROI	SAAS	TQM	ERP

Find out by typing the acronym followed by "stands for" in the Google search box or Chrome address bar—and then be sure your readers also know them before you use them without defining them.

LO 3 Write concretely and use active verbs.

Use Concrete Language

Good business communication is marked by words that tend to form sharp and clear meanings in the mind. These are the concrete, specific words.

Concrete is the opposite of abstract. While abstract words are vague, concrete words stand for things the reader can see, feel, taste, or smell. Concrete words hold interest because they refer to the reader's experience.

Communication in brief

Lost in Translation

When considering using slang in cross-cultural messages, consider this lesson about how even a seemingly straightforward word can go wrong:

Some interesting problems can arise when attempts are made to reach what are thought to be single-minded markets supposedly speaking a common language. Spanish is probably the most vivid example of a language that, while it has many commonalities throughout its use in different places, also contains certain words that have marked variations in meaning. As a result, the message that's meant to be conveyed isn't necessarily the message that's received.

To illustrate, according to Philip Cateora in his book *International Marketing*, the word *ball* translates in Spanish as *bola*. *Bola* means ball in several countries, a lie or fabrication in several others, while in yet another, it's a vulgar obscenity. Tropicana brand orange juice, he writes, was advertised as *Jugo de China* in Puerto Rico, but when marketed to the Cuban population of Miami, Florida, it failed to make a dent in the market. To the Puerto Rican, *China* translated into orange, but none of the Cubans in Miami were interested in buying what they perceived to be Chinese juice.

Source: Michael White, *A Short Course in International Marketing Blunders* (Novato, CA: World Trade Press, 2002) 40–41, 22, *ebrary*, University of Cincinnati, Web, 9 Mar. 2010.

> "Overuse of the verb "to be" and passive voice can sap the energy from your sentences."

Sample concrete nouns are *chair, desk, computer, Lance Armstrong,* and the *Empire State Building.* Some abstract nouns are *administration, negotiation, wealth, inconsistency, loyalty, compatibility, conservation, discrimination, incompetence,* and *communication.* Note how difficult it is to visualize what the abstract words stand for.

Concreteness is related to being specific. Notice how much clearer the specific words are in the following examples:

Abstract	Specific
A significant loss	A 53 percent loss
The leading company	First among 3,212 competitors
The majority	62 percent
In the near future	By noon Thursday

Now let us see the difference concreteness makes in the clarity of longer passages. Here is an example of abstract wording:

It is imperative that the firm practice extreme conservatism in operating expenditures during the coming biennium. The firm's past operating performance has been ineffectual for the reason that a preponderance of administrative assignments have been delegated to personnel who were ill equipped to perform in these capacities. Recently instituted administrative changes stressing experience in operating economies have rectified this condition.

Written for concreteness, this message might read as follows:

We must reduce operating expenses at least $2 million during 2011–12. Our $1,350,000 deficit for 2009–10 was caused by the inexperience of our two chief administrators, Mr. Sartan and Mr. Ross. We have replaced them with Ms. Pharr and Mr. Kunz, who have had 13 and 17 years, respectively, of successful experience in operations management.

As you can see, specific wording is not only easier to understand; it is also more informative.

Prefer Active Verbs

Of all parts of speech, verbs do the most to make your writing interesting and lively, for a good reason: they contain the action of the sentence.

But not all verbs add vigor to your writing. Overuse of the verb "to be" and passive voice can sap the energy from your sentences. To see the difference between writing that relies heavily on forms of "to be" and writing that uses active verbs, compare the following two passages (the forms of "to be" and their replacements are italicized):

There *are* over 300 customers served by our help desk each day. The help desk personnel's main tasks *are* to answer questions, solve problems, and educate the callers about the software. Without their

technology in brief

Grammar and Style Checkers Help Writers with Word Selection

Today, word processors will help writers with grammar and style as well as with spelling. By default, Word checks spelling and grammar automatically, using red and green underlines to distinguish between them. But as you see in the grammar settings screen shots here, writers can specify whether or not they want help and even which rules are applied to their documents. And they can choose to correct as they go along or to correct on demand. Although grammar and style checkers are not as accurate as spelling checkers, they will identify words, phrases, and sentences that could be improved. In fact, they often provide a way to fix problems along with an explanation of correct usage.

In the example shown here, the checker found the use of passive voice and suggested a change to active voice. However, the writer must decide whether to accept the suggestion or ignore it. The writer needs to determine whether this passive voice was used intentionally for one of the reasons discussed in this chapter or whether it was used by accident and should be changed.

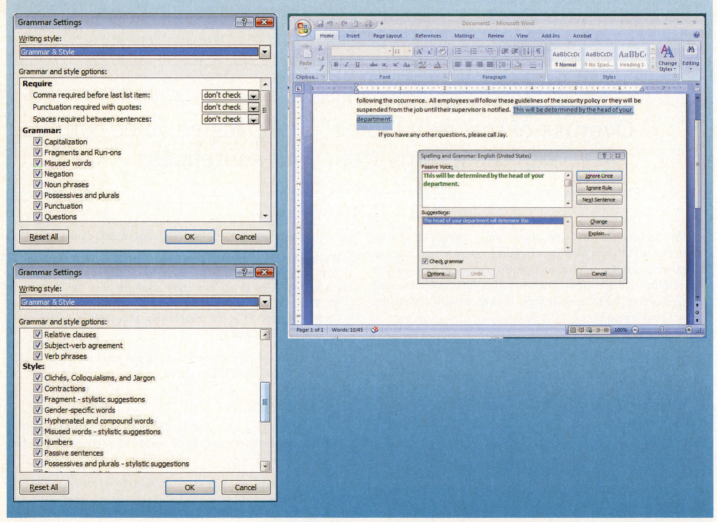

expert work, our customer satisfaction ratings *would be* much lower than they *are.*

Our help desk personnel *serve* **over 300 customers each day. They** *answer* **questions,** *solve* **problems, and** *educate* **the users about the** software. Without their expert work, our customer satisfaction ratings *would drop* significantly.

As these examples show, using active verbs adds impact to your writing, and it usually saves words as well.

In addition to minimizing your use of "to be" verbs, you can make your verbs more active by using what grammarians refer to as *active voice*. As you may recall from your grammar teacher, a sentence with a verb that can take a direct object (the recipient of the action) can be written either in a direct (active) pattern or an indirect (passive) pattern. For example, the sentence "the auditor inspected the books" is in active voice. In passive voice, the sentence would read: "The books were inspected by the auditor." Notice how more energetic the active-voice version is. For further support of the advantages of active over passive voice, compare the following sentences:

Passive	Active
The results were reported in our July 9 letter.	We reported the results in our July 9 letter.
This policy has been supported by our union.	Our union supported this policy.
The office will be inspected by Mr. Hall.	Mr. Hall will inspect the office.
Hardware sales were increased 30 percent by the latest promotion.	The latest promotion increased hardware sales by 30 percent.

The suggestion to prefer active voice does not mean passive voice is incorrect or you should never use it. Sometimes passive voice is preferable. For example, when the doer of the action is unimportant to the message, passive voice properly de-emphasizes the doer:

Advertising is often criticized for its effect on price.

Petroleum is refined in Texas.

Passive voice may enable you to avoid accusing your reader of an action:

The damage was caused by exposing the material to sunlight [instead of "You caused . . ."].

The desired color was not specified in your order [instead of "You did not specify . . ."].

Passive voice also may be preferable when the performer is unknown, as in this example:

During the past year, the equipment has been sabotaged seven times.

Yet another situation in which passive voice may be preferable is one in which the writer does not want to name the performer:

Two complaints have been made about you.

In general, though, your writing will be clearest and liveliest when you write sentences in the "who does what?" (subject, verb, object) order.

Communication in brief

Everything You Wanted to Know about Active and Passive Voice

Writers are often confused by the terms *active voice* and *passive voice*. Here's the lowdown:

Broadly speaking, there are two main categories of verbs in English: those that can take direct objects and those that can't. To illustrate, the verb *repair* can take a direct object (that is, you can repair something), while the verb *happen* cannot (you can't happen anything).

Sentences with verbs that can take direct objects are the ones that can be written in either active or passive voice. When you write in active voice, the sentence is in "who + does/did what + to what/whom" order, as in this for example:

An authorized technician repaired the new laser printer,
　　[who]　　　[did what]　　　[to what]

When you write the same idea in passive voice, the direct object moves to the start of the sentence and bumps the real subject to a phrase at the end of it (or out of it altogether). With this move, you now have

The new laser printer was repaired by an authorized
　　[what]　　　[had something done to it]
technician.
　　[by whom]

Or even just

The new laser printer was repaired.
　　[what]　　　[had something done to it]

As you can see, inverting the word order this way makes the sentence less energetic, more roundabout, and sometimes less informative.

You can find instances of passive voice in your own writing by looking for two- and three-word verbs that consist of

• a form of the verb to be (for example, *is, was, has been, will be*) and

• a verb in past-tense form (for example, *installed, reduced, chosen, sent*).

When you find such verbs—*was installed, has been reduced, will be chosen*—see if your meaning would be clearer and sharper if you wrote in the active voice instead, with the doer of the action in the subject position.

Avoid Overuse of Camouflaged Verbs

An awkward construction that should be avoided is the camouflaged verb. When a verb is camouflaged, the verb describing the action in a sentence takes the form of a noun. Then other words have to be added. For example, suppose you want to write a sentence in which *eliminate* is the action to be expressed. If you use the noun form of this verb, *elimination,* you must add more words—perhaps *was effected*—to have a sentence. Your sentence might then be "Elimination of the surplus was effected by the staff." The sentence is indirect and

passive. Using the verb *eliminate* yields this sharper sentence: "The staff eliminated the surplus."

Again, writing sentences in the "who does what?" order will give them the most clarity and impact. Involved, strained, and monotonous sentences often result from other structures.

LO 4 Write with clarity and precision by selecting the right words and by using idioms correctly.

Select Words for Precise Meanings

Obviously, writing requires considerable knowledge of the language being used. But beyond basic familiarity with vocabulary, good writers possess a sensitivity to words' shades of meaning. Words, like people, have personalities. Some are forceful and some timid; some are positive and some negative; some are formal and some informal. Your task as a writer is to choose the words that will best achieve the desired effects with your intended readers.

be sensitive to connotation Consider the differences among *tycoon, industry giant, successful entrepreneur,* and *prominent business executive.* All four labels indicate a person who has acquired wealth and power in business. But they differ in terms of their *connotation,* or the contexts and values they suggest. *Tycoon* calls to mind the robber barons of the late 19th and early 20th centuries, with their diamond tie

Give your writing impact by using strong verbs.

Non-native speakers have particular trouble with idiomatic expressions in foreign languages.

Consider the English verbal phrase "put up with." If you're a native English speaker, it makes clear sense to you—but imagine how nonsensical it might sound to a non-native speaker hearing or reading it for the first time.

On the other hand, choosing the appropriate preposition to describe going "to" a certain place can be challenging for a non-native French speaker. The preposition changes depending on whether you are using it with the name of a city or island ("á Paris"), with the feminine name of a country ("au Japon" [Japan]), with the masculine name of a country ("en Belgique" [Belgium]), with the name of a continent ("en Amerique du Sud" [South America]), with the masculine name of a state or region ("dans le Nevada"), or with the feminine name of a state or region ("en Californie" [California])!

When communicating cross-culturally, be careful to check your wording against a good phrase dictionary or another expert source. Likewise, when communicating with an inexperienced user of your language, try to keep idiomatic expressions to a minimum and be tolerant of errors in idiom that he or she may make.

---

pins and ruthless business practices, whereas *prominent business executive* suggests a less flashy, less greedy person who has achieved success within the constraints of a corporation. Similarly, *fired, dismissed, canned, separated, terminated,* and *discharged* refer to the same action but have different connotations.

Being aware of words' social and emotional associations will make you a more skillful and effective writer.

Faulty Idiom	Correct Idiom
authority about	authority on
comply to	comply with
different than	different from
get a feel on	get a feel for
equally as bad	equally bad
in accordance to	in accordance with

> ## Some word choices are unwise, some are awkward, and some are just plain wrong.

do not confuse similar words Knowledge of language also enables you to use words that carry the right *denotation* or primary meaning. For example, *fewer* and *less* mean the same to some people. But careful users select *fewer* to mean "a smaller number of items" and *less* to mean a smaller amount. The verbs *affect* and *effect* are often used as synonyms. But *affect* means "to influence" and *effect* means "to bring to pass." You can read about more confusing word pairs on your chapter review cards.

use correct idioms In your effort to be a precise writer, you should use idioms correctly. By *idioms* we mean word combinations that have become standard in a language. For example, "independent of" is good idiomatic usage; "independent from" is not. Similarly, you "agree to" a proposal, but you "agree with" a person. Here are some additional illustrations:

As you can see, some word choices are unwise, some are awkward, and some are just plain wrong. If you're unsure which word you need or how a certain word will come across, consult a good dictionary.

LO 5 Use words that do not discriminate against others.

Avoid Discriminatory Wording

Although discriminatory words are not directly related to writing clarity, our review of word selection would not be complete without some mention of them. By discriminatory words we mean words that do not treat all people equally and with respect. More specifically, they are words that refer negatively to groups of people, such as by gender, race, nationality, sexual orientation, age, or disability. Such words run contrary to acceptable views of fair play and human decency. They do not promote good business ethics or good business and thus have no place in business communication.

The following review of the major forms of discriminatory words should help you achieve equitable and inclusive writing.

use gender-neutral words Take care not to use words that discriminate on the basis of gender. While sometimes sexist wording is directed against males, it is more likely to discriminate against women. Our language developed in a society in which it was customary for women to work in the home and for men to be the wage earners and decision makers. But times have changed. The language you use in business needs to acknowledge the gender-diverse nature of most workplaces today.

This means avoiding words implying that only one gender can be in charge or perform certain jobs. Such job titles as *fireman, waitress, congressman,* and *chairman* should be replaced with the more neutral labels *firefighter, server, representative,* and *chairperson.* It also means avoiding modifiers that call attention to gender, as in *lady lawyer* or *male nurse.* And when tempted to use such masculine-specific words as *manpower* and *man-made,* see if you can find a more neutral expression (*personnel, manufactured*).

DID YOU KNOW?

In 2008, women comprised 46.5 percent of the total U.S. labor force, and 39 percent of these women worked in management, professional, and related occupations.

Source: "Quick Stats on Women Workers, 2008," *US Department of Labor, Women's Bureau,* US DOL, 2010, Web, 9 Mar. 2010.

You can avoid such problems in three ways (see Exhibit 4.1). First, you can reword the sentence to eliminate the offending word. Thus, the preceding example could be reworded as follows: "The typical State University student eats lunch at the student center." Here are other examples:

Sexist	Gender-Neutral
If a customer pays promptly, *he* is placed on our preferred list.	A customer who pays promptly is placed on our preferred list.
When an unauthorized employee enters the security area, *he* is subject to dismissal.	An unauthorized employee who enters the security area is subject to dismissal.
A supervisor is not responsible for the damage if *he* is not negligent.	A supervisor who is not negligent is not responsible for the damage.

A second way to avoid sexist use of the masculine pronoun is to make the reference plural. Fortunately, the English language has plural pronouns (*their, them, they*) that refer to both sexes. Making the references plural in the examples given above, we have these nonsexist revisions:

If customers pay promptly, *they* are placed on our preferred list.

When unauthorized employees enter the security area, *they* are subject to dismissal.

Supervisors are not responsible for the damage if *they* are not negligent.

WE MADE WORKFORCE DIVERSITY ONE OF OUR TOP GOALS BECAUSE IT'S THE RIGHT THING TO DO.

THAT'S WHY. THAT'S THE ONLY REASON.

OF COURSE, WE DID NEED MORE GOOD IDEAS, GOOD EMPLOYEES, AND GOOD CUSTOMERS TOO.

Source: GRANTLAND® Copyright Grantland Enterprises, www.grantland.net

A third way to avoid sexist use of *he, his,* or *him* is to substitute any of a number of neutral expressions. The most common are *he or she, he/she, s/he, you, one,* and *person.* Using neutral expressions in the problem sentences, we have these revisions:

If a customer pays promptly, *he or she* is placed on our preferred list.

When an unauthorized employee enters the security area, *he/she* is subject to dismissal.

You are not responsible for the damage if *you* are not negligent.

Perhaps the most troublesome words are the masculine pronouns (*he, his, him*) when they are used to refer to both sexes, as in this example: "The typical State University student eats *his* lunch at the student center." Assuming that State is coeducational, the use of *his* excludes the female students. Historically, of course, the word *his* has been considered generic—that is, it can refer to both sexes. But many modern-day businesspeople do not agree and are offended by this use of the masculine pronoun.

▼ **EXHIBIT 4.1** Getting Around *He, His,* and *Him*

You can avoid sexist use of *he, his,* and *him* by
- eliminating the personal pronoun altogether.
- using the plural personal pronouns (*they, their, them*).
- using a neutral expression, such as *he or she* or *you.*

You should use the "he or she" type of expressions with caution, however. They tend to be awkward, particularly if they are used often. Certainly, you should avoid sentences like this one: "To make an employee feel he/she is doing well by complimenting her/him insincerely confuses her/him later when he/she sees his/her co-workers promoted ahead of him/her."

Examples of the sexist use of words abound. In deciding which words to avoid and which to use, you will have to rely on your best judgment. Remember that your goal should be to use words that are fair and that do not offend.

avoid words that stereotype by race, nationality, or sexual orientation
Words that stereotype all members of a group by race, nationality, or sexual orientation are especially unfair, and frequently they reinforce stereotypical beliefs about this group. Members of any minority vary widely in all characteristics. Thus, it is unfair to suggest that Jews are miserly, that Italians are Mafia members, that Hispanics are lazy, that African Americans can do only menial jobs, that gay men are effeminate and so on. Unfair references to minorities are sometimes subtle and not intended, as in this example: "We conducted the first marketing tests in the low-income areas of the city. Using a sample of 200 African-American families, we. . . ." These words unfairly suggest that only African Americans live in low-income areas.

Also unfair are words suggesting that a minority member has struggled to achieve something that is taken for granted in the majority group. Usually well intended, words of this kind can carry subtle discriminatory messages. For example, a reference to a Chinese human resources manager may suggest that it is unusual for a Chinese person to have skills in this area.

Eliminating unfair references to minority groups from your communication requires two basic steps. First, you must consciously treat all people equally, without regard to their minority status. Refer to minority membership only in those rare cases in which it is a vital part of the message to be communicated. Second, you must be sensitive to the effects of your words. Ask yourself how those words would affect you if you were a member of the minorities to which they refer. If you could be offended, find more neutral words.

avoid words that stereotype by age
Your avoidance of discriminatory wording should be extended to include discriminating on the basis of age—against both the old

In business today, men and women, and people of all races and ages work side by side in roles of mutual respect. It would be unfair as well as counterproductive to use words that discriminate against any of them.

and the young. While those over 55 might be retired from their first jobs, many lead lives that are far from the sedentary roles in which they are sometimes depicted. They also are not necessarily feeble, forgetful, or behind the times. While some do not mind being called *senior citizens,* others do. Be careful with terms such as *mature* and *elderly* as well; perhaps *retired, experienced,* or *veteran* would be better received. Likewise, when tempted to refer to someone as *young* (*young accountant, accomplished young woman*), be sure that calling attention to the person's age is defensible.

Also be careful when using one of the popular generational labels in your writing. While it makes sense for the popular management literature to use such labels as *Baby Boomer* and *Millennial* as short-hand references to different generations, the same labels can seem discriminatory in business messages. Your co-worker Frank probably does not want to be referred to as the "Baby Boomer in the group," and your manager Courtney probably will not appreciate your saying that she holds the opinions she does because she's a "Generation X-er." As we have suggested, use such labels only when relevant and appropriate.

> " Words that stereotype all members of a group by race, nationality, or sexual orientation are unfair. "

How Diverse Is Too Diverse?

Can your employer tell you what to wear, outlaw decorated fingernails, or forbid the display of such body art as tattoos and piercings?

According to EmployeeIssues.com, a website about employee rights, the answer is yes—as long as the appearance policies are clearly stated in writing and are applied fairly to all employees.

Just as employers can require the use of uniforms, they can delineate what kinds of personal clothing will be acceptable on the job.

For example, they might define "business casual" in a way that explicitly excludes T-shirts, shorts, flip-flops, and the like. And as long as tattoos and body piercings aren't required by your religion, they can be grounds for being disciplined or even fired—as long as the rules have been clearly stated.

Looking professional need not mean selling out your cultural or ethnic heritage, argues Kali Evans-Raoul, founder of an image consultancy for minorities. Everyone must "balance self-expression with workplace realities," she asserts. Just as one doesn't wear a uniform at home, one shouldn't expect to bring one's entire personal look to work.

To avoid conflicts over your on-the-job identity, your best bet is to try to choose an employer whose values align with your own. Then find and abide by that company's appearance policy.

Sources: "Dress Cody Policy," *Employee-Issues.com*, EmployeeIssues.com, 2003–2010, Web, 9 Nov. 2010; Dan Woog, "Your Professional Image: Balance Self-Expression with Workplace Expectations," *Monster.com*, Monster.com, 2010, Web, 9 Mar. 2010.

The first step toward avoiding discriminatory writing is to put yourself in the reader's shoes.

avoid words that typecast those with disabilities People with disabilities are likely to be sensitive to discriminatory words. We often see or read about those with disabilities exceeding the performance of an average person, and common sense tells us not to stereotype these people. However, sometimes we do anyway. Just as with age, we need to avoid derogatory labels and apologetic or patronizing behavior. For example, instead of describing someone as *deaf and dumb*, use *deaf*. Avoid slang terms such as *fits, spells, attacks*; use *seizures, epilepsy*, or other objective terms. Adjectives such as *crippled* and *retarded* should be avoided. Work to develop a nonbiased attitude, and show it through carefully chosen words.

Some Final Words about Words

There's a lot to keep in mind when selecting the most appropriate words. Under time pressure, it can be tempting to take a shortcut and settle—as Mark Twain once put it—for the best word's "second cousin." But remember: Business and business relationships can be won or lost with one word choice. The effort to say what you mean as clearly, readably, and appropriately as you can is effort well spent.

WRITING CLEAR SENTENCES

When you sit down to write a given message, you have many bits of information at hand. How will you turn them into a clear, coherent message?

When editing your message, it can help to print a copy and make corrections manually.

Your first task will probably be grouping and ordering the information—that is, planning the message's overall organization or structure. But sooner or later, writing a successful message comes down to figuring out how to stitch your contents together in a series of sentences. How much information will you put into each sentence? And in what form and order will that information be?

The advice that follows will help you answer these questions and enhance your chances of communication success.

LO 6 Write short, clear sentences by limiting sentence content and economizing on words.

Limit Sentence Content

Business audiences tend to prefer simple, efficient sentences over long, complex ones. Having too much to do in too little time is a chronic problem in business. No one, whether executive or entry-level employee, wants to read writing that wastes time.

Favoring short sentences can save your readers time. It can also prevent miscommunication. Readability research tells us that the more words and the more relationships there are in a sentence, the greater is the possibility for misunderstanding. This finding suggests that the mind can hold only so much information at one time. Thus, to give it too much information in your sentences is to risk falling short of your communication

technology in brief

Readability Statistics Help Writers Evaluate Document Length and Difficulty

Grammar and style checkers give writers the option of viewing readability statistics. These statistics report the number of words, characters, paragraphs, and sentences in a document along with averages of characters per word, words per sentence, and sentences per paragraph.

The report you see here was generated for a scholarly manuscript. It reports an average of 18.5 words per sentence, a bit high for a business document but probably at an acceptable level for a scholarly document's readers. The Flesch-Kincaid score confirms that the reading grade level is 9.4, too high for business documents but appropriate for a scholarly audience. However, the Flesch Reading Ease score might give the writer cause to review the document for accessibility, even for its targeted audience. The 59.3 score is slightly below the 60–70 range that Microsoft recommends.

Readability Statistics		?	✕
Counts			
Words			1625
Characters			7716
Paragraphs			30
Sentences			85
Averages			
Sentences per Paragraph			3.8
Words per Sentence			18.5
Characters per Word			4.5
Readability			
Passive Sentences			9%
Flesch Reading Ease			59.3
Flesch-Kincaid Grade Level			9.4
		OK	

purpose. The following two versions of the same content illustrate the point:

One Long Sentence

Some authorities in human resources object to expanding normal salary ranges to include a trainee rate because they fear that through oversight or prejudice, probationers may be kept at the minimum rate longer than is warranted and because they fear that it would encourage the spread from the minimum to maximum rate range.

Shorter and Clearer Sentences

Some authorities in human resources object to expanding the normal salary range to include a trainee rate, for two reasons. First, they fear that through oversight or prejudice, probationers may be kept at the minimum rate longer than is warranted. Second, they fear that expansion would increase the spread between the minimum and the maximum rate range.

Surely the vast majority of business readers would prefer the revised version, with its shorter sentences and helpful transitional words.

Bear in mind, though, that what constitutes a short, readable sentence is related to the reader's ability. Readability studies suggest that writing intended to communicate with the middle-level adult reader should average about 16 to 18 words per sentence. For more advanced readers, the average may be higher, while for less advanced readers, it should be lower. You

DID YOU KNOW?

A study found that 95 percent of executives and managers make a to-do list for each day, but 99 percent of them do not complete the tasks on those lists. This is the busy environment in which they'll be reading your messages.

Source: Chuck Martin, *Tough Management: The 7 Winning Ways to Make Tough Decisions Easier, Deliver the Numbers, and Grow the Business in Good Times and Bad* (New York: McGraw-Hill, 2005) xiv, print.

will need to gauge what sentence length is best for each situation.

Moreover, a preference for short sentences should not mean that you should use all short sentences. In fact, you should avoid overusing them. The overuse of short sentences results in a choppy, elementary-sounding effect. You should write easily understood sentences that also maintain a smooth flow of ideas.

Let's consider an example. The following sentence from an employee handbook is much too long:

When an employee has changed from one job to another job, the new corresponding coverages will be effective as of the date the change occurs, unless, however, if due to a physical disability or infirmity as a result of advanced age, an employee is changed from one job to another job and such change results in the employee's new job rate coming within a lower hourly job-rate bracket in the table, in which case the employee may, at the discretion of the company, continue the amount of group term life insurance and the amount of accidental death and dismemberment insurance that the employee had prior to such change.

So many words and relationships are in the sentence that they cause confusion. The result is vague communication at best—complete miscommunication at worst.

Now look at the message written in all short sentences. The meanings may be clear, but the choppy effect is distracting and irritating. Imagine reading a long document written in this style.

An employee may change jobs. The change may result in a lower pay bracket. The new coverage is effective when this happens. The job change must be because of physical disability. It can also be because of infirmity. Old age may be another cause. The company has some discretion in the matter. It can permit continuing the accidental death insurance. It can permit continuing the dismemberment insurance.

The following paragraph takes a course between these two extremes. Clearly, it is an improvement. Generally, it relies on short sentences, but it combines content items where appropriate.

The new insurance coverage becomes effective when because of disability, infirmity, or age an employee's job change results in lower pay. But at its discretion, the company may permit the old insurance coverage to continue.

The upcoming sections on conciseness, management of emphasis, and sentence unity can help you decide how much content each sentence should carry.

Don't write like a faceless bureaucrat!

Business Etiquette—It Depends on Where You Are

Most people are aware that certain unwritten rules for professionalism govern people's business interactions. Those with whom we do business expect us to show respect through our actions, words, and even appearance.

But what is considered appropriate will vary from situation to situation, industry to industry, and country to country. For example, in a small informal company, relatively casual clothing and relaxed behavior would be expected, and anyone behaving too formally would be considered stiff and rude. In a more formal setting, such as a bank or the executive offices of a large organization, what one should wear, say, or even laugh at would be more constrained.

Cross-cultural communication requires additional considerations. For example, according to a website researched by MBA students at the University of Texas–Dallas, it is considered rude in China for women to wear high heels or wear short-sleeved clothing while doing business, or for men to wear anything besides a conservative business suit. The Chinese are also offended by large hand movements, being pointed at while spoken to, and any actions involving touching the mouth.

To learn good business etiquette, consult such sources as Beverly Langford's *The Etiquette Edge: The Unspoken Rules for Business Success* (New York: AMACOM, 2005) and Jeanette S. Martin and Lillian H. Cheney's *Global Business Etiquette: A Guide to International Communication and Customs* (Westport, CT: Praeger, 2008). And then adapt their advice to your specific situation.

Source: "China," *InternationalBusinessCenter.org*, International Business Center, 1998–2008, Web, 10 Mar. 2010.

Economize on Words

Related to limiting sentence content is economizing on words. Anything you write can be expressed in many ways, some shorter than others. In general, the shorter wordings save the reader time and are clearer and more interesting.

Sometimes business writers mistakenly strive for a droning, "blah-blah-blah" effect, believing that it makes them sound more official or businesslike. But readers are more impressed by clear, efficient language than by flabby prose. To avoid the latter, consider the following kinds of excess verbiage and edit them out of your own writing.

Take the Monotony Test

If your verbs are strong, your sentences vary in length, and you emphasize the right ideas, your writing will have an interesting and inviting rhythm.

So read your writing aloud. If you find your voice lapsing into a monotone, you probably need to apply one or more of the guidelines presented in this chapter.

cluttering phrases An often used uneconomical wording is the cluttering phrase. This is a phrase that can be replaced by shorter wording without loss of meaning. The little savings achieved in this way add up.

Here is an example of a cluttering phrase:

In the event that payment is not made by January, operations will cease.

The phrase *in the event that* is uneconomical. The little word *if* can substitute for it without loss of meaning:

If payment is not made by January, operations will cease.

Similarly, the phrase that begins the following sentence adds unnecessary length:

In spite of the fact that they received help, they failed to exceed the quota.

Although makes an economical substitute:

Although they received help, they failed to exceed their quota.

Too many simple sentences create an elementary-sounding style, so combine ideas where appropriate for your adult readers.

The following partial list (with suggested substitutions) of cluttering phrases should help you cut down on their use.

Cluttering Phrase	Shorter Substitute
At the present time	Now
During the time	While
For the purpose of	For
For the reason that	Because, since
In the amount of	For
In the meantime	Meanwhile
In the near future	Soon
In very few cases	Seldom
In view of the fact that	Since, because
With regard to, with reference to	About

surplus words To write economically, eliminate words that add nothing to sentence meaning. As with cluttering phrases, we often use meaningless extra words as a matter of habit. Eliminating these surplus words sometimes requires recasting a sentence, but sometimes they can just be left out.

The following is an example of surplus wording from a business report:

I am writing to tell you that the records for the past years show a steady increase in special appropriations.

The beginning words make an obvious point and add nothing to the meaning of the sentence. Notice how dropping them makes the sentence stronger—and without loss of meaning:

The records for the past years show a steady increase in special appropriations.

Here is a second example:

His performance was good enough *to enable him* to qualify for the promotion.

The words *to enable* add nothing and can be dropped:

His performance was good enough to qualify him for the promotion.

The following sentences further illustrate the use of surplus words. In each case, the surplus words can be eliminated without changing the meaning.

There Is, There Are . . . Do You Really Need Them?

One common way of writing a wordy sentence with a weak verb is to start it with *There is* or *There are.*

Which of these two sentences seems to have the sharper wording?

There are many reasons why people visit our Web site.

People visit our Web site for many reasons.

The next time you're tempted to start a sentence with *There is* or *There are,* stop and think: Can you say the same thing more efficiently by just starting with the real subject of the sentence?

Contains Surplus Words	Eliminates Surplus Words
There are four rules *that* should be observed.	Four rules should be observed.
The machines *that were* damaged by the fire were repaired.	The machines damaged by the fire were repaired.
By *the* examining *of* production records, they found the error.	By examining production records, they found the error.
The president *is of the opinion that* the tax was paid.	The president *believes* the tax was paid.
It is essential that the income be used to retire the debt.	The income *must* be used to retire the debt.
He criticized everyone he *came in contact with.*	He criticized everyone he *met.*

unnecessary repetition of words or ideas Repeating words obviously adds to sentence length. Such repetition sometimes serves a purpose, as when it is used for emphasis or special effect. But all too often it is without purpose, as this sentence illustrates:

We have not received your payment covering invoices covering June and July purchases.

It would be better to write the sentence like this:

We have not received your payment covering invoices for June and July purchases.

Another example is this one:

He stated that he believes that we are responsible.

The following sentence eliminates one of the *that*s:

He stated that he believes we are responsible.

Repetitions of ideas through the use of different words that mean the same thing (*free gift, true fact, past history*) also add to sentence length. Such redundancies are illogical and can rarely be defended.

To Use *That* or Not to Use *That*?

How easy is it to read the following sentence without making a misstep?

> We found the reason for our poor performance was stiff competition from a local supplier.

In such a sentence, adding the word *that* where it is implied would help:

> We found that the reason for our poor performance was stiff competition from a local supplier.

In your quest for an economical sentence, do not eliminate *that* when it actually adds clarity.

Here are other examples of redundancies and ways to eliminate them:

Needless Repetition	Repetition Eliminated
Please *endorse your name on the back* of this check.	Please *endorse* this check.
We must assemble *together* at 10:30 AM *in the morning.*	We must assemble at 10:30 AM.
One should know the *basic fundamentals* of clear writing.	One should know the *fundamentals* of clear writing.
The *consensus of opinion* is that the tax is unfair.	The *consensus* is that the tax is unfair.

Determine Emphasis in Sentence Design

The sentences you write should give the right emphasis to the different pieces of content. Any written business communication contains a number of items of information, not all of which are equally important. Some are very important, such as a conclusion in a report or the objective in a message. Others are relatively unimportant. Your task as a writer is to form your sentences to communicate the importance of each item.

Sentence length affects emphasis. Short, simple sentences tend to carry more emphasis than long, involved ones. They stand out and call attention to their contents. Longer sentences tend to give less emphasis to their contents simply because they contain more material.

When a sentence contains two or more ideas, the ideas share emphasis. How they share it will depend on how you construct the sentence. If two ideas are presented equally (in independent clauses, for example), they get about equal emphasis. But if they are not presented equally (for example, in an independent and a dependent clause), the independent clause will get more emphasis than the other elements.

The Right EmPHAsis on the Right SyllAble

Common usage determines which syllable in a word gets the accent. But in sentences and paragraphs, you decide what to emphasize. Consider the matter carefully, with your readers and your desired effect in mind.

To illustrate the varying emphasis you can give information, consider this example. You have two items of information to write. One is that the company lost money last year. The other is that its sales volume reached a record high. You could present the information in at least three ways. First, you could give both items equal emphasis by placing them in separate short sentences:

The company lost money last year. The loss occurred in spite of record sales.

Second, you could present the two items in the same sentence with emphasis on the lost money.

Although the company enjoyed record sales last year, it lost money.

Third, you could present the two items in one sentence with emphasis on the sales increase:

Although the company lost money last year, it enjoyed record sales.

Which way should you choose? The answer depends on what you want to emphasize. You should think the matter through and follow your best judgment. But the point is clear: Your choice makes a difference.

Two Ways to Manage Emphasis

Coordinate: Put equally important information into equal structures (for example, both in main clauses).

Subordinate: Put less important information into phrases and dependent clauses that modify the main idea.

The following paragraphs illustrate the importance of thinking logically to determine emphasis. In the first, each item of information gets the emphasis of a short sentence and none stands out. However, the items are not equally important and do not deserve equal emphasis. Notice, also, the choppy effect that the succession of short sentences produces.

The main building was inspected on October 1. Mr. George Wills inspected the building. Mr. Wills is a vice president of the company. He found that the building has 6,500 square feet of floor space. He also found that it has 2,400 square feet of storage space. The new store must have a minimum of 6,000 square feet of floor space. It

must have 2,000 square feet of storage space. Thus, the main building exceeds the space requirements for the new store. Therefore, Mr. Wills concluded that the main building is adequate for the company's needs.

In the next paragraph, some of the items are subordinated, but not logically. The really important information does not receive the emphasis it deserves. Logically, these two points should stand out: (1) the building is large enough and (2) storage space exceeds minimum requirements. But they do not stand out in this version:

Mr. George Wills, who inspected the main building on October 1, is a vice president of the company. His inspection, which supports the conclusion that the building is large enough for the proposed store, uncovered these facts. The building has 6,500 square feet of floor space and 2,400 square feet of storage space, which is more than the minimum requirement of 6,000 and 2,000 square feet, respectively, of floor and storage space.

The third paragraph shows good emphasis of the important points. The short beginning sentence emphasizes the conclusion. The supporting facts that the building exceeds the minimum floor and storage space requirements receive main-clause emphasis. The less important facts, such as the reference to George Wills, are treated subordinately. Also, the most important facts are placed at the points of emphasis—the beginning and ending.

Vice President George Wills inspected the main building on October 1 and concluded that it is large enough for the new store. The building's 6,500 square feet of floor space exceed the minimum requirement by 500 square feet. The 2,400 square feet of storage space exceed the minimum requirement by 400 square feet.

The preceding illustrations show how sentence construction can determine emphasis. You can make items stand out, you can treat them equally, or you can deemphasize them. The choices are yours. But what you do must be the result of sound thinking about your purpose and your readers, not simply a matter of chance.

LO 8 Employ unity and logical wording to make sentences clear.

Give the Sentences Unity

Good sentences have unity. For a sentence to have unity, all of its parts must combine to form one clear thought. In other words, all the components of a sentence should have a logical reason for being together.

Business leaders are communicating more and more outside the office. They want and need their incoming messages to communicate easily and quickly.

Stringy and See-Saw Sentences

If you try to load down a sentence with too much information, you can wind up with a stringy sentence like this:

While we welcome all applications, we are particularly interested in candidates who have at least three years' experience, although we will consider those with less experience who have a degree in the field or who have earned a certificate from an industry-certified trainer, and we will also consider fluency in Italian a plus.

A see-saw sentence is one that goes back and forth between two points, like this:

A blog can add visibility to a business, although it can be labor intensive to maintain, but the time spent on the blog could be worthwhile if it generates a buzz among our potential customers.

In these cases, whittle the sentences down to readable size, use helpful transitional phrases (*in addition, on the other hand*), and don't switch directions too often.

Here, for example, are more easy-to-follow versions of the problem sentences.

While we welcome all applications, we are particularly interested in candidates who (1) have at least three years' experience or (2) have less experience but have earned a degree or certificate in the field. Fluency in Italian is also a plus.

A blog can add visibility to a business. True, maintaining a blog takes time, but if the blog generates a buzz among our potential customers, the time will be well spent.

> # " All the components of a sentence should have a good reason for being together. "

Violations of unity in sentence construction are usually caused by two problems: (1) unrelated ideas and (2) excessive detail.

unrelated ideas Placing unrelated ideas in a sentence is the most obvious violation of unity. Putting two or more ideas in a sentence is not grammatically wrong, but the ideas must have a reason for being together. They must combine to complete the single goal of the sentence.

You can give unity to sentences that contain unrelated ideas in three basic ways: (1) You can put the ideas in separate sentences, (2) you can make one of the ideas subordinate to the other, or (3) you can add words that show how the ideas are related. The first two of these techniques are illustrated by the revisions of the following sentence:

Mr. Jordan is our sales manager, and he has a degree in law.

Perhaps the two ideas are related, but the words do not tell how. A better arrangement could be to put each in a separate sentence:

Mr. Jordan is our sales manager. He has a law degree.

Or the two ideas could be kept in one sentence by subordinating one to the other. In this way, the main clause provides the unity of the sentence.

Mr. Jordan, our sales manager, has a law degree.

Adding words to show the relationship of ideas is illustrated in the revision of the following example:

Our production increased in January, and our equipment is wearing out.

The sentence has two ideas that seem unrelated. One way of improving it is to make a separate sentence of each idea. A closer look reveals, however, that the two ideas really are related, but the words do not show how. The following revision brings out the relationship:

Even though our equipment is wearing out, our production increased in January.

These contrasting pairs of sentences further illustrate the technique:

Unrelated Material	Improved
Our territory is the southern half of the state, and our salespeople cannot cover it thoroughly.	Our territory, the southern half of the state, is so big that our salespeople cannot cover it thoroughly.
Using the cost-of-living calculator is simple, but no tool will work well unless it is explained clearly.	Using the cost-of-living calculator is simple, but, like any tool, it will not work well unless it is explained clearly.

excessive detail Putting too much detail into one sentence tends to hide the central thought. If the detail is important, you should put it in a separate sentence.

This suggestion strengthens another given earlier in the chapter—that you use short sentences. Long sentences, full of detail, run the risk of lacking unity, as illustrated in these contrasting examples:

Excessive Detail	Improved
Our New York offices, considered plush in the 1990s but now badly in need of renovation, as is the case with most offices that have not been maintained, have been abandoned.	Considered plush in the 1990s, our New York offices have not been maintained properly. Because the repairs would have been too costly, we have abandoned them.
We have attempted to trace the Plytec insulation you ordered from us October 1, and about which you inquired in your October 10 message, but we have not yet been able to locate it, although we are sending you a rush shipment immediately.	We are sending you a rush shipment of Plytec insulation immediately. Following your October 10 inquiry, we attempted to trace your October 1 order but were unable to locate it.
In 2007, when I, a small-town girl from a middle-class family, began my studies at Bradley University, which is widely recognized for its business administration program, I set as my goal a career with a large public company.	A small-town girl from a middle-class family, I entered Bradley University in 2007. I selected Bradley because of its widely recognized business administration program. From the beginning, my goal was a career with a large public company.

Word Sentences Logically

At some point, you've probably had a teacher write "awkward" beside one or more of your sentences. Often, the cause of such a problem is illogical wording. The paragraphs that follow will help you avoid some of the most common types of illogical sentences. But keep in mind that many awkward sentences defy efforts to label them. The only guards against these kinds of sentences are your own good ear and careful editing.

mixed constructions Sometimes illogical sentences occur when writers mix two different kinds of sentences.

For example, can you describe what's wrong with the following sentence about cutting costs?

First we found less expensive material, and then a more economical means of production was developed.

If you said that the first half of the sentence used active voice but the second half switched to passive voice, you're right. Shifts of this kind can make a sentence hard to follow. Notice how much easier it is to understand this version:

First we found less expensive material, and then we developed a more economical means of production.

There's a similar problem in the following sentence:

The consumer should read the nutrition label, but you often don't take the time to do so.

Did you notice that the point of view changed from third person (*consumer*) to second (*you*) in this sentence? The following revision would be much easier to follow:

Consumers should read nutrition labels, but they often don't take the time to do so.

Sometimes we start writing one kind of sentence and then change it before we get to the end, illogically fusing parts of two different sentences together. Here's an example:

Because our salespeople are inexperienced caused us to miss our quota.

Rewriting the sentence in one of the following ways (by either changing the subject or changing the predicate) would eliminate the awkwardness:

Because our salespeople are inexperienced, we missed our quota.

Our inexperienced salespeople caused us to miss our quota.

These sentences further illustrate the point:

Mixed Construction	Improved
Some activities that the company participates in are affordable housing, conservation of parks, and litter control.	Some causes the company supports are affordable housing, conservation of parks, and litter control.
Job rotation is when you train people by moving them from job to job.	Job rotation is a training method in which people are moved from job to job.
Knowing that she objected to the price was the reason we permitted her to return the goods.	Because we knew she objected to the price, we permitted her to return the goods.
My education was completed in 2008, and then I began work as a manager for Home Depot.	I completed my education in 2008 and then began work as a manager for Home Depot.
The cost of these desks is cheaper.	The cost of these desks is lower. (*or* These desks are cheaper.)

incomplete constructions   Certain words used early in a sentence signal that the rest of the sentence will contain a certain kind of content. Be careful to fulfill your reader's expectations.

For example, the following sentence, while technically a sentence, is incomplete:

She was so happy with the retirement party we gave her.

She was so happy . . . that what? That she sent everyone a thank-you note? That she made a donation to the library in the company's name? In a sentence like this, either complete the construction or leave "so" out.

Or consider the incomplete opening phrase of this sentence:

As far as time management, he is a master of multitasking.

You can rectify the problem in one of two ways:

As far as time management goes [*or* is concerned], he is a master of multitasking.

As for time management, he is a master of multitasking.

dangling/misplaced modifiers   Putting modifiers in the wrong place or giving them nothing to modify in the sentence is another common way that sentence logic can go awry. Consider this sentence:

Believing the price would drop, the purchasers were instructed not to buy now.

The sentence seems grammatically correct . . . but it doesn't make sense. It looks as though the purchasers believed the price would drop—but if they did, why did someone else have to tell them not to buy? The problem is that the people whom the opening phrase is supposed to modify have been left out, making the opening phrase a dangling modifier.

> Putting modifiers in the wrong place or giving them nothing to modify in the sentence is another common way that sentence logic can go awry.

You can correct his problem by putting the right agents after the opening phrase:

Believing the price would drop, we instructed our purchasers not to buy now.

What makes this sentence hard to follow?

We have compiled a list of likely prospects using the information we gathered at the trade show.

Surely the "prospects" aren't really the ones using the information. The sentence would be clearer if the final phrase were more logically placed, as in

Using the information we gathered at the trade show, we have compiled a list of prospects in the Chicago area.

faulty parallelism Readers expect the same kinds of elements in a sentence to be worded in the same way. Faulty parallelism violates this logical expectation.

How might you make the similar items in this sentence more parallel in wording?

They show their community spirit through yearly donations to the United Way, giving free materials to Habitat for Humanity, and their employees volunteer at local schools.

Here's one way:

They show their community spirit by donating yearly to the United Way, giving free materials to Habitat for Humanity, and volunteering at local schools.

Other rules of grammar besides those mentioned here can help you avoid illogical constructions and write clear sentences. You can review these rules by studying the online material about correctness and completing the diagnostic exercise there to test your understanding of them.

WRITING CLEAR PARAGRAPHS

Skillful paragraphing is also important to clear communication. Paragraphs show where topics begin and end, thus helping the reader mentally organize the information. Strategic paragraphing also helps certain ideas stand out.

Designing paragraphs requires the ability to organize and explain information. It also involves anticipating your readers' likely reactions and structuring your content for the desired effect. The following advice will help you use paragraphing to your best advantage.

LO 9 Compose paragraphs that are short and unified, use topic sentences effectively, and communicate coherently.

Give the Paragraphs Unity

Like sentences, paragraphs should have unity. When applied to paragraph structure, unity means that a paragraph sticks to a single topic or idea, with everything in the paragraph developing this topic or idea. When you have finished a paragraph, you should be able to say, "Everything in this paragraph belongs together because every part concerns every other part."

A violation of unity is illustrated in the following paragraph from an application letter. As the goal of the paragraph is to summarize the applicant's coursework, all the sentences should pertain to coursework. By shifting to personal qualities, the

third sentence (in italics) violates paragraph unity. Taking this sentence out would correct the problem.

At the university I studied all the basic accounting courses as well as specialized courses in taxation, international accounting, and computer security. I also took coursework in the behavioral areas, with emphasis on human relations. *Realizing the value of human relations in business, I also actively participated in organizations, such as Sigma Nu (social fraternity), Alpha Kappa Psi (professional fraternity), Intramural Soccer, and A Cappella.* I selected electives to round out my general business education, choosing courses in investments, advanced business report writing, financial policy, and management information systems. The enclosed résumé provides a complete list of my business-related coursework.

Keep Paragraphs Short

As a general rule, you should keep your paragraphs short. This suggestion complements the suggestion about unity, because unified paragraphs tend to be short.

As noted earlier, paragraphs help the reader follow the writer's organization plan. Writing marked by short paragraphs identifies more of the details of that plan. In addition, such writing is inviting to the eye. People simply prefer to read writing with frequent paragraph breaks.

Give every paragraph a clear focus.

How long a paragraph should be depends on its contents—on what must be included to achieve unity. Readability research has suggested an average length of eight lines for longer papers such as reports. Shorter paragraphs are appropriate for messages.

Keep in mind that these are general suggestions. Some good paragraphs may be quite long—well over the average. Some paragraphs can be very short—as short as one line. One-line paragraphs are an especially appropriate means of emphasizing major points in business messages. A one-line paragraph may be all that is needed for a goodwill closing comment or an attention-grabbing opening.

A good rule to follow is to question the unity of all long paragraphs—say, those longer than 10 lines. If after looking over such a paragraph you conclude that it has unity, leave it as it is. But you will sometimes find more than one topic. When you do, make each topic into a separate paragraph.

Make Good Use of Topic Sentences

One good way of organizing paragraphs is to use topic sentences. The topic sentence expresses the main idea of a paragraph, and the remaining sentences build around and support it. In a sense, the topic sentence serves as a headline for the paragraph, and all the other sentences supply the story. True, not every paragraph must have a topic sentence. Some paragraphs, for example, introduce ideas, relate succeeding items, or present an assortment of facts that lead to no conclusion. The central thought of such paragraphs is difficult to put into a single sentence. Even so, you should use topic sentences whenever you can. Using topic sentences forces you to find the central idea of each paragraph and helps you check for paragraph unity.

Where the topic sentence should be in the paragraph depends on the subject matter, the reader's expectations, and the writer's plan, but you basically have three choices: the beginning, end, or middle. The following sections illustrate these possibilities.

topic sentence first The most common paragraph arrangement begins with the topic sentence and continues with the supporting material. In fact, the arrangement is so

appropriate for business information that one company's writing manual suggests that it be used for virtually all paragraphs.

To illustrate the writing of a paragraph in which the topic sentence comes first, take a paragraph reporting on economists' replies to a survey question asking their view of business activity for the coming year. The facts to be presented are these: 13 percent of the economists expected an increase; 28 percent expected little or no change; 59 percent expected a downturn; 87 percent of those who expected a downturn thought it would come in the first quarter. The obvious conclusion—and the subject for the topic sentence—is that the majority expected a decline in the first quarter. Following this reasoning, we would develop a paragraph like this:

A majority of the economists consulted think that business activity will drop during the first quarter of next year. Of the 185 economists interviewed, 13 percent looked for continued increases in business activity, and 28 percent anticipated little or no change from the present high level. The remaining 59 percent looked for a recession. Of this group, nearly all (87 percent) believed that the downturn would occur during the first quarter of the year.

topic sentence last The second most common paragraph arrangement places the topic sentence at the end, usually as a conclusion. Paragraphs of this kind present the supporting details first and then lead readers to the conclusion, as in this example:

The significant role of inventories in the economic picture should not be overlooked. At present, inventories represent 3.8 months' supply. Their dollar value is the highest in history. If considered in relation to increased sales, however, they are not excessive. In fact, they are well within the range generally believed to be safe. *Thus, inventories are not likely to cause a downward swing in the economy.*

topic sentence within the paragraph A third arrangement places the topic sentence somewhere within the paragraph. This arrangement is rarely used, but sometimes it is appropriate, as in this example:

Numerous materials have been used in manufacturing this part. And many have shown quite satisfactory results. *Material 329, however, is superior to them all.* When built with material 329, the part is almost twice as strong as when built with the next best material. It is also three ounces lighter. Most important, it is cheaper than any of the other products.

> "The topic sentence serves as a headline for the paragraph, and all the other sentences supply the story."

Leave Out Unnecessary Detail

You should include in your paragraphs only the information needed to achieve your purpose.

You can best judge what to include by putting yourself in your reader's place. What additional information might be helpful or persuasive? What information does he or she need? How will it be used? If you follow this procedure, you will probably leave out much that you originally intended to use.

The following paragraph from a message to an employee presents excessive information.

In reviewing the personnel records in our company database, I found that several items in your file were incomplete. The section titled "work history" has blanks for three items of information. The first is for dates employed. The second is for company name. And the third is for type of work performed. On your record only company name was entered, leaving two items blank. Years employed or your duties were not indicated. This information is important. It is reviewed by your supervisors every time you are considered for promotion or for a pay increase. Therefore, it must be completed. I request that you log in to the company portal and update your personnel record at your earliest convenience.

The message says much more than the reader needs to know. The goal is to have the reader update the personnel record, and everything else is of questionable value. This revised message is better:

A recent review of the personnel records showed that yours is incomplete. Please log in to the company portal at your earliest convenience to update your record.

Make Paragraphs Coherent

Like well-made sentences, well-made paragraphs move the reader logically and smoothly from point to point. They clearly indicate how the different bits of information are related to each other in terms of logic and the writer's apparent purpose. This quality of enabling readers to proceed easily through your message, without side trips and backward shifts, is called *coherence*.

The best way to give your message coherence is to arrange its information in a logical order—an order appropriate for the strategy of the case. So important are such decisions to message writing that we devote whole chapters to different patterns of organization. But logical organization is not enough. Various techniques are needed to tie the information together. These techniques are known as transitional devices. Here we will discuss three major ones: repetition of key words, use of pronouns, and the use of transitional words (Exhibit 4.2).

repetition of key words By repeating key words from one sentence to the next, you can smoothly connect successive ideas. The following sentences illustrate this transitional device (key words

> Like well-made sentences, well-made paragraphs move the reader logically and smoothly from point to point.

in italics). The sentences come from a message refusing a request to present a lecture series for an advertising clinic.

Because your advertising clinic is so well planned, I am confident that it can provide a really *valuable* service to practioners in the community. To be truly *valuable,* I think you will agree, the program must be given the time a thorough preparation requires. As my time for the coming week is heavily committed, may I recommend that you invite Seth Greenley to conduct the ad-writing session?

Avoid Vague *This*

When using the word *this* to refer back to a preceding idea, use it with a noun—for example, "this plan," "this improvement"—to make the reference clear.

use of pronouns Because pronouns refer to words previously used, they make good transitions between ideas. The demonstrative pronouns (*this, that, these, those*) can be especially helpful. The following sentences (with the demonstrative pronouns in italics) illustrate this technique.

Ever since the introduction of our Model V nine years ago, consumers have suggested only one possible improvement—voice controls. During all *this* time, making *this* improvement has been the objective of Atkins research personnel. Now we proudly report that *these* efforts have been successful.

transitional words When you talk in everyday conversation, you connect many of your thoughts with transitional words. But when you write, you may not use them enough. Be alert for places where providing such words will help move your readers through your paragraphs.

Among the commonly used transitional words are *in addition, besides, in spite of, in contrast, however, likewise, thus, therefore, for example,* and *also.* (You can find a more extensive list on page 236 and on the Words and Style page of the BC Resources online.) These words bridge thoughts by indicating the nature of the connection between what has been said and what will be said next.

Notice how the transitional expressions (in italics) in the following paragraph signal the relations among the parts and move the reader steadily forward through the ideas:

Three reasons justify moving from the Crowton site. *First,* the building rock in the Crowton area is questionable. The failure of recent

The language used in a message communicates more than the message. It tells how friendly, how considerate, how careful the writer is—and more.

geologic explorations in the area appears to confirm suspicions that the Crowton deposits are nearly exhausted. *Second*, the distances from the Crowton site to major markets make transportation costs unusually high. Obviously, any savings in transportation costs will add to company profits. *Third*, the outdatedness of much of the equipment at the Crowton plant makes this an ideal time for relocation. The old equipment at the Crowton plant could be scrapped.

The transition words *first, second,* and *third* bring out the paragraph's pattern of organization and make it easy for the reader to follow along.

Keep in mind that transitional devices can also be used between paragraphs—to tie thoughts together, to keep the focus of the message sharp, and to move the reader smoothly from point to point. Strive for coherence on both the paragraph and the document level.

WRITING FOR A POSITIVE EFFECT

As Chapter 1 made clear, every business message has a human-relations dimension. Using an appropriate style involves managing your tone as well as your contents. You need to strive both for clarity and for positive emotional effects in order to achieve your communication purpose.

Getting positive effects with your messages is largely a matter of skillful writing and of understanding how people respond to words. Keeping certain attitudes and techniques in mind can help. The following sections review these attitudes and techniques.

LO 10   Use a conversational style that eliminates rubber stamps.

Use a Conversational Style

One technique that helps build goodwill is to write in conversational language. Such language is warm and natural. Because it is the language we use most, it is also easily understood.

Writing conversationally is not as easy as you might think. When faced with a writing task, you can be tempted to change character and write in stiff and stilted words. The result is a cold and unnatural style—one that doesn't produce the goodwill effect you want your messages to have. The following examples illustrate this problem and how to correct it.

Stiff and Dull	Conversational
Enclosed herewith is the brochure about which you make inquiry.	Enclosed is the brochure you asked about.
This will acknowledge receipt of your May 10th order for four dozen Docker slacks. Please be advised that they will be shipped in accordance with your instructions by UPS on May 16.	Four dozen Docker slacks should reach your store by the 18th. As you instructed, they were shipped today by UPS.
Submitted herewith is your notification of our compliance with subject standards.	Attached is notification of our compliance with the standards.

technology in brief

Grammar and Style Checkers Help Writers Identify Clichés, Colloquialisms, and Jargon

While not perfect, grammar and style checkers can help writers identify some clichés, colloquialisms, and jargon that creep into their writing. The checker here illustrates that it found a cliché and offers two suggestions for correcting it. Clicking the Explain button will bring up the reason behind the suggestion. Although this software can help, writers still need to be able to identify the trite and overused expressions the software misses. Also, writers need to be able to recast the sentences for clarity and sincerity.

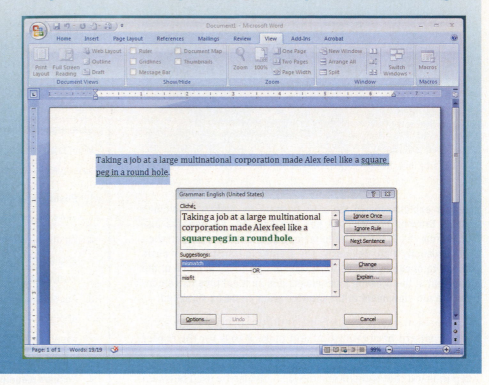

Cut Out "Rubber Stamps"

Rubber stamps (also called *clichés*) are expressions used by habit every time a certain type of situation occurs. They are used without thought and are not adapted to the specific situation. As the term indicates, they are used much as you would use a rubber stamp.

Because they are used routinely, rubber stamps communicate the effect of routine treatment, which is not likely to impress readers favorably. Such treatment tells readers that the writer has no special concern for them—that the present case is being handled in the same way as others. In contrast, words specially selected for the case show the writer's concern for and interest in the readers. Clearly, specially selected wording is the better choice for producing a goodwill effect.

Some examples of rubber stamps you have no doubt heard before are listed below. These phrases, while perhaps once appropriate, have become stale with overuse:

If I can be of further assistance, please do not hesitate to ask.

This will acknowledge receipt of . . .

This is to inform you that . . .

Thank you for your time.

It has come to my attention . . . (which is negative as well as stale)

You do not need to know all the rubber stamps to stop using them. You need only to write in the language of good conversation and treat your readers like the individuals they are.

LO 11 Use the you-viewpoint to build goodwill.

Use the You-Viewpoint

Writing from the you-viewpoint (also called *you-attitude*) is another technique for building goodwill in written messages.

Six Chix by Kathyrn LeMieux

In a broad sense, you-viewpoint writing emphasizes the reader's interests and concerns. It emphasizes *you* and *your* and de-emphasizes *we* and *our*. But it is more than a matter of just using second-person pronouns. *You* and *your* can appear prominently in sentences that emphasize the we-viewpoint, as in this example: "If you do not pay by the 15th, you must pay a penalty." Likewise, *we* and *mine* can appear in sentences that emphasize the you-viewpoint, as in this example: "We will do whatever we can to protect your investment." The point is that the you-viewpoint is an attitude of mind that places the reader at the center of things.

The following examples illustrate the value of using the you-viewpoint. Imagine the contrasting effects that the difference in wording would create.

We-Viewpoint	You-Viewpoint
We are pleased to have your new account.	Your new charge account is now open for your convenience.
Our policy prohibits us from permitting outside groups to use our equipment except on a cash-rental basis.	Our policy of cutting operating costs by renting our equipment helps us make efficient use of your tax dollars.
We have been quite tolerant of your past-due account and must now demand payment.	If you are to continue to enjoy the benefits of credit buying, you must clear your account now.
We have received your report of May 1.	Thank you for your report of May 1.
Please submit your January report so that we may complete our records.	So that your file may be completed, please send us your January report.
We require that you sign the sales slip before we will charge to your account.	For your protection, you are charged only after you have signed the sales slip.

Some critics of the you-viewpoint point out that it can be insincere and manipulative. It is better, they say, just to "tell it like it is."

Without question, the you-viewpoint can be used to the point of being insincere, and it can be used to pursue unethical goals. Our advice is to use the you-viewpoint when it is friendly and sincere and when your goals are ethical. In such cases, using the you-viewpoint is "telling it like it is." If you have your readers' feelings genuinely in mind, writing from the you-viewpoint should come naturally.

LO 12 Accent the positive through word choice and positioning to achieve goodwill and other desired effects.

Accent the Positive

In most situations, it is better to use positive than negative wording in your business messages.

This is not to say that negative words have no place in business writing. Such words are powerful, and you will sometimes want to use them. But positive words tend to put the reader in a cooperative frame of mind, and they emphasize the pleasant

In face-to-face communication, words, voice, facial expressions, and gestures combine to create the desired communication effect. In writing, the printed word alone must do the job.

aspects of the goal. They also create the goodwill that helps build relationships.

Consider the case of a company executive who had to deny a local civic group's request to use the company's meeting facilities. To soften the refusal, the executive could let the group use a conference room, which might be somewhat small for its purpose. The executive came up with this totally negative response:

We *regret* to inform you that we *cannot* permit you to use our auditorium for your meeting, as the Sun City Investment Club asked for it first. We can, however, let you use our conference room, but it seats *only* 60.

The negative words are italicized. First, the positively intended message "We *regret* to inform you" is an unmistakable sign of coming bad news. "*Cannot* permit" contains an unnecessarily harsh meaning. And notice how the good-news part of the message is handicapped by the limiting word *only*.

Had the executive searched for more positive ways of covering the same situation, he or she might have written

Although the SunCity Investment Club has reserved the auditorium for Saturday, we can offer you our conference room, which seats 60.

Not a single negative word appears in this version. Both approaches achieve the primary objective of denying a request, but their effects on the reader would differ sharply. There is no question about which approach does the better job of building goodwill.

Parent, Child, or Adult?

In the 1950s, psychologist Eric Berne developed a model of relationships that he called "Transactional Analysis." It has proven to be so useful that it is still popular today.

At the core of this model is the idea that in all our transactions with others (and even within ourselves), people occupy one of three positions: parent, child, or adult.

• A *parent* is patronizing, spoiling, nurturing, blaming, criticizing, and/or punishing.
• A *child* is uninhibited, freely emotional, obedient, whining, irresponsible, and/or selfish.
• An *adult* is reasonable, responsible, considerate, and flexible.

Significantly, the "self" that one projects invites others to occupy the complementary position. Thus, acting "parental" leads others to act "childish" and vice versa, while acting "adult" invites others to be adults.

In both internal and external business messages, strive for "adult–adult" interactions. Your courtesy and professionalism will be likely to elicit the same from your readers.

In general, you should be wary of strongly negative words. These words convey unhappy and unpleasant thoughts, and such thoughts usually detract from your goal. They include such words as *mistake, problem, error, damage, loss,* and *failure,* as well as words that deny—words such as *no, do not, refuse,* and *stop.* Try also to avoid wording that blames the reader or focuses on what you cannot do. The following examples illustrate (negative wording is in italics):

Negative	Positive
You *failed* to give us the fabric specifications of the chair you ordered.	To complete your order, please check your choice of fabric on the enclosed card.
Smoking is *not* permitted anywhere except in the lobby.	Smoking is permitted in the lobby only.
We *cannot* deliver until Friday.	We can deliver the goods on Friday.
We *regret* to inform you that we must deny your request for credit.	For the time being, we can serve you on a cash basis only.
You should have known that the camera lens *cannot* be cleaned with tissue, for it is clearly explained in the instructions.	The instructions explain why the camera lens should be cleaned only with a nonscratch cloth.

The effort to accentuate the positive can involve more than word choice; it can also involve skillful management of emphasis. As we advised earlier in this chapter, use sentence structure to your advantage. If you have positive information, putting it in the main clause of the sentence—or even in a short sentence all by itself—will emphasize it. If you have negative information, you might be able to de-emphasize it by putting it in a phrase or dependent clause, as in the following sentence:

While your plan is not feasible at this time, we encourage you to submit it again next year when we should have more resources for implementing it.

"We're a Limited Partnership. We're limited by Allen's pessimism, Elizabeth's abrasive personality, and Dave's refusal to work weekends."

Source: Copyright © Randy Glasbergen. Reprinted with permission.

Another way to manage emphasis is to consider carefully where to put the positive and negative news.

The beginnings and endings of a writing unit usually carry more emphasis than the center parts. This rule of emphasis applies whether the unit is the message, a paragraph of the message, or a sentence within the paragraph (see Exhibit 4.3.). Some authorities think that the reader's fresh mental energy explains beginning emphasis. Some say that the last parts stand out because they are the most recent in the reader's mind. Whatever the explanation, research has suggested that this emphasis technique works.

If we were to use this technique in the example just provided, we might write a paragraph like this:

In light of the current budget crunch, we approved those suggestions that would save money while not costing much to implement. While your plan is not feasible at this time, we hope you will submit it again next year when we should have more resources for implementing it.

▼ **EXHIBIT 4.3** Emphasis by Position

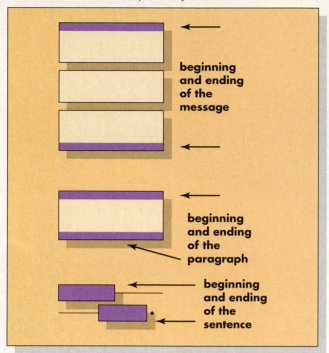

beginning
and ending
of the
message

beginning
and ending
of the
paragraph

beginning
and ending
of the
sentence

As with use of the you-viewpoint, emphasis on the positive, when overdone, can lead to fake and manipulative messages. The technique is especially questionable when it causes the reader to overlook an important negative point in the message—the discontinuation of a service, for example, or information about an unsafe product.

Do not let your effort to please the reader lead you to be dishonest or insincere. That would be not only morally wrong; it would also be a bad way to do business. On the other hand, you should not be naïve about the nature of reality, either. What we represent in our communication—whether data, events, people, or situations—does not come to us possessing one and only one meaning. Most phenomena can be rightly perceived in multiple ways. In your quest to achieve your communication purpose and build goodwill, think before you let negative feelings make their way into your messages. You will often be able to depict the glass as half full rather than as half empty, and you will probably find that your own perspective has improved in the process. ■

When ethical and appropriate, view the glass as half full, not as half empty.

Get Online

mhhe.com/FlatleyM2e

for study materials including quizzes and Internet resources.

writing good-news and
neutral messages

Most business messages use a direct organizational plan. That is, the message leads with its most important point and then moves to additional or supporting information. If you recall what Chapter 1 observed about the nature of business, you will understand why. Communication is central to organized human activity. Especially in business, people need to know what to do, why, and how. They undertake any job understanding that they have a certain function to perform, and they need information to be able to perform it well. When external audiences interact with companies, they also expect and need certain kinds of information presented as quickly as possible. It is fair to say that direct messages are the lifeblood of virtually any business activity. ■

LEARNING OBJECTIVES

L01 Properly assess the reader's likely reaction to your message.

L02 Describe the general plan for direct-order messages.

L03 Write clear, well-structured routine requests for information.

L04 Write direct, orderly, and friendly favorable responses.

L05 Compose adjustment grants that regain any lost confidence.

L06 Write order acknowledgments and other thank-you messages that build goodwill.

L07 Write direct claims that objectively and courteously explain the facts.

L08 Write clear and effective operational communications.

There are, of course, unlimited kinds of direct messages. Each business is unique in some ways, and each, therefore, will have developed its own direct-message types—its preferred purposes, patterns, styles, and formats for these messages. Still, there is a basic plan for the direct message. Moreover, certain situations calling for a direct approach have occurred so often that we can identify plans for several common types of these messages.

This chapter first describes a general plan for writing all messages of this type. Then we adapt this general plan to some of the more common business situations—external and internal—that it can organize. We also show why each of these situations requires special treatment and how to handle each one. By noting these special requirements, you will be able to adapt to any related situation.

LO 1 Properly assess the reader's likely reaction to your message.

PRELIMINARY ASSESSMENT

As discussed in Chapter 1, any messages other than those for the most mechanical, routine circumstances require careful thinking about the situation, your readers, and your goals. When determining your message's basic plan, a good beginning is to assess your reader's probable reaction to what you have to say. If the reaction is likely to be negative, an indirect organization plan may be in order. These plans are discussed in the following chapters. But if the reaction is likely to be positive, or even neutral, your best approach is likely to be a direct one—that is, one that gets to the objective right away without delaying an explanation or conditioning words. The general plan for this direct approach is the following.

LO 2 Describe the general plan for direct-order messages.

THE GENERAL DIRECT PLAN

Beginning with the Objective

Begin with your objective. If you are seeking information, start by asking for it. If you are giving information, start giving it. Whatever your key point is, lead with it.

In some cases, you might need to open with a brief orienting phrase, clause, or even sentence, especially if your reader is not expecting to hear from you or is not familiar with you or your company. You may need to preface your main point with a few words of background, but get to the point as soon as possible. For example, the sentence "We have received your May 7 inquiry" does nothing but state the obvious. Keep any prefatory remarks brief and get to the real message without delay. Then stop the first paragraph. Let the rest of the message fill in the details.

Covering the Remaining Part of the Objective

Whatever else must be covered to complete the objective makes up the bulk of the remainder of the message. If you cover all of your objective in the beginning (as in an inquiry in which a single question is asked), nothing else is needed. If additional questions, answers, or information is needed, you cover it systematically—perhaps listing questions or arranging information by paragraphs. If these parts have their own explanations or commentary, you include them. In short, you cover everything else that needs to be covered.

Ending with Adapted Goodwill

End the message with an appropriately friendly comment as you would if you were having a face-to-face conversation with the reader.

These final goodwill words will receive the best reader reaction if they are customized to fit the message. True, such general closes as "A prompt reply will be appreciated" and "Thank you for your time and consideration" are positive, because they

> "If you are seeking information, start by asking for it. If you are giving information, start giving it."

workplace scenario

Writing Routine Inquiries

Play again the role of the assistant to the vice president for operations of Pinnacle Manufacturing Company. Your duties involve helping your boss cover a wide assortment of activities. Many of these activities require written messages.

At the moment, your boss is working with a group of Pinnacle executives to select offices for a new regional headquarters. They have chosen the city. Now they must find the best possible offices in this city. As chair of this committee, your boss has accepted responsibility for finding office locations from which to choose. Of course, your boss has delegated much of the work to you.

Already you have found three possible office suites in the chosen city. Now you must get the pertinent information about each so that the executives can make their selection. The first of these you found in the classified advertisements of the local newspaper. It is a 3,200-square-foot office suite, but the ad tells little more. So now you must write the advertiser a routine inquiry seeking the information the management team needs.

express a friendly thank-you. There is nothing wrong with a thank-you sincerely expressed here or elsewhere. The problem is in the routine, rubber-stamp nature of many of these expressions. A more positive reaction results from an individually tailored expression that fits the message—for example: "If you will answer these questions about Ms. Hill right away, she and I will be most grateful."

Be aware, though, that phrases such as "as soon as possible" or "at your convenience" may have very different meanings for you and your reader. If you need your response by a specific date or time, give your reader that information as well as a reason for the deadline so that your reader understands the importance of a timely response. You may say, for example, "Your answers to these questions by July 1 will help Ms. Hill and us as we meet our deadline for filling the accounting position."

Now let us see how you can adapt this general plan to fit the more common direct message situations.

LO 3 Write clear, well-structured routine requests for information.

ROUTINE INQUIRIES

Choosing from Two Types of Beginnings

The opening of the routine inquiry should focus on the main objective, as recommended in the preceding section. Since your objective is to ask for information, begin with a question. This opening question can be either of two types: specific or general.

First, it can be one of the specific questions to be asked (assuming that more than one question needs to be asked). Preferably it should be a question that sets up the other questions. For example, if your objective is to get information about the office

suites described in the Workplace Scenario, you might begin with these words:

Can you please send me additional information about the floor plan of the office suite that you advertised in Monday's *Sentinel Times*?

Businesspeople frequently shake hands to show goodwill at the end of a meeting. Writers show goodwill at the close of messages with positive words and a courteous tone.

In the body of the message, you would include additional specific questions concerning the suite.

Or, the opening question could be a general request for information. The specific questions would follow. This beginning sentence illustrates a general request:

Will you please send me a description of the features of the 3,200-square-foot office suite advertised in Monday's *Daily Journal*?

Whether you open with a specific or a general question, be sure your reader has a clear sense of your message's purpose.

Informing and Explaining Adequately

To help your reader answer your questions, you may need to include explanation or information. If you do not explain enough or if you misjudge the reader's knowledge, you make the reader's task difficult. For example, answers to your questions about office space for Pinnacle Manufacturing may depend on characteristics or specific needs of the company. Without knowing how Pinnacle Manufacturing will use the space, even the best

realtor or property manager may not know how to answer your questions or perhaps direct you to other office space that better meets your needs.

Where and how you include the necessary explanatory information depend on the nature of your message. Usually, a good place for general explanatory material is before or after the direct request in the opening paragraph. This information helps reduce any startling effect that a direct opening question might have. It often fits logically into this place, serving as a qualifying or justifying sentence for the message.

In messages that ask more than one question, include any necessary explanatory material with the questions. If this is the case, the explanation fits best with the questions to which it pertains. Such messages may alternate questions and explanations in the body of the message.

Structuring the Questions

After you ask your initial question and provide any relevant background information, your message will take one of two directions. If your inquiry involves only one question, you have achieved your objective, and you may move to a goodwill

> **If you do not explain enough or if you misjudge the reader's knowledge, you make the reader's task difficult.**

Answering inquiries that do not include adequate explanation can be frustrating.

ending to finish your message. If you have to ask several questions, develop an organized, logical list in the body of your message.

Make sure the questions stand out. You can do this in a number of ways. First, you can make each question a separate sentence with a bullet—a symbol (for example, ●, ○, ■) used to call attention to a particular item. Combining two or more questions in a sentence de-emphasizes each and invites the reader to overlook some questions.

Second, you can give each question a separate paragraph whenever your explanation and other comments about each question justify a paragraph.

Third, you can order or rank your questions with numbers. By using words (e.g., *first, second, third*), numerals (e.g., 1, 2, 3), or letters (e.g., *a, b, c*), you make the questions stand out. Also, you provide the reader with a convenient check and reference guide for answering.

> # Avoid questions that can be answered with a simple *yes* or *no* unless you really want a simple *yes* or *no* answer.

Fourth, you can structure your questions in question form. True questions stand out. Sentences that merely hint at a need for information do not attract much attention. The "It would be nice if you would tell me. . ." and "I would like to know. . ." types are really not questions. They do not ask—they merely suggest. The questions that stand out are those written in question form: "Will you please tell me. . . ?" "How much would one be able to save. . . ?" "How many contract problems have you had. . . ?"

Avoid questions that can be answered with a simple *yes* or *no* unless you really want a simple *yes* or *no* answer. For example, the question "Is the chair available in blue?" may not be what you really want to know. A better wording probably is "In what colors is the chair available?" Often you'll find that you can combine a yes/no question and its explanation to get a better, more concise question. To illustrate, the wording "Does the program run with Windows? We use Windows Vista." could be improved with "Does the program run with Windows Vista?"

Ending with Goodwill

The goodwill ending described in the general plan is appropriate here, just as it is in most business messages. And we must emphasize again that the closing words do the most toward creating goodwill when they fit the specific message. Remember to include important deadlines and reasons for them as well.

Reviewing the Order

In summary, the plan recommended for the routine inquiry message is as follows:

- Focus directly on the main point—either a specific question that sets up the entire message or a general request for information.
- Include necessary explanation—wherever it fits.
- If a number of questions are involved, ask them.
- Make the questions stand out (using bullets, numbering, paragraphing, question form).
- End with goodwill words adapted to the individual case.

technology in brief

Picture Bullets Add a Bit of Flair

Word processing applications allow writers to list items easily with bullets or numbers. Writers generally use numbers to show ordering or ranking and bullets to list unranked or equal items. One way to add interest to lists is to use picture bullets, an easy task today. Rather than selecting one of the six standard bullets, writers can easily customize them with pictures. Microsoft Word includes a nice selection of picture bullets in various colors and styles, some that you see below. However, writers can also select other images to import for use

as a bullet. By simply pointing and clicking on the image to import, a writer instantly creates a bullet and resizes it automatically for bullet use.

In a message to its members meeting in Incline Village, NV, the executive director of the Association for Business Communication might use one picture bullet to list items members should bring with them for tours of the area. The writer might suggest that members bring these items:

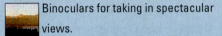 Binoculars for taking in spectacular views.

■ All-weather jacket with a hood for protection from sudden showers.

■ Cameras with wide lenses for panoramic photos.

The same message might use a different picture bullet for a list of items for a side trip to the casinos. Clearly, these bullets could add interest through color and convey differentiation of the lists as well. Through careful use, picture bullets can help writers present lists that get attention.

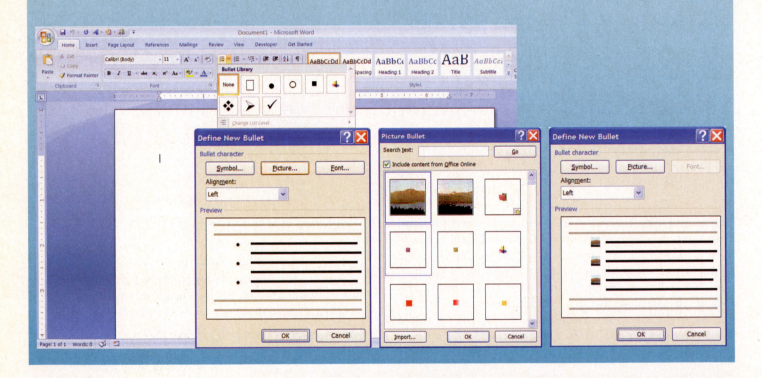

Contrasting Examples

The following two routine inquiry messages on pages 101 and 102 illustrate bad and good examples for requesting information about office space for a new Pinnacle regional headquarters (recall the Workplace Scenario). The first example follows the indirect pattern. The second is direct. Here they are presented as letters, as indicated by the "Dear" in the salutation and the "Sincerely" closing, but the points they make apply to inquiries in other media as well.

In addition, you can study the two Case Illustrations (pages 104–105). The margin comments of these examples help you see how the examples follow the advice in this chapter.

the indirect message The less effective message begins slowly and gives obvious information. Even if the writer thinks that this information needs to be communicated, it does not deserve the emphasis of the opening sentence. The writer gets to the point of the message in the second paragraph, but there are no questions here—just topics. The items of information the writer wants do not stand out but are listed in rapid succession in one sentence. The close is selfish and stiff.

the direct and effective message The second example (page 102) begins directly by asking for information. The explanation is brief but complete. The questions, with explanation worked in where needed, are made to stand out; thus, they help to make answering easy. The message closes with a courteous and appropriate request for quick action.

LO 4 Write direct, orderly, and friendly favorable responses.

Writing inquiries requires that one use careful wording so the reader understands clearly what is being asked.

GENERAL FAVORABLE RESPONSES

As you read the first example, note that it is tagged with a red light. We use this icon throughout the text wherever we show bad examples. The good examples are marked by a green light.

When you answer inquiries favorably, your primary goal is to tell your readers what they want to know. Because their reactions to your goal will be favorable, directness is in order.

Dear Mr. Piper:

We have seen your advertisement for 3,200 square feet of office space in the *Daily Journal*. As we are interested, we would like additional information.

Specifically, we would like to know the interior layout, annual cost, availability of transportation, length of lease agreement, escalation provisions, and any other information you think pertinent.

If the information you give us is favorable, we will inspect the property. Please send your reply.

Sincerely,

This letter's indirect and vague beginning makes it slow, and the questions do not stand out.

Beginning with the Answer

As you can deduce from the preceding examples, directness here means giving the readers what they want at the beginning. When a response involves answering a single question, you begin by answering that question. When it involves answering two or more questions, one good plan is to begin by answering one of them—preferably the most important. In the Workplace Scenario (p. 103), this opening would get the response off to a fast start:

Yes, you can use Eco-Treat to prevent mildew.

An alternative possibility is to begin by stating that you are giving the reader what he or she wants—that you are complying with the request. Actually, this approach is really not direct because it delays giving the information requested. But it is a favorable beginning that does respond to the inquiry, and it does not run the risk of sounding abrupt, which is a criticism of direct beginnings. These examples illustrate this type of beginning:

Thank you for your inquiry about Eco-Treat.

Here are the answers to your questions about Eco-Treat.

Identifying the Message Being Answered

Because this type of message is a response to another message, you should identify the message you are answering.

"First the good news—if I cure you, I'll become world famous."

Such identification helps the reader recall or find the message being answered. If you are writing an email response, the original message is appended to your message. Hardcopy messages may use a subject line (Subject: Your April 2 inquiry about Eco-Treat), as illustrated in the sample formats on the text website. Or you can refer to the message incidentally in the text ("as requested in your April 2 inquiry"). Preferably you should make this identification early in your message.

This direct and orderly letter begins with the request and uses a bulleted list to order the questions.

Dear Mr. Piper:

Will you please answer the following questions about the 3,200-square-foot office suite advertised in the June 28 issue of the *Daily Journal?* It appears that this space may be suitable for the new regional headquarters we are opening in your city in August.

- Is the layout of these offices suitable for a work force of two administrators, a receptionist, and seven office employees? If possible, please send us a diagram of the space.
- What is the annual rental charge?
- What housekeeping, maintenance, and utilities costs are included?
- What is the nature of the walls and flooring?
- What access is available to mass transportation and the airport?
- What are your requirements for length of lease agreement?
- Will you send us photos of the interior and exterior of the building?

We look forward to learning about your property. We hope to secure a space by July 21 that meets our needs.

Sincerely,

Logically Arranging the Answers

If you are answering just one question, you have little to do after handling that question in the opening. You answer it as completely as the situation requires, and you present whatever explanation or other information is needed. Then you are ready to close the message.

If, on the other hand, you are answering two or more questions, the body of your message becomes a series of answers. As in all clear writing, you should work for a logical order, perhaps answering the questions in the order your reader used in asking them. You may even number your answers, especially if your reader numbered the questions. Or you may decide to arrange your answers by paragraphs so that each stands out clearly.

Skillfully Handling the Negatives

When your response concerns some bad news along with the good news, you need to handle the bad news with care. Bad news stands out. Unless you are careful, it is likely to receive more emphasis than it deserves. In routine, direct-order messages, you will need to subordinate the bad news and emphasize the good news.

How Routine Responses Were Written in the Late 1800s

The following model letter for answering routine inquiries appears on page 75 of O. R. Palmer's *Type-Writing and Business Correspondence.* Published in 1896, the book was a leader in its field.

Dear Sirs:

Your favor of Dec. 18th, enclosing blue prints for tank, received. In reply thereto we beg to submit the following:

[*Here was a listing of materials for the tank.*]

Trusting that our price may be satisfactory to you, and that we shall be favored with your order, we beg to remain,

Very truly yours,

To give proper emphasis to the good- and bad-news parts, you should use the techniques discussed in Chapter 4, especially positioning. That is, you should place the good news in positions of high emphasis—at paragraph beginnings and endings and at the beginning and ending of the message as a whole. You should place the bad news in secondary positions such as the second paragraph. In addition, you should

workplace scenario

Writing Favorable Responses

Continue in your role as assistant to the vice president for operations of Pinnacle Manufacturing Company and answer some of the messages sent to you.

You answer most of the incoming messages favorably. That is, you tell the reader what he or she wants to know. In today's inbox, for example, you have a typical problem of this type. It is a message from a prospective customer for Pinnacle's

Eco-Treat paint. In response to an advertisement, this prospective customer asks a number of specific questions about Eco-Treat. Foremost, she wants to know whether the paint is really mildew-proof. Do you have evidence of results? Do you guarantee results? Is the paint safe? How much does a gallon cost? Will one coat do the job?

You can answer all but one of the questions positively. Of course, you will report this one negative point (that two coats are needed to do most jobs), but you will take care to give it only the emphasis it deserves. The response will be primarily a good-news message. Because the reader is a good prospect, you will work for the best goodwill effect.

case illustration

A Routine Inquiry
(Getting Information about a Training Program)

This email message is from a company training director to the director of a management-training program. The company training director has received literature on the program but needs additional information. The message seeks this information.

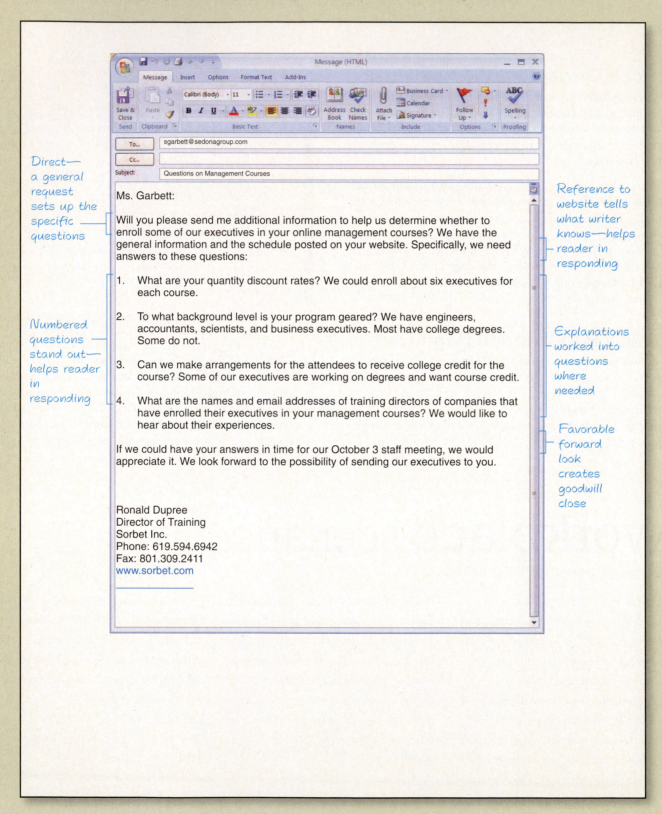

Direct—a general request sets up the specific questions

Numbered questions stand out—helps reader in responding

Reference to website tells what writer knows—helps reader in responding

Explanations worked into questions where needed

Favorable forward look creates goodwill close

To... sgarbett@sedonagroup.com
Cc...
Subject: Questions on Management Courses

Ms. Garbett:

Will you please send me additional information to help us determine whether to enroll some of our executives in your online management courses? We have the general information and the schedule posted on your website. Specifically, we need answers to these questions:

1. What are your quantity discount rates? We could enroll about six executives for each course.

2. To what background level is your program geared? We have engineers, accountants, scientists, and business executives. Most have college degrees. Some do not.

3. Can we make arrangements for the attendees to receive college credit for the course? Some of our executives are working on degrees and want course credit.

4. What are the names and email addresses of training directors of companies that have enrolled their executives in your management courses? We would like to hear about their experiences.

If we could have your answers in time for our October 3 staff meeting, we would appreciate it. We look forward to the possibility of sending our executives to you.

Ronald Dupree
Director of Training
Sorbet Inc.
Phone: 619.594.6942
Fax: 801.309.2411
www.sorbet.com

A Routine Inquiry
(An Inquiry about Hotel Accommodations)

This fax message to a hotel inquires about meeting accommodations for a professional association. In selecting a hotel, the company's managers need answers to specific questions. The message covers these questions.

Visit us: www.womensmedia.com

TO: Ms. Connie Briggs, Manager
COMPANY: Drake Hotel
FAX: 312.787.1431
DATE: July 17, 2011

FROM: Patti Wolff, Chair of the Site Selection Committee
COMPANY: WomensMedia.com
PHONE: 619.401.9600
FAX: 619.401.9444
EMAIL: pwolff@womensmedia.com

TOTAL PAGES *(including cover):* 1

Direct—a courteous general request that sets up the specific question

COMMENTS: Will you please help WomensMedia.com decide whether we can hold our annual meeting at the Drake hotel?

Explanation of situation provides background information

We have selected Chicago for our 2013 meeting, which will be held August 16, 17, and 18. In addition to the Drake, the conference committee is considering the Marriott and the Hilton. In order to decide, we need the following information:

Can you accommodate a group of about 600 employees on these dates? They will need about 400 rooms.

What size room blocks do you offer? We need assurance of having available a minimum of 450 rooms, and we could guarantee 400. Would you be willing to set aside this size block of rooms?

Specific questions—with explanations where needed

Questions stand out—in separate paragraphs

What are your charges for conference rooms? We will need eight for each of the three days, and each should have a minimum capacity of 60. For the half-hour business meeting on the 18th, we will need a large ballroom with a capacity of at least 500.

Do you offer a discount on room rates for conference attendees? If so, what size conference qualifies, and what is the discount?

Also, will you please send me your menu selections and prices for group dinners? On the 17th we host our presidential dinner. About 500 can be expected for this event.

Individually tailored goodwill close

As meeting plans must be announced by September, may we have your response right away? We look forward to the possibility of being with you in 2013.

technology in brief

Shortcut Tools Help Writers Improve Productivity and Quality

Shortcuts help writers save time and improve quality. One of the easiest to use is the AutoCorrect tool in Word (shown here) or the similar QuickCorrect tool in WordPerfect. This tool will automatically replace a word entered with another word set up to replace that particular word. The default setting is generally set up to correct common misspellings and typos. However, it also can be used to expand acronyms or phrases used repeatedly.

If you worked frequently with the Association for Business Communication, you might set up the AutoCorrect tool to replace the acronym ABC with the full name, as you see at the right. Not only will this shortcut enable you to save time, but it also will improve the quality of your message by inserting a correctly spelled and typed replacement every time.

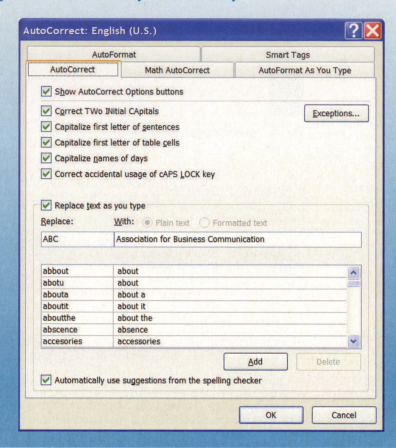

use space emphasis to your advantage. This means giving less space to bad-news parts and more space to good-news parts. You also should select words and build sentences that communicate the effect you want. Generally, this means using positive words and avoiding negative words. Your overall goal should be to present the information in your response so that your readers feel good about you and your company. If the bad news is the focus of your message or if your objective is to deliver bad news, you should use the indirect approach discussed in Chapter 6.

Considering Extras

To create goodwill, as well as future business, you should consider including extras with your answers. These are the things you say and do that are not actually required. Examples are a comment or question showing an interest in the reader's question, some additional information that may prove valuable, and a suggestion for the use of the information supplied. In fact, extras can be anything that helps your response do more than skim the surface with hurried, routine answers. Such extras frequently make the difference between success and failure in the goodwill effort.

Illustrations of how extras can be used to strengthen the goodwill effects of a message are as broad as the imagination. A business executive answering a college professor's request for information on company operations could supplement the requested information with suggestions of other sources. A technical writer could clarify highly technical answers with simpler explanations. In the Eco-Treat problem, additional information (say, how much surface area a gallon covers) would be helpful. Such extras encourage readers to take the extra step in building a business relationship with you.

Closing Cordially

As in the other direct messages, your ending should be cordial, friendly words that fit the one case. For example, you might close the Eco-Treat message with these words:

If I can help you further in deciding whether Eco-Treat will meet your needs, please email me again.

technology in brief

ClearContext Helps One Manage Email, Tasks, and Calendar

While numerous studies have predicted the growing volume of messages we will all be getting in the future, a variety of tools are being developed to help us handle them more efficiently. These tools vary in their approach to the solution, too, from discouraging message sending to using various organizing strategies with add-ins for the messaging tools we're already using. One of these latter tools is ClearContext, an add-in for Microsoft Outlook. As you can see in this screen shot, it offers a dashboard where one can see at a glance an organized, color-coded presentation of appointments, tasks, and prioritized emails.

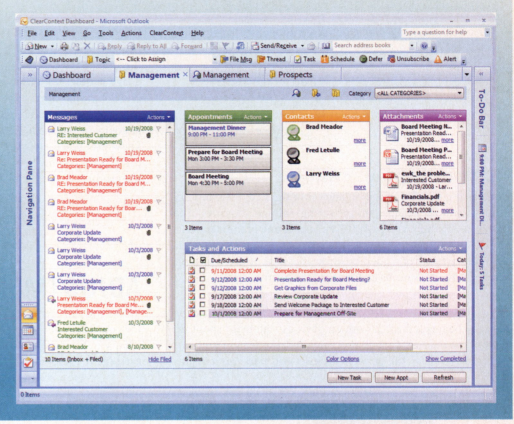

Subject: Your inquiry of April 3

Ms. Motley

I have received your April 3 message, in which you inquire about our Eco-Treat paint. I want you to know that we appreciate your interest and will welcome your business.

In response to your question about how many coats are needed to cover new surfaces, I regret to report that two are usually required. The paint is mildew-proof. We do guarantee it. It has been well tested in our laboratories. It is safe to use as directed.

George Moxley

This email is indirect and ineffective.

Reviewing the Plan

When we review the preceding special considerations, we produce the following plan for the favorable response message:

- Begin with the answer or state that you are complying with the request.
- Identify the message being answered either incidentally or in a subject line.
- Continue to respond in a way that is logical and orderly.
- De-emphasize any negative information.
- Consider including extras.
- End with a friendly comment adapted to your reader.

Contrasting Illustrations

Contrasting email messages in answer to the Eco-Treat inquiry illustrate the techniques of answering routine inquiries. The first message shown on page 107 violates many of the standards set in this and earlier chapters. The second message below meets the requirements of a good business message. It takes into account the reader's needs and the writer's business goals.

an indirect and hurried response The ineffective message begins indirectly with an obvious statement about receipt of the inquiry. Though well intended, the second sentence continues to delay the answers. The second paragraph begins to give the desired information, but it emphasizes the most negative answer by position and by wording. This answer is followed by hurried and routine answers to the other questions asked. Only the barest information is presented. There is no goodwill close.

effectiveness in direct response The better message begins directly with the most favorable answer. Then it presents the other answers, giving each the emphasis and positive language it deserves. It subordinates the one negative answer by position, volume of treatment, and sentence structure. More pleasant information follows the negative answer. The close is goodwill talk with some subtle selling strategy added. "We know that you'll enjoy the long-lasting beauty of this mildew-proof paint" points positively to purchase and successful use of the product.

LO 5 Compose adjustment grants that regain any lost confidence.

ADJUSTMENT GRANTS

When you can grant an adjustment, the situation is a happy one for your customer. You are correcting an error. You are doing what you were asked to do. As in other positive situations, a message written in the direct order is appropriate.

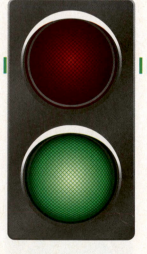

This direct email answers the reader's question immediately and uses positive language.

Subject: Your April 3 inquiry about Eco-Treat

Ms. Motley:

Yes, Eco-Treat paint will prevent mildew or we will refund your money. We know it works because we have tested it under all common conditions. In every case, it proved successful.

When you carefully follow the directions on each can, Eco-Treat paint is guaranteed safe. As the directions state, you should use Eco-Treat only in a well-ventilated room—never in a closed, unvented area.

One gallon of Eco-Treat is usually enough for one-coat coverage of 500 square feet of previously painted surface. For the best results on new surfaces, you will want to apply two coats. For such surfaces, you should figure about 200 square feet per gallon for a long-lasting coating.

We sincerely appreciate your interest in Eco-Treat, Ms. Motley. This mildew-proof paint will bring you five years or more of beautiful protection.

George Moxley

In most face-to-face business relations, people communicate with courteous directness. You should write most business messages this way.

Considering Special Needs

The adjustment-grant message has much in common with the message types previously discussed. You begin directly with the good-news answer. You refer to the message you are answering and you close on a friendly note, but because the situation stems from an unhappy experience, you have two special needs. One is the need to overcome the negative impressions that the experience leading to the adjustment has formed in the reader's mind. The other is the need to regain any confidence in your company, its products, or its service that the reader may have lost from the experience.

need to overcome negative impressions To understand the first need, just place yourself in the reader's shoes. As the reader sees it, something bad has happened—goods have been damaged, equipment has failed, or sales have been lost. The experience has not been pleasant. Granting the adjustment will take care of much of the problem, but some negative thoughts may remain. You need to work to overcome any such thoughts.

You can attempt to do this using words that produce positive effects. For example, in the opening you can do more than just give the affirmative answer. You can add goodwill, as in this example:

The enclosed check for $189.77 is our way of proving to you that we value your satisfaction.

Throughout the message you should avoid words that recall unnecessarily the bad situation you are correcting. You especially want to avoid the negative words that could be used to describe what went wrong—words such as *mistake, trouble, damage, broken,* and *loss.* Even general words such as *problem, difficulty,* and *misunderstanding* can have unpleasant connotations. Negative language makes the customer's complaint the focus of your message. Your goal is to move the customer beyond the problem and to the solution—that the customer is going to have his or her claim granted. You can only do this if you use positive, reader-centered language.

Also negative are the apologies often included in these messages. Even though well intended, the somewhat conventional

workplace scenario

Writing Adjustment Grants

Continuing in your role with Pinnacle, this time you received an email message from an unhappy customer. It seems that Ms. Bernice Watson, owner of Tri-Cities Hardware, is upset because some of the 30 Old London lampposts she ordered from Pinnacle arrived in damaged condition. "The glass is broken in 17 of the units," she writes,

"obviously because of poor packing." She had ordered the lights for a special sale. In fact, she notes, she had even featured them in her advertising. The sale begins next Friday. She wants a fast adjustment—either the lamps by sale time or her money back.

Of course, you will grant Ms. Watson's request. You will send her an email message

saying that the goods are on the way. And because you want to keep this customer, you will try to regain any lost confidence with an honest explanation of the problem. This message is classified as an adjustment grant.

A Routine Response Message
(Favorable Response to a Professor's Request)

This email message responds to a professor's request for production records that will be used in a research project. The writer is
giving the information wanted but must restrict its use.

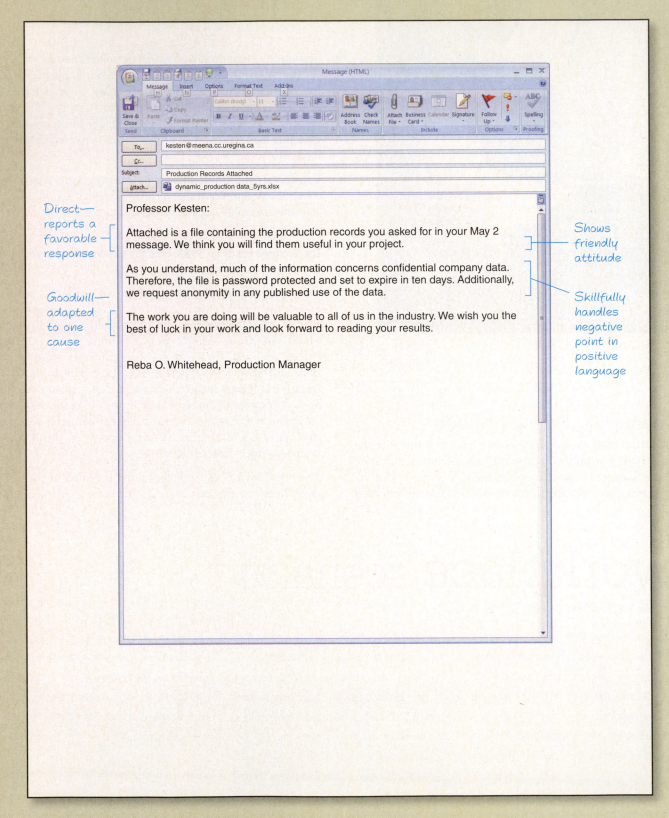

Direct—
reports a
favorable
response

Goodwill—
adapted
to one
cause

Shows
friendly
attitude

Skillfully
handles
negative
point in
positive
language

To.. | kesten@meena.cc.uregina.ca

Cc...

Subject: | Production Records Attached

Attach... | dynamic_production data_5yrs.xlsx

Professor Kesten:

Attached is a file containing the production records you asked for in your May 2
message. We think you will find them useful in your project.

As you understand, much of the information concerns confidential company data.
Therefore, the file is password protected and set to expire in ten days. Additionally,
we request anonymity in any published use of the data.

The work you are doing will be valuable to all of us in the industry. We wish you the
best of luck in your work and look forward to reading your results.

Reba O. Whitehead, Production Manager

A Routine Response Message
(A Request for Detailed Information)

Answering an inquiry about a company's experience with executive suites, this letter numbers the answers as the questions were numbered in the inquiry. The opening appropriately sets up the numbered answers with a statement that indicates a favorable response.

Merck & Co., Inc.
One Merck Drive
P.O. Box 100, WS1A-46
Whitehouse Station, NJ 08889
http://www.merck.com

August 7, 2011

Ms. Ida Casey, Sales Manager
Liberty Insurance Company
1165 Second Ave.
Des Moines, IA 50318-9631

Dear Ms. Casey:

Direct— tells that writer is complying

Following is the information about our use of temporary executive suites that you requested in your August 3 fax. For your convenience, I have numbered my responses to correspond with the sequence you used.

Sets up listing

Orderly listing of answers

1. Our executives have mixed feelings about the effectiveness of the suites. At the beginning the majority opinion was negative, but it appears now that most of the antagonism has faded.

2. The suites option definitely has saved us money. Rental costs in the suburbs are much less than downtown costs; annual savings are estimated at nearly 30 percent.

3. The transition did create a morale problem among those remaining downtown even after we assured them that their workloads would not increase.

Complete yet concise answers

4. We began using executive suites at the request of several sales representatives who had read about other companies using them. We pilot-tested the program in one territory for a year using volunteers before we implemented it companywide.

5. We are quite willing to share with you the list of facilities we plan to use again. Additionally, I am enclosing a copy of our corporate policy, which describes details of use.

Friendly— adapted to the one case

If after reviewing this information you have any other questions, please write me again or contact our sales representatives for firsthand information. I wish you the best of luck in implementing these suites in your operations.

Offers extra to build goodwill

Sincerely,

David M. Earp

David M. Earp
Office Manager

Enclosure

"we sincerely regret the inconvenience caused you . . ." type of comment is of questionable value. It emphasizes the negative happenings for which the apology is made. If you sincerely believe that you owe an apology or that one is expected, you can apologize and risk the negative effect. But do it early and move on, and don't repeat it at the end. In most instances, however, your efforts to correct the problem will show adequate concern for your reader's interests.

need to regain lost confidence Except in cases in which the cause of the difficulty is routine or incidental, you also will need to regain the reader's lost confidence. Just what you must do and how you must do it depend on the facts of the situation. You will need to survey the situation to see what they are. If something can be done to correct a bad procedure or a product defect, you should do it. Then you should tell your reader what has been done as convincingly and positively as you can. If what went wrong was a rare, unavoidable event, you should explain this. Sometimes you will need to explain how a product should be used or cared for. Sometimes you will need to resell the product. Of course, whatever you do must be ethical—supported by truth and integrity.

Reviewing the Plan

Applying these two special needs to the general plan previously reviewed, we come up with this specific plan for the message granting an adjustment:

- Begin directly—with the good news.
- Incidentally identify the message that you are answering.
- Avoid negatives that recall the problem.
- Regain lost confidence through explanation or corrective action.
- End with a friendly, positive comment.

Contrasting Adjustments

The following adjustment messages (below and next page), which respond to the workplace scenario on page 109 illustrate these techniques. The first, with its indirect order and grudging tone, is ineffective. The directness and positiveness of the second clearly make it the better message.

a slow and negative approach The ineffective message begins with an obvious comment about receiving the

This email is indirect and negative.

Subject: Your Broken Old London Lights

Ms. Watson,

We have received your May 1 claim reporting that our shipment of Old London lamppost lights reached you with 17 broken units. We regret the inconvenience caused you and can understand your unhappiness.

Following our standard practice, we investigated the situation thoroughly. Apparently the fault is the result of an inexperienced temporary employee's negligence. We have taken corrective measures to assure that future shipments will be packed more carefully.

I am pleased to report that we are sending replacements today. They should reach you before your sale begins. Our driver will pick up the broken units when making delivery.

Again, we regret all the trouble we caused you.

Stephanie King

The next work you take from your in-box is an order for paints and painting supplies. It is from Mr. Tony Lee of the Central City Paint Company, a new customer whom Pinnacle has been trying to attract for months. You usually acknowledge orders with routine messages, but this case is different. You feel the need to welcome this new customer and to cultivate him for future sales.

After checking your current inventory and making certain that the goods will be on the way to Lee today, you are ready to write him a special acknowledgment and thank him for his business.

claim. It recalls vividly what went wrong and then painfully explains what happened. As a result, the good news is delayed for an additional paragraph. Finally, after two delaying paragraphs, the message gets to the good news. Though well intended, the close leaves the reader with a reminder of the trouble.

the direct and positive technique The better message below uses the subject line to identify the transaction. The opening words tell the reader what she most wants to hear in a positive way that adds to the goodwill tone of the message. With reader-viewpoint explanation, the message then reviews what happened. Without a single negative word, it makes clear what caused the problem and what has been done to prevent its recurrence. After handling the essential matter of picking up the broken lamps, the message closes with positive resale talk removed from the problem.

LO 6 Write order acknowledgments and other thank-you messages that build goodwill.

ORDER ACKNOWLEDGMENTS

In the course of your professional career, you will find yourself in situations where business and social etiquette require thank-you messages. Such messages may be long or short, formal or informal. They may be also combined with other purposes such as confirming an order. In this section we focus on one specific kind of thank-you message—the order acknowledgement—as well as more general thank-you messages for other business occasions.

Subject: Your May 1 Email on Invoice 1248

Ms. Watson:

Seventeen carefully packed Old London lamppost lights should reach your sales floor in time for your Saturday promotion. Our driver left our warehouse today with instructions to special deliver them to you on Friday.

Because your satisfaction with our service and products is our top priority, we have thoroughly checked our shipping procedures. It appears that the shipment to you was packed by a temporary employee who was filling in for a hospitalized veteran packer. We now have our veteran packer back at work and have taken measures to ensure better performance by our temporary staff.

As you know, the Old London lamppost lights have become one of the best-selling products in the lighting field. We are confident they will contribute to the success of your sale.

Stephanie King

This email message is direct and positive. It focuses on the solution rather than the problem.

An Adjustment Grant Message
(Explaining a Human Error)

This email message grants the action requested in the claim of a customer who received a leather computer case that was monogrammed incorrectly. The writer has no excuse because human error was to blame. His explanation is positive and convincing.

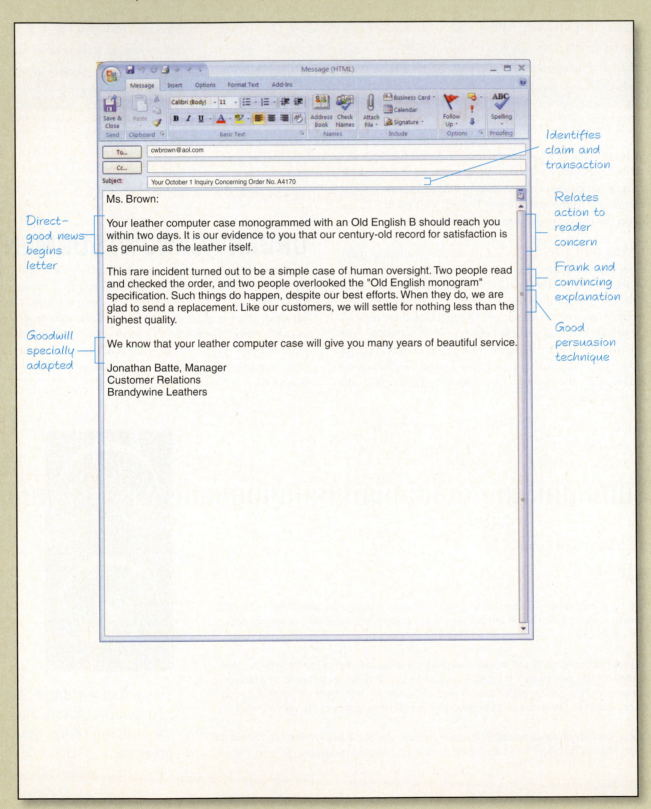

To... cwbrown@aol.com

Cc...

Subject: Your October 1 Inquiry Concerning Order No. A4170 — *Identifies claim and transaction*

Ms. Brown:

Direct—good news begins letter — Your leather computer case monogrammed with an Old English B should reach you within two days. It is our evidence to you that our century-old record for satisfaction is as genuine as the leather itself. — *Relates action to reader concern*

This rare incident turned out to be a simple case of human oversight. Two people read and checked the order, and two people overlooked the "Old English monogram" specification. Such things do happen, despite our best efforts. When they do, we are glad to send a replacement. Like our customers, we will settle for nothing less than the highest quality. — *Frank and convincing explanation*

Goodwill specially adapted — We know that your leather computer case will give you many years of beautiful service. — *Good persuasion technique*

Jonathan Batte, Manager
Customer Relations
Brandywine Leathers

Online Order Acknowledgment

This email message thanks the reader for her order and invites her to participate in this company's online product review.

From: Gardeners Supply [mailto:gardeners@e-news.gardeners.com]
Sent: Thursday, January 08, 2012 9:08 AM
To: KATHRYN.RENTZ@UC.EDU
Subject: Tell Us What You Think About Our Products

GARDENER'S
SUPPLY COMPANY

New Feature: Customer Reviews

Dear Kathryn,

Thanks the reader — Thank you for your purchase from Gardener's Supply. We hope you are enjoying your items and that this year's garden will be your best ever!

Your satisfaction with our products is important to us, and we want to hear what you have to say about them. We recently added customer reviews to our Web site, which helps us improve our product selection and helps other gardeners find the best products to suit their needs. — *Moves to another goal of the message*

Adds a reader benefit and incentive — We're hoping you'll take a moment to rate and review some or all of the items you have purchased from us. Other gardeners will appreciate your opinions and advice, and you may also enjoy reading what fellow gardeners have to say!

Each time you submit a product review to our Web site, your name will be entered in a monthly drawing for a $1000 prize (see information below).

Here are the item(s) you recently purchased. Just click on an item to write a review.

Men's Waterproof Gloves

★ **Rate and review it**

Glove Set, 3 Pairs

★ **Rate and review it** — *Makes participation easy by providing links*

Provides a quick visual confirmation of the order

Builds goodwill with a forward-looking ending — Thank you for your time and consideration,

The Employee-Owners at Gardener's Supply

Copyright @2008 America's Gardening Resource, Inc.

technology in brief

Tables Help Writers Organize Data for Easy Reading

Setting up tables within a document is an easy task. The tables feature allows writers to create tables as well as to import spreadsheet and database files. In both instances, you can arrange information in columns and rows, inserting detail in the cells. Headings can be formatted and formulas can be entered in the cells. The table you see here could be one the writer created for use in a favorable response to an inquiry about possible locations for a meeting in Chicago.

Organizing information with tables makes it easier for both the writer and the reader. A careful writer will include column and row labels as needed, helping the reader extract information both quickly and accurately.

Hotel Name	Address	Convention Room Rate for Standard Rooms	Guest Rating
Chicago Marriott Downtown	540 North Michigan Avenue, Chicago, IL 60611-3869	$409	4.2
Drake Hotel	140 East Walton Street, Chicago, IL 60611-1545	$309	4.3
Palmer House Hilton	17 East Monroe Street, Chicago, IL 60603-5605	$252	4.4

Source: Hotels.com.

> Individually written acknowledgments are sometimes justified, especially with new accounts or large orders.

Order Acknowledgments

Acknowledgments are sent to let people who order goods know the status of their orders. Most acknowledgments are routine. They simply tell when the goods are being shipped. Many companies use form or computer-generated messages for such situations. Some use printed, standard notes with check-off or write-in blanks, but individually written acknowledgments are sometimes justified, especially with new accounts or large orders.

Skillfully composed acknowledgments can do more than acknowledge orders, though this task remains their primary goal. These messages also can build goodwill through their warm, personal, human tone. They can make the reader feel good about doing business with a company that cares and want to continue doing business with that company. To maintain this goodwill for repeat customers, you will want to revise your form acknowledgments regularly.

Directness and Goodwill Building in Order Acknowledgments

Like the other direct messages in this chapter, the acknowledgment message appropriately begins with its good news—that the goods are being shipped. And it ends on a goodwill note. Except when some of the goods ordered must be delayed, the remainder of the message is devoted to goodwill building. This goodwill building can begin in the opening by emphasizing the reader's receipt of the goods rather than merely sending the goods:

The Protect-O paints and supplies you ordered April 4 should reach you by Wednesday. They are leaving our Walden warehouse today by DHL Freight.

It also can include a warm expression of thanks for the order, especially when a first order is involved. Anything else you can say that will be helpful to the reader is appropriate in this regard—information about new products or services, for example. A specially adapted forward look to continued business relations is an appropriate goodwill gesture in the close.

Tact in Order Acknowledgments

Sometimes the task of acknowledging is complicated by your inability to send the goods requested right away. You could be out of them, or perhaps the reader did not give you all the information you need to send the goods. In either case, a delay is involved. In some cases, delays are routine and expected and do not pose a serious problem. In these situations, you can use the direct approach. However, you will still want to minimize any negative news so that your routine message does not become a negative-news message. You can do this by using positive language that focuses on what *can* or *will* happen rather than what *didn't* or *won't* happen.

In the case of a vague order, for example, you should handle the information you need without appearing to accuse the reader of giving insufficient information. To illustrate, you gain nothing by writing "You failed to specify the color of phones you want." But you gain goodwill by writing "So that we can send you precisely the phones you want, please check your choice of colors on the space below." This sentence handles the matter positively and makes the action easy to take. It also shows a courteous attitude.

Similarly, you can handle back-order information tactfully by emphasizing the positive part of the message. For example, instead of writing "We can't ship the ink jet cartridges until the 9th," you can write "We will rush the ink jet cartridges to you as soon as our stock is replenished by a shipment due May 9." If the back-order period is longer than the customer expects or longer than the 30 days allowed by law, you may choose to give your customer an alternative. You could offer a substitute product or service. Giving the customer a choice builds goodwill.

In some cases delays will lead to major disappointments, which means you will have to write a bad-news message. A more complete discussion of how to handle such negative news is provided in Chapter 6.

Summarizing the Structure of Order Acknowledgments and Other Thank-You Messages

To write an order acknowledgment or thank-you message:

- Use the direct order: Begin by thanking the reader for something specific (e.g., an order).
- Continue with your thanks or with further information.
- Use positive, tactful language to address vague or back orders.
- If appropriate, achieve a secondary goal (e.g., reselling or confirming a mutual understanding).
- Close with a goodwill-building comment, adapted to the topic of the message.

> " . . . you will still want to minimize any negative news so that your routine message does not become a negative-news message. "

Dear Mr. Lee:

Your April 4 order for $1,743.30 worth of Protect-O paints and supplies has been received. We are pleased to have this nice order and hope that it marks the beginning of a long relationship.

As you instructed, we will bill you for this amount. We are shipping the goods today by DHL Freight.

We look forward to your future orders.

Sincerely,

This one delays the important news.

workplace scenario

Writing Claim Messages

Introduce yourself to claim messages by playing the role of Ms. Bernice Watson, one of Pinnacle's customers and the owner of Tri-Cities Hardware. For the past few days you have been preparing for your annual spring promotion. You have ordered widely, and you have advertised the items to be featured. All has gone well until today when Pinnacle's shipment of Old London lamp-post lights arrived. You ordered 30, and the glass coverings on 17 of them are broken. Obviously, the lamps were poorly packed.

Now you must make a fast claim for adjustment. You will send Pinnacle an email message requesting replacement by the sale date or your money back. This message is classified as a claim.

Contrasting Acknowledgments

The following two messages (below and next page) show bad and good technique in acknowledging Mr. Lee's order. As you would expect, the good version follows the plan described in the preceding paragraphs.

slow route to a favorable message
The bad example on the previous page begins indirectly, emphasizing receipt of the order. Although intended to produce goodwill, the second sentence further delays what the reader wants most to hear. Moreover, the letter is written from the writer's point of view (note the "we" emphasis).

fast-moving presentation of the good news
The better message below begins directly, telling Mr. Lee that he is getting what he wants. The remainder of the message is a customer welcome and subtle selling. Notice the good use of reader emphasis and positive language. The message closes with a note of appreciation and a friendly, forward look.

LO 7 Write direct claims that objectively and courteously explain the facts.

DIRECT CLAIMS

Occasionally things go wrong between a business and its customers (e.g., merchandise is lost or broken during shipment, customers are inaccurately billed for goods or services). Such situations are not routine for a business; for most businesses, the routine practice is to fulfill their customers' expectations.

The direct message gives the good news immediately and creates goodwill with positive language.

Dear Mr. Lee:

Your selection of Protect-O paints and supplies was shipped today by DHL Freight and should reach you by Wednesday. As you requested, we are sending you the invoice, which is for $1,743.30, including sales tax.

Because this is your first order from us, I welcome you to the Protect-O circle of dealers. Our representative, Ms. Cindy Wooley, will call from time to time to offer whatever assistance she can. She is a highly competent technical adviser on paint and painting.

Here in the home plant we also will do what we can to help you profit from Protect-O products. We'll do our best to give you the most efficient service. And we'll continue to develop the best possible paints—like our new Eco-Treat line. As you will see from the enclosed brochure, Eco-Treat is a real breakthrough in mildew protection.

We genuinely appreciate your order, Mr. Lee. We are determined to serve you well in the years ahead.

Sincerely,

Because claim messages are not about routine circumstances and because they involve unhappy news, many are written in the indirect approach discussed in Chapter 6. Nevertheless, there are some instances where directness in writing a claim is appropriate, and for this reason we discuss the direct claim in this chapter.

Using Directness for Claims

Most businesses want to know when something is wrong with their products or services so they can correct the matter and satisfy their customers. Many times the easiest and quickest way for you to address these claims is simply to call the company directly to settle the matter. Sometimes, though, you may want to write a claim if you need a written record of the request. Or, depending on a company's phone options for accessing customer service, a written claim sent via email or the company website may be more efficient than a phone call. When writing a claim for issues where you anticipate no resistance from your reader in granting an adjustment of your claim, you may use the direct approach (e.g., adjusting an incorrect charge to an invoice). Be sure that when you write the claim, you keep your tone objective and professional so that you preserve your reader's goodwill. If you use words such as *complaint* or *disappointment*, you will compromise your chances of receiving an adjustment quickly.

> " When you write the claim keep your tone objective and professional to preserve your reader's goodwill. "

Organizing the Direct Claim

Because you anticipate the reader will willingly grant your request, a direct claim begins with the claim, moves to an explanation, and ends with a goodwill closing.

beginning a direct claim The direct claim should open with just that—the direct claim. This should be a polite but direct statement of what you need. If the statement sounds too direct, you may soften it with a little bit of explanation of your claim, but the direct claim should be at the beginning of your message, as in this example:

Please adjust the invoice (# 6379) for our May 10 order to remove the $7.50 shipping charge.

explaining the issue The body of the direct claim should provide the reader with any information he or she might need to understand your claim. To continue with the same example, we might write the following brief middle paragraph:

Because our order totaled $73.50, we were able to take advantage of your offer for free shipping on orders of $50 or more and should not have been charged a shipping fee.

providing a goodwill closing Your close should end with an expression of goodwill. A simple ending like the following can suffice: Please send a corrected copy of the invoice

Subject: Our Order No. 7135

Mr. Goetz:

As your records will show, on March 7 we ordered 30 Old London lamppost lights (our Order No. 7135). The units were received by us on March 14 (your Invoice No. 715C).

At the time of delivery, our shipping and receiving supervisor noticed that some of the cartons had broken glass inside. Upon further inspection, he found that the glass on 17 of the lamps was broken. Further inspection showed that your packers had been negligent as there was insufficient packing material in each carton.

It is hard for me to understand a shipping system that permits such errors to take place. We had advertised these lights for our annual spring promotion, which begins next Saturday. We want the lights by then or our money back.

Megan Adami

This one delays the claim and focuses on the problem.

to me at jsmith@americanmortgage.com. We look forward to continued business with National Office Supplies.

Contrasting Examples of Claim Messages

The two email messages on pages 119 and 120 show contrasting ways of handling Tri-Cities Hardware's problem with the Old London lamppost lights. The first is slow and harsh. The second is courteous, yet to the point and firm.

a slow and harsh message The first message starts slowly with a long explanation of the situation. Some of the details in the beginning sentence are helpful, but they do not deserve the emphasis that this position gives them. The problem is not described until the second paragraph. The wording here is clear but much too strong. The words are angry and insulting, and the writer talks down to the reader. Such words are more likely to produce resistance than acceptance. The negative writing continues into the close, leaving a bad final impression.

a firm yet courteous message The second message follows the plan suggested in preceding paragraphs. A subject line quickly identifies the situation. The claim message begins with a clear statement of the claim. Next, in a tone that shows, it uses objective language to tell what went wrong. The ending is rational and shows that the writer is interested in resolving the issue, not placing blame or blaming the reader.

Since unanticipated problems occur in business, writing a clear, complete, and fair-minded claim will usually solve them.

[A firm yet courteous message . . . uses objective language to tell what went wrong.]

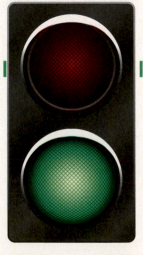

The direct message presents the request immediately & uses objective language.

Subject: Broken Glass in 17 Old London Lampposts (Invoice 1248)

Please send 17 lampposts to replace the ones that arrived today with broken glass coverings. We need the lampposts by Saturday, as we have advertised them for our annual spring promotion. If replacement is not possible, we request a refund for the broken units.

At the time of delivery, our shipping and receiving manager noticed broken glass in some of the cartons. He believes insufficient packing material caused the glass to break. We can return the broken lamps or dispose of them as you request.

I know that situations such as this can occur despite all precautions, and I am confident that you will replace the units with your usual courtesy.

workplace scenario

Writing Operational Messages

Continuing in your role as assistant to the vice president for operations of Pinnacle Manufacturing Company, write a request for cost information for a meeting at the Timber Creek Lodge.

Your boss, Becky Pharr, held a meeting with Remigo Ruiz this morning about the upcoming sales meeting in Colorado. During that meeting Remigo agreed to gather specific cost estimates for travel, room and board, recreation, and meeting rooms. Write a reminder message that your boss can send him requesting the information needed and specifying the exact kind of information she needs.

Operational communications are those messages that are sent within a business. They are messages to and from employees that get the work of the business done. This kind of message usually takes the form of a memo or email message, but it can also be a document posted on a bulletin board, mailed to employees, uploaded to a company intranet or portal, or distributed as a handout.

> ". . . Remember that being frank doesn't mean being impolite."

LO 8 Write clear and effective operational communications.

OPERATIONAL COMMUNICATIONS

The formality of operational messages ranges widely. At one extreme are the informal, casual memorandum and email exchanges between employees concerning work matters. At the other are formal documents communicating company policies, directives, and procedures. Then, of course, there are the various stages of formality in between.

Casual Operational Messages

The documents at the bottom of the formality range typically resemble conversation. Usually they are quick responses to work needs. Rarely is there time or need for careful construction and wording. The goal is simply to exchange the information needed in conducting the company's work.

Frankness describes the tone of these highly casual messages as well as many of the messages at more formal levels. The participants exchange information and views forthrightly. They write with the understanding that all participants are working for a common goal—usually what is best for the company. They know that people working together in business situations want and expect straightforward communication.

Still, remember that being frank doesn't mean being impolite. Even in quick messages you should build goodwill with a positive, courteous tone.

Moderately Formal Messages

Messages in the midlevel formality range tend to resemble the messages discussed earlier in this chapter. Usually they require more care in construction. And usually they follow a direct pattern. The most common arrangement begins with the most important point and follows with details. Thus, a typical beginning sentence is a topic (theme) statement. In messages in memorandum form, the opening repeats the subject-line information and includes the additional information needed to identify the situation. The remainder of the message consists of a logical, orderly arrangement of the information covered. When the message consists of items in sequence, the items can be numbered and presented in this sequence.

Suggestions for writing the somewhat formal internal messages are much the same as those for writing the messages covered previously. Exhibit 5.1 of a hard-copy memorandum illustrates a direct, concise, and visually appealing message moderately formal message in response to the workplace scenario above. It is moderately formal, distinctly above casual writing. Yet it is conversational. It is clearly written and organized in direct order, beginning with the objective and then systematically and clearly covering the vital bits of information. It is straightforward yet courteous.

This message is moderately formal but conversational.

DATE: April 1, 2011
TO: Remigo Ruiz
FROM: Becky Pharr
SUBJECT: Request for Cost Information Concerning Meeting at Timber Creek Lodge

As we discussed in my office today, please get the necessary cost information for conducting our annual sales meeting at the Timber Creek Lodge, Timber Creek Village, Colorado. Our meeting will begin on the morning of Monday, June 5; we should arrange to arrive on the 4th. We will leave after a brief morning session on June 9.

Specifically, we'll need the following information:

- Travel costs for all 43 participants, including air travel to Denver and ground travel between the airport and the lodge. I have listed the names and home towns of the 43 participants on the attached sheet.

- Room and board costs for the five-day period, including cost with and without dinner at the lodge. As you know, we are considering the possibility of allowing participants to purchase dinners at nearby restaurants.

- Costs for recreational facilities at the lodge.

- Costs for meeting rooms and meeting equipment (projectors, lecterns, and such). We will need a room large enough to accommodate our 43 participants.

I'd like to have the information by April 15. If you need additional information, please contact me at ✕3715 or Pharr@pinnacle.com.

Highly Formal Messages

The most formal of the operational messages deserve our special attention. These are the messages presenting policies, directives, and procedures. Usually written by executives for their subordinates, these administrative messages are often compiled in manuals, perhaps kept in loose-leaf form and updated as new material is developed.

These higher-level messages are more formally written than most of the internal communications. Their official status explains why. Usually they follow a direct order, although the nature of their contents can require variations. The goal should be to arrange the information in the most logical order for quick understanding. Since the information frequently involves a sequence of information points, numbering these points can be effective. And since these documents must be clearly understood and followed, the writing must be clear to all, including those with low verbal skills. Exhibit 5.2 presents a well written, highly formal operational message.

▼ **EXHIBIT 5.2** Example of a Highly Formal Operational Message

This message is clear and builds good relations with employees.

DATE: June 10, 2011
TO: All Employees
FROM: Terry Boedeker, President
SUBJECT: Energy Conservation

To help us keep costs low, the following conservation measures are effective immediately:

- Thermostats will be set to maintain temperatures of 78 degrees Fahrenheit throughout the air-conditioning season.

- Air conditioners will be shut off in all buildings at 4 PM Monday through Friday.

- Air conditioners will be started as late as possible each morning to have buildings at the appropriate temperature within 30 minutes after the start of the workday.

- Lighting levels will be reduced to approximately 50- to 60-foot candles in all work areas. Corridor lighting will be reduced to 5- to 10-foot candles.

- Outside lighting levels will be reduced as much as possible without compromising safety and security.

In addition, will each of you help with this conservation effort? Specifically, I ask that you do the following:

- Turn off lights not required in performing work.

- Keep windows closed when the cooling system is operating.

- Turn off all computer monitors and printers at the end of the day.

I am confident that these measures will reduce our energy use significantly. Your efforts to follow them are appreciated.

Even though this message is straightforward, note the writer's courtesy and his use of *us* and *our*. When writing direct messages, skillful managers make use of such strategies for maintaining good relations with employees. Remembering this goal becomes especially important in situations where managers have news to convey or requests to make that employees may not be ready to accept. In fact, in these situations an indirect order will be more appropriate, as Chapters 6 and 7 will discuss. For most operational communication, however, the direct order will be both expected and appreciated.

Summarizing the Structure of Operational Messages

Applying these special considerations to the general plan for direct messages, we arrive at this specific plan for operational communication.

This indirect message wastes time and dwells on the negative.

Subject: Inconsistent Shipping Policies

Pinnacle Manufacturing has been incurring increasing freight expenses and a decline in freight revenue over the last two years, impacting our ability to achieve our financial goals. The warehouse team has done a lot of research into the reasons behind this increase, and it has come to our attention that a very considerable number of shipments are going out of Cedar Rapids (1) as unbillable to the customer, and/or (2) as overnight shipments rather than ground.

Pinnacle Manufacturing only has one product for which shipping is not billed to the Customer— the Chem-Treat paint. In all other cases, product shipments are supposed to be billed to the customer. **Therefore, effective immediately, except for Chem-Treat shipments, which by contract provide for free overnight (weekday delivery) shipping, Pinnacle Manufacturing will bill the customer for all shipments of products. Finance will screen all orders to ensure that they indicate billable shipping terms.**

Pinnacle Manufacturing's overnight shipping falls into a few categories, including shipments of products to customers and shipments of marketing materials to prospects and customers. There are no customer programs or marketing programs for which Pinnacle Manufacturing offers overnight shipping (except Chem-Treat). **Therefore, effective immediately, except for Chem-Treat shipments, which by contract provide for overnight (weekday delivery) shipping, Pinnacle Manufacturing will not ship products overnight to customers unless the overnight shipping is billed to the customer. Also effective immediately, shipments of sales/marketing materials are to be shipped ground, not overnight.**

This policy change will impact some of your work processes, requiring you to be more planful in getting products shipped to customers in a businesslike and timely manner, and challenging you to prevent last-minute rush situations. I suspect that much of the freight performance situation, from a financial point of view, is an awareness issue for our Cedar Rapids team. I thank each of you in advance for adherence to this policy. We are fortunate to have an excellent distribution team in Cedar Rapids. That team needs all of our help so that their high quality shipping and inventory control performance becomes matched by strong financial performance.

Exceptions to the billable shipping-only and no overnight shipping policies must be brought to me for approval prior to entering the order.

Dean Young

VP, Operations

> ## AS IN ALL CONTACTS, YOU SHOULD END YOUR MESSAGE WITH APPROPRIATE AND FRIENDLY GOODWILL WORDS THAT PROMOTE A PROFESSIONAL IMAGE.

To write an operational message, writers should do the following:

- Organize in the direct order.
- Choose the appropriate tone (formal or informal) and communication medium.
- Be clear and courteous.
- Order the information logically.

OTHER DIRECT MESSAGE SITUATIONS

In the preceding pages, we have covered the most common direct message situations. Others occur, of course. You should be able to handle them with the techniques that have been explained and illustrated.

This direct message will be easy to read and reference. Its tone is straightforward but courteous.

Subject: Refresher on Our Shipping Policy

Please remember that our shipping policy is as follows:

Shipping Charges:
- *Chem-Treat paint* is the only product for which shipping is **not** billed to the customer.
- *All other product shipments* (including sales/marketing materials) **are** billed to the customer.

Overnight Shipping:
- Sales/marketing materials are to be shipped ground, not overnight.
- *Chem-Treat paint* may be shipped overnight at **no charge** to the customer, as provided by contract.
- *All other overnight product shipments* **are billed** to the customer.

Billing our customers accurately and consistently for shipping improves customer satisfaction with our service. In addition, the increased freight revenue will help us achieve our financial goals and control our shipping and inventory costs.

To ensure that your customers receive their products quickly, refer to the shipping and mailing timeline on Pinnacle's intranet.

The Finance Department will be screening all shipment invoices to make sure that shipments are billed accurately. If you have questions regarding the shipping policy or require an exception, please contact me at Ext. 555.

Dean Young

VP, Operations

In handling such situations, remember that whenever possible, you should get to the goal of the message right away. You should cover any other information needed in good logical order. You should carefully choose words that convey just the right meaning. More specifically, you should consider the value of using the you-viewpoint, and you should weigh carefully the differences in meaning conveyed by the positive or negative tone of your words. As in all contacts, you should end your message with appropriate and friendly goodwill words that promote a professional image. ■

Get Online

mhhe.com/FlatleyM2e

for study materials including quizzes
and Internet resources.

writing
bad-news
messages

six

Like all human resources professionals, Joan McCarthy, Director of Human Resources Communication for Comcast Cable, sometimes has to deliver negative news to employees, whether it's about health-care coverage, organizational change, or other issues. Her advice? "Balance, not spin, is the key. Frequent, candid communication that balances the good with the bad will go much further toward restoring and maintaining employee trust than the most creative 'spin.'"

Sometimes McCarthy will state negative news directly, while other times she takes a more gradual approach. Whichever pattern you use, "it's important to communicate openly and honestly," she advises. But you should also balance out the negative by "reinforcing the positive, putting the news in perspective, and showing what the organization is doing to help." In these ways you can "communicate bad news in a way that preserves your company's credibility and keeps employee trust and morale intact."

This chapter contains additional strategies for minimizing the negative impact of bad news, whether you're delivering it to internal or external readers. ◼

LEARNING OBJECTIVES

LO1 Determine which situations require using the indirect order for the most effective response.

LO2 Write indirect-order messages following the general plan.

LO3 Write an indirect claim that obtains an adjustment while maintaining goodwill.

LO4 Use tact and courtesy in refusals of requests.

LO5 Write adjustment refusals that minimize and overcome bad impressions.

LO6 Write negative announcements that maintain goodwill.

SITUATIONS REQUIRING INDIRECTNESS

As Chapter 5 mentions, handling tricky communication tasks often requires using the indirect order. This order is especially effective when you must say "no" or convey other disappointing news. The main reason for this approach is that negatives are received more positively when an explanation precedes them. An explanation may even convince the reader that the writer's position is correct. In addition, an explanation cushions the shock of bad news. Not cushioning the shock makes the message unnecessarily harsh, and harshness destroys goodwill.

You may want to use directness in some bad-news situations. If you think that your negative answer will be accepted routinely, you might choose directness. For example, in many buyer–seller relationships in business, both parties expect backorders and order errors to occur now and then. Thus, messages

Using a Strategic Buffer

Indirect messages presenting bad news often begin with a strategic buffer. By *buffer* we mean an opening that identifies the subject of the message but does not indicate overtly that negative news is coming. That is, it raises the topic of the message but does not indicate what the rest of the message will say about it.

A buffer can be neutral or positive. A neutral buffer might simply acknowledge your receipt of the reader's earlier message and indicate your awareness of what it said. A positive buffer might thank the reader for bringing a situation to your attention or for being a valued customer or employee. You do need to use care when opening on a positive note. You do not in any way want to raise the reader's expectations that you are about to deliver the news that he or she may be hoping for. That would only make your task of maintaining good relations more difficult.

Some may argue that not starting with good news is, for savvy readers, a clear tip-off that bad news is coming. If this is the case, then why not just start with the bad news? True, for some

> ## Not cushioning the shock makes the message unnecessarily harsh, and harshness destroys goodwill.

reporting this negative information are considered routine and are written in the direct order. You also might choose directness if you know your reader well and feel that he or she will appreciate frankness. But such instances are less common than those in which indirectness is the preferable strategy.

As in the preceding chapter, we first describe a general plan. Then we adapt this plan to specific business situations—four in this case. First is an indirect claim, which builds on the routine or neutral claim you learned about in Chapter 5. Second, is the refusal of a request, a common message type in business. Next we cover a special type of refusal—the refusal of a request for adjustment. Finally, we cover negative announcements, which are a form of bad-news messages with unique characteristics.

THE GENERAL INDIRECT PLAN

While the following five-part plan won't apply to all negative messages, you'll find it helpful for most of them.

readers in some bad-news situations, a direct approach may be the best. For example, if you are writing to tell customers that there is a defective part in a car they have purchased and that they should return the car to the dealership immediately for repairs, it would be almost unethical not to feature this important information in the opening paragraph. Most readers in most situations, however, appreciate a more gradual introduction to the message's main negative point. It gives them a chance to prepare for the news—and even if they suspect that it will be negative, the use of a buffer indicates consideration for their feelings.

Setting Up the Negative News

For each case, you will have thought through the facts involved and decided that, to some extent, you will have to say "no" or present some other kind of negative news. You then have to figure out how you will present your reasons in such a way that your reader will accept the news as positively as possible. Your strategy might be to explain the fairness of a certain action. It might be to present facts that clearly make the decision necessary. Or you might cite the expert opinion of authorities whom

Particularly when conveying negative news, you should bear in mind the important concept of *face*, as defined by conflict-management specialists Kathy Domenici and Stephen W. Littlejohn:

We use the metaphor of *face* to designate the universal desire to present oneself with dignity and honor. The idea of face probably originated in China, where it referred to respectability in terms of character and success. . . .

Face can be "lost," "maintained," "protected," or "enhanced." These outcomes are accomplished through the work of communication, or facework. We define *facework* as *a set of coordinated practices in which communicators build, maintain, protect, or threaten personal dignity, honor, and respect.* Constructive facework is a vital aspect of all interpersonal communication. If we do it well, we build relationships, we reinforce our own

competence as communicators, and we make interaction more rewarding and less distressing.

Every element of a negative-news message—from the use of a buffer-type opening paragraph to a goodwill ending—can help you do positive facework with your reader.

Source: *Facework: Bridging Theory and Practice* (Thousand Oaks, CA: Sage, 2006) 10–11, print.

> It might even be possible to show that your reasons for the negative decision will actually benefit the reader in the long run.

both you and your reader respect. It might even be possible to show that your reasons for the negative decision will actually benefit the reader in the long run.

Whatever explanatory strategy you have chosen, these reasons should follow your buffer and precede the negative news itself. In other words, the paragraph after the buffer should start explaining the situation in such a way that, by the time the negative news comes, the reader is prepared to receive it in the most favorable light possible. Examples of how to accomplish this follow.

A buffer in a bad-news message helps you let your reader down easy.

Presenting the Bad News Positively

Next, you present the bad news. If you have developed your reasoning convincingly, this bad news should appear as a logical outcome. And you should present it as positively as the situation

will permit. In doing so, you must make certain that the negative message is clear—that your positive approach has not given the wrong impression.

Strange as it may sound, one useful technique is to present your reasoning impersonally—that is, in first and third person rather than second person. To illustrate, in a message refusing a request for a refund, one could write these negative words: "Since you have broken the seal, state law prohibits us from returning the product to stock." Or one could write these more positive words emphasizing first and third person: "State law prohibits us from returning to stock all such products with broken seals."

It is sometimes possible to take the sting out of negative news by linking it to a reader benefit. For example, if you preface a company policy with "in the interest of fairness" or "for the safety of our guests," you are indicating that all your patrons, including the reader, get an important benefit from your policy.

Your efforts to present this part of the message positively should stress the positive word emphasis described in Chapter 4. In using positive words, however, you must make certain your words truthfully and accurately convey your message. Your goal is to present the facts in a positive way and not to mislead.

Offering an Alternative Solution

For almost any negative-news situation, there is something you can do to help the reader with his or her problem.

If someone seeks to hold an event on your company grounds and you must say "no", you may be able to suggest other sites. If someone wants information that you cannot give, you might know of another way that he or she could get similar information. If you cannot volunteer your time and services, perhaps you know someone who might, or perhaps you could invite the reader to make the request again at a later, better time. If you have to announce a cutback on an employee benefit, you might be able to suggest ways that employees can supplement this benefit on their own. Taking the time to help the reader in this way is a sincere show of concern for the reader's situation. For this reason, it is one of your most powerful strategies for maintaining goodwill.

Giving the reader an alternative way to solve his or her problem helps build goodwill in a negative message.

Ending on a Positive Note

Since even a skillfully handled bad-news presentation can be disappointing to the reader, you should end the message on a forward-looking note. Your goal here is to shift the reader's thoughts to happier things—perhaps what you would say if you were in face-to-face conversation with the person. Preferably your comments should fit the one case, and they should not recall the negative message. They should make clear that you value your relationship with the reader and still regard it as a positive one.

Following are adaptations of this general plan to four of the more common negative-message situations. From these applications you should be able to see how to adapt this general plan to almost any other negative-message situation.

LO 3 Write an indirect claim that obtains an adjustment while maintaining goodwill.

INDIRECT CLAIMS

As you've learned in Chapter 5's section on writing claim messages, things can go wrong in business. In situations where an obvious error has been made, a claim message can directly request a correction and then supply the facts that support it. But in cases where you anticipate resistance to a claim, you must prepare the reader to entertain your request with an open mind. Otherwise, you might push your reader into a "no" response right from the beginning.

Anticipating your reader's likely response requires carefully thinking through the circumstances. If a large amount of money or time will be involved in correcting the problem, you can expect your reader to be resistant. Or if the facts of the case are somewhat unusual and the company is unlikely to have a policy that covers them, you can expect to have to explain the facts before making your request. To take a third possibility, times may be tight, making it likely that your reader will look for any excuse to avoid the extra expense that an adjustment would entail. As many of us know from experience, there are many reasons why a company might refuse an adjustment request. If you think there is any possibility at all, choose the indirect pattern.

What makes this indirect message particularly tricky is that you are writing about a negative subject. Somehow, you must discuss what happened without alienating the reader. The following advice should help.

Choosing the Right Tone

As you learned in Chapter 5, your goal in writing either a direct or an indirect claim is to obtain the remedy you want. With indirect claims, indirectness will help soften the sting of the situation while preparing the reader to accept your request for a remedy. As with the direct claim, you will not advance your cause with accusatory, subjective language. You still need to

workplace scenario

Writing Indirect Claims

Play the role of Jeff Sutton, owner and president of Sutton Creative Services. You've just received a bill from Regal Banquet Center for the winter-holiday party that your company held there last week. It's for $1,410, which you had agreed to pay for an elegant three-course meal, plus drinks, for your 27 employees.

The food was as good as its reputation, but there were two problems. First, the room for the party was much too warm. You complained to the servers but to no avail.

You would have opened windows to correct the problem yourself, but the room you were given did not have any windows (something you weren't happy about either). Second, there was apparently a shortage of servers on the night of your event. Some of your employees had to wait a long time for their food, while those who had their food first either had to start eating before the others or let their food get cold while waiting for all to be served. This ragged timing ruined the

dinner, and it also threw off the timing of the program you had planned.

You were embarrassed by these problems. They reflected poorly on you and your efforts to thank your employees for their work. While you understand that unexpected problems can arise, you just don't think you should have to pay the full amount for this experience. You'll need to write an indirect claim message asking for an adjustment to your bill.

> ## An objective presentation of facts helps lead the reader through them and perhaps even to see the reasonableness of the remedy you will request.

You will present the facts objectively and logically, enabling the reader to understand the seriousness and leading him or her to agree that the remedy you want is a fair one.

Beginning the Indirect Claim with a Buffer

Even an indirect claim needs to identify the problem early, starting with a dramatic statement of the problem in either the subject line or opening paragraph would likely give undue emphasis to the negative situation. Starting with a buffer that identified the subject could help absorb some of that blow. For example, if the contractor has used the wrong paint color in your new suite of offices, you might begin your indirect claim with the following subject line:

> Subject: Customized paint for new office building

You might then follow the subject line with this opening:

> Opening: When our paint crew chief informed me yesterday that the painting of the new office suite was complete, I discovered that the color of the walls did not match the customized color we had chosen.

The goal is to identify the topic and convey a general sense that something is wrong while keeping the reader open to facts you will be presenting next.

Describing the Problem Clearly

Although the situation is a bad one, you need to describe the facts objectively and order them logically. If you were the one who spent hours planning the company's move to its new location only to see it fall apart because the contractor specified the wrong paint color, you must avoid using overly emotional words to describe the problem. The words you use should be presented factually and courteously. They should cover the problem completely and accurately, giving the reader the information he or she needs to remedy the situation appropriately.

If there were consequences from unsatisfactory products or services, you need to report them explicitly. This beginning illustrates this point:

> Getting the painting done on time affects many other contractors' ability to complete their work and their costs. This will undoubtedly affect the costs on every part of the project, not just the painting.

Notice that the writer simply states facts with the words "done on time" and "affects many other contractors" rather than accuse the reader of being incompetent or a poor manager. An objective presentation of facts helps lead the reader through them and perhaps even to see the reasonableness of the remedy you will request.

Requesting the Correction

Unlike the routine or neutral claim where you can often leave the correction to the reader's judgment and sense of fairness, the remedy for indirect claims is usually best handled by asking for what you believe is a fair and reasonable remedy. One way to know whether or not your remedy is reasonable is to decide if, after receiving it, you'd be willing to do business with that company again. In the case of our workplace scenario, a reader may simply call for an assurance that future dinners at the restaurant be held in comfortable rooms and fully staffed. Or he or she may ask for a full refund, a partial refund, a free meal, a discount on a future event, or even a combination of these. The facts you present should logically lead your reader to your request.

Closing with Goodwill

Despite the negative topics of indirect claims your goal in closing is still to maintain goodwill. This can be achieved by keeping your request for a specific remedy reasonable. Ending with a positive, forward-looking relationship works, too.

Outlining the Indirect Claim Message

Summarizing the preceding points, we arrive at this outline for the indirect claim message:

- Identify the subject of the message while keeping the reader in an open frame of mind.

- Present the facts objectively and logically.

- Identify a reasonable solution or alternatives that would satisfy you.

- Close with a positive, success-conscious statement that maintains goodwill.

Contrasting Examples of Indirect Claim Messages

The following two messages show contrasting ways of handling Jeff Sutton's problem with the Regal Banquet Center. The first is blunt and harsh. The second is courteous, yet clear and firm.

This example is harsh due to its extreme use of negative words and its accusatory tone.

Subject: Bill Adjustment

To whom it may concern:

I just received a bill for $1,410 for the winter party that I held for my employees at the Regal Banquet Center. I absolutely refuse to pay this amount for the subpar job you did of hosting this event.

First, you put us in an unpleasant room with no windows even though we had made our reservations weeks in advance. The room was also much too warm. I asked your staff to adjust the temperature, but apparently they never did. Since the room didn't have any windows, we just had to sit there and swelter in our dress clothes. As if this weren't bad enough, it took the servers so long to bring all our food out that some people had finished eating before others were even served. This made a complete mess of the nice dinner and the scheduled program.

I had heard good things about your center but now regret that I chose it for this important company event. The uncomfortable and chaotic experience reflected poorly on me and on my appreciation for my employees. Enclosed is my payment for $1,000, which I feel is more than fair.

Sincerely,

Jeff Sutton, Owner and President
Sutton Creative Services

Enclosure

a blunt and harsh message From the very beginning, the first message—a letter that the reader is returning along with his reduced payment—is insulting. "To whom it may concern" shows that the writer regards the reader as a person. It also transfers from the writer to the clerk opening the message the power to decide who gets the letter. The opening paragraph is a further affront, blurting out the writer's stance in angry language. The middle of the message continues in this negative vein, accusing the reader with *you* and *your* and using emotional language. The negative writing continues through the close, leaving a bad final impression. Such wording is more likely to produce resistance than cooperation.

a firm yet courteous message The second message follows the plan suggested in preceding paragraphs. A subject line quickly identifies the situation. The claim message begins with a lead-in to the problem. Next, in a tone that shows firmness without anger, it tells what went wrong. Then it requests a specific remedy. The ending uses subtle persuasion by implying confidence in the reader. The words used here leave no doubt about the writer's interest in a continued relationship.

LO 4 Use tact and courtesy in refusals of requests.

REFUSED REQUESTS

The refusal of a request is definitely bad news. Your reader has asked for something, and you must say no. Your primary goal, of course, is to present this bad news. You could do this easily with a direct refusal. But as a courteous and caring businessperson, you have the secondary goal of maintaining goodwill. To achieve this second goal, you must convince your reader that the refusal is fair and reasonable.

Developing the Strategy

Finding a fair and reasonable explanation involves carefully thinking through the facts of the situation. First, consider why you are refusing. Then, assuming that your reasons are just, try to find the best way of explaining them to your reader. In doing this, you might well place yourself in your reader's shoes. Try to imagine how the explanation will be received. What comes out of this thinking is the strategy you should use in your message.

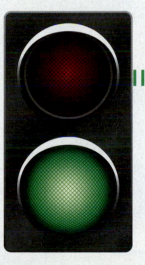

This more tactful but honest email invites the reader to do what is fair and retains goodwill.

Subject: Invoice #3712 for Sutton Party on 12/12/11

Dear Ms. Sanchezs:

I held my company's annual holiday party at your facility on the evening of December 12. I have now received the invoice for the event, in the amount of $1,410. While the food was exceptional, I must say that we did not have a good experience.

The room we were given for the event was Salon C. As you know, the room has no windows and is not one of your more attractive rooms. Because we had made our reservation two months in advance, I expected a more pleasant environment for this special event. The location also had the drawback of making the temperature hard to control. The servers were sympathetic but were unable to keep the room from getting too warm. This made for an uncomfortable evening for my 27 employees.

It also appeared that not enough servers had been scheduled for our party. The fare was elegant, but it was served with such ragged timing that some guests had finished eating before others had even started. We also had to start the after-dinner program in the middle of the meal.

Overall, the event was not a very impressive "thank-you" to my hard-working employees. In light of these circumstances, a revised invoice of $1,000 is fair for an experience that I am sure did not represent the Regal's typical level of customer service.

Sincerely yours,

Jeff Sutton, President and Owner
Sutton Creative Services

workplace scenario

When you do give an apology, make sure it is sincere, like the one offered by Toyota executives because of acceleration plus braking problems with their cars.

One often-used explanation is that company policy forbids compliance. This explanation may work, but only if the company policy is defensible and clearly explained. Often you must refuse simply because the facts of the case justify a refusal—that is, you are right and the reader is wrong. In such cases, your best course is to review the facts, taking care not to accuse or insult and appealing to the reader's sense of fair play. There are other explanations, of course. You select the one that best fits your situation.

Setting Up the Explanation in the Opening

Having determined the explanation, you begin the message with words that set up discussing it. For example, take the case described in the workplace scenario above—refusing an association's request for a donation. The following opening meets this case's requirements well:

> Your organization is doing a commendable job of educating its needy children. Like many other worthy efforts, it deserves the help of those who are in a position to give it.

This on-subject beginning comment clearly marks the message as a response to the inquiry. It implies neither a yes nor a no answer. The second statement sets up the explanation, which will point out that the company is not in a position to give. Also, it puts the reader in an agreeable or open frame of mind—ready to accept the explanation that follows.

Presenting the Explanation Convincingly

As with the general plan, you next present your reasoning. To do this you use your best persuasion techniques: positive wording, proper emphasis, convincing logic, and supporting detail. In general, you use all your presentation skills in your effort to convince your reader.

Handling the Refusal Positively

Your handling of the refusal follows logically from your reasoning. If you have built the groundwork of explanation and fact convincingly, the refusal comes as a logical

Maintaining goodwill with negative messages is often difficult with U.S. readers, even if one uses the indirect approach recommended in this chapter. But it can be even more difficult if you are corresponding with an Asian reader.

As intercultural business communication experts Linda Beamer and Iris Varner point out, "Asian cultures are renowned for saying yes. In fact, in Japan, Westerners have heard *yes* and gone home happy when the Japanese really meant *no*."

Why does this happen? Beamer and Varner explain:

Saying *no* is more difficult for high-context cultures [cultures where communicators depend heavily on contextual cues to interpret words' meanings]. As when they communicate about problems, they would rather not actually have to put a refusal into words. In Chinese, a *no* may reside in the words "That may be difficult." The Japanese equivalent to that would be a drawn-out hissing breath and drawn-out words. . . .

No in high-context cultures is frequently couched in an expression that turns the situation around. For example, a person who has to refuse an invitation to dine out with a business associate may say by way of refusal, "You must be very tired and want to have a quiet evening." This way, the refused person does not lose face, although the refusal is clearly understood in a high-context culture.

Be careful to learn about such communication preferences on the part of your readers when preparing cross-cultural negative-news messages.

Source: *Intercultural Communication in the Global Workplace*, 5th ed. (McGraw-Hill/Irwin: New York, 2011) 194–195, print.

Telling people news they don't want to hear requires your most careful communication effort.

conclusion and as no surprise. If you have done your job well, your reader may even support the refusal. Even so, because the refusal is the most negative part of your message, you should not give it too much emphasis. You should state it quickly, clearly, and positively. You should also try to keep it away from positions of emphasis, such as paragraph endings.

To state the refusal quickly, you should use as few words as possible. Laboring over the refusal for three or four sentences when a single clause would do gives it too much emphasis.

You might even be able to make the message clear without stating the negative news explicitly. For example, if you are refusing a community member's request to use your company's retreat facility for a fundraiser, you will convey "no" clearly if you say that you must restrict the use of the facility to employees only and then go on to offer alternative locations. You must be sure, though, that your message leaves no doubt about your answer. Being unclear the first time will leave you in the position of writing an even more difficult, more negative message.

To state the refusal positively, you should study carefully the effects of your words. Such harsh words as *I refuse, will not*, and *cannot* stand out. So do such timeworn apologies as "I deeply regret to inform you . . ." and "I am sorry to say. . . ." You can usually phrase your refusal in terms of a positive statement of policy. For example, instead of writing "your insurance does not cover damage to buildings not connected to the house," write "your insurance covers damage to the house only." Or instead of writing "We must refuse," a wholesaler could deny a

> # THE BEST CLOSING SUBJECT MATTER DEPENDS ON THE FACTS OF THE CASE, BUT IT SHOULD BE POSITIVE TALK THAT FITS THE ONE SITUATION.

When refusing a request, remember how disappointing "no" can be and do all you reasonably can to spare your reader's feelings.

discount by writing "We can grant discounts only when. . . ." In some cases, your job may be to educate the reader. Not only will this be your explanation for the refusal, but it also will build goodwill.

Using a Compromise When Practical

If the situation justifies a compromise, you can use it in making the refusal positive. More specifically, by saying what you can do (the compromise), you can clearly imply what you cannot do. For example, if you write "The best we can do is to (the compromise) . . . ," you clearly imply that you cannot do what the reader requested. Such statements contain no negative words and usually are as positive as the situation will permit.

Closing with Goodwill

Even a skillfully handled refusal is the most negative part of your message. Because the news is disappointing, it is likely to put your reader in an unhappy frame of mind. That frame of mind works against your goodwill goal. To leave your reader with a feeling of goodwill, you must shift his or her thoughts to more pleasant matters.

This bad example of a refusal is harsh because of its directness and its selfish focus on the writer's interests.

Subject: Your request for donation

Ms. Cangelosi:

We regret to inform you that we cannot grant your request for a donation to the association's scholarship fund.

So many requests for contributions are made of us that we have found it necessary to budget a definite amount each year for this purpose. Our budgeted funds for this year have been exhausted, so we simply cannot consider additional requests. However, we will be able to consider your request next year.

We deeply regret our inability to help you now and trust that you understand our position.

Mark Stephens

The best closing subject matter depends on the facts of the case, but it should be positive talk that fits the one situation. For example, if your refusal involves a counterproposal, you could say more about the counterproposal. Or you could make some friendly remark about the subject of the request as long as it does not remind the reader of the bad news. In fact, your closing subject matter could be almost any friendly remark that would be appropriate if you were handling the case face to face. The major requirement is that your ending words have a goodwill effect.

Ruled out are the timeworn, negative apologies. "Again, may I say that I regret that we must refuse" is typical of these. Also ruled out are the equally timeworn appeals for understanding, such as "I sincerely hope that you understand why we must make this decision." Such words sound selfish and emphasize the bad news.

Fitting the General Plan to Refused Requests

Adapting the preceding analysis to the general plan, we arrive at the following outline for the refused request:

- Begin with words that indicate a response to the request, are neutral about the answer, and set up the strategy.

- Present your justification or explanation, using positive language and you-viewpoint.

- Refuse as positively as possible.

- Include a counterproposal or compromise when appropriate.

- End with an adapted goodwill comment.

Contrasting Refusals

The advantage of the indirect order in refusal messages is illustrated by the contrasting examples at the bottom of pages 136 and 137. Both refuse clearly. But only the one that uses the indirect order is likely to gain reader goodwill.

harshness in the direct refusal The first example states the bad news right away. This blunt treatment puts the reader in an unreceptive frame of mind. The result is that the reader is less likely to accept the explanation that follows. The explanation is clear, but note the unnecessary use of negative words (*exhausted, regret, cannot consider*). Note also how the closing words leave the reader with a strong reminder of the bad news.

tact and courtesy in an indirect refusal The second example skillfully handles the negative message. Its opening words are on subject and neutral. They set up the explanation that follows. The clear and logical explanation ties in with the opening. Using no negative words, the explanation leads smoothly to the refusal. Note that the refusal also is handled without negative words and yet is clear. The friendly close fits the one case.

LO 5 Write adjustment refusals that minimize and overcome bad impressions.

Subject: Your scholarship fund request

Ms. Cangelosi,

Your efforts to build the scholarship fund for the association's needy children are most commendable. We wish you success in your efforts to further this worthy cause.

At Pinnacle we are always willing to assist worthy causes whenever we can. That is why every January we budget for the year the maximum amount we are able to contribute to such causes. Then we distribute that amount among the various deserving groups as far as it will go. Since our budgeted contributions for this year have already been made, we are placing your organization on our list for consideration next year.

We wish you the best of luck in your efforts to help educate the deserving children of the association's members.

Mark Stephens

This refusal using the indirect approach is better.

Saying "No" from a "Yes" Position

Negotiation expert William Ury explains why our efforts to say "no" are often stress inducing and ineffective:

We humans are reaction machines. And our Nos tend to be reactive. We accommodate out of fear and guilt. We attack out of anger. We avoid out of fear. To get ourselves out of this three-A trap, we need to become proactive, forward-looking, and purposeful.

Ury recommends first letting your negative feelings have their say inside your head. Once they subside, you can think about your "yes"—the things you want to protect and affirm by saying "no." From this position of thinking about the things you care about, you are better able to say "no" with calmness and grace. And then you can invite your readers to consider alternative solutions.

In short, "a positive No," Ury says, "is a *Yes! No. Yes?* The first Yes expresses your interests, the No asserts your power, and the second Yes furthers your relationship."

Source: *The Power of a Positive No: Save the Deal, Save the Relationship—and Still Say No* (New York: Bantam Dell, 2008) 28, 17, print.

The challenge will be to say "no" while still making possible an ongoing, positive relationship with the reader.

ADJUSTMENT REFUSALS

Adjustment refusals are a special type of refused request. Your reader has made a claim asking for a remedy. Usually you grant claims because you want to correct any error for which you are responsible. But sometimes the facts do not justify a correction. In these cases, you must say "no."

Determining the Strategy

The primary difference between this and other refusal messages is that in these situations, as we are defining them, your company will probably have clear, reasonable guidelines for what should and should not be regarded as legitimate requests for adjustment. You will, therefore, not have to spend much time figuring out why you cannot grant the reader's request. You will have good reasons to refuse. The challenge will be to do so while still making possible an ongoing, positive relationship with the reader.

Setting Up Your Reasoning

With your strategy in mind, you begin with words that set it up. Since this message is a response to one the reader has sent, you also acknowledge this message. You can do this with a date reference early in the message. Or you can do it with words that clearly show you are writing about the specific situation.

One good way of setting up your strategy is to begin on a point of common agreement and then explain how the case at hand is an exception. To illustrate, a case involving a claim for adjustment for failure of an air conditioner to perform properly might begin thus:

> You are correct in believing that an 18,000 BTU Whirlpool window unit should cool the ordinary three-room apartment.

The explanation that follows this sentence will show that the apartment in question is not an ordinary apartment.

Another strategy is to build the case that the claim for adjustment goes beyond what can reasonably be expected. A beginning such as this one sets it up:

workplace scenario

Refusing Adjustment Requests

Sometimes your job at Pinnacle involves handling an unhappy person. Today you have to do that, for the morning email has brought a strong claim for adjustment on an order for Pinnacle's Do-Craft fabrics. The claim writer, Ms. Arlene Sanderson, explains that a Do-Craft fabric her upholstering company used on some outdoor furniture has faded badly in less than 10 months. She even includes photographs of the fabric to prove her point. She contends that the product is defective, and she wants her money back—all $2,517 of it.

Inspection of the photographs reveals that the fabric has been subjected to strong sunlight for long periods. Do-Craft fabrics are for inside use only. Both the Pinnacle brochures on the product and the catalog description stress this point. In fact, you have difficulty understanding how Ms. Sanderson missed it when she ordered from the catalog. Anyway, as you see it, Pinnacle is not responsible and should not refund the money. At the same time, you want to keep Ms. Sanderson as a repeat customer. Now you must write the message that will do just that. The following discussion tells you how.

> ## "One good way of setting up your strategy is to begin on a point of common agreement and then explain how the case at hand is an exception."

Assisting families to enjoy beautifully decorated homes at budget prices is one of our most satisfying goals. We do all we reasonably can to reach it.

The explanation that follows this sentence will show that the requested adjustment goes beyond what can be reasonably expected.

Making Your Case

In presenting your reasons for refusal, explain your company's relevant policy or practice. Without accusing the reader, call attention to facts that bear on the case—for example, that the item in question has been submerged in water, that the printed material warned against certain uses, or that the warranty has expired. Putting together the policy and the facts should lead logically to the conclusion that the adjustment cannot be granted.

Refusing Positively and Closing Courteously

As in other refusal messages, your refusal derives from your explanation. It is the logical result. You word it clearly, and you make it as positive as the circumstances permit. For example, this one is clear, and it contains no negative words:

> For these reasons, we can pay only when our employees pack the goods.

If a compromise is in order, you might present it in positive language like this:

© 2008 Ted Goff www.tedgoff.com

"Sorry, we believe that the customer is only right some of the time under certain circumstances, and none of them apply to you."

In view of these facts, the best we can do is repair the equipment at cost.

As in all bad-news messages, you should end this one with some appropriate, positive comment. You could reinforce the message that you care about the reader's business or the quality of your products. In cases where it would not seem selfish, you could write about new products or services that the reader might be interested in. Neither apologies nor words that recall the problem are appropriate here.

A Refused Request
(Turning Down a Speaking Invitation)

This example shows good strategy in turning down a request to speak at a convention.

On-subject beginning—compliment gains reader's favor

Offer of alternative—shows concern, builds goodwill

Goodwill close—adapted to this one case

Conveys the subject but not the bad news

Setup for explanation

Reasonable, convincing explanation

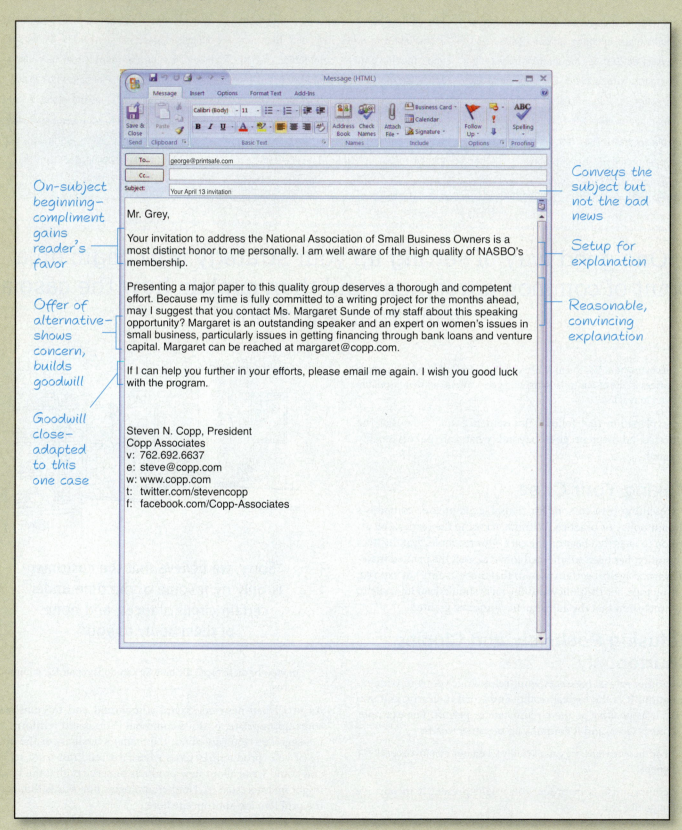

> **To...** george@printsafe.com
>
> **Cc...**
>
> **Subject:** Your April 13 invitation
>
> Mr. Grey,
>
> Your invitation to address the National Association of Small Business Owners is a most distinct honor to me personally. I am well aware of the high quality of NASBO's membership.
>
> Presenting a major paper to this quality group deserves a thorough and competent effort. Because my time is fully committed to a writing project for the months ahead, may I suggest that you contact Ms. Margaret Sunde of my staff about this speaking opportunity? Margaret is an outstanding speaker and an expert on women's issues in small business, particularly issues in getting financing through bank loans and venture capital. Margaret can be reached at margaret@copp.com.
>
> If I can help you further in your efforts, please email me again. I wish you good luck with the program.
>
>
> Steven N. Copp, President
> Copp Associates
> v: 762.692.6637
> e: steve@copp.com
> w: www.copp.com
> t: twitter.com/stevencopp
> f: facebook.com/Copp-Associates

Adapting the General Plan

When we apply these special considerations to the general plan, we come up with the following specific plan for adjustment refusals:

- Begin with words that are on subject, are neutral about the decision, and set up your strategy.

- Present the strategy that explains or justifies, being factual and positive.

- Refuse clearly and positively, perhaps including a counterproposal.

- End with positive, forward-looking, friendly words.

Contrasting Adjustment Refusal Messages

The two messages at the bottom of pages 142 and 143 illustrate bad and good treatment of Pinnacle's refusal to return money

Neither apologies nor words that recall the problem are appropriate in your conclusion.

technology in brief

Email Templates Allow Writers to Reuse and Customize Messages

Templates allow writers to reuse frequently repeated text. Whether your message is a monthly status report for your boss or a refusal message to people wanting to reserve a room in your fully booked hotel, you can create a template that allows you to reuse and customize the basic message. In Outlook 2007 and 2010, it's an easy task. After you've written the message the first time, save it as an Outlook template. The next time you need it, you can bring it up from the Tools menu by clicking Forms and selecting Choose Form. Then select User Templates to bring up your list of

templates and click on one. When the message opens you can enter text in any of the placeholders you've created for variable information, and you can modify any generic information to customize the message to fit the particular use.

Spending a little extra time creating and polishing your original message will

help ensure that you are only reusing well-written messages.

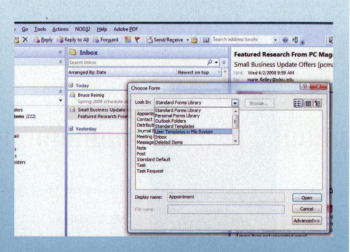

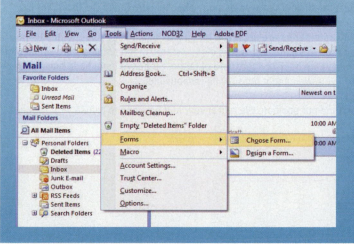

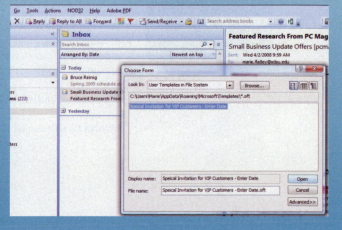

workplace scenario

Writing Negative Announcements

In your role as assistant to Pinnacle's vice president for administration, you have been given the difficult assignment of writing a bad-news message for your boss. She has just returned from a meeting of the company's top executives in which the decision was made to deduct 25 percent of the employees' medical insurance premiums from their paychecks. Until now, Pinnacle has paid it all. But the rising cost of health coverage is forcing the company to cut back on these benefits, especially since Pinnacle's profits have declined for the past several quarters. Something has to give if Pinnacle is to remain competitive while also avoiding lay-offs. The administrators decided on a number of cost-cutting measures including this reduction in Pinnacle's payment for employee medical insurance. The message you will write to Pinnacle employees is a negative announcement.

for the faded fabric. The bad one, which is blunt and insulting, destroys goodwill. The good one, which uses the techniques described in the preceding paragraphs, stands a fair chance of keeping goodwill.

bluntness in a direct refusal The bad email begins bluntly with a direct statement of the refusal. The language is negative (*regret, must reject, claim, refuse, damage, inconvenience*). The explanation is equally blunt. In addition, it is insulting ("It is difficult to understand how you failed . . ."). It uses little tact, little you-viewpoint. Even the close is negative, recalling the bad news.

tact and courtesy in an indirect refusal The well-written good message begins with friendly talk on a point of agreement that also sets up the explanation. Without accusations, anger, or negative words, it reviews the facts of the case, which free the company of blame. The refusal is clear, even though it is made by implication rather than by direct words. It is skillfully handled. It uses no negatives, and it does not receive undue emphasis. The close shifts to helpful suggestions that fit the one case—suggestions that may actually result in a future sale. Friendliness and resale are evident throughout the message, but especially in the close.

The bad email shows little concern for the reader's feelings.

Subject: Your May 3 claim for damages

Ms. Sanderson,

I regret to report that we must reject your request for money back on the faded Do-Craft fabric.

We must refuse because Do-Craft fabrics are not made for outside use. It is difficult for me to understand how you failed to notice this limitation. It was clearly stated in the catalog from which you ordered. It was even stamped on the back of every yard of fabric. Since we have been more than reasonable in trying to inform you, we cannot possibly be responsible.

We trust that you will understand our position. We regret very much having to refuse your request.

Marilyn Cox, Customer Relations

NEGATIVE ANNOUNCEMENTS

Occasionally, businesses must announce bad news to their customers or employees. For example, a company might need to announce that prices are going up, that a service or product line is being discontinued, or that a branch of the business is closing. Or a company might need to tell its employees that the company is in some kind of trouble, that people will need to be laid off, or, as in the workplace scenario on page 142, that employee benefits must be reduced. Such announcements generally follow the instructions previously given in this chapter.

When making a negative announcement, remember that an indirect, tactful approach is usually better than a blunt "loud" approach.

Determining the Strategy

When faced with the problem of making a negative announcement, your first step should be to determine your overall strategy. Will you use direct or indirect organization?

In most cases the indirect (buffer) arrangement will be better. This route is especially recommended when it is reasonable to expect that the readers would be surprised, particularly disappointed, or even angered by a direct presentation. When planning an indirect announcement, you will need to think about what kind of buffer opening to use, what kind of explanation to give, how to word the news itself, and how to leave your readers feeling that you have taken their interests into account.

Setting Up the Bad News

As with the preceding negative message types, you should plan your indirect beginning carefully. You should think through the situation and select a strategy that will set up or begin the explanation that justifies the announcement. Perhaps you will begin by presenting justifying information. Or maybe you will start with complimentary or cordial talk focusing on the good relationship that you and your readers have developed. Whatever you choose should be what will be most likely to prepare your reader to accept the coming bad news.

Subject: Your May 3 message about Do-Craft fabric

Ms. Sanderson,

Certainly, you have a right to expect the best possible service from Do-Craft fabrics. Every Do-Craft product is the result of years of experimentation. And we manufacture each yard under the most careful controls.

Because we do want our fabrics to please, we carefully inspected the photos of Do-Craft Fabric 103 you sent us. It is apparent that each sample has been subjected to long periods in extreme sunlight. Since we know that Do-Craft fabrics cannot withstand exposure to sunlight, we clearly state this in all our advertising, in the catalog from which you ordered, and in a stamped reminder on the back of every yard of the fabric. Under the circumstances, all we can do at this point is suggest that you change to one of our outdoor fabrics. As you can see from our catalog, all of the fabrics in the 200 series are recommended for outdoor use.

You may also be interested in the new Duck Back cotton fabrics listed in our 500 series. These plastic-coated cotton fabrics are a great value, and they resist sun and rain remarkably well. If we can help you further in your selection, please contact us at service@pinnacle.com.

Marilyn Cox, Customer Relations

This better email is indirect, tactful, and helpful.

An Adjustment Refusal Letter (Refusing a Refund for a Woman's Dress)

An out-of-town customer bought an expensive dress from the writer and mailed it back three weeks later, asking for a refund. The customer explained that the dress was not a good fit and that she really did not like it anymore. But perspiration stains on the dress proved that she had worn it. This letter skillfully presents the refusal.

MARIE'S *Fashions*

103 BREAKER RD. HOUSTON, TX 77015 713-454-6778 Fax: 713-454-6771
www.mariesfashion.com - facebook.com/mariesfashion - twitter.com/mariesfashion

February 19, 2011

On-subject opening—neutral point from claim letter

Ms. Maud E. Krumpleman
117 Kyle Avenue E
College Station, TX 77840-2415

Dear Ms. Krumpleman:

We understand your concern about the St. John's dress you returned February 15. As always, we are willing to do as much as we reasonably can to make things right.

Setup of explanation

Review of facts—supports writer's position

What we can do in each instance is determined by the facts. With returned clothing, we generally give refunds. Of course, to meet our obligations to our customers for quality merchandise, all returned clothing must be in resalable condition. As you know, our customers expect only the best from us, and we insist that they get it. Thus, because the perspiration stains on your dress would prevent its resale, we must consider the sale final. We are returning the dress to you. With it you will find a special alteration voucher that assures you of getting the best possible fit free of charge.

Good restraint—no accusations, no anger

Positive language in refusal

Emphasis on what store can do helps restore goodwill

Friendly goodwill close

So, whenever it is convenient, please allow us to alter this beautiful St. John's creation to your requirements. We look forward to serving you.

Sincerely,

Marie O. Mitchell

Marie O. Mitchell
Owner

dm

case illustration

A Negative Announcement
(Reporting a Price Increase)

Here a TV cable company informs a customer of a rate increase. The cordial opening makes friendly contact that leads to an explanation of the action. Then the news is presented clearly yet positively. The goodwill close continues the cordiality established earlier in the message.

Heartland Cable TV, Inc.

37411 Jester Road, Kansas City, MO 64106

Ph: 815.555.1212
Fax: 815.555.1213
www.heartlandcabletv.com

March 14, 2011

Ms. Ellen Butler
396 Scott Street
Kansas City, MO 64109

Dear Ms. Butler:

Cordial opening → Your cable company has been working extra hard to provide you with the highest-quality TV entertainment. We think we have succeeded. The quantity of our programming is continually expanding, and Heartland has become a leader in HD broadcast and recording technology.

We have also been working hard to keep the cost of these services as low as possible and continue to maintain high standards. Last year we were able to do this and pass along savings of up to 20 percent on two of our premium services. As you may have heard in the news, our costs continue to increase. Thus, in order to continue to maintain our goals of high quality at the lowest possible cost, we are announcing a price adjustment effective April 1. The monthly cost of your basic package of 59 stations will increase $1.50 (from $37.99 to $39.49) The cost of all premium services (for example, HBO, Cinemax, and HD packages) will remain the same.   ← **Explanation to set up bad news** / **Bad news presented in terms of reader interests**

Positive information to end the paragraph →

In our continuing efforts to improve your total entertainment value, we are planning a number of exciting new projects. Watch our monthly cable guide for announcements about these.   ← **Friendly forward look**

Cordial words to end → We appreciate your business and assure you that we will continue to bring you the very best in service and entertainment.

Sincerely,

Carlos H. Rodriguez

Carlos H. Rodriguez
President

> # TRY TO AVOID STARTING YOUR EXPLANATION WITH WORDS THAT SIGNAL THE BAD NEWS, SUCH AS *UNFORTUNATELY* OR *HOWEVER.*

Explaining the Situation

In most cases, the opening paragraph will enable you to continue with background reasons or explanations in the next paragraph, before you present the negative news. When writing this part, try to avoid beginning with words that signal the bad news, such as *unfortunately* or *however*. Instead, just start describing the situation that has led to the need for a negative announcement. You might even think of starting this part as if you were beginning a story, explaining things that have happened that have brought you or your company up to this present moment. Tell the readers enough about the situation so that they'll see you are doing the best you can—and with their interests at heart—under the circumstances.

Positively Presenting the Bad News

As in other negative situations, you should use positive words and avoid unnecessary negative comments when presenting the news itself. Since this is an announcement, however, you must make certain that you cover all the factual details involved. People may not be expecting this news. They will, therefore, want to know the whys and whats of the situation. And if you want them to believe that you have done all you can to prevent the negative situation, you will need to provide evidence that this is true. If there are actions the readers must take, these should be covered clearly as well. All questions that may come to the readers' minds should be anticipated and covered.

Directness here sends a negative message.

To our employees:

Pinnacle management sincerely regrets that effective February 1 you must begin contributing 25 percent of the cost of your medical insurance. As you know, in the past the company has paid the full amount.

This decision is primarily the result of the rising costs of health insurance, but Pinnacle's profits also have declined the last several quarters. Given this tight financial picture, we needed to find ways to reduce expenses.

We trust that you will understand why we must ask for your help with cutting costs to the company.

Sincerely,

Focusing on Next Steps
or Remaining Benefits

In many cases negative news will mean that things have changed. Customers may no longer be able to get a product that they have relied upon, or employees may have to find a way to pay for something that they have been getting for free. For this reason, a skillful handling of a negative announcement will often need to include an effort to help people solve the problem that your news just created for them. In situations where you have no further help to offer—for example, when announcing certain price increases—you can still help people feel better about your news by calling attention to the benefits that they will continue to enjoy. You can focus on the good things that have not changed and perhaps even look ahead to something positive or exciting on the horizon.

Closing on a Positive
or Encouraging Note

The ending words should cement your effort to cover the matter positively. They can be whatever is appropriate for this one situation—a positive look forward, a sincere expression of gratitude, an affirmation of your positive relationship with your readers.

Reviewing the Plan

Applying the preceding instructions to the general plan, we arrive at this specific plan for negative announcements written in indirect order:

- Start with a buffer that begins or sets up justification for the bad news.

- Present the justification material.

- Give the bad news positively but clearly.

- Help solve the problem that the news may have created for the reader.

- End with appropriate goodwill talk.

Contrasting Negative
Announcements

Compare the good and bad examples on the preceding page and this page. The bad one uses directness, which in some

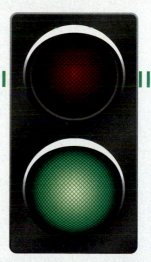

This indirect example follows the bad-news pattern.

To All Employees:

Companies all across the United States, no matter how large or small, are struggling to keep up with the rising cost of health care insurance. Legislators, health care providers, and businesspeople everywhere are struggling to find solutions to the skyrocketing cost of health insurance premiums.

We are feeling this situation here in our own company. The premiums that we pay to cover our health benefits have increased by 34 percent over the last two years, and our future expenditures are unknown as lawsuits and details of the recently passed health care bill are untangled in the next few years. Meanwhile, as you know, our sales have been lower than usual for the past several quarters.

For the short term, it is imperative that we find a way to cut overall costs. Your management has considered many options and rejected such measures as cutting salaries and reducing personnel. Of the solutions that will be implemented, the only change that affects you directly concerns your medical insurance. On **March 1** we will begin deducting 25 percent of the cost of the premium. The other savings measures will be at the corporate level.

Jim Taylor in the Human Resources Office will soon be announcing an informational meeting about your insurance options. Switching to spousal coverage, choosing a less expensive plan with higher deductibles, or setting up a flexible spending account may be right for you. You can also see Jim after the meeting to arrange a personal consultation. He is well versed in the many solutions available and can give you expert advice for your situation.

Our health care benefits have long been some of the best in our city and in our industry, and those who continue with the current plan will not see any change in their medical coverage or their co-pays. Your management regards a strong benefits program as critical to the company's success, and we will do all we can to maintain these benefits while keeping your company financially viable. We will appreciate your cooperation and understanding.

Sincerely,

A Direct Negative Message (A Message Announcing the Discontinuance of a Program)

A company has decided to drop a Preferred Customer program and has decided to tell their customers directly while announcing a new program.

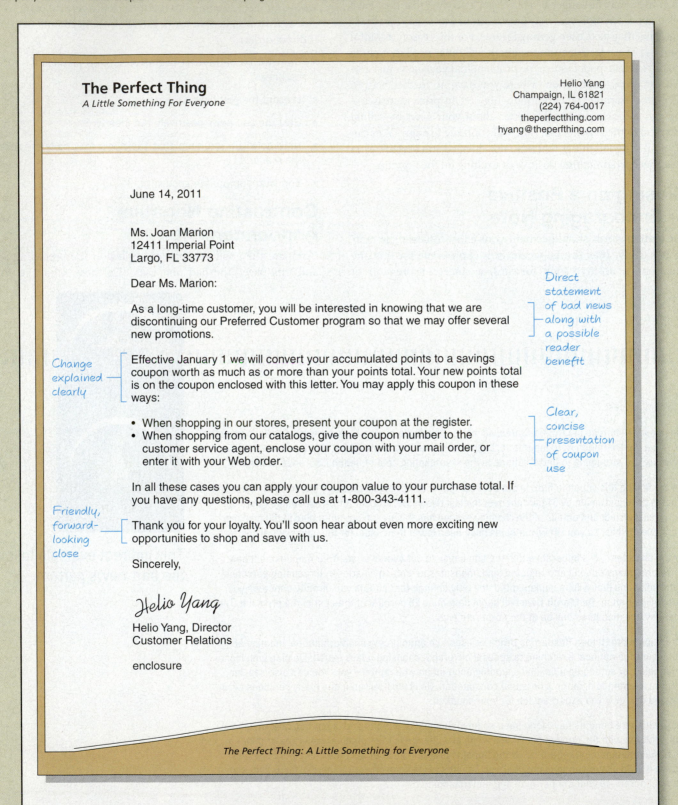

The Perfect Thing
A Little Something For Everyone

Helio Yang
Champaign, IL 61821
(224) 764-0017
theperfectthing.com
hyang@theperfthing.com

June 14, 2011

Ms. Joan Marion
12411 Imperial Point
Largo, FL 33773

Dear Ms. Marion:

As a long-time customer, you will be interested in knowing that we are discontinuing our Preferred Customer program so that we may offer several new promotions.

Direct statement of bad news along with a possible reader benefit

Effective January 1 we will convert your accumulated points to a savings coupon worth as much as or more than your points total. Your new points total is on the coupon enclosed with this letter. You may apply this coupon in these ways:

Change explained clearly

• When shopping in our stores, present your coupon at the register.
• When shopping from our catalogs, give the coupon number to the customer service agent, enclose your coupon with your mail order, or enter it with your Web order.

Clear, concise presentation of coupon use

In all these cases you can apply your coupon value to your purchase total. If you have any questions, please call us at 1-800-343-4111.

Thank you for your loyalty. You'll soon hear about even more exciting new opportunities to shop and save with us.

Friendly, forward-looking close

Sincerely,

Helio Yang

Helio Yang, Director
Customer Relations

enclosure

The Perfect Thing: A Little Something for Everyone

circumstances may be acceptable but clearly is not in this case. The good one follows the pattern just discussed.

directness alarms the readers The bad example clearly upsets the readers with its abrupt announcement in the beginning. The readers aren't prepared to receive the negative message. Probably they don't understand the reasons behind the negative news. The explanation comes later, but the readers are not likely to be in a receptive mood when they see it. The message ends with a repetition of the bad news.

convincing explanation begins a courteous message The better example follows the recommended indirect pattern. Its opening words begin the task of convincing the readers of the appropriateness of the action to be taken. After more convincing explanation, the announcement flows logically. Perhaps it will not be received positively by all recipients, but it is a reasonable deduction from the facts presented. After the announcement comes an offer of assistance to help readers deal with their new situation. The last paragraph reminds readers of remaining benefits and reassures them that management understands their interests. It ends on an appreciative, goodwill note.

© 2008 Ted Goff
www.tedgoff.com

"I don't know why you're upset with us. Didn't we provide you with excellent excuses?"

Using Directness in Some Cases

In some cases it is likely that the reader will react favorably to a direct presentation of the bad news. If, for example, the negative news is expected (as when the news media have already revealed it), its impact may be viewed as negligible. There is also a good case for directness when the company's announcement will contain a remedy or announce new benefits that are designed to offset the effects of the bad news. As in all announcements with some negative element, this part must be handled in good positive language. Also, the message should end on a goodwill note. A store's announcement discontinuing a customer-reward program is illustrated in the Case Illustration.

OTHER INDIRECT MESSAGES

The negative-news type of indirect message covered in the preceding pages is very common. But there are other indirect types, such as persuasive messages and job applications which are positive. They are covered in subsequent chapters. You should be able to handle all indirect types that you encounter by adapting the techniques explained and illustrated in these chapters. ■

Get Online

mhhe.com/FlatleyM2e

for study materials including quizzes and Internet resources.

chapter seven

writing persuasive messages + **proposals**

Everything you write on the job will have some kind of persuasive purpose—to convince the reader of your professionalism, convey an appealing company image, promote good relations, and the like. But in some situations, persuasion will be your central goal. In these cases, your readers will hold a certain position, and your task will be to move them from this position to one that is more favorable to you and/or your company. Meeting this challenge requires careful analysis, strategic thinking, and skillful writing.

Because you will be proposing something that your reader probably does not already agree with or want to do, it is often best to organize persuasive messages in an indirect order. Preparing the reader to accept your idea is a much better strategy than blurting out the idea from the start and then having to argue uphill through the rest of the message. Ideally, you should organize each persuasive message so that, from the subject line to the end, your readers will agree with you. If you

continued on p. 152

LEARNING OBJECTIVES

LO1 Describe important strategies for writing any persuasive message.

LO2 Write skillful persuasive requests that begin indirectly, develop convincing reasoning, and close with goodwill and action.

LO3 Discuss ethical concerns regarding sales messages.

LO4 Describe the planning steps for direct mail or email sales messages.

LO5 Compose sales messages that gain attention, persuasively present appeals, and effectively drive for action.

LO6 Write well-organized and persuasive proposals.

continued from p. 151

try to have them on your side from start to finish, you'll have your best chance of success.

In the following pages we first provide some general advice for effective persuasion. We then explain how the indirect order is used in two kinds of persuasive messages: the persuasive request and the sales message. Finally, we cover another important category of persuasive writing: proposals. These, as you will see, can use either the direct or indirect pattern, depending on whether they are invited or uninvited. ■

LO 1 Describe important strategies for writing any persuasive message.

GENERAL ADVICE ABOUT PERSUASION

All our previous advice about adapting your messages to your readers comes into play with persuasive messages—only more so. Moving your reader from an uninterested or even antagonistic position to an interested, cooperative one is a major accomplishment. To achieve it, keep the following advice in mind.

Know Your Readers

For any kind of persuasive message, thinking about your subject from your readers' point of view is critical. To know what kind of appeals will succeed with your readers, you need to know as much as you can about their values, interests, and needs. Companies specializing in email and direct-mail campaigns spend a great deal of money to acquire such information. Using a variety of research techniques, they gather demographic information (such as age, gender, income, and geographic location) and psychographic information (such as social, political, and personal preferences) on their target audience. They also develop mailing lists based on prior shows of interest from consumers and purchase mailing lists from other organizations that have had success with certain audiences.

But even an individual tasked with writing an internal or external persuasive message can increase the chances for success by learning as much as possible about the intended readers. He or she can talk with the customer service people about the kinds of calls they're getting, study the company's customer database, chat with people around the water cooler or online, and run ideas past colleagues. Good persuasion depends on knowledge as well as on imagination and logic.

Choose and Develop Targeted Reader Benefits

No one is persuaded to do something for no reason. Sometimes their reasons for acting are related to *tangible* or measurable rewards. For example, they will save money, save time, or acquire some kind of desired object. But often, the rewards that persuade are *intangible*. People may want to make their lives easier, gain prestige, or have more freedom. Or perhaps they want to identify with a larger cause, feel that they are helping others, or do the right thing. In your quest for the appeals that will win your readers over, do not underestimate the power of intangible benefits, especially when you can pair them with tangible rewards.

When selecting the reader benefits to feature in your persuasive messages, bear in mind that such benefits can be *intrinsic, extrinsic,* or a combination. Intrinsic benefits are benefits that readers will get automatically by complying with your request. For example, if you are trying to persuade people to attend your company's awards dinner, the pleasure of sharing in their colleagues' successes will be intrinsic to the event. Door prizes would be an extrinsic benefit. We might classify the meal itself as a combination—not really the main feature of the event but definitely central to it. Intrinsic benefits are tightly linked to what you're asking people to do, while extrinsic ones are added on and more short-lived.

Let intrinsic benefits do the main work of your persuasive effort. Focusing too much on extrinsic benefits can actually cheapen your main benefits in the readers' eyes.

When presenting your reader benefits, be sure the readers can see exactly how the benefits will help them. The literature on selling makes a useful distinction between product *features* and reader *benefits*. If you say that a wireless service uses a certain kind of technology, you're describing a feature. If you say that the technology results in fewer missed or dropped calls, you're describing a benefit.

Knowing your readers enables you to target their interests.

Extrinsic benefits like door prizes can add incentive, but intrinsic benefits are usually more persuasive.

Make Good Use of Three Kinds of Appeals

The first acknowledged expert on persuasion, the Greek philosopher Aristotle, lived almost 2,500 years ago, but many of his core concepts are still widely taught and used. Of particular value is his famous categorizing of persuasive appeals into three kinds: those based on *logic* (logos), those based on *emotion* (pathos), and those based on the *character* of the speaker (ethos). All three kinds come into play in every persuasive message—in fact, one might say, in every kind of message. But as the writer of a persuasive message, you will need to think especially carefully about how to manage these appeals and which ones to emphasize given your intended audience.

In practice, these three kinds of appeals often cannot be neatly separated, but to get a sense of your options, you might benefit from thinking about each in turn. What kind of logical appeals might you use—saved money? Saved time? A more dependable or effective product? How about emotional appeals? Higher status? More sex appeal? Increased popularity? And don't neglect appeals based on character. What kind of image of yourself and your company will resonate with the reader? Should you get a celebrity or expert to endorse your product or to serve as the spokesperson? Not only when planning but also when revising your persuasive message, assess your appeals. Be sure to choose and develop the ones most likely to persuade your audience.

Benefits persuade by enabling readers to envision the features of the recommended product or action in their own worlds.

One common technique for achieving this goal is to use what we call *scenario painting,* or a description that pictures the reader in a sample situation enjoying the promised benefits. Here is an example of scenario painting from the Carnival Cruise Lines website:

Think your schedule is too tight to take a fun-filled vacation? Our Baja Mexico sailings are just the cruises to change your mind. You can experience the tropical beauty of Baja with a 3-day weekend cruise to Ensenada. Relax in the privacy of Ensenada's private beaches before hitting the fashionable shops of Avenida Primera for new jewelry—duty-free, of course.

Have an extra day to spare? Our 4-day Baja cruises visit Catalina Island. Who knows? You may spot some of Hollywood's elite while sunning on the golden beaches of California's Emerald Island.

Scenario painting is very common in sales messages, but you can also use it to good advantage in other persuasive messages, even internal ones. Whatever your persuasive situation or strategy, be sure to provide enough detail for readers to see how they will benefit from what you are asking them to do.

Painting a vivid scene showing the benefits can help you persuade.

Make It Easy for Your Readers to Comply

Sometimes writers focus so much on creating persuasive appeals that they put insufficient thought into making the requested action as clear and easy to perform as possible. If you want people to give money or buy your product, tell them where and how to do it, and supply a postage-paid preaddressed mailing envelope or an ecommerce-enabled Web address if applicable. If you want employees to give suggestions for improving products or operations, tell them exactly where and how to submit their ideas and make it easy for them to do so. If you want people to remember to work more safely or conserve on supplies, give them specific techniques for achieving these goals and include auxiliary reminders at the actual locations where they need to remember what to do. Making the desired action both specific and easy to perform is a key part of moving your readers from resistance to compliance with your request.

With this general advice in mind, we now turn to the three main types of persuasive writing in business: persuasive requests, sales messages, and proposals.

LO 2 Write skillful persuasive requests that begin indirectly, develop convincing reasoning, and close with goodwill and action.

PERSUASIVE REQUESTS

Many times in your work life you will need to make persuasive requests. Perhaps, as in the scenario below, you will be asked to write a fund-raising message. Perhaps you will need to ask your management for another staff position or

Take it from the Greeks: ethos, logos, and pathos can all help you persuade.

workplace scenario

Making Persuasive Requests

Introduce yourself to the next business message situation by returning to your hypothetical position at Pinnacle. As a potential executive, you spend some time working for the community. Pinnacle wants you to do this volunteer work for the sake of good public relations. You want to do it because it is personally rewarding.

Currently, as chair of the fund-raising committee of the city's Junior Achievement program, you head all efforts to get

financial support for the program from local businesspeople. You have a group of workers who will call on businesspeople. But personal calls take time, and there are many people to call on.

At its meeting today, the Junior Achievement board of directors discussed the problem of contacting businesspeople. One director suggested using a letter to sell them on giving money. The board accepted the idea with enthusiasm. With just as much

enthusiasm, it gave you the assignment of writing the letter.

As you view the assignment, it is not a routine letter-writing problem. Although the local businesspeople are probably generous, they are not likely to part with money without good reason. In fact, their first reaction to a request for money is likely to be negative. So you will need to overcome their resistance in order to persuade them. Your task is indeed challenging.

WHETHER WRITTEN TO INTERNAL OR EXTERNAL READERS, REQUESTS THAT ARE LIKELY TO BE RESISTED REQUIRE A SLOW, DELIBERATE APPROACH.

for special equipment. You may need to persuade a potential client to join you in a meeting so that you can demonstrate the benefits of your products. Or maybe you will be trying to persuade your employees to change their behavior in some way.

Whether written to internal or external readers, requests that are likely to be resisted require a slow, deliberate approach. You must persuade the reader that he or she should grant the request before making the request. More specifically, you must present facts and logical reasoning that support your case. And you must do it convincingly. Such a presentation requires that you begin by developing a plan.

Many times in your career you will need to ask for something. This chapter tells you how.

Determining the Persuasive Plan

Developing your persuasive plan involves three interrelated tasks: determining what you want, figuring out your readers' likely reactions, and deciding upon a persuasive strategy that will overcome reader objections and evoke a positive response.

Think carefully about your actual goals for your persuasive requests. A request for a one-time-only donation might be written very differently from a request that is intended to create a long-time, multiple donor. If you were convincing employees to leave the parking places next to the building for customers' use, you would write a very different message if you cared about maintaining the employees' goodwill than you would if you simply wanted to order them to comply. Your goals, considered in the context of your organization's goals and your relationship with your readers, are key shapers of your persuasive message.

As we have said, thinking about your readers' needs and interests is paramount when planning any persuasive message. Considering everything you know about your readers, put yourself in their shoes. Look at the request as they are likely to see it. Figure out what's in it for them, and anticipate their likely objections. From this thinking and imagining, your plan should emerge.

The specific plan you develop will depend on the facts of the case. You may be able to show that your reader stands to gain in time, money, or the like. Or you may be able to show that your reader will benefit in goodwill or prestige. In some cases, you may persuade readers by appealing to their love of beauty, excitement, serenity, or other emotions. In different cases, you may be able to persuade readers by appealing to the pleasant feeling that comes from doing a good turn. You decide on the benefits that will be most likely to win over your readers.

A special kind of persuasive request is one that casts the request as a problem–solution message. With this strategy, you first present a problem that you and the readers share—a form of the *common-ground* persuasion technique—and then show how doing as you propose will solve the problem for all concerned. Many fund-raising letters start with this ploy, giving us striking facts about the current economic climate, the environment, or living conditions in a certain area of the world. But this strategy can also be a powerful one for internal audiences who might not be receptive to a straightforward proposal for action but who share your opinion that something needs to be done.

A persuasive request situation is a special opportunity for analysis, creativity, and judgment. With careful use of all three, you can plan messages that will change your readers' minds and move them to action.

Gaining Attention in the Opening

In the indirect messages discussed in Chapter 6, the goal of the opening is to set up the explanation. The same goal exists in persuasive requests. Your beginning should lead to your central strategy. But the opening of a persuasive request has an additional goal: to gain attention.

You need to draw your reader in with the opening of your persuasive message because you are writing to a person who has not invited your message and may not agree with your goal. An interesting beginning is a good step toward getting this person into a receptive mood.

Planning an Appealing Argument

One of the most prominent scholars in the field of logic, British philosopher Stephen Toulmin, created a model for argument that many have found useful. Understanding its three main components—**claim**, **evidence**, and **warrant**—can help you write more persuasively.

A **claim** is an assertion. For example, if you are trying to sell your lawn-treatment services, your main claim might be "Our services will help you have a healthier, greener lawn."

The **evidence** is what backs up the claim. To continue with the same example, you might provide details about your chemicals, "before" and "after" pictures, and customer testimonials. To be persuasive, the evidence needs to be *believable*, *sufficient*, and *clearly relevant* to the claim.

The **warrant** is the unspoken value or assumption that makes the evidence convincing for your particular audience. To value all the evidence in our example, the readers would need to believe that chemicals are a good way to make a lawn healthy, that the grass should look lush and homogenous, and that other customers' opinions are important. Our argument would not work with people who worry that chemicals are bad for the environment, believe that a lawn should have a natural look, or do not care what strangers think.

When planning a persuasive appeal, start by considering the warrant—the values that your targeted readers hold. Then make your claims and choose your evidence based on those values.

> ## If you are writing your request in the form of a problem–solution message, you should start with a goal that you and the readers share.

Determine what your reader will find compelling. It might be a statement that arouses curiosity or emotion, such as this one:

While you and I dined heartily last night, 31 orphans at San Pablo Mission had only dried beans to eat.

Or it might be a statement offering or implying a reader benefit:

Even a newspaper or a cup of coffee costs more than 11 cents a day!

Yet that's about the cost of our discounted CET-PBS membership, which is all it takes to keep public television alive and well in our community.

Because questions get people thinking, they are often effective openings, as in the following examples:

From the cover letter of a questionnaire seeking the opinions of medical doctors:

What, in your opinion as a medical doctor, is the value of electronic records to the practice of medicine?

From a message seeking the cooperation of business leaders in promoting a fair:

What would your profits be if 300,000 free-spending visitors came to our town during a single week?

If you are writing your request in the form of a problem–solution message, you should start with a goal that you and the readers share. For example, let's say that one of your project managers has retired and that you want a certain member of the office staff to be promoted into the position. The challenge is that no office person in your company has ever broken into the managerial ranks, so any direct proposal to the company's executives to promote your candidate will, you feel sure, be met with this objection. To get the executives on your side from the beginning, you could start your message with facts that everyone can agree upon: that someone has retired, that his or her duties are important, that someone capable needs to be found, and fast. Your subject line for an email along these lines might be something like, "Reassigning Jim Martin's Duties" (which everyone supports), not "Promoting Kathy Pearson" (which your readers will resist unless you have prepared them for the idea).

Whatever the case, the form of indirectness that you choose for your opening should engage your readers right away and get them thinking along the lines that will lead to their approval of your request.

Developing the Appeal

Following the opening, you should proceed with your goal of persuading. Your task here is a logical and orderly presentation of the reasoning you have selected.

Try to draw your reader in right from the start of your persuasive message.

As with any argument intended to convince, you should do more than merely list points. You should help convey the points with convincing details. Since you are trying to penetrate a neutral or resistant mind, you need to make good use of the you-viewpoint. You need to pay careful attention to the meanings of your words and the clarity of your expression. You need to use logic and emotion appropriately and project an appealing image. And, because your reader may become impatient if you delay your objective, you need to make every word count.

Making the Request Clearly and Positively

After you have done your persuading, move to the action you seek. You have tried to prepare the reader for what you want. If you have done that well, the reader should be ready to accept your request.

As with negative messages, your request requires care in word choice. You should avoid words that detract from the request. You also should avoid words that bring to mind images and ideas that might work against you. Words that bring to mind reasons for refusing are especially harmful, as in this example:

I am aware that businesspeople in your position have little free time to give, but will you please consider accepting an assignment to the board of directors of the Children's Fund?

The following positive tie-in with a major point in the persuasion strategy does a much better job:

Because your organizing skills are so desperately needed, will you please serve on the board of directors of the Children's Fund?

Whether your request should end your message will depend on the needs of the case. Although the ending is a point of emphasis, in some cases you will profit by following the request with words of explanation. This procedure is especially effective when a long persuasion effort is needed. In such cases, you simply cannot present all your reasoning before stating your goal. On the other hand, you may end less involved presentations with the request. Even in this case, however, you may want to follow the request with one last appeal. As illustrated in the sample messages on pages 158 and 159, this strategy associates the request with the advantage that saying "yes" will give the reader.

Summarizing the Plan for Requests

From the preceding discussion, the general plan for persuasive requests can be summarized as follows:

- Open with words that (1) gain attention and (2) set up the strategy.

- Develop the appeal using persuasive language and the you-viewpoint.

- Make the request clearly and without negatives (1) either at the end of the message or (2) followed by words that recall the persuasive appeal.

One last appeal can result in success.

case illustration

A Persuasive External Request (Asking for Information about Employment Applicants)

In this letter a trade publication editor seeks information from an executive for an article on desirable traits of job applications. Granting the request will require time and effort from the executive, so indirect persuasion is appropriate.

FastTrack
Jumpstarting Your Business Career

November 20, 2012

Ms. Adelade O. Romano
Director of Human Resources
Chalmers-DeLouche, Inc.
17117 Proden Road
St. Paul, MN 55108

Dear Ms. Romano:

Question opening gets attention

What clues have you found in employment applications that help you assess a person's character and desirability to your firm?

Opening topic sets up explanation

Explanation follows logically

Young people entering business are eager for any clue that will put them on the other side of the fence. They want to know what goes on in your mind when you are judging the people behind the letters. In our column "Applications That Talk," we want to send a message especially to those people. To make the article as practical as possible, we are drawing our information from people in the field who really know.

Explanation is straight-forward—appeals subtly to good feeling from helping others

Request evolves from presentation of appeal

A mutual friend of ours, Max Mullins, told me of your recent efforts to find the most desirable person behind 250 applications. What specific points did you look for in these applications? What clues distinguished some people from the others? When the going got hard, what fine points enabled you to make your final choice? The young professionals of today are eager for answers to such questions.

You can help solve their problem if you will jot down your personal comments on a diverse sample of these applications and allow me to interview you about your judgments. All applicant information would of course be kept confidential.

Clear statement of the request

Final words recall basic appeal

Will you share your insights with me and with hundreds of young professionals? If so, please call or email me to set up an interview time that is convenient for you. It is just possible, that through this article you will contribute to the success of a future leader in your own company. At least, you will be of service to the many young people who are trying to get "that" job that is so important to them right now.

Sincerely,

Charlotte C. Clayton

Charlotte C. Clayton
Associate Editor

enclosures

405 Perrin Ave.
Austin, TX 78716
512-437-7080
Clayton@fasttrack.com

A Persuasive Internal Request (Persuading Employees to Donate Blood)

The writer wants employees to participate in the company's annual blood drive. He needs to convince them of the importance of the drive and overcome their likely objections. This message will be distributed to employees' mailboxes in reusable internal-mail envelopes.

AMBERLY
Engineering & Construction

Department of Community Relations
Mail Location 12
123 Jackson Street
Edison, Colorado 80864
(719) 777-4444
CommunityRelations@Amberly.com

February 27, 2012

Opens with an attention-getting, you-focused question

Did you help save Brad Meyer's life?

Tells an engaging story with specific details

A few years ago, an employee of Amberly was driving to a friend's wedding when an oncoming car, operated by a drunk driver, swerved across the center line. Brad doesn't remember the crash. But he does remember two months spent in the hospital, two months of surgery and therapy.

Uses a character-based appeal; invites the reader to identify with these "lifesavers"

Without the help of people like us, Brad would not have lived. Some Amberly employees save lives regularly. We're blood donors. Please be a lifesaver and join us on Friday, March 19th, for Amberly's annual blood drive.

Your help is needed for a successful drive.

Avoids words such as "draw blood" or "needle" that would bring unpleasant thoughts to mind

Giving blood is simple. The entire process will take less than 45 minutes.

Giving blood is safe. Experienced health professionals from the Steinmetz Blood Center will be on-site to conduct the procedure exactly as they would in a clinic setting.

Addresses likely reader objections

Giving blood is convenient. The Steinmetz staff will be in Room 401, Building B, between 9:00 A.M. and 3:00 P.M. To save time, make an appointment to donate. Call the Steinmetz Blood Center at 777-1170.

Giving blood is important. Nobody knows who will need blood next, but one thing is certain—it will be available only if healthy, caring people take time to give it. Brad's accident required 110 units—more than 12 gallons—of blood. Because 110 people set aside 45 minutes, Brad Meyer has a lifetime of minutes to be grateful.

Recalls the emotion-based opening and links it to a logical appeal: you or someone in your family might benefit

Take a few moments now to make your pledge on the reverse side of this letter. Then return it to the Community Relations department, Mail Location 12, by March 15th. You can track the campaign's success by clicking the Amberly Lifesavers link on the intranet homepage.

Makes the requested action clear and easy

From Brad and from other families—like yours and mine—who might need it in the days to come,

Thank you,

John M. Piper

John M. Piper
Director, Community Relations

Revised and printed with permission from Dr. Joseph A. Steger, President Emeritus, University of Cincinnati.

Contrasting Persuasive Requests

The persuasive request is illustrated by contrasting letters that ask businesspeople to donate to Junior Achievement. The message below is direct and weak in its persuasion; the second version (page 161), which follows the recommended approach, produced better results.

a selfish blunt approach The weaker letter begins with the request. Because the request is opposed to the reader's wishes, the direct beginning is likely to get a negative reaction. In addition, the comments about how much to give tend to lecture rather than suggest. Some explanation follows, but it is weak and scant. In general, the letter is poorly written. It makes little use of the you-viewpoint. Perhaps its greatest fault is that the persuasion comes too late. The selfish close is a weak reminder of the action requested.

skillful persuasion in an indirect order The second message shows good anticipation of the readers' likely reactions. Its opening generates interest and sets up the persuasion strategy. Notice the effective use of the you-viewpoint throughout. Not until the reader has been sold on the merits of the request does the message ask the question. It does this clearly and directly. The final words leave the reader thinking about the benefits that a "yes" answer will give.

The Ingredients of Successful Fundraising

Expert fundraiser Jerold Panas conducted several focus groups to find out what makes a fundraiser successful and effective. The answers boiled down to "three Es"—plus one "I":

- Empathy—the ability to understand the audience's values and interests
- Energy—the determination to put sufficient work into the fundraising effort
- Enthusiasm—the fundraiser's obvious commitment to the cause
- Integrity—the fundraiser's sincerity and truthfulness

Source: *Asking: A 59-Minute Guide to Everything Board Members, Volunteers, and Staff Must Know to Secure the Gift* (Medfield, MA: Emerson & Church, 2007) 17–20, print.

This direct, bland approach is not likely to persuade.

Dear Mr. Williams:

Will you please donate to the local Junior Achievement program? We have set $50 as a fair minimum for businesses to give. But larger amounts would be appreciated.

The organization badly needs your support. Currently, about 900 young people will not get to participate in Junior Achievement activities unless more money is raised. Junior Achievement is a most worthwhile organization. As a business leader, you should be willing to support it.

If you do not already know about Junior Achievement, let me explain. Junior Achievement is an organization for high school youngsters. They work with local business executives to form small businesses and then operate them. In the process, the students learn about our economic system. This is a good thing, and it deserves our help.

Hoping to receive your generous donation,

SALES MESSAGES

One of the most widely disseminated forms of business communication is the sales message. It is such an important component of most businesses' sales strategies that it has become an elaborate, highly professionalized genre, backed by extensive consumer research. Think about the typical sales letter that you receive. Careful attention has been paid to the message on the envelope, the kinds of pieces inside, and the visual appeal of those pieces, as well as to the text of the letter itself. This material is often coordinated with other media, such as television commercials, email, and Internet postings. Clearly, advertising professionals produce many of these sales messages, as well as much of the fundraising literature that we receive. Why, then, should you study sales writing?

As a businessperson, you will often find yourself in the position of helping to shape a major sales campaign. You may well have valuable insight into your product's benefits and your potential customers. You need to be familiar with

Face-to-face selling is only part of the picture. Many sales occur through mail, email, and the Internet.

Dear Mr. Williams:

Right now—right here in our city—620 teenage youngsters are running 37 corporations. The kids run the whole show; their only adult help comes from business professionals who advise them.

Last September these young people applied for charters and elected officers. They then created plans for business operations. For example, one group planned to build websites for local small businesses. Another elected to conduct a rock concert. Yet another planned to publish electronic newsletters for area corporations. After determining their plans, the kids issued stock—and sold it, too. With the proceeds from stock sales, they began their operations. Now they are operating. This May they will liquidate their companies and account to their stockholders for their profits or losses.

What's behind these impressive accomplishments? As you've probably guessed, it's Junior Achievement. Since 1919, this nonprofit organization has been teaching school kids of all ages about business, economics, and entrepreneurship. Thanks to partnerships between volunteers and teachers, these kids gain hands-on experience with real business operations while learning the fundamentals of economics and financial responsibility. They also learn cooperation and problem solving. It's a win–win situation for all involved.

To continue to succeed, Junior Achievement needs all of us behind it. During the 13 years the program has been in our city, it has had enthusiastic support from local business leaders. But with over 900 students on the waiting list, our plans for next year call for expansion. That's why, as a volunteer myself, I ask that you help make the program available to more youngsters by contributing $50 (it's deductible). By helping to cover the cost of materials, special events, and scholarships, you'll be preparing more kids for a bright future in business.

Please make your donation now by completing our online contribution form at <www.juniorachievement. org>. You will be doing a good service—for our kids, for our schools, and for our community.

Sincerely,

This indirect, interesting, detailed letter has a much greater chance of success.

workplace scenario

Designing Sales Messages

Introduce yourself to the next message type by assuming the role of Anthony A. Killshaw, a successful restaurant consultant. Over the past 12 years, you have acquired an expert knowledge of restaurant operations. You have made a science of virtually every area of restaurant activity: menu design, food control, purchasing, kitchen organization, service. You also have perfected a simple system for data gathering and analysis that quickly gets to the heart of most operations' problems. Testimonials from a number of satisfied clients prove that the system works.

Knowing that your system works is one thing. Getting this knowledge to enough prospective clients is another. So you have decided to publicize your work by writing restaurant managers and telling them about what you have to offer.

At the moment your plan for selling your services is hazy. But you think you will do it by email. It's a fast and easy way to reach your potential customers, you think. They will be more likely to read your message than if you used direct mail. Probably you will use a basic message that will invite the readers to look at your website. The

website conveys the details—much more than you could get into the message.

Because sales writing requires special skills, you have decided to use the help of a local advertising agency—one with good experience with this type of selling. However, you have a pretty good idea of what you want, so you will not leave the work entirely up to the agency's personnel. You will tell them what you want included, and you will have the final word on what is acceptable.

---

the conventions for sales messages and to be able to offer your own good ideas for their success.

In addition, knowledge of selling techniques can help you in many of your other activities, especially the writing of other kinds of business messages. In a sense most of them involve selling something— an idea, a line of reasoning, your company, yourself. Sales techniques are more valuable to you than you might think. After you have studied the remainder of this chapter, you should see why.

Questioning the Acceptability of Sales Messages

We begin our discussion of sales messages by noting that they are a controversial area of business communication, for two main reasons: they are often unwanted, and they sometimes use ethically dubious persuasive tactics. You probably know from your own

Persuasive requests and sales messages arrive uninvited. They have goals that are likely to encounter reader resistance. Unless they appeal to the reader's interests right away, they are likely to end up in a recycle bin.

experience that direct-mail sales literature is not always received happily. Called "junk" mail, these mailings often go into the wastebasket without being read. Even so, they must be successful—the direct-mail business is still going strong.

Sales messages sent by email appear to be creating even more hostility among intended customers. Angrily referred to as "spam," unsolicited email sales messages have generated strong resistance among email users.

Perhaps it is because these messages clutter up in-boxes. Maybe it is because mass mailings place a heavy burden on Internet providers, driving up costs to the users. Or perhaps the fact that they invade the reader's privacy is to blame. There are the downright unethical practices of some email advertisers who use "misleading subject lines and invalid email addresses to thwart filtering attempts and get respondents to open them."[1] Whatever the explanation, the resistance is real. You will need to consider these objections any time you use this sales medium.

Fortunately, a more acceptable form of email selling has developed. Called *permission email* or *opt-in email marketing,* it permits potential customers to sign up for email promotions on a company's website or offer their email addresses to a catalog, phone marketer, or other recipient. The potential customers may be asked to indicate the products, services, and specific topics of their interest. The marketers can then tailor their messages to the customer and the customer will receive only what he or she wants. According to a recent white paper by eMarketer, building permission-based email distribution lists is one of the most important steps in waging successful emarketing campaigns.[2] Such practices can help address the problem of unwanted email sales messages.

As for the charge that persuasive messages use unfair persuasive tactics, this is, unfortunately, sometimes the case. The unfair tactics could range from deceptive wording and visuals to the omission of important information to the use of emotional elements that impair good judgment. In a Missouri court case, Publishers Clearing House was found guilty of deception for direct mail stating that the recipients were already winners when in fact they were not.[3] To consider a different example, one linen supply company sent a letter to parents of first-year college students telling them that the students would need to purchase extra-long sheets, offered by this company, to fit the extra-long beds on campus—but omitted the information that only one dorm out of four had such beds. And it is well documented that images, because they work on a visceral level, persuade in ways that tend to bypass the viewers' reasoned judgment, leading some to question the ethics of such elements.[4]

Any persuasive message is, by its very nature, biased. The writer has a favored point of view and wants to persuade the reader to adopt it. Therefore, considering the ethical dimension of your communication, while important for all types of messages, is especially critical for persuasive messages. Let your conscience

Begin work on a sales message by thoroughly studying the product or service to be sold.

and your ability to put yourself in the readers' shoes guide you as you consider how to represent your subject and win others to your cause.

LO 4 Describe the planning steps for direct mail or email sales messages.

Preparing to Write a Sales Message

Before you can begin writing a sales message, you must know all you can about the product or service you are selling. You simply cannot sell most goods and services unless you know them and can tell the prospects what they need to know. Before prospects buy a product, they may want to know how it is made, how it works, what it will do, and what it will not do. Clearly, a first step in sales writing is careful study of your product or service.

In addition, you should know your readers. In particular, you should know about their needs for the product or service. Anything else you know about them can help: their economic status, age, nationality, education, and culture. The more you know about your readers, the better you will be able to adapt every element of your sales message to them.

In large businesses, a marketing research department or agency typically gathers information about prospective customers. If you do not have such help, you will need to gather this information on your own. If time does not permit you to do the necessary research, you may have to follow your best logic. For example, the nature of a product can tell you something about its likely buyers. Industrial equipment would probably be bought by people with technical backgrounds. Expensive French perfumes and cosmetics would probably be bought by people in high-income brackets. Burial insurance would appeal to older members of the lower economic strata. If you are purchasing a mailing list, you usually receive basic demographics

Many marketing firms use focus groups to learn about prospective customers.

Logical appeals are more rational. These include strategies based on saving money, making money, doing a job better, and getting better use from a product. Illustrating a rational appeal (saving money) are these words from a message selling magazine subscriptions:

We're slashing the regular rate of $36 a year down to only $28, saving you a full 22 percent. That means you get 12 information-filled new issues of *Science Digest* for only $2.33 a copy. You save even more by subscribing for 2 or 3 years.

Appeals based on character persuade by implying such arguments as "I use this product, so you should, too" or "I am an authority, so you should do what I recommend." Ads that employ sports figures, music stars, or experts to sell their products

such as age, sex, race, education, income, and marital status of those on the list. Sometimes you know more—interests, spending range, or consumption patterns.

Determining the Central Appeal

With your product or service and your prospects in mind, you are ready to create the sales message. This involves selecting and presenting your persuasive appeals, whether emotional, logical, character based, or a combination. But for most sales messages, one appeal should stand out as the main one—mentioned in the beginning, recalled in the middle, and reiterated at the end. While other benefits can be brought in as appropriate, the message should emphasize your central, best appeal.

Emotional appeals—those designed to appeal to our senses and emotions—can be found in almost any sales message, but they predominate in messages for goods and services that do not perform any discernable rational function. Illustrating emotional appeal is the following example from a message that attempts to sell perfume by linking the romance of faraway places with the product's exotic scent:

Linger in castle corridors on court nights in London. Dance on a Budapest balcony high above the blue Danube. Seek romance and youth and laughter in charming capitals on five continents. And there you'll find the beguiling perfume that is fragrance Jamais.

A well-known spokesperson can add character appeal.

> ## You should consider those appeals that fit your product or service and your readers best.

---

are relying heavily on character-based appeals. Companies themselves often convey an appealing "character" in their sales campaigns. Note how the following excerpt from a sales letter for *Consumer Reports* magazine uses the company's identity to persuade:

Consumer Reports is on your side. We're a nonprofit consumer protection organization with no commercial interests whatsoever. To put it bluntly, we don't sell out to big companies and private interest groups—we're accountable to no one except to consumers. And when you're not beholden to advertisers (like other so-called consumer protection publications), you can tell it like it is.

People may also buy a certain product because they want to identify with, and be identified with, a certain successful, socially responsible, or "cool" company as projected in the company's sales messages.

In any given case, many appeals are available to you. You should consider those that fit your product or service and your readers best. Such products as perfume, style merchandise, candy, and fine food lend themselves to emotional appeals. On the other hand, such products as automobile tires, tools, and industrial equipment are best sold through rational appeals. And almost any product could be promoted through a character-based appeal. Often a combination of appeals is your best strategy, but be sure that they work together to create a coherent effect.

How the buyer will use the product may be a major basis for selecting a sales strategy. Cosmetics might well be sold to the final user through emotional appeals. Selling cosmetics to a retailer (who is primarily interested in reselling them) would require rational appeals. A retailer would be interested in their emotional qualities only to the extent that these would entice customers to buy. A retailer's main questions about the product are "Will it sell?," "What turnover can I expect?," and "How much money will it make for me?"

Determining the Makeup of the Mailing

When you write a sales message to be sent by mail or email, a part of your effort is in determining the makeup of the mailing. To know what you want to say in your main message, you'll need to decide what kinds of additional pieces will be included and how they will support the main piece.

Consider, for example, a direct-mail campaign by Scotts Lawn-Service (see the case illustration on page 169). The mailing comes

> ## TO KNOW WHAT YOU WANT TO SAY IN YOUR MAIN MESSAGE, YOU'LL NEED TO DECIDE WHAT KINDS OF ADDITIONAL PIECES WILL BE INCLUDED AND HOW THEY WILL SUPPORT THE MAIN PIECE.

Direct mail messages can include a lot of extras beyond the main message.

in a 9-inch by 12-inch white envelope with the words "LAWN ANALYSIS ENCLOSED FOR (the recipient's address)" on the front. Both the kind of envelope used and the wording on it convey the image of a personalized official document.

Inside are these three 7½-inch by 10½-inch pages:

- A top page that includes the main sales letter on the front, with bold letters in the top right corner advertising a **"FREE No-Obligation Lawn Analysis for (the resident's address)."** On the back are six testimonials under the heading **"Here's what our customers say about Scotts LawnService."**

- A second page, on glossy paper, that has "before" and "after" pictures of a lawn under the heading **"Now you can enjoy a thick, green, beautiful lawn . . . *and Scotts LawnService will do the work!"*** On the back are various character appeals for the company, under the heading **"Here's why you can expect more from Scotts LawnService than any other lawn service."**

- A replica of a "FREE LAWN ANALYSIS" form "TO BE COMPLETED FOR (the recipient's) FAMILY at (the recipient's address)," with "SAMPLE" stamped (or appearing to be stamped) across the form.

The final piece is a return envelope with a detachable form to fill out and return. Both parts advertise again the "FREE No-Obligation Lawn Analysis."

The author of this elaborate mailing determined that the free lawn analysis would be the immediate selling point, with the main reader benefit being the beautiful lawn that the analysis would lead to. With these decisions made, the writer could then decide what to place in the foreground of the letter, what other pieces to include, and how to coordinate the letter with the other pieces. Even if someone else, such as a graphic artist or desktop publishing expert, will be designing the pieces of your mailing, you will need to plan how all parts of the sales package will work together, especially for a complex mailing like this one.

Email sales messages can use all the publishing features available on the computer. The message can be presented creatively with color, font variations, box arrangements, artwork, and more. It may include links to support material as well as to the ordering procedure. And it may have attachments. Just as with a direct-mail package, the email sales package uses many elements to persuade and to make available all the information a reader needs to complete the sale.

LO 5 Compose sales messages that gain attention, persuasively present appeals, and effectively drive for action.

Gaining Attention

The beginnings of all sales messages have one basic requirement: to gain attention. If they do not, they fail. Because sales messages are sent without invitation, they are not likely to be received favorably. In fact, they may even be unwanted. Unless they gain attention early, the messages will not be read.

With direct mail, the envelope containing the message is the first attention getter. All too often the reader recognizes the mailing as an uninvited sales message and promptly discards it. For this reason many direct-mail writers place an attention getter on the envelope. It may be the offer of a gift ("Your gift is enclosed"). It may present a brief sales message ("12 months of *Time* at 60% off the newsstand price"). It may present a picture and a message (a picture of a cruise ship and "Tahiti and more at 2-for-1 prices"). An official-appearing envelope sometimes is used. So are brief and simple messages such as "Personal,"

"Sensitive material enclosed," and "May we have the courtesy of a reply." The possibilities are many.

With email, of course, there is no envelope. The attention begins with the from, to, and subject fields. As one authority explains, you should clearly tell who you are and identify your company.[5] Many "spam" messages disguise these identities, and you hope your readers will not regard your message as spam. You should also address the reader by name. Though some readers will delete the message even with this clear identification, the honesty conveyed will induce some to read on.

The subject line in email messages is the main place for getting attention. Here honesty and simplicity should be your guide. The subject line

Often the envelope begins the persuasive effort.

> ## "With direct mail, the envelope containing the message is the first attention getter."

should tell clearly what your message is about, and it should be short. It should avoid sensational wording, such as "How to earn $60,000 the first month." In addition, avoiding sensationalism involves limiting the use of solid caps, exclamation points, dollar signs, and "free" offers. In fact, you risk having spam filters block your message or send it to the junk folder of your readers' computers if you use "free" or other words and phrases commonly used in spam. An email with the subject line "Making your restaurant more profitable" that is sent to a researched list of restaurant managers and owners is much more likely to be opened and read than a message with the subject line "You have to read this!" that is sent to thousands of readers indiscriminately.

Holding Attention in the Opening

The first words of your message also have a major need to gain attention. The reader must be moved to read on. What you do here can be creative, but the method you use should help set up your strategy. It should not just gain attention for attention's sake. Attention is easy to gain if nothing else is needed. In a sales letter, a small explosion set off when the reader opens the envelope would gain attention. So would an electric shock or a miniature stink bomb. But these methods would not be likely to help sell your product or service.

One of the most effective attention-gaining techniques is a statement or question that introduces a need that the

product will satisfy. For example, a rational-appeal message to a retailer would clearly tap his or her strong needs with these opening words:

Here is a proven best-seller—and with a 12 percent greater profit.

Another appealing attention getter is this beginning of an email sales message promoting eFax.com's Web-conferencing service:

Give us 30 days and we'll show you a whole different kind of Web meeting: seamless, productive, free of software crashes . . . and, dare we say, even fun.

This paragraph of a message selling a fishing vacation at a lake resort illustrates an emotional-appeal approach:

Your line hums as it whirs through the air. Your line splashes and dances across the smooth surface of the clear water as you reel. From the depth you see the silver streak of a striking bass. You feel a sharp tug. The battle is on!

As you can see, the paragraph casts an emotional spell, which is what emotional selling should do. A different tack is illustrated by the following example. It attracts interest by telling a story and using character-based appeal:

In 1994 three enterprising women met to do something about the lack of accessible health information for women.

Whatever opening strategy you choose, it should introduce or lead into your central selling point.

> ## IN NO AREA OF BUSINESS COMMUNICATION IS THE USE OF THE YOU-VIEWPOINT MORE IMPORTANT THAN IN SALES WRITING.

Learn from the Blogging Pros

Want to learn how professional bloggers persuade their readers?

Check out copyblogger.com, one of the most popular blogs on the Internet. With a free subscription, you can access tutorials, learn about different media for advertising, and read such articles as these:

"Ten Timeless Persuasive Writing Techniques"
"The Seven Harsh Realities of Social Media Marketing"
"How Twitter Makes You a Better Writer"
"Five Grammatical Errors that Make You Look Dumb"*

You can also read readers' responses to the articles, search for topics you're interested in, and click on links to related websites.

*As of 15 Apr. 2010 at <http://www.copyblogger.com/>.

Building a Persuasive Case

With the reader's attention gained, you proceed with the sales strategy that you have developed. In general, you establish a need. Then you present your product or service as fulfilling that need.

The plan of your sales message will vary with each case. But it is likely to follow certain general patterns determined by your choice of appeals. If your main appeal is emotional, for example, your opening has probably established an emotional atmosphere that you will continue to develop. Thus, you will sell your product based on its effects on your reader's senses. You will describe the appearance, texture, aroma, and taste of your product so vividly that your reader will mentally see it, feel it—and want it. In general, you will seek to create an emotional need for your product.

If you select a rational appeal as your central theme, your sales description is likely to be based on factual material. You should describe your product based on what it can do for your reader rather than how it appeals to the senses. You should write matter-of-factly about such qualities as durability, savings, profits, and ease of operation.

When using character-based appeals, you will emphasize comments from a well-known, carefully selected spokesperson. Or, if the character being promoted is that of the company itself, you will provide evidence that your company is expert and dependable, understands customers like "you," and stands behind its service or product.

The writing that carries your sales message can be quite different from your normal business writing. Sales writing usually is highly conversational, fast moving, and aggressive. It even uses techniques that are incorrect or inappropriate in other forms of business writing: sentence fragments, one-sentence paragraphs, folksy language, and the like. As the case illustrations show, it also uses mechanical emphasis devices (underscore, capitalization, boldface, italics, exclamation marks, color) to a high degree. It can use all kinds of visuals and graphic devices as well as a variety of fonts. And its paragraphing often appears choppy. Any sales message is competing with many other messages for the intended reader's attention. In this environment of information overload, punchy writing and visual effects that enable quick processing of the message's main points have become the norm in professional sales writing.

Stressing the You-Viewpoint

In no area of business communication is the use of the you-viewpoint more important than in sales writing. A successful sales message bases its sales points on reader interest. You should liberally use and imply the pronoun *you* throughout the sales message as you present your well-chosen reader benefits.

Like a good attorney, you should build a strong case with your words when trying to persuade.

A Direct-Mail Message (Selling a Lawn-Care Service)

This sales letter uses all three types of appeals (logical, emotional, and character based). It also comes with several other pieces—including "before" and "after" pictures, customer testimonials, and a sample "free lawn analysis" form with the customer's name and address printed on it.

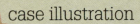

Scotts
LawnService®
271 2nd Street
Saddle Brook, NJ 07663

Announces the immediate benefit that will lead to the main benefit: a beautiful lawn

FREE No-Obligation
Lawn Analysis for
14111 Scottslawn Rd-Attn Dan Adams

March 27, 2012

The Adams Family
14111 Scottslawn Rd-Attn Dan Adams
Marysville, OH 43041-0001

Makes it seem as though Scotts may have already looked at the customer's lawn

YOU'LL BE SEEING OUR TRUCK ON SCOTTSLAWN ROAD A LOT THIS YEAR!

Dear Adams Family,

Do you know what's wrong with your lawn?

What do you need to do now to protect your lawn from unsightly weeds, insects you can't even see, and damaging turfgrass diseases? Call Scotts LawnService®! We have developed NEW Ortho Weed-B-Gon Pro® and Ortho® Max™ Pro Insect Control to handle tough weed and insect lawn problems.

Uses "social proof"—do what so many of your neighbors are doing

Sign up for Scotts LawnService like so many of your neighbors who had those problems. You'll see us treating their lawns throughout the season.

Uses you-viewpoint; suggests that you need to call in the experts

Now you can have a Scotts LawnService professional inspect your lawn for potential problems.

Builds Scotts' ethos as a company of knowledgeable professionals

We'll carefully examine your lawn and give you a detailed report on what we find, and what you need to do to keep your lawn thick, green and healthy.

And there's absolutely no cost and no obligation for this FREE Lawn Analysis.

Simply call us Toll Free at 1-800-736-0205 within the next 14 days, and Scotts LawnService will arrange for your FREE Lawn Analysis. It's easy, and you don't have to be home. We'll also include our recommendations for a Scotts LawnService program that's right for your lawn, plus a no-obligation price quote.

Makes several logical appeals

Appeals to emotion and logic and builds trust in the Scotts professionals

If you decide to become a Scotts LawnService customer, we'll put together a program that will give you the beautiful lawn you've always wanted. We use Scotts® slow-release, professional fertilizers on your lawn – and you can really see the difference in the results.

We'll evaluate your lawn during every visit, foreseeing and solving problems that may occur and taking personal responsibility for its progress. That's why Scotts LawnService offers you a Satisfaction Guarantee.

Requested action is clear and easy, and linked to the main benefit

Call Scotts LawnService now or mail in the slip enclosed in the postage-paid envelope to request your FREE No-Obligation Lawn Analysis. It's the first step to having a thick, green, healthy lawn you can be proud of.

Sincerely,

Mike Pribanic

Mike Pribanic
North Jersey, Branch Manager

A final reminder of the main benefit and the easy first step

P.S. It's so important to start early—to enjoy a beautiful lawn all season long. Please provide your phone number on the request slip, detach, and mail in the enclosed postage-paid envelope. For faster service, call 1-800-736-0205 to receive your FREE No-Obligation Lawn Analysis.

Communication in brief

Sales-Related Insights from Behavioral Economics

A relatively new specialty in the field of economics is behavioral economics—the study of seemingly irrational factors that affect consumers' decisions. Being aware of such factors can make you a better sales writer.

Here are four useful behavioral-economics insights from Ned Welch, a consultant for McKinsey & Company:

- *"Make a product's cost less painful."* Parting with money is a form of loss, so try to minimize the perception of that loss. One way to do so, Welch says, is "allowing consumers to delay payment." Some customers may simply not be able to afford a large outlay of money all at once, but even if they can, they tend to find immediate payments "viscerally unpleasant." Offering even small delays in payment can help increase the chances of a sale. Another strategy is to influence consumers' perception of which pot the money is coming out of. According to Welch, "windfall gains and pocket money are usually easiest for consumers to spend," in comparison to paychecks or savings. Even thought the dollars from all these sources are equal in value, consumers don't perceive them that way. This may be a reason why the only-pennies-a-day appeal works; a few cents can be perceived as pocket money, whereas the dollar amount seems more like a dip into one's income or savings.

- *"Harness the power of a default option."* People don't want to give up something they already have, so if you can devise an offer that enables people to continue to keep something that's "theirs"—for example, telling them that a gift is already reserved for them—you can make your appeals more persuasive.

- *"Don't overwhelm consumers with choice."* Doing so can undercut purchasing. In one study cited by Welch, in-store customers who sampled 24 jams bought many fewer jars than customers who sampled only 6 jams. Offering too many choices makes the customer work too hard and also "increase[s] the likelihood that each choice will become imbued with a 'negative halo'—a heightened awareness that every option requires you to forgo desirable features" of the other options. The lesson? Offer a few choices and make each one appealing.

- *"Position your preferred option carefully."* What people are willing to pay is influenced by the product's context. For example, people tend to buy the second-most expensive or the second-cheapest wine at restaurants; "customers who by the former feel they're getting something special but not going over the top," Welch explains, while "those who buy the latter feel they are getting a bargain but not being cheap." You might consider this tendency when offering various levels of giving in a fundraising message, for example.

Source: Adapted with permission from "A Marketer's Guide to Behavioral Economics," *McKinsey Quarterly*, McKinsey & Company, Feb. 2010, Web, 15 Apr. 2010.

> ## In persuasive messages, every word can influence how the reader will respond to the request.

The techniques of you-viewpoint writing in sales messages are best described through illustration. For example, assume you are writing a sales message to a retailer. One point you want to make is that the manufacturer will help sell the product with an advertising campaign. You could write this information in a matter-of-fact way: "HomeHealth products will be advertised in *Self* magazine for the next three issues." Or you could write it based on what the advertising means to the reader: "Your customers will read about HomeHealth products in the next three issues of *Self* magazine." Viewing things from the reader's perspective will strengthen your persuasiveness. The following examples further illustrate the value of presenting facts as reader benefits:

Facts	You-Viewpoint Statements
We make Aristocrat hosiery in three colors.	You may choose from three lovely shades.
The Regal weighs only a few ounces.	The Regal's featherlight touch makes vacuuming easier than ever.
Lime-Fizz is a lime flavored carbonated beverage.	Your customers will keep coming back for the refreshing citrus taste of Lime-Fizz.
Baker's Dozen is packaged in a rectangular box with a bright bull's-eye design.	Baker's Dozen's new rectangular package fits compactly on your shelf, and its bright bull's-eye design will catch the eyes of your customers.

> ## You must make sure that you present enough information to complete the sale.

Word Artistry

Remember *scenario painting* from the first part of this chapter? It's especially useful for creating vivid sales messages.

You may also want to make use of scenario painting, putting the reader in a simulated context that brings out the product's appeal. The J. Peterman clothing company is famous for this technique, exemplified in the following excerpt from an advertisement for women's Beautiful People Pants:

Nikki Beach, Mangos, Club Bed, Wet Willies.

The constant whirl of South Beach.

Into the night it goes.

Is it morning yet?

After their beauty sleep until noon, the beautiful people spend the next day shopping, drinking mimosas, and sizing up the competition.

If you were to walk past in these pants, you would pass muster.

Choosing Words Carefully

In persuasive messages, every word can influence how the reader will respond to the request. Try putting yourself in your reader's place as you select words for your message. Some words, while closely related in meaning, have significantly different emotional effects. For example, the word *selection* implies a choice while the word *preference* implies a first choice. Here are some examples where a single adjective changes the effect of a sentence:

The NuPhone's *small* size . . .

The NuPhone's *compact* size . . .

The NuPhone's *sleek* size . . .

Framing your requests in the positive is also a proven persuasive technique. Readers will tend to opt for solutions to problems that avoid negatives. Here are some examples:

Original Wording	Positive Wording
Tastee ice cream has nine grams of fat per serving.	Tastee ice cream is 95 percent fat free.
Our new laser paper keeps the wasted paper from smudged copies to less than 2 percent.	Our new laser paper ensures smudge-free copies over 98 percent of the time.

Including All Necessary Information

Of course, the information you present and how you present it are matters for your best judgment. But you must make sure that you present enough information to complete the sale. You

An Email Sales Message (Persuading Professionals to Attend a Seminar)

This message uses logical and character-based appeals. Note how short paragraphs, bold text, and underlining facilitate quick reading and generate excitement.

From: "Advertising Club of Cincinnati" <jethompson001@msn.com>
To: <Kathryn.Rentz@uc.edu>
Sent: Thursday, April 17, 2011 8:00 AM
Subject: ExactTarget Roadshow Comes to West Chester!

Sender's name and subject line are likely to appeal to readers on this organization's mailing list

To view this email as a Web page, go here.

We pledge allegiance to great ideas.

Colorful "letterhead" and catchy tagline generate interest

ExactTarget. The New eMarketing Essentials
One day seminars sponsored by Omniture and Salesforce.com
Register Now $59 Early Bird Special

Dear ADCLUB Member (or Member-To-Be):

Are you wondering if integrating your CRM and web analytics programs with email can help increase your marketing ROI?

Opening question with professional lingo invites further reading

The answer is YES. And, ExactTarget, one of ADCLUB Cincinnati's longtime trusted business partners, can show you how.

Character appeal adds to the persuasion

ExactTarget is launching a road show—**Route 1 to 1: The New eMarketing Essentials**—and it's coming your way! ExactTarget, Omniture, Salesforce.com, and SLI Systems are joining forces to make sure your CRM, web analytics, and email integrations drive highly-effective marketing return from day one. And thanks to our partnership, there's a special deal just for you!

Spend one day with ExactTarget and learn how to take your email marketing program to new heights.

View Agenda & Register Now!

Link here makes action easy to take

Logical appeals are the core of the message

ExactTarget's one day **Route 1 to 1** seminar series teaches you how to leverage your CRM and web analytics data and:

- Engage prospects
- Maximize marketing ROI
- Drive higher sales
- Increase "return-on customer"
- Build brand loyalty

Register for the Cincinnati Seminar! It's being held at the fabulous Savannah Center in West Chester. (The first 20 people to enter the code **R1T1ADCLUB** receive $20 off registration)

Yet another opportunity to register

A clever act-now strategy

Yet more reader benefits

In addition to presentations from ExactTarget's email thought leaders, top industry experts and analysts will provide one-to-one marketing technology insight. ExactTarget clients will also be on-site to share real-life examples of their B2B and B2C email marketing success.

See you there!

Best regards,

Judy

Judy Thompson
Executive Director
ADCLUB Cincinnati

P.S. The first 20 ADCLUB Cincinnati registrants will receive a $20 discount! Just enter the code R1T1ADCLUB while registering.

Reminder to act now

Special thanks to our Sponsors!

Gold Sponsor	Silver Sponsor	Bronze Sponsors
red echo post	GREENEBAUM	 CREATIVES ON CALL STEINHAUSER

These ads further contribute to the organization's credibility

Thanks, also to our ADCLUB Partners:
Cincy, Exact Target, Millcraft Paper, Primax Studio, Radisson Hotel, & Visual Aids Electronics

One final character appeal

 AAF

ADCLUB Cincinnati is proud to be affiliated with the American Advertising Federation. For more information, go to www.aaf.org.

This email was sent to: Kathryn.Rentz@uc.edu

This email was sent by: **Advertising Club of Cincinnati**
602 Main Street, Suite 806 Cincinnati, OH, 45202 USA

Go here to leave this mailing list or modify your email profile. We respect your right to privacy. View our policy.

Provides reader with opt-out choice

Powered by
ExactTarget.
Learn more.

> ## "AFTER YOU HAVE DEVELOPED YOUR READER'S INTEREST IN YOUR PRODUCT OR SERVICE, THE NEXT LOGICAL STEP IS TO DRIVE FOR THE SALE."

should leave none of your readers' questions unanswered. Nor should you fail to overcome any likely objections. You must work to include all such basic information in your message, and you should make it clear and convincing.

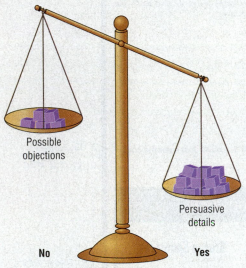

Give your readers enough information to tip them toward yes.

As we say, you will also need to decide how to apportion your information across all the pieces in your mailing or the layout of a screen. With direct mail, you should use your letter to do most of the persuading, with any enclosures, attachments, or links providing supplementary information. These supplements might provide in-depth descriptions, price lists, diagrams, and pictures—in short, all the helpful information that does not fit easily into the letter. You may want to direct your readers' attention to these other pieces with such comments as "you'll find comments from your satisfied neighbors in the enclosed brochure," "as shown on page 7 of the enclosed catalog," or "you'll see testimonials of satisfied customers in the blue shaded boxes."

When you send the sales message by email, the supporting information must be worked into the message or presented in links or attachments that you invite the reader to view. You must take care to avoid the appearance of too much length or clutter when working this material into the message. By skillfully chunking the message visually (see the case illustration on pages 172 and 173), you can reduce the effect of excessive length. And by making the boxes attractive with imaginative use of color, font selection, and formatting, you

can enhance the effectiveness of the presentation. In either mail or email selling, your goal is to give the readers all they need to know to complete a sale while allowing them the option of reading only as much as they desire.

Driving for the Sale

After you have developed your reader's interest in your product or service, the next logical step is to drive for the sale. After all, this is what you have been working for all along. It is a natural conclusion to the sales effort you have made.

How to word your drive for the sale depends on your strategy. If your selling effort is strong, your drive for action also may be strong. It may even be worded as a command ("Order your copy today—while it's on your mind"). If you use a milder selling effort, you could use a direct question ("May we send you your copy today?"). In any event, the drive for action should be specific and clear. For best effect, it should take the reader through the motions of whatever he or she must do. Here are some examples:

Just check your preferences on the enclosed order card and drop it in the mail today.

To start enjoying *House and Garden*, just call 1-888-755-5265. Be sure to have your promo code handy to receive your 40 percent discount.

As in this Habitat for Humanity example, most sales mailings consist of a letter and a coordinated group of support pieces.

From: Angie's List [angieslist@angieslist.com
Sent: Monday, March 01, 2010 10:17 AM
To: Rentz, Kathryn (rentzkc)
Subject: Plumbing disasters are a hassle

Join Angie's List today and save $20 on an annual membership or waive the activation fee!
Use promo code **PIPES2** by 3/7.

Trouble viewing the images in this e-mail? Go here.
Add angieslist@angieslist.com to your address book. I Update E-mail Preferences.

Join 1 ——→ **Angie's list.**

Ready for a thaw?
Maybe not.

This winter, a series of storms have taken a toll on the plumbing in homes across the country. If you encounter a plumbing issue or emergency, check Angie's List to find the best local plumbers to fix your problem.

If your pipes have frozen, be careful! Pipes occasionally burst when they've frozen, but the ice will prevent telltale leaks. Once it thaws, you could have a major problem on your hands that requires the attention of a skilled plumbing professional. Find one today, when you join Angie's List.

Hope to see you on the List soon!

Sincerely,

Angie Hicks

Angie Hicks, co-founder

Join Angie's List with promo code PIPES2 by 3/7 and save $20 on an annual membership or waive the activation fee!

Join 3 ——→ **JOIN NOW**

Join Angie's List with promo code PIPES2 by 3/7
and save $20 on an annual membership or waive
the activation fee!

Continue with PayPal ←—— Join 2

If you have a friend you'd like to invite to Angie's List, pass this e-mail and offer along to them.

Source: Reprinted with permission.

Similarly, in email selling you will need to make the action easy. Make it a simple click—a click to an order form or to the first part of the ordering process. Words such as these do the job well: "Just click on the button below to order your customized iPhone case now!" and "You can download our free new catalog of business gifts at <http://thankyoutoo.com>." Many sales emails, such as the one shown in Exhibit 7.1, make the desired action easy by including multiple places for readers to perform it.

Because readers who have been persuaded sometimes put things off, you should urge immediate action. "Do it now" and "Act

Communication in brief

Persuasive Strategies Vary Across Cultures

When writing persuasive messages, be especially careful to adapt your messages to the culture of the intended readers.

For example, while sales letters in English and Chinese use many of the same core elements, there are also these crucial differences:

- English sales letters often use attention-getting headlines and postscripts that pressure readers to act, while Chinese sales letters do not use these seemingly harsh strategies.

- Both types of letters contain a salutation, but it is more formal in Chinese letters (for example, "Honored Company" instead of "Dear Mr. Smith"). Furthermore, Chinese letters follow the salutation with polite words of greeting, whereas English letters go directly into sales talk.

- English letters tend to describe the product's benefits by using "you," whereas the Chinese, finding the use of "you" disrespectful, tend to use "we" (as in "Our consistent goal is to produce comfortable luxury cars of high standard and good quality").

- Both types of letters extol the benefits of the product, but Chinese letters use fewer details, especially about price.

- When making the actual request, Chinese letters are less pushy than English letters, favoring such mild language as "If you are interested in our products, please contact us."

- Both types of letters use a complimentary close, but instead of "Sincerely yours," the Chinese attempt to promote cooperation and mutual respect with such closings as "wishing you good health."

Source: Zhu Yunxia, "Building Knowledge Structures in Teaching Cross-Cultural Sales Genres," *Business Communication Quarterly* 63.4 (2000): 49–69, print.

> ## A sales message can use a postscript as a part of its design.

today" are versions of this technique, although some people dislike the commanding tone of such words. Even so, this type of action is widely used. A milder and generally more acceptable way of urging action is to tie it in with a practical reason for doing it now. Here are some examples:

. . . to take advantage of this three-day offer.

. . . so that you can be ready for the Christmas rush.

. . . so that you can immediately begin enjoying. . . .

Another effective technique for the close of a sales message is to use a few words that recall the main appeal. Associating the action with the benefits that the reader will gain by taking it adds strength to your sales effort. Illustrating this technique is a message selling Maxell DVDs to retailers. After building its sales effort, the message asks for action and then follows the action request with these words:

. . . and start taking your profits from the fast-selling Maxell DVDs.

Another illustration is a message selling a fishing resort vacation that follows its action words with a reminder of the joys described earlier:

It's your reservation for a week of battle with the fightingest bass in the Southland.

Adding a Postscript

Unlike other business messages where a postscript (P.S.) appears to be an afterthought, a sales message can use a postscript as a part of its design. It can be used effectively in a number of ways: to urge the reader to act, to emphasize the major appeal, to invite attention to other enclosures, to suggest that the reader pass along the sales message, and so on. Postscripts effectively used by professionals include the following:

PS: Don't forget! If you ever think that *Action* is not for you, we'll give you every cent of your money back. We are that confident that *Action* will become one of your favorite magazines.

PS: Hurry! Save while this special money-saving offer lasts.

PS: Our magazine makes a distinctive and appreciated gift. Know someone who's having a birthday soon?

PS: Click now to order and automatically enter our contest for a Nexus One smartphone.

Offering Name Removal to Email Readers

Until January 1, 2004, it was a courtesy to offer the recipients of commercial email the option of receiving no further emails from the sender. Now, thanks to the so-called CAN-SPAM Act, it is a legal requirement as well.[6] Consider placing this invitation in a prominent place—perhaps even before the main message (Exhibit 7.1 does so with the link "Update Email Preferences"). According to one authority, "This is the equivalent of asking, 'Is it OK if we come in?'"[7]

- Drive for the sale by urging action now and recalling the main appeal.

- Possibly add a postscript.

- In email writing, offer to remove the party contacted from your email list to comply with legal requirements.

Reviewing the General Sales Plan

From the preceding discussion, a general plan for the sales message emerges. This plan is similar to the classic AIDA (attention, interest, desire, action) model that direct-mail copywriters developed almost a century ago. It should be noted, however, that in actual practice, sales messages vary widely. Creativity and imagination are continually leading to innovative techniques. Even so, the general prevailing plan is the following:

- Gain favorable attention.

- Create desire by presenting the appeals, emphasizing supporting facts, and emphasizing reader viewpoint.

- Include all necessary information—using a coordinated sales package (brochures, leaflets, links, and other appended parts).

Evaluating Contrasting Examples

The two email sales messages on this page and the next show bad and good efforts to sell Killshaw's restaurant consulting services.

weakness in an illogical plan Although the subject line of the weak sales message presents the main appeal, it is dull and general. The opening statement is little more than an announcement of what the consultant does. Then, as a continuation of the opening, it offers the services to the reader. Such openings do little to gain attention or build desire. Next comes a routine, I-viewpoint review of the consultant's services. The explanation of the specific services offered is little better. Although the message tells what the consultant can do, it is dull. The drive for action is more a hint than a request. The closing words do suggest a benefit for the reader, but the effort is too little too late.

Subject: A plan to increase profits

Ms. Collins,

You have probably heard in the trade about the services I provide to restaurant management. I am now pleased to be able to offer these services to you.

From 12 years of experience, I have learned the details of restaurant management. I know what food costs should be. I know how to find other cost problems, be they on the buying end or the selling end. I know how to design menu offerings for the most profitability. I have studied kitchen operations and organization. And I know how the service must be conducted for best results.

From all this knowledge, I have perfected a simple system for analyzing a restaurant and finding its weaknesses. This I do primarily from guest purchasing records, invoices, and an on-site analysis. As explained on my website (http://www.restaurantimp.com), my system finds the trouble spots. It shows exactly where to correct all problems.

I can provide you with the benefits of my system for only $1,500—$700 now and $800 when you receive my final report on your operations. If you will fill out and return by email the information requested on my website, I will show you how to make more money.

Larry Kopel, Consultant

This me-focused message is short on appealing reader benefits.

skillful presentation of a rational appeal The better message follows the conventional sales pattern described in the preceding pages. Its main appeal is rational, which is justified in this case. Its subject line gains interest with the main claim of the message presented in you-viewpoint language. The beginning sentence continues this appeal with an attention-holding testimonial. The following sentences explain the service quickly—and interestingly. Then, through good you-viewpoint writing, the reader learns what he or she will get from the service. This part is loaded with reader benefits (profits, efficiency, cost cutting). Next, after the selling has been done, the message drives for action. The last sentence ties in the action with its main benefit—making money. A note about how to "unsubscribe" is both courteous and in compliance with U.S. federal law.

PROPOSALS

Proposals share certain characteristics with reports. Both genres require that information be carefully gathered and presented. Visually, they can seem quite similar; at their most formal, they use the same kinds of prefatory material (title page, letter of transmittal, table of contents, and so forth). And proposals sometimes use the direct pattern that most reports use. But proposals differ from reports in one essential way: Proposals are intentionally *persuasive*. Proposal writers are not providing

The you-viewpoint and better details give this message strong appeal.

Subject: A proven cost-analysis system that guarantees you more profits

Ms. Collins,

"Killshaw is adding $35,000 a year to my restaurant's profits!"

With these words, Bill Summers, owner of Boston's famed Pirate's Cove, joined the hundreds of restaurant owners who can point to proof in dollars that my cost-analysis system will add to your profits.

My time-proven plan to help you increase profits is a product of 12 years of intensive research, study, and consulting work with restaurants all over the nation. I found that where food costs exceed 40 percent, staggering amounts slip through restaurant managers' fingers. Then I tracked down the causes of these losses. I can find these trouble spots in your business—and I'll prove this to you in extra income dollars!

To make these extra profits, all you do is send me your guest purchasing records, invoices, and bills for a 30-day period and allow me to observe your operations for one day. After analyzing my findings, I will write you an eye-opening report that will tell you how much money your restaurant should make and how to make it.

From the report, you will learn in detail just what menu items are causing your higher food costs. And you will learn how to correct them. You will know what "best-sellers" are paying their way—and what "poor movers" are eating into your profits. You will also learn how to improve your operational efficiency. All in all, you'll get practical suggestions that will show you how to cut costs, build volume, and pocket a net 10 to 20 percent of sales.

For a more detailed explanation of this service, review the information presented on my website (http://www.restaurantimp.com/). Then let me prove to you, as I have to so many others, that I can add money to your income this year. This added profit can be yours for the modest investment of $1,500 ($700 now and the other $800 when you receive my profit plan report). Just email the information requested on my website and I'll do the rest.

That extra $35,000 or more will make you glad you did!

Larry Kopel, Consultant

You were sent this message because of your interest in the white paper you recently downloaded from our site. If you wish to be removed from our list, please click unsubscribe.

workplace scenario

Writing Proposals

Play the role of Evan Lockley, vice president of account management at Whitfield Organizational Research. Your company collects internal information for businesses that want to improve their management techniques, their information flow, employee morale, work processes, and so forth. To keep a steady stream of clients coming in, Whitfield must write numerous proposals for performing this kind of research.

As the manager of client accounts and the lead proposal writer at Whitfield, you now sit down to write a proposal for RT Industries. This company is about to implement an enterprise resource planning (ERP) system. This implementation will require employees in every functional area of the business—from purchasing to inventory to design, manufacturing, and shipping—to learn the system and enter the data for their area. If the implementation is successful, the management at RT Industries will be able to tell, with the click of a few buttons, exactly how every facet of the business is doing. But implementing such a system is a major, and potentially disastrous, organizational change, and RT knows it. That's why they want to pay an organizational research firm to track the implementation and make sure it's as successful as possible. RT has invited Whitfield, along with other firms, to bid on this job.

You and one of your principal researchers have visited with the implementation team at RT Industries to learn more about the system they've chosen and their particular concerns. Whitfield has experience tracking such organizational changes, so you feel your odds of winning this client are good. But now you need to make your case. How can you craft a proposal that will make as positive an impression as possible? How can you make sure the readers at RT Industries will choose you over the competition? Read on to see how to write a persuasive proposal.

information objectively. They are writing to get a particular result, and they have a vested interest in that result. The following sections provide an introduction to the main types of proposals and offer guidelines for preparing them.

Types of Proposals

Proposals can vary widely in purpose, length, and format. Their purpose can be anything from acquiring a major client to getting a new copier for your department. They can range from one page to hundreds of pages. Their physical format can range from an email message or letter to a long, highly structured report. They are usually written, but they can be presented orally or delivered in both oral and written form. As with other kinds of business communication, the context will determine the specific traits of a given proposal. But all proposals can be categorized as either internal or external, and either solicited or unsolicited (Exhibit 7.2). It is with the unsolicited type that indirect organization is most often used.

internal or external
Proposals can be either *internal* or *external*. That is, they may be written for others within your organization or for readers outside your organization.

The reasons for internal proposals differ, but you will almost surely find yourself having to write them. They are a major means by which you will get what you need in order to do or

▼ **EXHIBIT 7.2** Types of Proposals

- *Internal* or *external*
- *Solicited* or *unsolicited*

enhance your job or to effect an important change in your organization. Whether you want a computer upgrade, an improved physical environment, specialized training, travel money, or additional staff members, you will usually need to make your case to management. Of course, much of what you need as an employee will already be provided by your company. But when resources are tight, as they almost always are, you will have to persuade your superiors to give you the money rather than allocating it to another employee or department. Even if your idea is to enhance company operations in some way—for example, to make a procedure more efficient or cost effective—you may find yourself having to persuade. Companies tend to be conservative in terms of change. The management wants good evidence that the trouble and expense of making a change will pay off.

In addition, as the practice of outsourcing has grown, many companies have adopted a system in which departments have to compete with external vendors for projects. As the director of technical publications for a company, for example, you may find yourself bidding against a technical-writing consulting firm for the opportunity, and the funding, to write the company's online documentation. If you are not persuasive, you may find yourself with a smaller and smaller staff and, eventually, no job yourself. Clearly, the ability to write a persuasive internal proposal is an important skill.

External proposals are also written for a variety of reasons, but the most common purposes are to acquire business for a company or money from a grant-awarding organization. Consulting firms—whether in training, financial services, information technology, or virtually any other business specialty—depend upon external proposals for their livelihood. If such firms cannot persuade companies to choose their services, they will not be in business for long. Companies that supply other companies with goods they need, such as uniforms, computers, or raw materials, may also need to prepare proposals to win clients. Business-to-business selling is a major arena for external proposals.

But external proposals are also central to other efforts. A company might propose to merge with another company; a city government might propose that a major department store choose the city for its new location; a university professor might write a proposal to acquire research funding. Many nonprofit and community organizations depend upon proposals for the grant money to support their work. They might write such proposals to philanthropic foundations, to wealthy individuals, to businesses, or to government funding agencies. Depending on the nature of the organization you work for, proficiency in external proposal writing could be critical.

technology in brief

Visuals Help Business Writers Add Interest to Sales Messages

Sales messages—both print and rich email—often include art and animation to increase their visual appeal as well as attract attention to the message. In one recent experiment comparing two types of visual email messages, an HTML and a video message, Holland America found that the video message resulted in a 33 percent higher click-through rate than the HTML mailing. Furthermore, once readers got to the site, the average stay was nine minutes compared to five minutes for the HTML message. Additionally, the video message was cost effective, costing only 20 percent more than the HTML message.*

Today's business writers need not be artists or professional photographers to use good visuals in their documents. Major software programs include bundled art, animation, photographs, and sounds; and scanners and easy-to-use programs are readily available to help writers create customized visuals. Additionally, on the Web, writers can find a vast assortment of specialists with products and services to help enhance their sales messages.

Here is a short list of a few websites. You'll find more on the textbook website as well.

- http://webclipart.about.com/
  A rich collection of links to websites for clip art, tutorials, hardware, and software.

- http://www.fotosearch.com/
  A meta search tool for finding professional photographs, illustrations, and videos.

- http://www.animationfactory.com/en/
  A subscription website for a variety of professionally prepared media.

- http://www.freeaudioclips.com/
  A site for free audio clips and links to software tools as well as a good search tool.

*Heidi Anderson, "Cruising to E-Mail Results," ClickZ, Incisive Interactive marketing LLC, 10 July 2003, Web, 15 Apr. 2010.

Whether solicited or unsolicited, proposals must do an effective job of presenting a complete picture of what is being proposed. You must work hard to meet readers' needs so readers can make decisions in your favor.

Many nonprofit organizations depend upon grant writing for their survival.

pages, depending upon the scope and complexity of the given project. As you might expect, their contents can also vary. But a lot of thought and research go into a good RFP. In fact, some RFPs—for instance, a company's request for proposals from IT firms to design and implement their technology infrastructure—need to be just as elaborately researched as the proposals being requested. Whatever the originating organization, the RFP needs to include a clear statement of the organization's

> ## "The primary means by which organizations solicit proposals is the request for proposals, or RFP."

solicited or unsolicited Another way to categorize proposals is *solicited* versus *unsolicited*. A solicited proposal is written in response to an explicit invitation from a company, foundation, or government agency that has certain needs to meet or goals to fulfill. An unsolicited proposal, as you can probably guess, is one that you submit without an official invitation to do so.

The primary means by which organizations solicit proposals is the request for proposals, or RFP (variations are requests for quotes—RFQs—and invitations for/to bid—IFBs or ITBs—both of which tend to focus only on price). These can range from brief announcements to documents of 50, 100, or more

need, the proposal guidelines (due date and time, submission process, and proposal format and contents), and the approval process, in addition to such helpful information as background about the organization.

When responding to an RFP, you should be careful to heed its guidelines. With some firms, your proposal gets eliminated if it arrives even one minute late or omits a required section. This is particularly true for proposals to the federal government, whose proposal guidelines are notoriously, and perhaps understandably, regimented (see Exhibit 7.3). On the other hand, most RFPs give you some latitude to craft your proposal in such a way that your organization can put its

With well-written proposals, businesses can win government contracts. But writers must follow the detailed guidelines carefully. The RFP for this relatively simple project is 91 pages long.

best foot forward. You will want to take advantage of this maneuvering room to make your proposal the most persuasive of those submitted. Of course, you will decide in the first place to respond only to those RFPs that give your organization (or, if it is an internal RFP, your department) a fighting chance to win.

In business situations, solicited proposals usually follow preliminary meetings between the parties involved. For example, if a business has a need for certain production equipment, its buyers might first identify likely suppliers by considering those they already know, by looking at industry material, or by asking around in their professional networks. Next they would initiate meetings with these potential suppliers to discuss the business's needs. Some or all of these suppliers would then be invited to submit a proposal for filling the need with its particular equipment. As you can see, the more relationships you have with companies that might use your goods or services, the more likely it is that they will invite you to a preliminary meeting and then invite you to bid. One expert, in fact, asserts that the success of a proposal depends even more on the conversations and relationships that led to the proposal than on the proposal itself.[8] Another advises that "proposals can be won (or lost) before the RFP hits the streets."[9]

Even if you are preparing a proposal for a government or foundation grant, it is wise—unless the RFP specifically forbids it—to call the funding source's office and discuss your ideas with a representative.

When writing unsolicited proposals, your job is harder than with solicited proposals. After all, in these scenarios, the intended reader has not asked for your ideas or services. For this reason, your proposal should resemble a sales message. It should quickly get the readers' attention and bring a need of theirs vividly to mind. It should then show how your product or services will answer the need. And from beginning to end, it should build your credibility. For example, if you want to provide training for a company's workforce, you should target your readers' training needs in the opening, use further details to elaborate on those needs, lay out the benefits of your

And the Most Overused Marketing Cliché Is . . .

In 2006, business author and speaker David Meerman Scott conducted a study to identify the most overused marketing expressions. After consulting with other PR professionals to create a list of candidates, he used Factiva's text-mining tools to look for these words and phrases in news releases issued by North American businesses between January and September.

Here were some of the most overused words and phrases in the 388,000 news releases studied:

Flexible
Robust
Easy to use
Cutting edge
Mission critical
Market leading

World class
Scalable
Industry standard
Turnkey
Groundbreaking

And the winning (or losing) expression? "Next generation."

In 2008, Scott studied 711,123 North American press releases and found that many of these same terms still ranked near the top—

along with "Innovate," "Leading Provider," "Leverage," and other tiresome expressions.

Instead of using this "gobbledygook," Scott advises, just explain in simple terms how your products "solve customer problems."

Sources: "The Gobbledygook Manifesto," *Change This*, 800-CEO-READ, 8 Aug. 2007, Web, 7 Apr. 2009; "Top Gobbledygook Phrases Used in 2008 and How to Avoid Them," *WebInkNow*, David Meerman Scott, 8 Apr. 2008, Web, 15 Apr. 2010.

> To succeed, proposals must be designed with the key decision makers in mind, emphasize the most persuasive elements, and present the contents in a readable format and style.

training plan, and get the readers to believe that yours is the best company for the job. Careful and strategic preparation of unsolicited proposals can result in much success.

As with solicited proposals, you should try, if at all possible, to make prior contact with a person in the organization who has some power to initiate your plan. All other things being equal, a proposal to someone you know is preferable to a "cold" proposal. It is best to view the unsolicited proposal as part of a larger relationship that you are trying to create or maintain.

Proposal Format and Contents

Every proposal is unique, but some generalizations can be made. To succeed, proposals must be designed with the key decision makers in mind, emphasize the most persuasive elements, and present the contents in a readable format and style.

format and formality

The physical arrangement and formality of proposals vary widely. The simplest proposals resemble formal email messages. Internal proposals (those written for and by people in the same organization) usually fall into this category, though exceptions exist. The more complex proposals

Wise Words from a Professional Proposal Writer

A proposal or grant is the beginning of a relationship. Essentially, the readers are interviewing your company or organization, trying to determine whether a basis for a positive, constructive alliance exists. Your proposal is the face you are presenting to the client or funding source. If they feel comfortable with your proposal, they will feel comfortable with your company or organization.

Source: Richard Johnson-Sheehan, *Writing Proposals*, 2nd ed. (New York: Pearson/Longman, 2008) 232–33, print.

may take the form of full-dress, long reports, including prefatory pages (title pages, letter of transmittal, table of contents, executive summary), text, and an assortment of appended parts. Most proposals have arrangements that fall somewhere between these extremes.

Because of the wide variations in the makeup of proposals, you would be wise to investigate carefully before designing a particular proposal. In your investigation, try to determine what format is conventional among those who will read it. Look to

Show your readers that your plan is a perfect fit for them.

see what others have done in similar situations. In the case of an invited proposal, review the request thoroughly, looking for clues to the preferences of the inviting organization. If you are unable to follow any of these courses, design a format based on your analysis of the audience and your knowledge of formatting strategies. Your design should be the one that you think is best for the one situation.

The same advice applies to your decisions about formality. Let your reader and the circumstances be your guide. Internal proposals tend to be less formal than external ones because the parties are often familiar with each other and because internal documents, in general, are less formal than external ones. If you are proposing a major initiative or change, however, using a formal presentation—whether oral, written, or both—may be in order. Likewise, external proposals, while they tend to be formal, can be quite informal if they are short and the two parties know each other well. Many successful business proposals are pitched in letter format. As with every other kind of message, knowledge of and adaptation to your reader are key.

content Whether you are writing an external or internal proposal or a solicited or unsolicited one, your primary goal is the same: to make a persuasive argument. Every element of your proposal—from the title to the cover letter to the headings and organization of your content to your writing style—needs to contribute to your central argument.

To be able to design your proposal according to this principle, you need to know your readers and their needs (which may be represented in an RFP). You also need to know how you can meet those needs. From these two sets of facts, you can develop your central argument. What is your competitive edge? Value for the money? Convenience? Reliability? Fit of your reader's needs or mission with what you have to offer? Some or all of the above? How you frame your argument will depend on how you think your proposal will be evaluated.

The reader of a business proposal will bring three basic criteria to the evaluation process:

- Desirability of the solution (Do we need this? Will it solve our problem?)

- Qualifications of the proposer (Can the author of the proposal, whether an individual or company, really deliver, and on time and on budget?)

- Return on investment (Is the expense, whether time or money, justified?)

If you can answer these three questions affirmatively from the point of view of your intended recipient, you have a good chance of winning the contract or your management's approval.

case illustration
An Internal Unsolicited Proposal (Asking for Funding for a Professional Resource)

This email proposal asks a company to sponsor an employee's membership in a professional organization. Starting with the subject line, the writer tries to avoid saying anything that the reader—in this case, the head of a corporate communications department—would disagree with. When enough background and benefits are given, the writer states the request and then describes the cost in the most positive terms. Offering to try the membership for one year helps the proposal seem relatively modest.

Establishes common ground with the reader

Names topics the reader cares about

After the indirect opening, clearly states the proposal

A comparison puts the cost in a favorable light

Asks for a trial membership— a modest request

Describes the subject in appealing terms

Establishes the credibility and value of the resource

Shows that the writer did his/her homework

Adds more details to show that this resource is a bargain

Costs are clear but are de-emphasized by being in the middle of the section

Explains how the proposal can save money

Ends with confidence and conviction

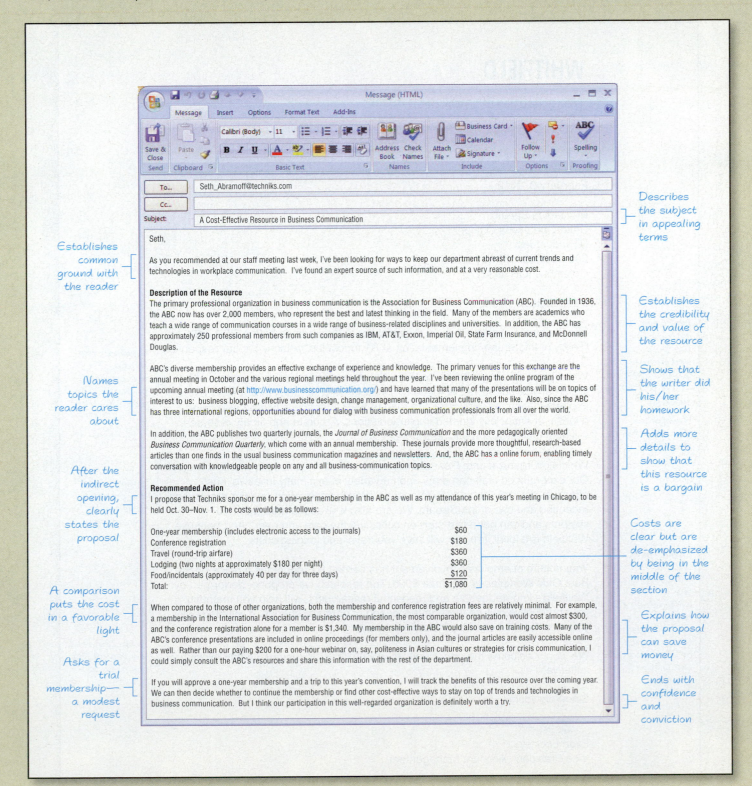

To... Seth_Abramoff@techniks.com

Cc...

Subject: A Cost-Effective Resource in Business Communication

Seth,

As you recommended at our staff meeting last week, I've been looking for ways to keep our department abreast of current trends and technologies in workplace communication. I've found an expert source of such information, and at a very reasonable cost.

Description of the Resource
The primary professional organization in business communication is the Association for Business Communication (ABC). Founded in 1936, the ABC now has over 2,000 members, who represent the best and latest thinking in the field. Many of the members are academics who teach a wide range of communication courses in a wide range of business-related disciplines and universities. In addition, the ABC has approximately 250 professional members from such companies as IBM, AT&T, Exxon, Imperial Oil, State Farm Insurance, and McDonnell Douglas.

ABC's diverse membership provides an effective exchange of experience and knowledge. The primary venues for this exchange are the annual meeting in October and the various regional meetings held throughout the year. I've been reviewing the online program of the upcoming annual meeting (at http://www.businesscommunication.org/) and have learned that many of the presentations will be on topics of interest to us: business blogging, effective website design, change management, organizational culture, and the like. Also, since the ABC has three international regions, opportunities abound for dialog with business communication professionals from all over the world.

In addition, the ABC publishes two quarterly journals, the *Journal of Business Communication* and the more pedagogically oriented *Business Communication Quarterly*, which come with an annual membership. These journals provide more thoughtful, research-based articles than one finds in the usual business communication magazines and newsletters. And, the ABC has a online forum, enabling timely conversation with knowledgeable people on any and all business-communication topics.

Recommended Action
I propose that Techniks sponsor me for a one-year membership in the ABC as well as my attendance of this year's meeting in Chicago, to be held Oct. 30–Nov. 1. The costs would be as follows:

One-year membership (includes electronic access to the journals)	$60
Conference registration	$180
Travel (round-trip airfare)	$360
Lodging (two nights at approximately $180 per night)	$360
Food/incidentals (approximately 40 per day for three days)	$120
Total:	$1,080

When compared to those of other organizations, both the membership and conference registration fees are relatively minimal. For example, a membership in the International Association for Business Communication, the most comparable organization, would cost almost $300, and the conference registration alone for a member is $1,340. My membership in the ABC would also save on training costs. Many of the ABC's conference presentations are included in online proceedings (for members only), and the journal articles are easily accessible online as well. Rather than our paying $200 for a one-hour webinar on, say, politeness in Asian cultures or strategies for crisis communication, I could simply consult the ABC's resources and share this information with the rest of the department.

If you will approve a one-year membership and a trip to this year's convention, I will track the benefits of this resource over the coming year. We can then decide whether to continue the membership or find other cost-effective ways to stay on top of trends and technologies in business communication. But I think our participation in this well-regarded organization is definitely worth a try.

A Solicited External Proposal (Selling Research Services)

A design and manufacturing company has invited research firms to propose plans for tracking its implementation of an enterprise resource planning (ERP) system—information technology that integrates all functions of the company, from job orders to delivery and from accounting to customer management. The midlevel formality of this proposal responding to the RFP is appropriate given the proposal's relative brevity and the two parties' prior meeting.

WHITFIELD
Organizational Research

7 Research Parkway, Columbus, OH 45319 614-772-4000 Fax: 614-772-4001
www.whitfieldresearch.com

February 3, 2012

Ms. Janice Spears
Chief Operations Officer
RT Industries
200 Midland Highway
Columbus, OH 45327

Dear Janice:

Identifies the context for the proposal and shows appreciation for being invited to submit.

Thank you for inviting Whitfield Organizational Research to bid on RFP 046, "Study of InfoStream Implementation at RT Industries." Attached is our response.

Reminds the reader of the previous, pleasant meeting.

Reinforces the need for the study.

We enjoyed meeting with you to learn about your goals for this research. All expert advice supports the wisdom of your decision to track InfoStream's implementation. As you know, the road of ERP adoption is littered with failed, chaotic, or financially bloated implementations. Accurate and timely research will help make yours a success story.

Whitfield Organizational Research is well qualified to assist you with this project. Our experienced staff can draw upon a variety of minimally invasive, cost-effective research techniques to acquire reliable information on your employees' reception and use of InfoStream. We are also well acquainted with ERP systems and can get a fast start on collecting the data you need. And because Whitfield is a local firm, we will save you travel and lodging costs.

Summarizes the proposing company's advantages.

Compliments the receiving company, shows the writer's knowledge of the company, and states the benefits of choosing the writer's company.

Your culture of employee involvement has earned RT Industries a place on the Best Ohio Workplaces list since 2006. The research we propose, performed by Whitfield's knowledgeable and respectful researchers, will help you maintain your productive culture through this period of dramatic change. It will also help you reap the full benefits of your investment.

We would welcome the opportunity to work with RT Industries on this exciting initiative.

Indirectly asks the reader for the desired action.

Sincerely yours,

Evan Lockley

Evan Lockley
Vice President, Account Management

enclosure

Response to RFP 046:
Study of InfoStream Implementation at RT Industries

Proposed by
Whitfield Organizational Research
February 3, 2012

Executive Summary

Provides a clear overview of the problem, purpose, and benefits.

RT Industries has begun a major organizational change with its purchase of InfoStream enterprise resource planning (ERP) software. To track the effect of this change on personnel attitudes and work processes in the company, RT seeks the assistance of a research firm with expertise in organizational studies.

Whitfield Organizational Research has extensive experience with personnel-based research, as well as familiarity with ERP software. We propose a four-part plan that will take place across the first year of implementation. It will yield three major deliverables: an initial, a midyear, and a year-end report. Our methodology will be multifaceted, minimally disruptive, and cost effective.

The results will yield a reliable picture of how InfoStream is being received and used among RT's workforce. Whitfield can also advise RT management on appropriate interventions during the process to enhance the success of this companywide innovation.

Project Goals

RT Industries has so far invested over $1.6 million and over 1,000 employee hours in the purchase of and management's training on InfoStream's ERP system. As RT integrates the system fully into its company of 800+ employees over the next 12 months, it will invest many additional dollars and hours in the project, with the total investment likely to top $2 million. Adopting such a system is one of the most wide-ranging and expensive changes a company can make.

Shows knowledge of the company; reminds readers of the investment they want to protect.

Reinforces the need for the study.

As Jeri Dunn, Chief Information Officer of Nestle USA, commented in *CIO Magazine* about her company's well-publicized troubles with their ERP software, "No major software implementation is really about the software. It's about change management." An ERP system affects the daily work of virtually everyone in the company. The most common theme in ERP-adoption failure stories—of which there are many—is lack of attention to the employees' experience of the transition. Keeping a finger on the pulse of the organization during this profound organizational change is critical to maximizing the return on your investment.

Our research will determine

- How well employees are integrating InfoStream into their jobs.
- How the new system is changing employees' work processes.
- How the system is affecting the general environment or "culture" in the company.

Statement of benefits, supported by clear logic.

Whitfield has designed a four-part, multimethod research plan to gather these data. Through our periodic reports, you will be able to see how InfoStream is

Whitfield Organizational Research

being integrated into the working life of the company. As a result, you will be able to make, and budget for, such interventions as strategic communications and additional training. You will also find out where employee work processes need to be adjusted to accommodate the new system.

Instituting a change of this magnitude *will* generate feedback, whether it is employee grumbling or constructive criticism. Whitfield associates will gather this feedback in a positive, orderly way and compile it into a usable format. The findings will enable RT's management to address initial problems and ward off future problems. The research itself will also contribute to the change management efforts of the company by giving RT's employee stakeholders a voice in the process and allowing their feedback to contribute to the initiative's success.

Deliverables

The information you need will be delivered as shown below. All dates assume a project start date of July 1, 2012.

Readers can see the products of the proposed research up front.

Approximate Date:	Deliverable:
October 1, 2012	Written report on **initial** study of 12–14 employees' work processes and attitudes and on companywide survey.
February 1, 2013	Written report at **midyear** on employees' work processes and attitudes and on companywide survey.
June 30, 2013	**Year-end** report (written and oral) on employees' work processes and attitudes and on companywide survey.

Anticipated Schedule/Methods

The research will take place from July 1, 2012, the anticipated go-live date for InfoStream at RT, to approximately June 30, 2013, a year later. As shown below, there will be four main components to this research, with Part III forming the major part of the project.

Gives details of the project in a readable format.

Research Part and Time Frame	Purpose	Methods
Part I (July '12)	Gather background information; recruit research participants	Gather data on RT (history, products/mission, organizational structure/culture, etc.). Interview personnel at RT and at InfoStream about why RT considered adopting an ERP system, why RT bought InfoStream, and how employees at RT have been informed about InfoStream. During this period we will also work with the COO's staff to recruit participants for the main part of the study (Part III).

Whitfield Organizational Research   3

Research Part and Time Frame	Purpose	Methods
Part II (July '12):	Obtain the perspective of the launch team on InfoStream	Focus-group interview with RT's launch team for InfoStream, with emphasis on their goals for and concerns about the implementation. Anticipated duration of this interview would be one hour, with participants invited to share any additional feedback afterward in person or by email.
Part III (July–Sept. '12; Nov. '12–Jan. '13; Mar.–May '13):	Assess the impact of InfoStream on employee work processes and attitudes	Conduct three rounds of 1–2 hour interviews with approximately 12–14 RT employees to track their use of InfoStream. Ideally, we will have one or two participants from each main functional area of the company, with multiple levels of the company represented.
Part IV (September '12, January '13, May '13)	Assess companywide reception of InfoStream	Conduct three Web-based surveys during the year to track general attitudes about the implementation of InfoStream.

This plan yields the following time line:

	7/12	8/12	9/12	10/12	11/12	12/12	1/13	2/13	3/13	4/13	5/13	6/13
Initial research	▓											
Focus group	▓											
1st round of interviews	▓	▓	▓									
1st web survey			▓									
Initial report				▓								
2nd round of interviews					▓	▓	▓					
2nd web survey							▓					
Mid-year report								▓				
3rd round of interviews									▓	▓	▓	
3rd web survey											▓	
Year-end report												▓

Time line makes it easy to see what will happen at each point.

Whitfield Organizational Research

Interview Structure and Benefits

While Parts I, II, and IV will provide essential information about the project and its reception, the most valuable data will come from Part III, the on-site interviews with selected RT employees. Gathering data in and about the subject's own work context is the only reliable way to learn what is really happening in terms of the employees' daily experience. Following is a description of our methodology for gathering these kinds of data:

Initial interview:

- Gather background information about the participants (how long they have worked at RT, what their jobs consist of, what kind of computer experience they've had, how they were trained on InfoStream).

- Ask them to show us, by walking us through sample tasks, how they use InfoStream.

- Ask them to fill out a questionnaire pertaining to their use of InfoStream.

- Go back over their answers, asking them to explain orally why they chose the answers they did.

- Ask them either to keep notes on or email us about any notable experiences they have with InfoStream.

- Take notes on any interruption, interactions, and other activities that occur during the interview.

Special section elaborates on the company's unique methodology; helps justify the most expensive part of the plan.

From data gained in these interviews, we will assess how well the participants' current work processes are meshing with InfoStream. We will also document how use of InfoStream is affecting the participants' attitudes and their interactions with other employees and departments. We will check our findings with the participants for accuracy before including these data in the initial report.

Midyear interview:

- Ask the participants if they have any notable experiences to relate about InfoStream and/or if any changes have occurred in the tasks they perform using InfoStream.

- Have the participants fill out the same questionnaire as in the first interviews.

- Discuss with participants the reasons for any changes in their answers since the first questionnaire.

- Observe any interactions or other activities that occur during the interview.

- Check our findings with the participants for accuracy before including these data in the midyear report.

Year-end interviews:

- Will be conducted in the same fashion as the second interviews.

- Will also include questions allowing participants to debrief about the project and about InfoStream in general.

Benefits of this interview method:

- Because researchers will be physically present in the employees' work contexts, they **can gather a great deal of information,** whether observed or reported by the employee, **in a short amount of time.**

- Because employees will be asked to elaborate on their written answers, the researcher **can learn the true meaning of the employees' responses.**

Whitfield Organizational Research   **5**

- Asking employees to verify the researcher's findings **will add another validity check and encourage honest, thorough answers.**

Specific Knowledge Goals

We will design the interviews and the companywide surveys to find out the extent to which

- InfoStream is making participants' jobs easier or harder, or easier in some ways and harder in others.
- InfoStream is making their work more or less efficient.
- InfoStream is making their work more or less effective.
- They believe InfoStream is helping the company overall.
- They are satisfied with the instruction they have received about the system.
- InfoStream is changing their interactions with other employees.
- InfoStream is changing their relations with their supervisors.
- InfoStream is affecting their overall attitude toward their work.

The result will be a detailed, reliable picture of how InfoStream is playing out at multiple levels and in every functional area of RT Industries, enabling timely intervention by RT management.

A tantalizing list of what the readers most want to know whets their desire to hire the proposing company.

Cost

Because we are a local firm, no travel or lodging expenses will be involved.

Research Component	Estimated Hours	Cost
Part I (background fact finding)	6 hours	$300
Part II (focus group with launch team)	3 hours (includes preparation and analysis)	$300
Part III (3 rounds of on-site interviews)	474 hours	$18,960
Part IV (3 rounds of web-based surveys)	48 hours	$1,920
Preparation of Reports	90 hours	$3,600
		Total: $25,080

Cost breakdown justifies the expense but is not so detailed that the readers can nitpick specific items.

Credentials

Whitfield Organizational Research has been recognized by the American Society for Training and Development as a regional leader in organizational consulting. We have extensive education and experience in change management, organizational psychology, quantitative and qualitative research methods, and team building. Our familiarity with ERP software, developed through projects with such clients as Orsys and PRX Manufacturing, makes us well suited to serve RT's needs. Résumés and references will be mailed upon request or can be downloaded from <www.whitfieldresearch.com>.

Efficient credentials section focuses only on those qualifications that are relevant to this situation.

When your proposal is uninvited, the challenge is harder.

When you have figured out what to propose and why, you need to figure out how to propose it. If the RFP provides strict guidelines for contents and organization, follow them. Otherwise, you have considerable discretion when determining your proposal's components. Although the number of content possibilities is great, you should consider including the eight topics listed below. They are broad and general, and you can combine or subdivide them as needed to fit the facts of your case. (See page 185 and pages 186–191 for two very different examples.)

1. *Writer's purpose and the reader's need.* An appropriate beginning is a statement of the writer's purpose (to present a proposal) and the reader's need (such as reducing turnover of field representatives). If the report is in response to an invitation, that statement should tie in with the invitation (for example, "as described in your July 10 announcement"). This proposal beginning illustrates these recommendations:

As requested at the July 10 meeting with Alice Burton, Thomas Cheny, and Victor Petrui in your Calgary office, Murchison and Associates present the following proposal for studying the high rate of turnover among your field representatives. We will assess the job satisfaction of the current sales force, analyze exit interview records, and compare company compensation and human resource practices with industry norms to identify the causes of this drain on your resources.

If a proposal is submitted without invitation, its beginning has an additional requirement: it must gain attention. As noted previously, uninvited proposals are much like sales messages. Their intended readers are not likely to be eager to read them. Thus, their beginnings must overcome the readers' reluctance.

> "Describing the reader's problem in ways that lead to your proposed solution helps your persuasive effort."

An effective start is to briefly summarize the highlights of the proposal with emphasis on its benefits. This technique is illustrated by the beginning of an unsolicited proposal that a consultant sent to prospective clients:

Is your social-marketing strategy working?

Twitter, blogs, Facebook, Linked In, online forums . . . such tools have come upon us very fast, and more are coming. Are you making the best use of them?

Using a three-step social-media audit, Mattox and Associates can find out. With access to your media and just one day of on-site interviews, our experts will tell you . . . [the rest of the proposal follows].

Your clear statement of the purpose and problem may be the most important aspect of the proposal. If you do not show right away that you understand what needs to be done and have a good plan for doing it, you may well have written the rest of your proposal in vain.

2. *Background.* A review of background information promotes an understanding of the problem. Thus, a college's proposal for an educational grant might benefit from a review of the college's involvement in the area to which the grant would be applied. A company's proposal of a merger with another company might review industry developments that make the merger desirable. Or a chief executive officer's proposal to the board of directors that a company be reorganized might present the background information that justifies the proposal.

3. *Need.* Closely related to the background information is the need for what is being proposed. In fact, background information may well be used to establish need. But because need can be presented without such support, we list it separately. You might wonder if this section applies in situations where an RFP has been issued. In such cases, won't readers already know what they need? In many cases the answer is no, not exactly. They may think they know, but you may see factors that they've overlooked. Plus, recasting their problem in ways that lead to your proposed solution helps your persuasive effort. And whatever the situation, elaborating on the receiving organization's needs enables your readers to see that *you* understand their needs.

4. *Description of plan.* The heart of a proposal is the description of what the writer proposes to do. This is the primary message of the proposal. It should be concisely presented in a clear and orderly manner, with headings and subheadings as needed. It should give sufficient detail to convince the reader of the plan's logic, feasibility, and appropriateness. It should also identify the "deliverables," or tangible products, of the proposal.

5. *Benefits of the proposal.* Your readers should easily be able to see how your proposed action will benefit them. A brief statement of the benefits should appear at the front of your proposal, whether in the letter of transmittal, executive

summary, opening paragraph, or all of the above. But you should elaborate on those benefits in the body of your proposal. You might do so in the section describing your plan, showing how each part will yield a benefit. Or you might have a separate section detailing the benefits. As with sales writing, the greater the need to persuade, the more you should stress the benefits.

As an example of benefits logically covered in proposals, a college's request for funding to establish a program for retraining the older worker could point to the profitability that such funding would give local businesses. And a proposal offering a consulting service to restaurants could stress such benefits as improved work efficiency, reduced employee theft, savings in food costs, and increased profits.

6. *Cost and other particulars*. Once you have pitched your plan, you need to state clearly what it will cost. You may also need to cover such other particulars as time schedules, performance standards, means of appraising performance, equipment and supplies needed, guarantees, personnel requirements, and the like. Remember that a proposal is essentially a contract. Anticipate and address any issues that may arise, and present your requirements in the most positive light.

7. *Evidence of ability to deliver*. The proposing organization must sometimes establish its ability to perform. This means presenting information on such matters as the qualifications of personnel, success in similar cases, the adequacy of equipment and facilities, operating procedures, environmental consciousness, and financial status. Whatever information will serve as evidence of the organization's ability to achieve what it proposes should be used. With an external proposal, resist the temptation to include long, generic résumés. The best approach is to select only the most persuasive details about your personnel. If you do include résumés, tailor them to the situation.

8. *Concluding comments*. In most proposals you should urge or suggest the desired action. This statement often occurs in a letter to the readers, but if there is no cover letter or the proposal itself is not a letter, it can form the conclusion of your proposal. You might also include a summary of your proposal's highlights or provide one final persuasive push in a concluding section.

Whatever you're writing—whether a proposal, request, sales message, or some other kind of message—the art of persuasion can be one of your most valuable assets. Adding the tips in this chapter to your problem-solving tools will help you prepare for all those times in your career when you will need others' cooperation and support. ■

© 2005 Ted Goff
www.tedgoff.com

new & Improved

"We need something to come after this part. Any ideas?"

researching + writing reports

How often you write reports in the years ahead will depend on the size and nature of the organization you work for. If you work for an organization with fewer than 10 employees, you will probably write only a few. But if you work for a midsize or larger organization, you are likely to write many. The larger the organization, the greater its complexity; and the greater the complexity, the greater the need for information to manage the organization.

The nature of the business can also influence the number and type of reports you will write. The Securities and Exchange Commission requires all publicly traded businesses to write certain financial reports at regular intervals. A consulting firm's main products are informational and advisory reports to its clients. A business performing work under government contracts will also have special reporting needs. The frequency with which you will write reports and the kinds you will write will depend on your employer. But you can be fairly certain that report writing will figure significantly in your business career. ■

workplace scenario

Introduce yourself to the subject of report writing by assuming the role of administrative assistant to the president of Technisoft, Inc. Much of your work at this large software company involves getting information for your boss. Yesterday, for example, you looked into the question of excessive time spent by office workers on Web surfing. A few days earlier, you worked on an assignment to determine the causes of unrest in one of the local branches. Before that assignment you investigated a supervisor's recommendation to change an evaluation process. You could continue the list indefinitely because investigating problems is a part of your work.

So is report writing because you must research and write a report on each of your investigations. You write these reports for good reasons. Written reports make permanent records. Thus, those who need the information contained in these reports can review and study them at their convenience. Written reports also can be routed to a number of readers with little effort. Unquestionably, such reports are a convenient and efficient means of transmitting information.

Your report-writing work is not unique to your job. In fact, report writing is common throughout the company. For example, the engineers often report on the technical problems they encounter. The accountants regularly report to management on the company's financial operations. From time to time, production people report on various aspects of operations. The salespeople regularly report on marketing matters. And so it is throughout the company. Such reporting is vital to your company's operations—as it is to the operations of all companies.

Writing to external audiences can also be critical to an organization's success. If the organization is a consulting firm, reports to the client may be its primary deliverable. If the company is publicly traded, it is required by law to publish financial reports to the government and to shareholders. Depending on the nature of its business, a company may have to research and write reports for various agencies about its impact on the environment, its hiring practices, or its compliance with quality standards.

Sometimes reports are written by individuals. Increasingly, however, they are prepared in collaboration with others. Even if one person has primary responsibility for a report, he or she will often need contributions from many people. Indeed, report writing draws on a wide variety of communication skills, from getting information to presenting it clearly.

This chapter and the following chapter will help you prepare for this vital form of business communication.

DEFINING REPORTS

You probably have a good idea of what reports are. Even so, you would be likely to have a hard time defining them. Even scholars' definitions range from one extreme to the other. Some define reports to include almost any presentation of information; others limit reports to only the most formal presentations. We use this middle-ground definition: *A business report is an orderly and objective communication of factual information that serves a business purpose.*

As an *orderly* communication, a report is prepared carefully. This care in their preparation distinguishes reports from casual exchanges of information. The *objective* quality of a report is its unbiased approach. Reports seek to present facts, and they avoid human biases as much as possible. The word *communication* in our definition is broad in meaning. It covers all ways of transmitting meaning: speaking, writing, using visuals, or a combination.

The basic ingredient of all reports is *factual information*. Factual information is based on events, statistics, and other data. Keep in mind that not all reports are business reports. Research scientists, medical doctors, ministers, students, and many others write them. To be classified as a business report, a report must *serve a business purpose.*

This definition is specific enough to be meaningful yet broad enough to account for the variations in reports. For example, some reports (information reports) do nothing more than present facts. Others (analytical reports) go a step further by including interpretations, sometimes accompanied by conclusions. Recommendation reports go further yet, presenting advice for future action. Some reports are highly formal both in writing style and in physical

> " To be classified as a business report, a report must *serve a business purpose.* "

appearance. And some reports are highly informal. Our definition permits all of these variations.

DETERMINING THE REPORT PROBLEM

Your work on a report logically begins with a need, which we refer to generally as the *problem* in the following discussion. Someone or some group (usually your superiors) needs information for a business purpose. Perhaps the need is for information only; perhaps it is for information and analysis; or perhaps it is for information, analysis, and recommendations. Whatever the case, someone with a need (problem) will authorize you to do the work. The work may be authorized orally or in writing.

After you have been assigned a report problem, your first task should be to get your problem clearly in mind. Elementary as this task may appear, all too often it is done haphazardly, which prevents a report from achieving its goal.

The Preliminary Investigation

Getting your problem clearly in mind is largely a matter of gathering all the information needed to understand it and then applying your best logic to it. Gathering the right information can involve many tasks depending on the problem. It may mean gathering material from company files, talking over the problem with experts, searching through print and digital sources, and discussing the problem with those who authorized the report. In general, you should continue this preliminary investigation until you have the information you need to understand your problem.

LO 1 State a problem and purpose clearly in writing.

Need for Clear Problem and Purpose Statements

Most reports contain a statement of the report's *problem* as well as its *purpose*. Clear problem and purpose statements are important for you as you plan and write the report and for those who receive the report.

For you, they serve as a touchstone, keeping you on track as you continue through the project. In addition, these statements can be reviewed, approved, and evaluated by people whose assistance may be valuable. Most important, putting the problem and purpose in writing forces you to think them through. Keep in mind, though, that no matter how clearly you try to frame the problem and your research purpose, your conception of them may change as you continue your investigation. As in other types of business writing, report writing often involves revisiting earlier steps (*recursivity*), as discussed in Chapter 2.

In your completed report, the problem and purpose statements will be an essential component of the report's introduction and such front matter as the letter of transmittal and executive summary; they will orient your readers and let them know where your report is headed.

The problem statement provides a clear presentation of your reason or motivation for writing the report. Problem statements are generally written as declarative statements: "Sales are decreasing at company."

But the problem statement is not the only statement that will guide your research. You will also need to write a purpose statement (also called the study's *objective*, *aim*, or *goal*). The purpose statement is often written in the form of a question or infinitive phrase. Thus, if your problem is that Company X wants to know why sales are decreasing, your purpose statement may be "to determine the causes of decreasing sales at Company X" or "What are the causes of decreasing sales at Company X?"

LO 2   List the factors involved in a problem.

DETERMINING THE FACTORS

After stating the problem, you look for the factors you must research in order to solve the problem.

Factors may be of three types. First, they may be subtopics of the overall topic about which the report is concerned. Second, they may be hypotheses that must be tested. Third, in reports that involve comparisons, they may be the bases on which the comparisons are made.

Hypotheses for Problems Requiring a Solution

Some reports concern why something bad is happening and perhaps how to correct it. In analyzing problems of this kind, you should seek explanations or solutions. Such explanations or solutions are termed *hypotheses*. Once formulated, hypotheses are tested, and their applicability to the problem is either proved or disproved.

To illustrate, assume that you have the problem of determining why sales at a certain store have declined. In preparing to investigate this problem, you would think of the possible explanations (hypotheses) for the decline. Your task would be one of studying, weighing, and selecting, and you would brainstorm such explanations as these:

Purpose statement: **To find out why sales at the Springfield store have declined.**

Hypotheses:
1. **Activities of the competition have caused the decline.**
2. **Changes in the economy of the area have caused the decline.**
3. **Merchandising deficiencies have caused the decline.**
4. **Changes in the environment (population shifts, political actions, etc.) have caused the decline.**

[After stating the problem, you look for the factors you must research in order to solve the problem.]

Use of Subtopics in Information Reports

If the problem concerns a need for information, you should determine the main areas about which information is needed. Illustrating this type of situation is a report that reviews Company X's activities during the past quarter. Clearly, this is an informational report—that is, it requires no analysis, no conclusion, no recommendation. It requires only that information be presented. The mental effort in this case is to determine which subdivisions of the overall topic should be covered. After thoroughly evaluating the possibilities, you might develop a plan like this:

Purpose statement: **To review operations of Company X from January 1 through March 31.**

Subtopics:
1. **Production**
2. **Sales and promotion**
3. **Financial status**
4. **Information technology**
5. **Product development**
6. **Human resources**

In the investigation that follows, you would test these hypotheses. You might find that one, two, or all apply. Or you might find that none are valid. If so, you would have to develop additional hypotheses for further evaluation.

Bases of Comparison in Evaluation Studies

When the problem concerns evaluating something, either singularly or in comparison with other things, you should look for the bases for the evaluation. That is, you should determine what characteristics you will evaluate. In some cases, the procedure may concern more than naming the characteristics. It also may include the criteria to be used in evaluating them.

Illustrating this technique is the problem for a company that seeks to determine which of three cities would be best for expansion. Such a problem obviously involves a comparison of the cities. The bases for comparison are the factors that determine success for the type of work involved. After a careful mental search for these factors, you might come up with a plan such as this:

Purpose statement (infinitive form): **To determine whether Y Company's new location should be built in City A, City B, or City C.**

> # SECONDARY RESEARCH MATERIALS ARE POTENTIALLY THE LEAST COSTLY, THE MOST ACCESSIBLE, AND THE MOST COMPLETE SOURCES OF INFORMATION. "

Report writing requires hard work and clear thinking in every stage of the process. To determine your problem and purpose and gather facts, you may need to consult many sources of information.

Comparison bases:
1. **Availability of skilled workers**
2. **Tax structure**
3. **Community attitude**
4. **Transportation facilities**
5. **Nearness to markets**

Each of the factors selected for investigation may have factors of its own. In the last illustration, for example, the comparison of transportation in the three cities may well include such subdivisions as water, rail, truck, and air. Workers may be compared by using such categories as skilled workers and unskilled workers or union and nonunion workers. Breakdowns of this kind may go still further. Skilled workers may be broken down by specific skills: engineers, programmers, technical writers, and graphic designers. The subdivisions could go on and on. Make them as long as they continue to be helpful.

LO 3 Explain the difference between primary and secondary research.

GATHERING THE INFORMATION NEEDED

You can collect the information you need for your report by using two basic forms of research: secondary research and primary research. Secondary research is research utilizing material that someone else has published in such resources as periodicals, brochures, books, and digital publications. This research may be the first form of research that you use in the preliminary investigation. Primary research is research that uncovers information firsthand. It is research that produces new findings such as surveys, interviews, and observations.

To be effective as a report writer, you should be familiar with the techniques of both secondary and primary research. The following pages describe these techniques.

LO 4 Gather secondary sources using direct and indirect research methods.

Conducting Secondary Research

Once you have determined the factors of your report, the first step in an orderly search for information is usually to collect the secondary information.

Secondary research materials are potentially the least costly, the most accessible, and the most complete sources of information. However, to take full advantage of the available materials, you must know what you are looking for and where and how to find it.

The task can be complex and challenging. You can meet the challenge if you become familiar with the general arrangement of a library or other repositories of secondary materials and if you learn the techniques of finding those materials. Also, research must be orderly if it is to be reliable and complete.

In the past, researchers used a card system to help them keep track of the sources they identified. This card system could be combined with and adapted to a computer system quite easily. The manual system of organization required that the researcher complete two sets of cards. One set was simply a bibliography card set, containing complete information about sources. A researcher numbered these cards consecutively as the sources were identified. A second set of cards contained the notes from each source. Each of these cards was linked to its source through the number of the source in the bibliography card set.

Since the computer systems in today's libraries often allow users to print, download, email, or transfer directly the citations they find from the indexes and databases, it makes sense to identify each with a unique number rather than recopy the source to a card. Not only is the resulting list more legible than one's handwriting, but it is also complete. Some researchers cut their printouts apart and tape them to a master sheet. Others enter these items in databases they build. And still others export items directly into specialty databases, letting the software organize and number them. With the widespread use of notebook and laptop computers, most researchers now take notes on computers rather than cards. These notes can be linked to the original source by number as in the manual system.

certain basic reference materials, you may be able to proceed directly to the information you seek. And if the direct approach does not work, there are several effective indirect methods of finding the material you need.

Taking the direct approach is advisable when you seek quantitative or factual information. The reference section of your library is where you should start. There, either on your own or with the assistance of a research librarian, you can discover any number of timely and comprehensive sources of facts and figures. Although you cannot know all these sources, as a business researcher you should be familiar with certain basic ones. These sources are available in either print or digital forms. You should be able to use both.

Encyclopedias Encyclopedias are the best-known sources of direct information and are particularly valuable when you are just beginning a search. They offer background material and other general information that give you a helpful introduction

> ## "Whether you use a manual, combined, or computer system for conducting secondary research, using an orderly system is essential."

Whether you use a manual, computer, or combined system for conducting secondary research, using an orderly system is essential.

To find secondary information efficiently, you can either go directly to it or go indirectly by starting with a resource that points or links you to it. To go directly to the information you need, you'll need to know both the kind of information you need and what kind of resource has that information. The next section covers the common types of direct sources before looking at ways to gather information indirectly.

taking the direct approach When you have determined the appropriate types of information for your research, you are ready for the next challenge. With the volume of material available, how will you find it? Many cost-conscious businesses are hiring professionals to find information for them. These professionals' charges range from $60 to $120 per hour in addition to any online charges incurred. Other companies like to keep their information gathering more confidential; some employ company librarians, and others expect their employees to gather the information. If you know little about how material is arranged in a library or online, you will waste valuable time on a probably fruitless search. However, if you are familiar with

to the area under study. Individual articles or sections of articles are written by experts in the field and frequently include a short bibliography.

Of the general encyclopedias, two worthy of special mention are *Encyclopedia Americana* and *Encyclopaedia Britannica*. *Britannica* online now requires a subscription at <britannica.com>. Others that are widely used are *Wikipedia* and *Infoplease*. Also helpful are such specialized encyclopedias as the *Encyclopedia of Banking and Finance and Insurance*, the *Encyclopedia of Business and Finance*, the *Encyclopedia of Small Business*, the *Concise Encyclopedia of Advertising*, the *Encyclopedia of Emerging Industries*, the *Encyclopedia of Macroeconomics*, and *Worldmark Encyclopedia of the Nations*.

Biographical directories A direct source of biographical information about leading figures of today or of the past is a biographical directory. The best-known biographical directories are *Who's Who in America* and *Who's Who in the World*, annual publications that summarize the lives of living people who have achieved prominence. Similar publications provide coverage by geographic area—*Who's Who in the East* and *Who's Who in the South and Southwest*, for example. For biographical information about prominent Americans of the past, the *Dictionary of American Biography* is useful. You also can find biographical information under the reference section of *LexisNexis Academic Universe* (see Exhibit 8.1). In addition to links to biographical directories, links to news stories about the person also are provided.

Specialized publications will help you find information on people in particular professions. Among the most important of these are *Who's Who in Finance and Industry*; *Standard & Poor's Register of Corporations, Directors, and Executives*; *Who's Who in Insurance*; and *Who's Who in Technology*. Nearly all business and professional areas are covered by some form of biographical directory.

Almanacs Almanacs are handy guides to factual and statistical information. Simple, concise, and selective in their presentation of data, they should not be underestimated as references. *The World Almanac and Book of Facts,* published by Funk & Wagnalls, is an excellent general source of facts and statistics. The *Time Almanac* is another excellent source for a broad range of statistical data. One of its strongest areas is information on the world. The *New York Times Almanac* presents much of its data in tables. It has excellent coverage of business and the economy.

Almanacs are available online as well. Infoplease.com offers broad coverage of topics, including a business section at <http://www.infoplease.com/almanacs.html>.

Trade directories For information about individual businesses or the products they make, buy, or sell, directories are the references to consult. Directories compile details in specific areas of interest and are variously referred to as *catalogs, listings, registers,* or *source books.* Two of the more comprehensive directories indispensable in general business research are *The Million Dollar Directory* (a listing of U.S. companies compiled by Dun & Bradstreet), and *Thomas-Net* (a listing of manufacturers, distributors, and service providers free on the Web at <http://www.thomasnet.com>). Directories that will help you determine links between parent entities and their subsidiaries include *America's Corporate Families* and *Who Owns Whom* (both compiled by Dun & Bradstreet) as well as the

▼ **EXHIBIT 8.1** Biographical Information on Lexis/Nexis

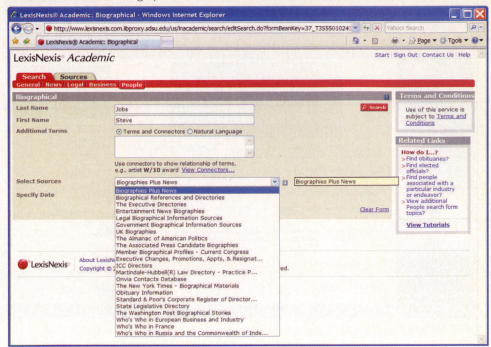

Today you can conduct much secondary research online by accessing a variety of databases, directories, and Internet sites.

The U.S. Census Bureau is a rich source of business information that is easily accessible.

Publications, a monthly list of general-interest publications that are sold to the public.

Routinely available are a number of specialized government publications that are invaluable in business research. These include *Census of Population and Housing, Annual Housing Survey, Consumer Income, Population Characteristics, Census of Governments, Census of Retail and Wholesale Trade, Census of Manufacturers, Census of Agriculture, Census of Construction Industries, Census of Transportation, Census of Service Industries,* and *Census of Mineral Industries.* The *Statistical Abstract of the United States* is another invaluable publication, as are the *Survey of Current Business,* the *Monthly Labor Review,* the *Occupational Outlook Quarterly,* and the

> # Because dictionaries reflect usage, you want to be sure the one you use is current.

Directory of Corporate Affiliations. Thousands of directories exist—so many, in fact, that there is a directory called *Directories in Print.*

Government publications Governments (national, state, local, etc.) publish hundreds of thousands of titles each year. In fact, the U.S. government is the world's largest publisher. Surveys, catalogs, pamphlets, periodicals—there seems to be no limit to the information that various bureaus, departments, and agencies collect and make available to the public. The challenge of working with government publications, therefore, is finding your way through this wealth of material to the specifics you need. That task sometimes can be so complex as to require indirect research methods. However, if you are familiar with a few key sources, the direct approach will often produce good results.

In the United States, it may be helpful to consult the *Monthly Catalog of U.S. Government Publications.* Issued by the Superintendent of Documents, it includes a comprehensive listing of annual and monthly publications and an alphabetical index of the issuing agencies. It can be searched online at <http://www.gpoaccess.gov/databases/>. The Superintendent of Documents also issues *Selected United States Government*

Federal Reserve Bulletin. To say the least, government sources are extensive.

Dictionaries Dictionaries are helpful for looking up meanings, spellings, and pronunciations of words or phrases. Electronic dictionaries add other options; they include pronunciation in audio files and let you find words when you know the meaning only. Dictionaries are available in both general and specialized versions. While it might be nice to own an unabridged dictionary, an abridged collegiate or desk dictionary will answer most of your questions.

You should be aware that the name *Webster* can be legally used by any dictionary publisher. Also, dictionaries often include added features such as style manuals, signs, symbols, and weights and measures. Because dictionaries reflect usage, you want to be sure the one you use is current. Not only are new words being added, but spellings and meanings change, too.

Several good dictionaries are the *American Heritage Dictionaries,* the *Random House Webster's College Dictionary,* and *Merriam-Webster's Collegiate Dictionary.* To have the most current dictionary available at your fingertips, you may want to subscribe to one such as Merriam-Webster at <http://www.m-w.com/>.

Specialized dictionaries concentrate on one functional area. Some business dictionaries are the *Dictionary of Business Terms, The Blackwell Encyclopedic Dictionary of Management Information Systems, The Blackwell Encyclopedic Dictionary of Accounting, The Blackwell Encyclopedic Dictionary of Business Ethics, The Blackwell Encyclopedic Dictionary of Finance,* the *Dictionary of Taxation,* the *Dictionary of International Business Terms,* the *Concise Dictionary of Business Management,* the *Dictionary of Marketing and Advertising,* the *Dictionary of Accounting,* the *Routledge Dictionary of Economics, A Dictionary of Business Management,* and the *Dictionary of Finance and Banking.* There are also dictionaries of acronyms, initialisms, and abbreviations. Two of these are the *Acronyms, Initialisms, and Abbreviations Dictionary* and the *Abbreviations Dictionary.*

Additional statistical sources Today's businesses rely heavily on statistical information. Not only is this information helpful in day-to-day business operations, but it also is helpful in planning future products, expansions, and strategies. Some of this information can be found in the publications previously mentioned, especially the government publications. More is available online and can be seen long before it is printed. Even more is available from the various public and private sources described in Exhibit 8.2.

Some of the basic comprehensive publications include the *Statistical Abstract of the United States* and *Standard & Poor's Statistical Service.* These sources are a starting point when you are not familiar with more specialized sources. They include historical data on American industry, commerce, labor, and agriculture; industry data by SIC/NAICS codes; and numerous indexes such as producer price indexes, housing indexes, and stock price indexes. Additionally, the *Statistical Abstract of the United States* contains an extremely useful guide to sources of statistics.

If you are not certain where to find statistics, you may find various guides useful. The *American Statistics Index* is an index to statistics published by all government agencies. It identifies the agency, describes the statistics, and provides access by category. The *Encyclopedia of Business Information Sources* provides a list of information sources along with names of basic statistical sources. The *Statistical Reference Index* publishes statistics from sources other than the government, such as trade and professional associations. These three directories will help direct you to specialized statistics when you need them.

Business information services Business services are private organizations that supply a variety of information to business practitioners, especially investors. Libraries also subscribe to their publications, giving business researchers ready access to yet another source of valuable, timely data.

> "Business services are private organizations that supply a variety of information to business practitioners, especially investors."

In order to facilitate the collection and retrieval of statistical data for industry, the U.S. government developed a classification system called the Standard Industrial Classification (SIC) code. In the 1930s, this system used a four-digit code for all manufacturing and nonmanufacturing industries.

In 1997, the U.S. government introduced a new industrial classification system—the North American Industry Classification System (NAICS)—to replace the SIC code. The new system is more flexible than the old one and accounts for changes in the global economy by allowing the United States, Mexico, and Canada to compare economic and financial statistics better. It has also been expanded to include new sectors such as the information sector; the health care and social assistance sector; and the professional, scientific, and technical services sector. The United States and Canada began using this system in 1997, and Mexico in 1998. The first NAICS-based statistics were issued in 1999.

Mergent, Inc., one of the best-known of such organizations, publishes a weekly *Manual* in each of five business areas: industrials, over-the-counter (OTC) industrials, international banks and finance, municipals, and governments. These reports primarily summarize financial data and operating facts on all major American companies, providing information that an investor needs to evaluate the investment potential of individual securities or of fields as a whole. *Corporation Records,* published by Standard & Poor's *NetAdvantage,* presents similar information in loose-leaf form. Both Mergent and Standard & Poor's provide a variety of related services, including *Moody's Investors Service* and *Value Line Investment Survey.*

Another organization whose publications are especially helpful to business researchers is The Gale Group, Inc. Gale provides several business services, including publications

How do I find business news and trends?

ABI Inform Complete on ProQuest

Business & Company Resource Center

Business & Industry Database (includes articles from over 900 trade publications)

Business Source Premier

Factiva (includes Dow Jones and Reuters Newswires and *The Wall Street Journal*, plus more than 8,000 other sources from around the world)

LexisNexis Academic, News and Business sections

Wilson OmniFile Full Text Mega

How do I find information about companies?

The Annual Reports Library (<http://www.zpub.com/sf/arl/>)

Business & Company Resource Center

Business Source Premier

Companies' own websites

D&B's (Dunn & Bradstreet's) *International Million Dollar Database*

D&B's *Million Dollar Database*

Factiva

Hoover's Online

LexisNexis Academic, Business section

Marketline (basic information about 10,000 global companies, including the United States)

Mergent Online (information about 25,000 U.S. and 35,000 international companies)

SEC Filings and Forms (EDGAR) (includes 10-K reports and annual reports)

Standard & Poor's NetAdvantage

Thomson Research (Disclosure provides information about 12,000 U.S. companies; Worldscope covers both U.S. and international company filings)

Value Line Research Center

How do I find information about particular industries?

Business Insight

Frost & Sullivan

Global Market Information Database

ICON Group International (see Industry Reports, Country Reports, and Culture Statistics)

IBISWorld

MarketLine

MarketResearch.com Academic

MergentOnline, Industry Reports

Plunkett Research Online

Standard & Poor's NetAdvantage, Industries section

How do I find biographical and contact information for business people?

American Business Directory (<http://library.dialog.com/bluesheets/html/bl0531.html>)

Biographical Dictionary of American Business Leaders

Biography Reference Bank

D&B's (Dunn & Bradstreet's) *Million Dollar Database*

LexisNexis Academic, Reference/Biographical Information section

Standard & Poor's NetAdvantage (see Register of Executives)

Who's Who in Finance and Business (includes Biography Resource Center)

How do I find information provided by the US government?

Business.gov (government rules and regulations, research, resources)

Fedstats (<http://www.fedstats.gov/>)

STAT-USA (includes State of the Nation Library)

U.S. Bureau of Labor Statistics (<http://www.bls.gov>; comprehensive employment and economic data, including *Monthly Labor Review* and *Occupational Outlook Handbook*)

U.S. Census Bureau (<http://www.census.gov>; links to *Statistical Abstract of the United States*)

U.S. Government Printing Office (<http://www.gpoaccess.gov>; comprehensive site for U.S. government publications)

U.S. Small Business Administration (<http://www.sba.gov/>)

How do I find out about other countries and international trade?

Economist Intelligence Unit—ISI Emerging Markets

Europa World Yearbooks

Global Market Information Database

SourceOECD (from the Organisation for Economic Cooperation and Development)

STAT-USA/Internet (<http://www.stat-usa.gov>)

U.S. Library of Congress, Country Studies (<http://lcweb2.loc.gov/frd/cs/cshome.html>)

U.S. State Department information (<http://www.state.gov>)

The World Factbook (<http://www.cia.gov/cia/publications/factbook/>)

WDI Online (the World Bank's World Development Indicators)

Yahoo!'s country links (<http://dir.yahoo.com/Regional/Countries/>)

How do I find information about cities?

American FactFinder (<http://factfinder.census.gov/home/saff/main.html?_lang=en>)

Cities' own websites

County and City Data Books (<http://www.census.gov/prod/www/abs/ccdbo.htm/>)

Sourcebook America (CD-ROM)

Cities of the World (4-volume reference book)

Source: Compiled with the assistance of Business Reference Librarians Wahib Nasrallah, University of Cincinnati, and Patrick Sullivan and Michael Perkins, San Diego State University.

featuring forecasts and market data by country, product, and company. Its online *Business and Company Resource Center* is particularly useful. This database provides access to hundreds of thousands of company records, allowing users to search by company name, ticker symbol, and SIC and NAICS codes. It provides links to the full text of news and magazine articles, company profiles, investment reports, and even legal actions and suits. Users can print the information as well as email it to others.

Exhibit 8.2 lists additional helpful resources, such as *Hoover's Online* and *Factiva*. Many can be accessed through your school library's website.

International sources In today's global business environment, we often need information outside our borders. Many of the sources we have discussed have counterparts with international information. *Principal International Businesses* lists basic information on major companies located around the world. *Major Companies of Europe* and *Japan Company Handbook* are two sources providing facts on companies in their respective areas. The *International Encyclopedia of the Social Sciences* covers all important areas of social science, including biographies of acclaimed persons in these areas. General and specialized dictionaries are available, too. Baron's *Dictionary of International Business Terms* includes commonly used business terms. You will even be able to find trade names in the *International Brands and Their Companies,* published by The Gale Group. For bibliographies and abstracts, one good source is the *Foreign Commerce Handbook*. Statistical information is available in such sources as the *Index to International Statistics and Statistical Yearbook,* and online at the United Nations Department of Economic and Social Affairs Statistical Division (<http://unstats.un.org/unsd/>). Additionally, the U.S. Bureau of Labor Statistics at <http://www.bls.gov/bls/other.htm> provides links to many countries' statistical portals. With the help of translation tools (see the textbook website), you can get information you want directly. In addition, libraries usually contain many references for information on international marketing, exporting, tax, and trade.

Today many colleges and some city libraries offer online access to virtual librarians. Sometimes you can get a direct answer especially for such questions as citing certain kinds of information in specific formats such as APA, Chicago, or MLA. Other times, virtual librarians will guide you in finding the information, making them an indirect method for finding information.

using indirect methods Sometimes you may not know what resource will provide the information you need. In these instances, prepare a list of key terms related to your topic. Then use these key terms to search for information using more general online catalogs, databases, or Internet search engines. These more general resources can guide you to specific sources on your topic. Once you find a specific source, keep a full bibliographic record to cite in your paper or project including names, dates, volume, issue, and page numbers.

Acquiring secondary materials should be orderly and thorough. You should not depend on the material that is readily at hand. You may need to use interlibrary loan services, for example, or gather company documents. Be sure you thoroughly check each source, taking time to review its table of contents, its index, and the endnotes or footnotes related to the pages you are researching. This will help you assess the reliability of the information as well as find additional resources.

The online catalog Today most libraries use online catalogs to list their holdings, providing numerous ways to locate sources. You can locate sources by the standard Keyword, Title, Author, and Subject options as well as a few other options. Becoming familiar with such catalogs is highly recommended, especially for the systems you access frequently. By using effective and efficient searching techniques, you will reap many rewards.

Two options you need to understand clearly are *Keyword* and *Subject*. When you select the Keyword option, the system will ask you to enter search terms and phrases. It will then search for only those exact words in several of each record's fields, missing all those records using slightly different wording. When you select Subject, the system will scan the Library of Congress subject heading for your search term. This means that for the most part you need to know the exact heading. To find possible Library of Congress subject headings for your topic, visit the Library of Congress Authorities webpage at <http://authorities.loc.gov> and click "Search Authorities." Sometimes the search engine will cross-reference headings such as suggesting you *See Intercultural Communication* whe[n] you enter *cross-cultural communication*. A Subject search [will] find all those holdings on the subject, including those [with] different wording such as *intercultural communicatio[n,] national communication, global communication,* [and divern]*sity*. If you ran multiple searches under the Key[word] using these terms, you would still miss those tit[les]

The government publications at the U.S. Department of Labor's website are up to date and easily accessible.

Online databases The online catalog helps you identify books and other holdings in your library. To find articles published in newspapers, magazines, or journals, you will need to consult an index, either a general one or one that specializes in the field you are researching. Most indexes today are available online and are updated regularly.

If you are like most business researchers today, you will start your search for periodical literature in an online database. As the sophistication and capacity of computer technology have improved, much of the information that was once routinely recorded in print form and accessed through directories, encyclopedias, and indexes is now stored digitally in computer files. These files, known as *databases*, are accessed through the use of search strategies. However, one first needs to identify which databases to use.

keywords, such as Frank Acuff's book *How to Negotiate Anything with Anyone around the World*. With a Subject search, you might even find a management book with a chapter on intercultural communication; however, the book's emphasis might be on something else, such as crisis management or conflict resolution.

The online catalog never gets tired. If you key in the words accurately, it will always produce a complete and accurate list of sources. In addition, you can modify or narrow your searches by publication date, language, material type, author, or title.

The online catalog is a useful source of information about your library's holdings. Learning how to use it effectively will save you time and will help your searches be fast and accurate.

While there are many databases produced by private and government information services, some of those most useful to business researchers are *ABI/Inform, Business Source Premiere, Factiva,* and *LexisNexis Academic. ABI/Inform* and *Business Source Premiere* are two of the most complete databases, providing access to hundreds of business research journals as well as important industry trade publications. Most of the articles are included in full-text form or with lengthy summaries. They allow basic, guided, and natural language searching. *Factiva,* on the other hand, provides access to current business, general, and international news, including access to various editions of *The Wall Street Journal.* It also includes current information on U.S. public companies and industries. Similarly, *LexisNexis* offers access to current business and international articles, providing them in full text. Additionally, it includes legal and reference information.

Hoover's Online is a subscription-based business information service that provides reliable, extensive, and high-quality information about companies.

last resort because it can eliminate potentially good sources. For example, if one were searching for articles on venture capital, using the NOT term in an attempt to eliminate DotCom companies might eliminate good articles where DotCom was mentioned as an aside or even an article that compared DotCom companies to other funded companies. If a search results in few citations, the OR operator can be used to expand the search by adding variations or synonyms to the basic search term.

To expand the search for articles on DotComs AND accountants, you might add accounting OR comptroller OR controller.

If you have difficulty thinking of terms to broaden your search, look at the keywords or descriptors of the items that have already been identified. Often these will give you ideas for additional terms to use. If the search still

> " If a search results in few citations, the OR operator can be used to expand the search by adding variations or synonyms to the basic search term. "

Once researchers know where to begin, their search skills become critical. A good command of Boolean logic combined with the knowledge of how to implement it in the databases (or Internet search engines) used will help researchers extract the information they need. Boolean logic uses three primary operators: AND, OR, and NOT. If search results yield more citations than you need, the results can be narrowed. Similar to the online catalog, most databases in the guided or advanced mode allow users to limit the search by article or publication type as well as by date, but the use of Boolean logic operators allows users to focus the subject matter more tightly, eliminating citations that are unrelated or tangential to the problem being discussed.

The operator AND is a narrowing term. It instructs the computer to find citations with both terms. The operator NOT is another narrowing term, instructing the computer to eliminate citations with a particular term. It should be used as a

comes up short, you need to check for spelling errors or variations. Becoming skilled at using Boolean logic will help you get the information you need when you need it.

The Internet The Internet is a network of networks. It operates in a structure originally funded by the National Science Foundation. However, no one organization owns or runs this globally connected network. Its users work together to develop standards, which are always changing. The network provides a wide variety of resources, including many useful to business. Since no one is officially in charge, finding information on the Internet can be difficult. Nevertheless, this network of loosely organized computer systems does provide some useful search and retrieval tools.

These tools can search for files as well as text on various topics. They can search both titles and the documents themselves. Since the Internet is a rapidly growing medium for publishing,

▼ **EXHIBIT 8.3** Illustration of an Individual Web Search Engine—Google

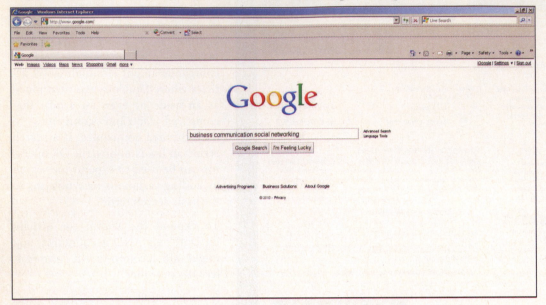

Source: Copyright © Google, Inc., reprinted with permission.

▼ **EXHIBIT 8.4** An Illustration of Results from a Basic Search

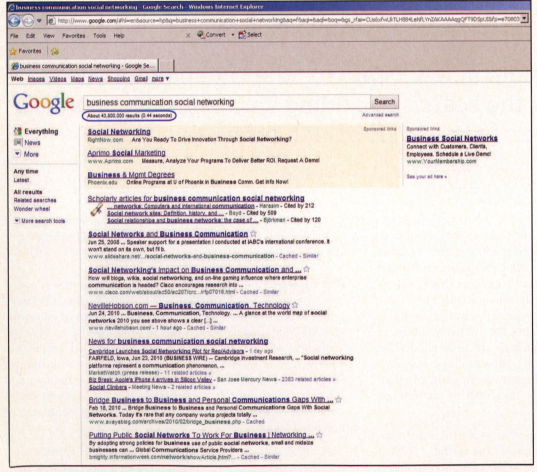

Source: Copyright © Google, Inc., reprinted with permission.

the browsers and major portals incorporate links to search tools. Most of the links currently are to individual search engines such as Google, Bing, ASK, and Yahoo! Most of these engines compile their indexes using human input, some use software robots, and some use a combination. Google, whose simple, clean screens you see in Exhibits 8.3 to 8.7 provides users with much more than the ability to search webpages. From the primary search page, users can search images, groups, directories, and news as well as link to advanced search and translation tools. In Exhibit 8.3, you may notice that the terms are entered without the Boolean operator AND. Google automatically ANDs all terms, freeing the user from having to add the operator each time a search is conducted. By hitting Enter (or clicking the Google Search button), you execute the search. Notice the result in Exhibit 8.4: 43.8 million results found in .44 of a second.

To limit this search, you could use the advanced search tool shown in Exhibit 8.5. Notice how the first search line (**all**) uses a built-in AND operator, and the third line (**at least one**) uses a built-in OR operator. Additionally, the advanced search allows its user to limit by language, English in this case, and by type of site, .gov here. When this search was run, its results were those shown in Exhibit 8.6: 143,000 links found in .25 of a second. To further limit the number of links, the user could click on the link *Similar* at the end of any result. It would return the screen you see in Exhibit 8.7 showing about 54 results related to the www.cisco.com site.

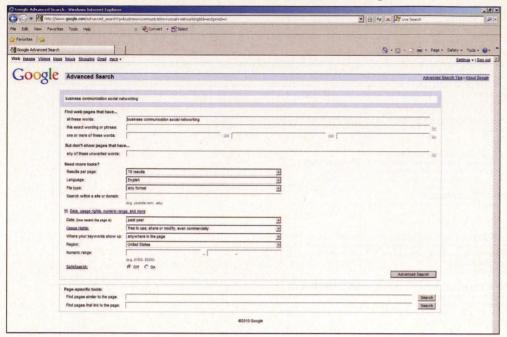

▼ **EXHIBIT 8.6** An Illustration of Results of an Advanced Search

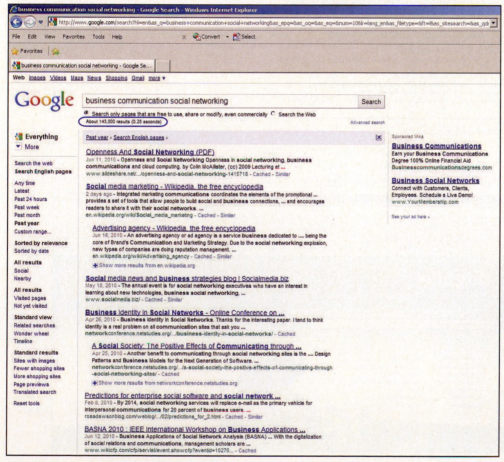

These are only a few of the features of Google. By thoroughly learning the special techniques and features of the search engines you use most frequently, you will find that they can help you immensely in finding the information you need.

As search engines evolve to meet the changing needs of the Internet's content and its users, new forms of these tools have emerged as well. Metasearch tools allow searchers to enter the search terms once, running the search simultaneously with several individual search engines and compiling a combined results page. Examples of these include Dogpile, Kartoo, Mamma, Metacrawler, and Search.com. You will find links to these and other search tools on the textbook website. Exhibits 8.8 and 8.9 illustrate how Dogpile searches various search engines for the phrase "business dining etiquette" and then combines the results and presents them in an easy-to-view form.

Another type of search tool that has emerged is the specialized search engine. Examples of these tools are Yahoo!: People Search for finding people, Deja.com for searching newsgroups, Edgar for finding corporate information, FindLaw for gathering legal information, and Mediafinder for finding print items. In addition, several blog indexes such as Google Blogs are useful sources of information on many subjects. There are specialty engines for finding information in finance, music, wireless, medicine, and more. These sites are sometimes referred to as the "invisible Web" or "deep Web."

Another form of gathering information from the Web is through use of digital personal agents or alerts. These agents allow users to define the kind of information they want to gather. The information gathered can be ready and waiting when users access their personal website,

▼ **EXHIBIT 8.7** An Illustration of Results of a Similar Pages Search

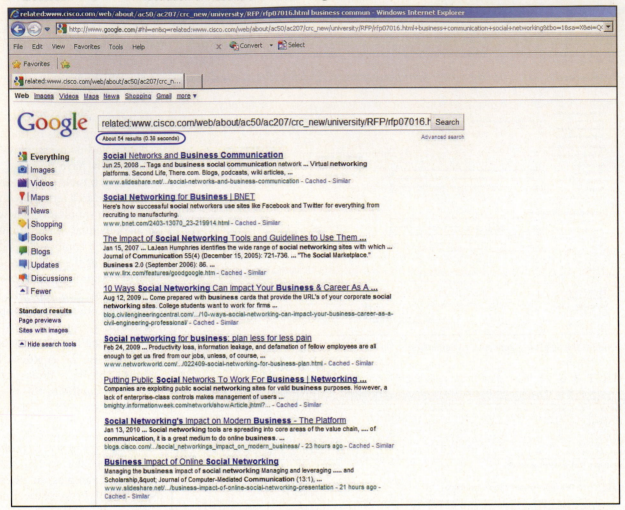

Source: Copyright © Google, Inc., reprinted with permission.

▼ **EXHIBIT 8.8** An Illustration of a Metasearch Engine—Dogpile

> # ALSO, YOU MUST RECOGNIZE THAT NOT ALL OF THE DOCUMENTS PUBLISHED ON THE WEB ARE INDEXED AND THAT NO SEARCH TOOL COVERS THE ENTIRE WEB.

such as at my.yahoo.com or iGoogle, or it can be delivered by email or text message in the form of "push technology." You are using push technology if you have news/traffic/weather updates sent to you.

While these tools assist users in finding helpful Web documents, it is crucial to remember that the tools are limited. You must evaluate the source of the information critically. Also, you must recognize that not all of the documents published on the Web are indexed and that no search tool covers the entire Web. Skill in using the tools plays a role, but judgment in evaluating the accuracy and completeness of the search plays an even more significant role.

LO 5   Evaluate website reliability.

evaluating sources and websites   Once you have located information sources, whether print or digital, you need to evaluate them. Primarily you are concerned that the sources you collect are complete, accurate, and reliable.

Most print sources include items such as author, title of publication, facts of publication, and date in a standard form; however, websites have not yet established a standard form. Additionally, the unmonitored digital media have introduced a slew of other factors one would want to consider in evaluating the credibility of the source as well as the reliability of the content. For example, most users of search engines do not understand the extent or type of bias introduced into the order in which search engines present their results; they often rely on one exclusively to find the most relevant sites when even the best of them only index a small fraction of the Internet content.

One experimental study found that users of website information were particularly susceptible to four types of misinformation: advertising claims, government misinformation, propaganda, and scam sites. Furthermore, the study found that users' confidence in their ability to gather reliable information was not related to their actual ability to judge the information appropriately. The results also revealed that level of education was not related to one's ability to evaluate website information accurately.[1]

One solution might be to limit one's use of information only to sites accessed through links from a trustworthy site, a site

▼ **EXHIBIT 8.9**   An Illustration of Results of a Metasearch

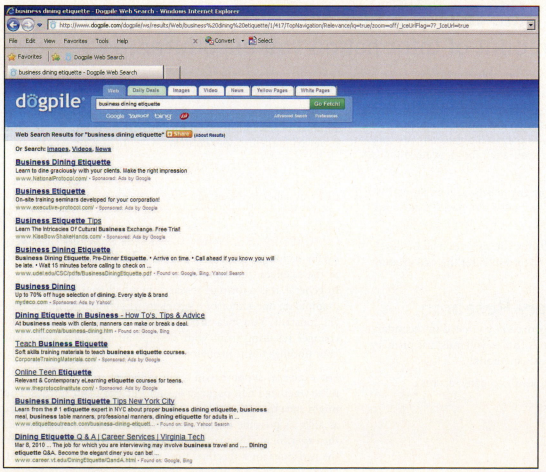

where others have evaluated the links before posting them. However, these sites are clearly not comprehensive and are often late in providing links to new sources. Therefore, developing the skill and habit of evaluating websites critically is probably a better choice. This skill can be honed by getting into the habit of looking at the purpose, qualifications, validity, and structure of the websites one uses.

- **Purpose.** Why was the information provided? To explain? To inform? To persuade? To sell? To share? What are the provider's biases? Who is the intended audience? What point of view does the site take? Could it possibly be ironic, a satire, or a parody?

- **Qualifications.** What are the credentials of the information provider? What is the nature of any sponsorship? Is contact information provided? Is it accurate? Is it complete—name, email address, street address, and phone? Is the information well written, clear, and organized?

- **Validity.** Where else can the information provided be found? Is the information from the original source? Has the information been synthesized or abstracted accurately and in correct context? Is the information timely? When was it created? When was it posted? Has the site already been validated? Who links

LO 6 Describe the procedure for searching through company records.

searching through company records
Since many of today's business problems involve various phases of company operations, a company's *transaction-level* internal records—production data, sales records, marketing information, accounting records, and the like—are frequently an excellent source of firsthand information.

There are no set rules on how to find and gather information through company records. Record-keeping systems vary widely from company to company. However, be sure to keep the following standards in mind as you conduct your investigation. First, as in any other type of research, you must have a clear idea of the information you need. Undefined, open-ended investigations are not appreciated—nor are they particularly productive. Second, you must clearly understand the ground rules under which you are allowed to review materials. Matters of confidentiality and access should be resolved before you start. And third, if you are not intimately familiar with a company's records or how

> " By critically evaluating the websites you use, you will be developing a skill that will help you effectively filter the vast amount of information you encounter. "

to it? (On Google, enter link:*url* to find links.) How long has the site existed? Is it updated regularly? Do the links work? Do they represent other views? Are they well organized? Are they annotated? Has the site received any ratings or reviews? Is cited information authentic?

- **Structure.** How is the site organized, designed, and formatted? Does its structure provide a particular emphasis? Does it appeal to its intended audience?

By critically evaluating the websites you use, you will be developing a skill that will help you effectively filter the vast amount of data you encounter.

Conducting Primary Research

When you cannot find the information you need in secondary sources, you must get it firsthand. That is, you must use primary research, which employs five basic methods:

1. A search through transaction-level company records.
2. Experimentation.
3. Observation.
4. Survey.
5. Qualitative research.

to access them, you must cooperate with someone who is. The complexity and sensitivity of such materials require that they be reviewed in their proper context.

LO 7 Conduct an experiment for a business problem.

conducting an experiment
The experiment is a very useful technique in business research. Originally developed in the sciences, the experiment is an orderly form of testing. In general, it is a form of research in which you systematically manipulate one factor of a problem while holding all the others constant. You measure quantitatively or qualitatively any changes resulting from your manipulations. Then you apply your findings to the problem.

For example, suppose you are conducting research to determine whether a new package design will lead to more sales. You might start by selecting two test cities, taking care that they are as alike as possible on all the characteristics that might affect the experiment. Then you would secure information on sales in the two cities for a specified time period before the experiment. Next, for a second specified time period, you would use the

technology in brief

Doing More Efficient Repeat Searching through Favorites

Most of the newest versions of today's browsers support tabs, enabling fast and efficient repeat searching. At the top of the illustration here, you can see that separate tabs were opened in Internet Explorer 8 to search *cross-cultural communication* in three different search engines—Alta Vista, Dogpile,

and Mamma. It also shows that adding the complete group of tabs to Favorites (called bookmarking in other browsers) can be done in one click. The middle illustration shows naming a folder *Cross-Cultural Searches* for the collection of tabs. Once they are saved there, you can repeatedly open all tabs in

the folder to run all the searches simultaneously by simply clicking the folder's arrow as shown in the bottom illustration.

Any search that you need to do repeatedly can be set up this way once and opened whenever you need to review the most recent results.

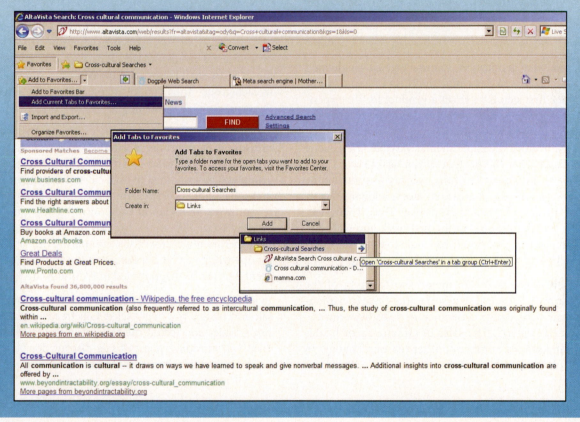

new package design in one of the cities and continue to use the old package in the other. During that period, you would keep careful sales records and check to make sure that advertising, economic conditions, competition, and other factors that might have some effect on the experiment remain unchanged. Thus, when the experimentation period is over, you can attribute any differences you found between the sales of the two cities to the change in package design.

Each experiment should be designed to fit the individual requirements of the problem. Nonetheless, a few basic designs underlie most experiments. Becoming familiar with two of the most common designs—the before–after and the controlled

before–after—will give you a framework for understanding and applying this primary research technique.

The before–after design   The simplest experimental design is the before–after design. In this design, illustrated in Exhibit 8.10, you select a test group of subjects, measure the variable in which you are interested, and then introduce the experimental factor. After a specified time period, during which the experimental factor has presumably had its effect, you again measure the variable in which you are interested. If there are any differences between the first and second measurements, you may assume that the experimental factor, plus any uncontrollable factors, is the cause.

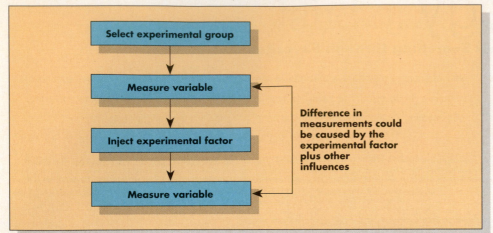

activity, other advertising, and so on. At best, you have determined only that point-of-sale advertising could influence sales.

The controlled before–after design

To account for influences other than the experimental factors, you may use designs more complex than the before–after design. These designs attempt to measure the other influences by including some means of control. The simplest of these designs is the controlled before–after design.

In the controlled before–after design, you select not one group, but two: the experimental group and the control group. Before introducing the experimental factor, you measure the variable to be tested in each group. Then you introduce the experimental factor into the experimental group only.

When the period allotted for the experiment is over, you again measure in each group the variable being tested. Any difference between the first and second measurements in the experimental group can be explained by two causes: the experimental factor and other influences. But the difference between the first and second measurements in the control group can be explained only by other influences, for this group was not subjected to the experimental factor. Thus, comparing the "afters" of the two groups will give you a measure of the influence of the experimental factor, as diagrammed in Exhibit 8.11.

In a controlled before–after experiment designed to test point-of-sale advertising, you might select Gillette razor blades and Schick razor blades and record the sales of both brands for one week. Next you introduce point-of-sale displays for Gillette only and you record sales for both Gillette and Schick for a second week. At

Consider the following application. Assume you are conducting research for a retail store to determine the effect of point-of-sale advertising. Your first step is to select a product for the experiment. You choose Gillette razor blades. Second, you record sales of Gillette blades for one week, using no point-of-sale advertising. Then you introduce the experimental variable: the Gillette point-of-sale display. For the next week you again record sales of Gillette blades; and at the end of that week, you compare the results for the two weeks. Any increase in sales would presumably be explained by the introduction of the display. Thus, if 500 packages of Gillette blades were sold in the first week and 600 were sold in the second week, you would conclude that the 100 additional sales can be attributed to point-of-sale advertising.

You can probably recognize the major shortcoming of the design. It is simply not logical to assume that the experimental factor explains the entire difference in sales between the first week and the second. The sales of Gillette razor blades could have changed for a number of other reasons: changes in the weather, holiday or other seasonal influences on business

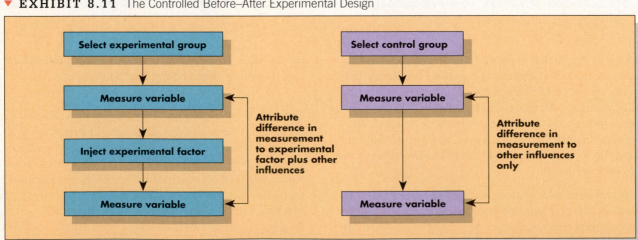

the end of the second week, you compare the results for the two brands. Whatever difference you find in Gillette sales and Schick sales will be a fair measure of the experimental factor, independent of the changes that other influences may have brought about.

For example, without point-of-sales displays in the control group, if 400 packages of Schick blades are sold the first week and 450 packages are sold the second week, the increase of 50 packages (12.5 percent) can be attributed to influences other than the experimental factor, the point-of-sale display. If 500 packages of Gillette blades are sold the first week and 600 are sold the second week, the increase of 100 can be attributed to both the point-of-sale display and other influences. To distinguish between the two, you note that other influences accounted for the 12.5 percent increase in the sales of Schick blades. Because of the experimental control, you attribute 12.5 percent of the increase in Gillette sales to other influences as well. An increase

Like all primary research techniques, observation must be designed to fit the requirements of the problem being considered. However, the planning stage generally requires two steps. First, you construct a recording form; second, you design a systematic procedure for observing and recording the information of interest.

The recording form may be any tabular arrangement that permits quick and easy recording of that information. Though observation forms are hardly standardized, one commonly used arrangement (see Exhibit 8.12) provides a separate line for each observation. Headings at the top of the page mark the columns in which the observer will place the appropriate mark. The recording form identifies the characteristics that are to be observed and requires the recording of such potentially important details as the date, time, and place of the observation and the name of the observer.

> ## Observation is seeing with a purpose. It consists of watching the events involved in a problem and systematically recording what is seen.

of 12.5 percent on a base of 500 sales is 63 sales, indicating that 63 of the 100 additional Gillette sales are the result of other influences. However, the sale of 37 additional packages of Gillette blades can probably be attributed to point-of-sale advertising.

LO 8 Design an observational study for a business problem.

---

using the observation technique Like the experiment, observation is a technique perfected in the sciences that is also useful in business research. Simply stated, observation is seeing with a purpose. It consists of watching the events involved in a problem and systematically recording what is seen. In observation, you do not manipulate the details of what you observe; you take note of situations exactly as you find them.

Note that observation as an independent research technique is different from the observation you use in recording the effects of variables introduced into a test situation. In the latter case, observation is a step in the experiment, not an end in itself. The two methods, therefore, should not be confused.

To see how observation works as a business technique, consider this situation. You work for a fast-food chain, such as McDonald's, that wants to check the quality and consistency of some menu items throughout the chain. By hiring observers, sometimes called mystery shoppers, you can gather information on the temperature, freshness, and speed of delivery of various menu items. This method may reveal important information that other data collection methods cannot.

The observation procedure may be any system that ensures the collection of complete and representative information. But every effective observation procedure includes a clear focus, well-defined steps, and provisions for ensuring the quality of the information collected. For example, an observation procedure for determining the courtesy of employees toward customers when answering the phone would include a detailed schedule for making calls, detailed instructions on what to ask, and provisions for dealing with different responses the observer might encounter. In short, the procedure would leave no major question unanswered.

Two additional primary research strategies—surveys and qualitative research—will receive extra attention in the following sections.

LO 9 Use sampling to conduct a survey.

Collecting Information by Survey

The premise of the survey as a method of primary research is simple: You can best acquire certain types of information by asking questions. Such information includes personal data, opinions, evaluations, and other important material. It also includes information necessary to plan for an experiment or an observation or to supplement or interpret the data that result.

Once you have decided to use the survey for your research, you have to make decisions about a number of matters. The first is the matter of format. The questions can range from

▼ **EXHIBIT 8.12**   Excerpt from a Common Type of Observation Recording Form

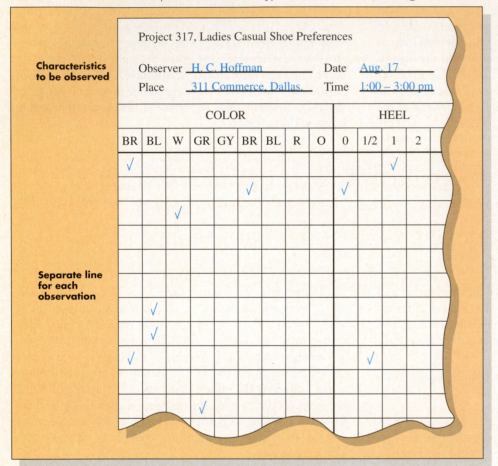

Quality-control supervisors spot-check a small percentage of products ready for distribution to determine whether production standards are being met. Auditors for large corporations sample transactions when examining the books. Sampling is generally used for economy and practicality. However, for a sample to be representative of the whole group, it must be selected properly.

Two important aspects to consider in sample design are controlling for sampling error and controlling for bias. Sampling error results when the sample is not representative of the whole group. While all samples have some degree of sampling error, you can reduce the error through techniques used to construct representative samples. These techniques fall into two groups: probability and nonprobability sampling.

probability sampling techniques   Probability samples are based on chance selection procedures. Every element in the population has a known nonzero probability of selection.[2] These techniques include simple random sampling, stratified random sampling, systematic sampling, and area or cluster sampling.

spontaneous inquiries to carefully structured interrogations. The next is the matter of delivery. The questions can be posed in a face-to-face interview, asked over the phone, or presented in printed or digital form.

But the most important is the matter of whom to survey. Except for situations in which a small number of people are involved in the problem under study, you cannot reach all the people involved. Thus, you have to select a sample of respondents who represent the group as a whole as accurately as possible. There are several ways to select that sample, as you will see.

sampling as a basis   Sampling theory forms the basis for most research by survey, though it has any number of other applications as well. Buyers of grain, for example, judge the quality of a multiton shipment by examining a few pounds.

Random sampling   Random sampling is the technique assumed in the general law of sampling. By definition, it is the sampling technique that gives every member of the group under study an equal chance of being included. To ensure equal chances, you must first identify every member of the group and then, using a list or some other convenient format, record all the identifications. Next, through some chance method, you select the members of your sample.

For example, if you are studying the job attitudes of 200 employees and determine that 25 interviews will give you the information you need, you might put the names of all 200 workers in a container, mix them thoroughly, and draw out 25. Since each of the 200 workers has an equal chance of being selected, your sample will be random and can be presumed to be representative.

Stratified random sampling Stratified random sampling subdivides the group under study and makes random selections within each subgroup. The size of each subgroup is usually proportionate to that subgroup's percentage of the whole. If a subgroup is too small to yield meaningful findings, however, you may have to select a disproportionately large sample. Of course, when the study calls for statistics on the group as a whole, the actual proportion of such a subgroup must be restored.

Assume, for example, that you are attempting to determine the curriculum needs of 5,000 undergraduates at a certain college and that you have decided to survey 20 percent of the enrollment, or 1,000 students. To construct a sample for this problem, first divide the enrollment list by academic concentration: business, liberal arts, nursing, engineering, and so forth. Then draw a random sample from each of these groups, making sure that the number you select is proportionate to that group's percentage of the total undergraduate enrollment. Thus, if 30 percent of the students are majoring in business, you will randomly select 300 business majors for your sample; if 40 percent of the students are liberal arts majors, you will randomly select 400 liberal arts majors for your sample; and so on.

Area or cluster sampling In area sampling, the items for a sample are drawn in stages. This sampling technique is appropriate when the area to be studied is large and can be broken down into progressively smaller components. For example, if you want to draw an area sample for a certain city, you may use census data to divide the city into homogeneous districts. Using an equal-chance method, you then select a given number of districts to include in the next stage of your sample. Next you divide each of the selected districts into subdistricts—city blocks, for example. Continuing the process, you randomly select a given number of these blocks and subdivide each of them into households. Finally, using random sampling once more, you select the households that will constitute the sample you will use in your research.

Area or cluster sampling is not limited to geographic division, however. It is adaptable to any number of applications. For example, it is an appropriate technique to use in a survey of the employees in a given industry. An approach that you may take in this situation is to randomly select a given number of companies from a list of all the companies in the industry. Then, using organization units and selecting randomly at each level, you break down

> "Area or cluster sampling is not limited to geographic division . . . It is adaptable to any number of applications."

Systematic sampling Systematic sampling, though not random in the strictest sense, is random for all practical purposes. It is the technique of taking selections at constant intervals (every nth unit) from a list of the items under study. The interval used is based, as you might expect, on the size of the list and the size of the desired sample. For example, if you want a 10 percent sample of a list of 10,000, you might select every 10th item on the list.

However, your sample would not really be random. By virtue of their designated place on the original list, items do not have an equal chance of being selected. To correct that problem, you might use an equal-chance method to determine what n to use. Thus, if you selected the number 7 randomly, you would draw the numbers 7, 17, 27, and so on to 9,997 to make up your sample. Or, if you wanted to draw every 10th item, you might first scramble the list and then select from the revised list numbers 10, 20, 30, and so on up to 10,000 and make up your sample that way.

Researchers frequently survey a sample of respondents who represent the group that is being studied.

technology in brief

Survey Tools Help Writers Lay Out, Analyze, and Report Results of Questionnaires

Survey tools, both software and Web-based tools, help you design professional-looking questionnaires as well as compile and analyze the data collected. Some tools such as those offered at Qualtrics.com and SurveyMonkey.com provide both free and purchase options. Software programs help with construction and layout of questionnaires and allow you to convert the questionnaires to html format for publishing on the Web easily. Web-based programs help you create, distribute, and manage data collection for online questionnaires.

Special data entry screens assist you in selecting the types of questions and desired layout. They then arrange the questionnaire automatically while giving you the freedom to move the questions to change the ordering and arrangement if desired. The tools also let you create open-ended questions. All of these questions can be saved in a library for reuse. Some of the tools even include libraries of surveys that can be adapted for one's particular use.

As shown, Qualtrics generates a variety of data, helping you see the results clearly and accurately as the questionnaires are being submitted.

Businesses can use these tools in a variety of applications, including training program evaluations, employee feedback on policies and procedures, longitudinal studies of ongoing practices such as network advertising revenues, opinion surveys of customers and potential customers, and feedback on customer satisfaction.

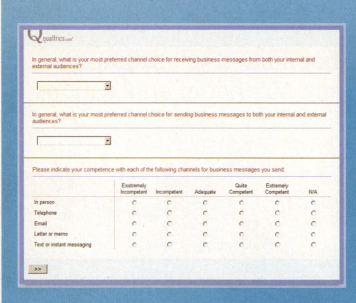

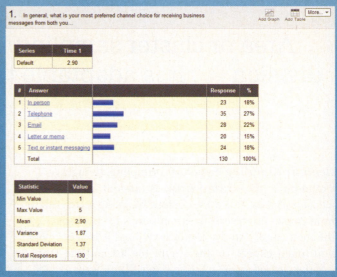

each of these companies into divisions, departments, sections, and so on until you finally identify the workers you will survey.

nonprobability sampling techniques
Nonprobability samples are based on an unknown probability of any one of a population being chosen. These techniques include convenience sampling, quota sampling, and referral sampling.[3]

Convenience sampling A convenience sample is one whose members are convenient and economical to reach.

When professors use their students as subjects for their research, they are using a convenience sample. Researchers generally use this sample to reach a large number quickly and economically. This kind of sampling is best used for exploratory research.

A form of convenience sampling is *judgment* or *expert* sampling. This technique relies on the judgment of the researcher to identify appropriate members of the sample. Illustrating this technique is the common practice of predicting the outcome of an election based on the results in a bellwether district.

Quota sampling Quota sampling is another nonrandom technique. Also known as *controlled sampling,* it is used whenever the proportionate makeup of the universe under study is available. The technique requires that you refer to the composition of the universe in designing your sample, selecting items so that your sample has the same characteristics in the same proportion as that universe. Specifically, it requires that you set quotas (actual numbers) for each characteristic that you want to consider in your research problem. Within those quotas, however, you will select individual items randomly.

Let us say that you want to survey a college student body of 4,000 using a 10 percent sample. As Exhibit 8.13 illustrates, you have a number of alternatives for determining the makeup of your sample, depending on the focus of your research. Keep in mind, though, that no matter what characteristic you select, the quotas the individual segments represent must total 100 percent and the number of items in the sample must total 400. Keep in mind also that within these quotas you will use

an equal-chance method to select the individual members of your sample.

Referral sampling Referral samples are those whose members are identified by others from a random sample. This technique is used to locate members when the population is small or hard to reach. For example, you might want to survey Six Sigma Black Belt certification holders. To get a sample large enough to make the study worthwhile, you could ask those from your town to give you the names of other Black Belt holders. Perhaps you are trying to survey the users of a project management application. You could survey a user group and ask those members for names of other users. You might even post an announcement on a blog or online forum asking for names.

LO 10 Construct a questionnaire, develop a working plan, and conduct a pilot study for a survey.

> # Referral samples are those whose members are identified by others from a random sample.

▼ **EXHIBIT 8.13** Example of a Quota Sample

	Number in Universe	Percent of Total	Number to Be Interviewed
Total student enrollment	4,000	100	400
Sex			
Male students	2,400	60	240
Female students	1,600	40	160
Fraternity, sorority membership			
Members	1,000	25	100
Nonmembers	3,000	75	300
Marital status			
Married students	400	10	40
Single students	3,600	90	360
Class rank			
Freshmen	1,600	40	160
Sophomores	1,000	25	100
Juniors	800	20	80
Seniors	400	10	40
Graduates	200	5	20

constructing the questionnaire Most orderly interrogation follows a plan of inquiry. This plan is usually worked out in a published (print or digital) form, called the *questionnaire.* The questionnaire is simply an orderly arrangement of the questions, with appropriate spaces provided for the answers. But simple as the finished questionnaire may appear to be, it is the subject of careful planning. You must plan so that the results are *reliable;* a test of a questionnaire's reliability is its repeatability with similar results. You also want your questionnaire to be *valid,* measuring what it is supposed to measure. It is, in a sense, the outline of the analysis of the problem. In addition, it must observe certain rules. These rules sometimes vary with the problem. The more general and by far the more important ones follow.

Avoid leading questions A leading question is one that in some way influences the answer. For example, the question "Is Dove your favorite bath soap?" leads the respondent to favor Dove. Some people who would say yes would name another brand if they were asked, "What is your favorite brand of bath soap?"

Make the questions easy to understand Questions that not all respondents clearly understand lead to error. Unfortunately, it is difficult to determine in advance just what respondents will not understand. As will be mentioned later, the best means of detecting such questions in advance is to test the questions before using them. But you can be on the alert for a few general sources of confusion.

One source of confusion is vagueness of expression, which is illustrated by the question, "How do you bank?" Who other than its author knows what the question means? Another source is using words respondents do not understand, as in the question "Do you read your house organ regularly?" The words *house organ* have a specialized, not widely known meaning, and *regularly* means different things to different people. Combining two questions in one is yet another source of confusion. For example, "Why did you buy a Ford?" actually asks two questions: "What do you like about Fords?" and "What don't you like about the other automobiles?"

Avoid questions that touch on personal prejudices or pride For reasons of pride or prejudices, people cannot be expected to answer accurately questions about certain areas of information. These areas include age, income status, morals, and personal habits. How many people, for example, would answer no to the question "Do you brush your teeth daily?" How many people would give their ages correctly? How many solid citizens would admit to fudging a bit on their tax returns?

But one may ask, "What if such information is essential to the solution of the problem?" The answer is to use less direct means of inquiry. To ascertain age, for example, investigators could ask for dates of high school graduation, marriage, or the like. From this information, they could approximate age. Or they could approximate age through observation, although this procedure is acceptable only if broad approximations would be satisfactory. They could ask for such harmless information as occupation, residential area, and standard of living and then use that information as a basis for approximating income. Another possibility is to ask range questions such as "Are you between 18 and 24, 25 and 40, or over 40?" This technique works well with income questions, too. People are generally more willing to answer questions worded by ranges rather than specifics. Admittedly, such techniques are sometimes awkward and difficult. But they can improve on the biased results that direct questioning would obtain.

Seek facts as much as possible Although some studies require opinions, it is far safer to seek facts whenever possible.

Human beings simply are not accurate reporters of their opinions. They are often limited in their ability to express themselves. Frequently, they report their opinions erroneously simply because they have never before been conscious of having them.

When opinions are needed, it is usually safer to record facts and then to judge the thoughts behind them. This technique, however, is only as good as the investigators' judgment. But a logical analysis of fact made by trained investigators is preferable to a spur-of-the-moment opinion.

A frequent violation of this rule results from the use of generalizations. Respondents are sometimes asked to generalize an answer from a large number of experiences over time. The question "Which magazines do you read regularly?" is a good illustration. Aside from the confusion caused by the word *regularly* and the fact that the question may tax the respondent's memory, the question forces the respondent to generalize. A better way to phrase it might be: "What magazines have you read this month?" The question could then be followed by an article-by-article check of the magazines to determine the extent of readership.

> People are generally more willing to answer questions worded by ranges rather than specifics.

Ask only for information that can be remembered Since the memory of all human beings is limited, the questionnaire should ask only for information that the respondents can be expected to remember. To make sure that this is done, you need to know certain fundamentals of memory.

Recency is the most important principle of memory. People remember insignificant events that occurred within the past few hours. By the next day, they will forget some. A month later they may not remember any. One might well remember, for example, what one ate for lunch on the day of the inquiry, and perhaps one might remember what one ate for lunch a day, or two days, or three days earlier. But one would be unlikely to remember what one ate for lunch a year earlier.

The second principle regarding memory is that significant events may be remembered over long periods. One may long remember the first day of school, the day of one's wedding, an automobile accident, a Christmas Day, and the like. In each of these examples there was an intense stimulus—a requisite for retention in memory.

A third principle of memory is that fairly insignificant facts may be remembered over long time periods through association with something significant. Although one would not normally remember what one ate for lunch a year earlier, for example, one might remember if the date happened to be one's wedding day, Christmas Day, or one's first day at college. Obviously, the memory is stimulated not by the meal itself but by the association of the meal with something more significant.

Plan the physical layout with foresight The overall design of the questionnaire should be planned to facilitate recording, analyzing, and tabulating the answers. Three major considerations are involved in such planning.

First, sufficient space should be allowed for recording answers. When practical, a system enabling the respondent to check an answer may be set up. Such a system must always provide for all possible answers, including conditional answers. For example, a direct question may provide for three possible answers: Yes _____, No _____, and Don't know _____.

Second, adequate space for identifying and describing the respondent should be provided. In some instances, such information as the age, sex, and income bracket of the respondent is vital to the analysis of the problem and should be recorded. In other instances, little or no identification is necessary.

Third, the best possible sequence of questions should be used. In some instances, starting with a question of high interest value may have psychological advantages. In other instances, it may be best to follow some other order of progression. Frequently, some questions must precede others because they help explain the others. Whatever the requirements of the individual case may be, however, careful and logical analysis should be used in determining the sequence of questions.

Use scaling when appropriate It is sometimes desirable to measure the intensity of the respondents' feelings about something (an idea, a product, a company, and so on). In such cases, some form of scaling is generally useful.

Of the various techniques of scaling, ranking and rating deserve special mention. These are the simpler techniques and, some believe, the more practical. They are less sophisticated than some others,[4] but the more sophisticated techniques are beyond the scope of this book.

The ranking technique consists simply of asking the respondent to rank a number of alternative answers to a question in order of preference (1, 2, 3, and so on). For example, in a survey to determine consumer preferences for toothpaste, the respondent might be asked to rank toothpastes A, B, C, D, and E in order of preference. In this example, the alternatives could be compared on the level of preference stated for each. This method of ranking and summarizing results is reliable despite its simplicity.

The rating technique graphically sets up a scale showing the complete range of possible attitudes on a matter and assigns number values to the positions on the scale. The respondent must then indicate the position on the scale that indicates his

▼ **EXHIBIT 8.14** Illustration of a Rating Question

1. What is your opinion of current right-to-work legislation?

Strongly oppose	Moderately oppose	Mildly oppose	Neutral	Mildly favor	Moderately favor	Strongly favor
○	○	○	○	○	○	○

or her attitude on that matter. Typically, the numeral positions are described by words, as the example in Exhibit 8.14 illustrates.

Because the rating technique deals with the subjective rather than the factual, it is sometimes desirable to use more than one question to cover the attitude being measured. Logically, the average of a person's answers to such questions gives a more reliable answer than does any single answer.

selecting the manner of questioning You can get responses to the questions you need answered in three primary ways: by personal (face-to-face) contact, by phone, or by mail (print or digital). You should select the way that in your unique case gives the best sample, the lowest cost, and the best results. By *best sample* we mean respondents who best represent the group concerned. And *results* are the information you need. As you can see in Exhibit 8.15, other factors will influence your choice.

developing a working plan After selecting the manner of questioning, you should carefully develop a working plan for the survey. As well as you can, you should anticipate and determine how to handle every possible problem. If you are conducting a mail or Web survey, for example, you need to develop an explanatory message that moves the subjects to respond, tells them what to do, and answers all the questions they are likely to

▼ **EXHIBIT 8.15** Comparison of Data Collection Methods

	Personal	Telephone	Online	Mail
Data collection costs	High	Medium	Low	Low
Data collection time required	Medium	Low	Medium	High
Sample size for a given budget	Small	Medium	Large	Large
Data quantity per respondent	High	Medium	Low	Low
Reaches high proportion of public	Yes	Yes	No	Yes
Reaches widely dispersed sample	No	Maybe	Yes	Yes
Reaches special locations	Yes	Maybe	No	No
Interaction with respondents	Yes	Yes	No	No
Degree of interviewer bias	High	Medium	None	None
Severity of nonresponse bias	Low	Low	High	High
Presentation of visual stimuli	Yes	No	Yes	Maybe
Field-worker training required	Yes	Yes	No	No

Source: Pamela L. Alreck and Robert B. Settle, *The Survey Research Handbook,* 3rd ed. (Burr Ridge, IL: McGraw-Hill/Irwin, 2004) 33, print. Reprinted with permission of The McGraw-Hill Companies.

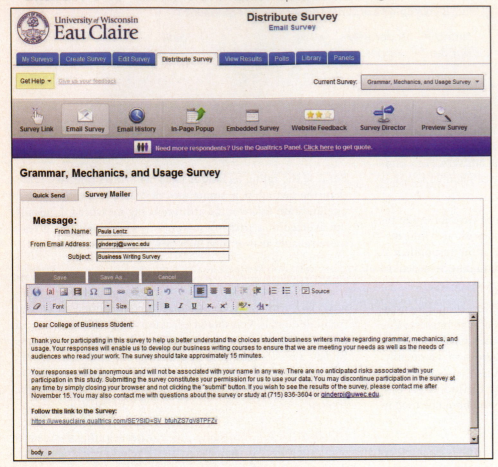

generate verbal data such as reviews of company records, personal interviews, focus groups, and direct observation. Qualitative research does not enable statistical analysis or the application of the findings to larger populations; rather, it enables one to interpret what the data mean at a more localized level.

conducting focus groups The purpose of a focus group is to bring together a group of people to find out their beliefs or attitudes about the topic of a research project. For instance, if you want to find information about how one of your company's products might be improved, you might gather a group of people who currently use your product and have them discuss what they like or don't like about it.

As the moderator of the discussion, you can structure the conversation and ask questions that will elicit useful data from the participants, or you can simply allow participants to voice their ideas. As you may have experienced, when people discuss a topic in a group, they often generate more or new ideas that they may not have done working individually. The focus group can create a sort of brainstorming session of ideas that yield rich data. Of course, as the moderator you also have to make sure that people can freely share their ideas. Some of the tips discussed in Chapter 10 for encouraging participation in writing projects and meetings may also help you facilitate focus groups. Because of advances in technology, focus groups can be conducted face to face, online, or even over the phone.

ask (see Exhibit 8.16). If you are conducting a personal or phone survey, you need to cover this information in instructions to the interviewers. You should develop your working plan before conducting the pilot study discussed in the following section. You should test that plan in the pilot study and revise it based on the knowledge you gain from the pilot study.

conducting a pilot study Before doing the survey, it is advisable to conduct a pilot study on your questionnaire and working plan. A pilot study is a small-scale version of the actual survey. Its purpose is to test what you have planned. Based on your experience in the pilot study, you modify your questionnaire and working plan for use in the full-scale survey that follows.

LO 11 Explain the use of qualitative strategies such as focus groups and personal interviews.

Conducting Qualitative Research

Qualitative researchers take a more interpretive approach to research. They begin with a more general question about what they want to learn and then study natural phenomena to gather insights into the phenomena or even to learn to ask different questions. Accordingly, they are likely to use research tools that

conducting personal interviews If you decide that talking with people one-on-one is the best way to gather data to answer your research question, you will likely conduct face-to-face interviews or phone interviews. People may be willing to share stories and opinions in a personal interview that they might not be comfortable sharing in a larger group.

Preparing for a personal interview is much like preparing for a survey. First, you need to decide whom to interview (your sample). Then you need to construct questions, as you would for a survey. However, the nature of the questions for a face-to-face interview will be a bit different. Many researchers prefer to use closed-ended questions in surveys. Closed-ended questions force the participants into giving only one possible response (e.g., answering a yes/no question, choosing an age range from a list provided by the researcher, or selecting a rating on a scale) and allow for quick data analysis. However, many researchers

> ## WHETHER YOU CONDUCT A PERSONAL INTERVIEW, CONVENE A FOCUS GROUP, OR OTHERWISE GATHER ORAL DATA, YOU NEED TO DECIDE HOW YOU WILL RECORD THE INTERACTIONS.

favor open-ended questions when they construct face-to-face interviews because the conversational nature of the interview setting enables participants to provide detailed, rich, and varied responses. Furthermore, open-ended questions in personal interviews provide the researcher with the opportunity to ask follow-up questions that they would not be able to ask participants taking a written survey.

Whether you conduct a personal interview, convene a focus group, or otherwise gather oral data, you need to decide how you will record the interactions. You cannot rely on your memory. Sometimes, simply taking notes is sufficient. Other times, you may want to video tape the session so that you can note nonverbal behaviors (e.g., tone, facial expressions, gestures) that influence the interpretation of a participant's response. Then transcribe the notes using a system for coding these nonverbal behaviors in the text of the transcript.

Evaluating and Reporting Data

Gathering information is one step in processing facts for your report. You also need to evaluate it. In the case of secondary research, ask yourself questions about the writer's credibility, including methods of collecting facts and ability to draw inferences from the facts presented. Does the author draw conclusions that can be supported by the data presented? Are the sources reliable? Are the data or interpretations biased in any way? Are there any gaps or holes in the data or interpretation? You need to be a good judge of the material and discard it if it does not meet your standard for quality.

As for primary research, this chapter has discussed how to plan and carry out primary data collection properly. Once you have good data to work with, you must interpret them accurately and clearly for your reader. The next major section provides advice for interpreting data.

If you are unsure of your reader's level of expertise in understanding descriptive statistics such as measures of central tendency and cross-tabulations, present the statistic and tell the reader what it means. In general, you can expect to explain the statistics from univariate, bivariate, and multivariate analyses. In many cases, graphics help tremendously because they clearly show trends and relationships. Statistical programs such as SPSS and SAS help you analyze, report, and graph your data. Finally, you have an ethical responsibility to present your data honestly and completely.

Omitting an error or limitation of the data collection is often viewed as seriously as hiding errors or variations from accepted practices. Of course, any deliberate distortion of the data, whether primary or secondary, is unethical. It is your responsibility to communicate the findings of the report accurately and clearly.

LO 12 Explain the guidelines for conducting ethical business research.

Conducting Ethical Business Research

Many companies, academic institutions, and medical facilities have guidelines for conducting research with human subjects and have institutional review boards (IRBs) that ensure employees comply with the laws and policies that govern research. Be sure that you are familiar with these policies before conducting research.

The main principle behind such policies is that participants in a research study have the right to informed consent. That is, they have the right to know the nature of their participation in the study and any associated risks. In addition, participation must be voluntary, and people have the right to discontinue their participation at any time during the study. Just because they agreed to participate at one point does not mean they are obligated to finish the project. Furthermore, participants need to know if their participation and data associated with them in the study are confidential (known only to the researcher and participant) or anonymous (known only to the participant).

Because protecting participants' rights can require you to develop a proposal to an IRB, an informed consent letter to the participants, and an informed consent form, be sure you build this process into the planning stage of your project.

LO 13 Explain the common errors in interpreting and develop attitudes and practices conducive to good interpreting.

INTERPRETING THE FINDINGS

The next major stage of the report-writing process is to interpret the information you've gathered. Actually, you will have done a good bit of interpreting already by the time you reach this stage. You had to interpret the elements of the situation to develop with your definition of the problem. You also had to

technology in brief

Citation Managers Help Writers Document Their Report Sources

One feature in Word 2007—the Reference tab—helps writers manage their sources. Although not as full-featured as dedicated citation managers such as ProCite, End-Note, or even the Web-based RefWorks, it can take some of the grunt work out of managing and citing sources.

When you select the type of source to cite, it will open a form prompting you for the information needed. Once you've entered the data and selected the form (APA, Chicago, MLA, etc.) you want to use, Word will insert your citation in proper format as well as create a Bibliography or Works Cited page for you.

The citation manager is helpful in ordering and punctuating your sources, but you still need to proofread for spelling, capitalization, accuracy of the information, and completeness of the citation.

Used wisely, though, this tool is effective for compiling and organizing sources. The online Supplementary Chapter E: "Documentation of Sources" explains this feature more thoroughly.

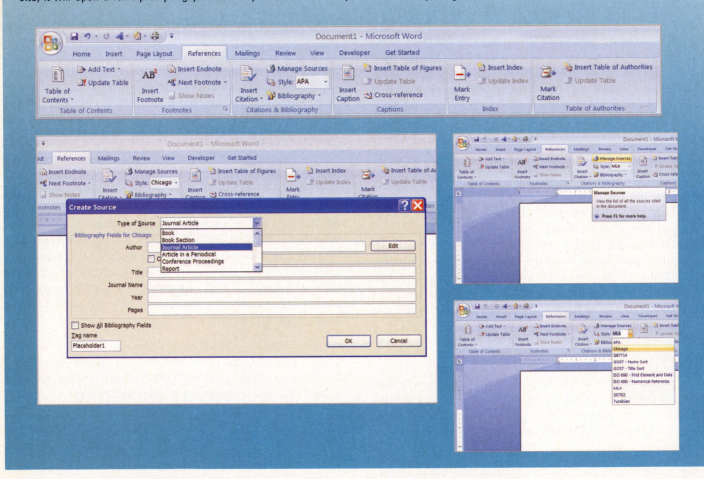

interpret your data as you were gathering them to make sure that you were getting appropriate and sufficient information. But when your research is finished, you will need to develop the interpretations that will guide the shape and contents of your report. To do this, keep both your problem and your readers in mind. Your findings will need to apply clearly to the given problem in order to be viewed as logical solutions, but they will also need to meet the readers' needs in order to be viewed as

relevant and helpful. If you have kept your reader-based problem statements and purpose in mind while doing your research, making logical, reader-based analyses of your data should follow naturally.

Interpretation is obviously a mental process, and how you interpret your data will vary from case to case. Still, the following general advice can help you with this process.

Interpreting facts requires not only analytical skills and objective judgment but consideration for ethical issues as well.

Advice for Avoiding Human Error

To avoid certain human tendencies that lead to error in interpretation, keep the following advice in mind:

1. *Report the facts as they are.* Do nothing to make them more or less exciting. Adding color to interpretations to make the report more interesting compromises integrity.

2. *Do not think that conclusions are always necessary.* When the facts do not support a conclusion, you should just summarize your findings and conclude that there is no conclusion. All too often report writers think that if they do not conclude, they have failed in their investigation.

3. *Do not interpret a lack of evidence as proof to the contrary.* The fact that you cannot prove something is true does not mean that it is false.

You're right. This report does make you look like a fool.

4. *Do not compare noncomparable data.* When you look for relationships between sets of data, make sure they have similarities—that you do not have apples and oranges.

5. *Do not draw illogical cause–effect conclusions.* The fact that two sets of data appear to affect each other does not mean they actually do. Use your good logic to determine whether a cause–effect relationship is likely.

6. *Beware of unreliable and unrepresentative data.* Much of the information to be found in secondary sources is incorrect to some extent. The causes are many: collection error, biased research, recording mistakes. Beware especially of data collected by groups that advocate a position (political organizations, groups supporting social issues, and other special interest groups). Make sure the sources you uncover are reliable. And remember that the interpretations you make are no better than the data you interpret.

7. *Do not oversimplify.* Most business problems are complex, and all too often we neglect some important parts of them.

8. *Tailor your claims to your data.* There's a tendency among inexperienced report writers to use too few facts to generalize far too much. If you have learned about a certain phenomenon, do not assume that your interpretations can automatically be applied to similar phenomena. Or if your research has revealed the source of a problem, do not assume that you can also propose solutions; finding solutions can be a separate research project altogether. Make only those claims that are well supported by your evidence, and when you are not sure how strong to make them, use such qualified language as "may be," "could be," and "suggest."

Appropriate Attitudes and Practices

In addition to being alert to the most likely causes of error, you can improve your interpretation of findings if you do the following:

1. *Maintain a judicial attitude.* Play the role of a judge as you interpret. Look at all sides of every issue without emotion or prejudice. Your primary objective is to form the most reliable interpretations of the situation.

2. *Consult with others.* Rarely is one mind better than two or more. Thus, you can profit by talking over your interpretations with others.

3. *Test your interpretations.* While the ultimate test of your interpretations' validity will be how well they hold up in their actual application to a company problem, you can perform two tests to help you make reasonable inferences from your data.

   • First is the *test of experience.* In applying this test, you use the underlying theme in all scientific methods—reason. You ponder each interpretation you make, asking yourself, "Does this appear reasonable in light of all I know or have experienced?"

   • Second is the *negative test,* which is an application of the critical viewpoint. You begin by making the interpretation that is directly opposite your initial one. Next, you examine the opposite interpretation carefully in light of all available evidence, perhaps even building a case for it. Then you compare the two interpretations and retain the one that is more strongly supported.

Statistical Tools in Interpretation

In many cases, the information you gather is quantitative—that is, expressed in numbers. Such data in their raw form usually are voluminous, consisting of tens, hundreds, even thousands of figures. To use these figures intelligently, you first must find ways of simplifying them so that your reader can grasp their general meaning. Statistical techniques provide many methods for analyzing data. By knowing them, you can improve your ability to interpret. Although a thorough review of statistical techniques is beyond the scope of this book, you should know the more commonly used methods described in the following paragraphs.

Possibly of greatest use to you in writing reports are *descriptive statistics*—measures of central tendency, dispersion, ratios, and probability. Measures of central tendency—the mean, median, and mode—will help you find a common value of a series that

interpretation, not a replacement for it. Whatever you do to reduce the volume of data deserves careful explanation so that the reader will receive the intended meaning.

LO 14 Organize information in outline form using time, place, quantity, factors, or a combination of these as bases for division.

ORGANIZING THE REPORT INFORMATION

When you have interpreted your information, you know the message of your report. Now you are ready to organize this message for presentation. Your goal here is to arrange the information in a logical order that meets your reader's needs.

The Nature and Benefits of Outlining

An invaluable tool at this stage of the process is an outline. A good one will group things that go together, order them logically, and relate ideas in terms of levels of generality (hierarchy).

> "In constructing your outline, you can use any system of numbering or formatting that will help you see the logical structure of your planned contents."

appropriately describes a whole. The measures of dispersion—ranges, variances, and standard deviations—should help you describe the spread of a series. Ratios (which express one quantity as a multiple of another) and probabilities (which determine how many times something will likely occur out of the total number of possibilities) also can help you convey common meaning in data analysis. Inferential and other statistical approaches are also useful but go beyond these basic elements. You will find descriptions of these and other useful techniques in the help documentation of your spreadsheet and statistics software as well as in any standard statistics reference source.

A word of caution, however: Your job as a writer is to help your reader interpret the information. Sometimes unexplained statistical calculations—even if elementary to you—may confuse the reader. Thus, you must explain your statistical techniques explicitly with words and visuals when needed. Use charts, tables, and other graphics when necessary to help your reader understand. You must remember that statistics are a help to

Although you can outline mentally, a written plan is advisable for all but the shortest reports. Time spent on outlining at this stage is time well spent, because it will make your drafting process more efficient and orderly. For longer reports, your outline will also form the basis for the table of contents.

If you have proceeded methodically thus far, you probably already have a rough outline. It is the list of topics that you drew up when planning how to research your problem. You may also have added to this list the findings that you developed when interpreting your data. But when it's time to turn your research plan into a report plan, you need to outline more deliberately. Your goal is to create the most logical, helpful pattern of organization for your readers.

In constructing your outline, you can use any system of numbering or formatting that will help you see the logical structure of your planned contents. If it will help, you can use the conventional or the decimal symbol system to mark the levels. The conventional system uses Roman numerals to show the major headings and letters of the alphabet and Arabic numbers to show the lesser headings, as illustrated here:

Conventional System
I. **First-level heading**
  A. **Second level, first part**
  B. **Second level, second part**
    1. **Third level, first part**
    2. **Third level, second part**
      a. **Fourth level, first part**
        (1) **Fifth level, first part**
          (a) **Sixth level, first part**
II. **First-level heading**
  A. **Second level, first part**
  B. **Second level, second part**
    Etc.

The decimal system uses whole numbers to show the major sections. Whole numbers followed by decimals and additional digits show subsections. That is, the digits to the right of the decimal show each successive step in the outline as in this example:

Decimal System
1.0 First-level heading
  1.1 Second level, first part
  1.2 Second level, second part
    1.2.1 Third level, first part
    1.2.2 Third level, second part
      1.2.2.1 Fourth level, first part
        1.2.2.1.1 Fifth level, first part
          1.2.2.1.1.1 Sixth level, first part

2.0 First-level heading
  2.1 Second level, first part
  2.2 Second level, second part
  Etc.

Bear in mind that at this stage the outline is a tool for you, even though it is geared toward your reader. Unless others will want to see an updated outline as you work, spend minimal time on its appearance. Allow yourself to change it, scribble on it, depart from it—whatever seems appropriate as your report develops. For example, you might want to note on your outline which sections will contain visuals, or to jot down a particularly good transition between sections that came to mind. The time to sweat over the outline's format and exact wording will be when you use it to create the headings and the table of contents for your finished report.

Organization by Division

One methodical way to create an outline is to use the process of dividing the contents into smaller and smaller sections. With this method, you begin by looking over all your information. You then identify its major parts. This first level of division gives you the major outline in Roman numerals (I, II, III, and so on as indicated in Exhibit 8.17).

Next, you find ways to subdivide the contents in each major section, yielding the second-level information (indicated by A, B, C).

technology in brief

Application Tools Assist the Writer in Both Identifying Factors and Outlining

Inspiration (or its Web-based version *mywebspiration.com*) is a concept-mapping tool aimed at helping business executives create and outline business documents. The example shown here demonstrates how individuals or groups can brainstorm the factors of a report that investigates going green in the office. Using either the diagram or outline view (or both shown here), a report writer would list as many ideas as possible. Later the items and relationships can be rearranged.

The software will update the outline symbols as changes are made. Users can toggle between the different views to work with the mode that works best for them.

When ready to write, users can export the outline or diagram to Word, RTF format, or Google Docs. You can also publish your work to a webpage, blog, or wiki.

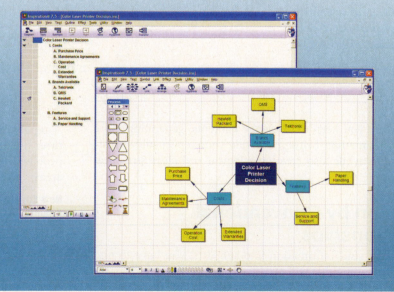

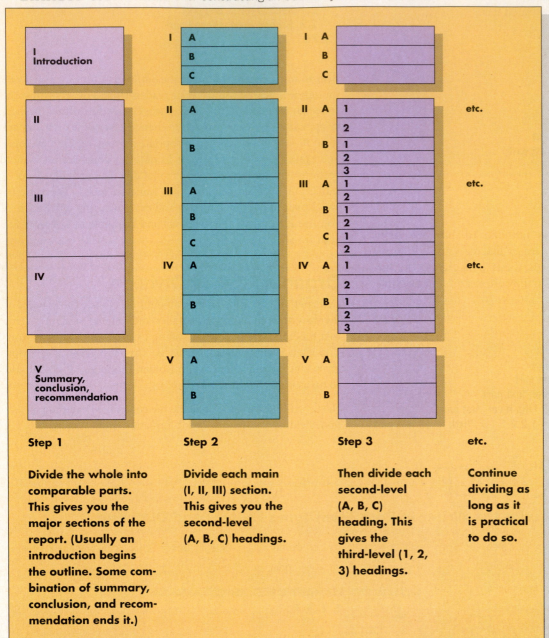

Step 1

Divide the whole into comparable parts. This gives you the major sections of the report. (Usually an introduction begins the outline. Some combination of summary, conclusion, and recommendation ends it.)

Step 2

Divide each main (I, II, III) section. This gives you the second-level (A, B, C) headings.

Step 3

Then divide each second-level (A, B, C) heading. This gives the third-level (1, 2, 3) headings.

etc.

Continue dividing as long as it is practical to do so.

Time, place, quantity, and factor are the general bases for these divisions.

Whenever the information you have to present has some time aspect, consider organizing it by *time*. In such an organization, the divisions are periods of time. These time periods usually follow a sequence. Although a past-to-present or present-to-past sequence is the rule, variations are possible.

A report on the progress of a research committee illustrates this possibility. The period covered by this report might be broken down into the following comparable subperiods:

The period of orientation, May–July

Planning the project, August

Implementation of the research plan, September–November

The happenings within each period might next be arranged in order of occurrence. Close inspection might reveal additional division possibilities.

If the information you have collected has some relation to geographic location, you may use a *place* division. Ideally, this division would be such that the areas are nearly equal in importance.

If practical, you keep dividing the contents, generating more levels. This method helps you divide your report into digestible chunks while also creating a logical and clear structural hierarchy.

Division by Conventional Relationships

In dividing your information into subparts, you have to find a way of dividing that will produce approximately equal parts. The divisions you select could be equal in length or importance.

A report on the U.S. sales program of a national manufacturer illustrates a division by place. The information in this problem might be broken down by these major geographic areas:

New England
Atlantic Seaboard
South
Southwest
Midwest
Rocky Mountains
Pacific Coast

Another illustration of organization by place is a report on the productivity of a company with a number of customer service branches. A major division of the report might be devoted to each of the branches. The information for each branch might be broken down further, this time by sections, departments, divisions, or the like.

Quantity divisions are possible for information that has quantitative values. To illustrate, an analysis of the buying habits of potential customers could be divided by such income groups as the following:

Under $30,000
$30,000 to under $45,000
$45,000 to under $60,000
$60,000 to under $85,000
$85,000 to under $100,000
$100,000 and over

Factor breakdowns are less easily seen than the preceding three possibilities. Problems often have few or no time, place, or quantity aspects. Instead, they require that certain information areas be investigated. Such areas may consist of questions that must be answered in solving a problem or of subjects that must be investigated and applied to the problem.

An example of a division by factors is a report that seeks to determine which of three locations is the best for a new office for property management. In arriving at this decision, one would need to compare the three locations based on the factors affecting the office location. Thus, the following organization would be a possibility:

Location accessibility
Rent
Parking
Convenience to current and new customers
Facilities

Combination and Multiple Division Possibilities

Not all division possibilities are clearly time, place, quantity, or factor. In some instances, combinations of these bases of division are possible. In a report on the progress of a sales organization, for example, the information collected could be arranged by a combination of quantity and place:

Areas of high sales activity
Areas of moderate sales activity
Areas of low sales activity

In some cases, the information can be organized in more than one way. For example, take the problem of determining the best of three locations for an annual sales meeting. The gathered information could be organized by site or by the bases of

comparison. Organized by sites, the bases of comparison would probably be the second-level headings:

Site A
 Airport accessibility
 Hotel accommodations
 Meeting facilities
 Favorable weather
 Costs
 Restaurant/entertainment options
Site B
 Airport accessibility
 (And so on)
Site C
 Airport accessibility
 (And so on)

Organized by bases of comparison, cities would probably be the second-level headings:

Airport accessibility
 Site A
 Site B
 Site C
Hotel accommodations
 Site A
 Site B
 Site C
Meeting facilities
 Site A
 Site B
 Site C

> ". . . some problems can be organized in more than one way."

At first glance, both plans appear logical. Close inspection, however, shows that organization by cities separates information that has to be compared. For example, you must examine three different parts of the report to find out which city has the best hotel accommodations. In the second outline, the information that has to be compared is close together. You can determine which city has the best hotel accommodations after reading only one section of the report.

Nevertheless, these two plans show that some problems can be organized in more than one way. In such cases, you must compare the possibilities carefully to find the one that best presents the report information.

LO 15 Turn an outline into a table of contents whose format and wording are logical and meaningful.

From Outline to Table of Contents

When you are ready to prepare the table of contents for your report, you will be, in essence, turning the outline that helped you write into an accessibility tool for the reader. Because it will be your public outline, the table of contents needs to be carefully formatted and worded.

Communication in brief

Contrasting Headings from a Sample Report

Talking Headings	Topic Headings
Orientation to the Problem	Introduction
Authorization by Board Action	Authorization
Problem of Locating a Woolen Mill	Purpose
Use of Miscellaneous Government Data	Sources
Factors as Bases of Problem Solution	Preview
Community Attitudes Toward the Woolen Industry	Community Attitudes
Favorable Reaction of All Towns to New Mill	Plant Location
Mixed Attitudes of All Towns Toward Labor Policy	Labor Policy
Labor Supply and Prevailing Wage Rates	Factors of Labor
Lead of San Marcos in Unskilled Labor	Unskilled Workers
Concentration of Skilled Workers in San Marcos	Skilled Workers
Generally Confused Pattern of Wage Rates	Wage Rates
Nearness to the Raw Wool Supply	Raw Wool Supply
Location of Ballinger, Coleman, and San Marcos in the Wool Area	Adequate Areas
Relatively Low Production Near Big Spring and Littlefield	Inadequate Areas
Availability of Utilities	Utilities
Inadequate Water Supply for All Towns but San Marcos	Water
Unlimited Supply of Natural Gas for All Towns	Natural gas
Electric Rate Advantage of San Marcos and Coleman	Electricity
General Adequacy of All Towns for Waste Disposal	Waste Disposal
Adequacy of Existing Transportation Systems	Transportation
Surface Transportation Advantages of San Marcos and Ballinger	Surface
General Equality of Airway Connections	Air
A Final Weighting of the Factors	Conclusions
Selection of San Marcos as First Choice	First Choice
Recommendation of Ballinger as Second Choice	Alternative Choice
Lack of Advantages in Big Spring, Coleman, and Littlefield	Other Possibilities

True, you will probably design the table of contents late in the report-writing process. We discuss it here as a logical conclusion to our discussion of outlining. But if others involved in the project want to see a well-prepared outline before your report is done, you can use the following advice to prepare that outline. Note also that what we say about preparing the headings for the table of contents also applies to writing the headings for the report sections. The two sets of headings—those in the table of contents and those in the report itself—should match exactly. Using the Outline view in Word with the Styles tool and Table of Contents generator will ensure that these are exact matches.

formatting decisions

Whatever format you used for your outline, you now need to choose a format for the presentation of your document that your reader will find instructive, readable, and appropriate.

An *instructive* format clearly indicates the hierarchy of the information. Rely mostly on form (font selection, size, style, and color) and placement to distinguish the levels of your contents.

A *readable* format uses ample vertical white space between topics and enables readers to see at a glance how the report is organized. Using leaders (dots with intervening spaces) between your topics and your page numbers can also enhance readability.

An *appropriate* format is one that your reader expects. Most business readers view the conventional outlining system (Roman numerals, letters, and Arabic numbers) and the decimal system (as in 1.2.1) as adding unnecessary clutter to the table of contents. Instead, they prefer the use of form and placement to show them how the parts relate to each other. However, in the military and some technical environments, the decimal system is expected, and in other contexts, your readers may want the full numerals and letters of the conventional system.

In our examples, we use a headings and subheadings format rather than numbering to indicate levels of information, but be sure to get a sense of what your particular readers will prefer.

topic or talking headings

In selecting the wording for your table of contents headings, you have a choice of two general forms: topic headings and talking headings. *Topic headings* are short constructions, frequently consisting of one or two words. They merely identify the topic of discussion. Here is a segment of a topic-heading table of contents:

Present armor unit
    Description and Output
    Cost
    Deficiencies
Replacement Effects
    Space
    Boiler Setting
    Additional Accessories
    Fuel

Like topic headings, *talking headings* (or *popular headings* as they are sometimes called) identify the subject matter covered. But they go a step further. They also indicate what is said about the subject. In other words, talking headings summarize the material they cover, as in this illustration:

Operation Analyses of Armor Unit
    Recent Lag in Overall Output
    Increase in Cost of Operation
    Inability to Deliver Necessary Steam
Consideration of Replacement Effects
    Greater Space Requirements
    Need for Higher Boiler Setting
    Efficiency Possibilities of Accessories
    Practicability of Firing Two Fuels

parallelism of construction As a general rule, you should write headings at each level of the table of contents in the same grammatical form. In other words, equal-level headings should be parallel in structure. This rule is not just an exercise in grammar; its purpose is to show similarity. As you will recall from the discussion of conventional relationships of data,

Or you could make all the headings sentences, like this:

Programmer Output Is Lagging.
Cost of Labor Is Increasing.
Information Technology Cannot Deliver Necessary Results.

conciseness in wording Your talking headings should be the shortest possible word arrangement that also can meet the talking requirement. Although the following headings talk well, their excessive lengths obviously impairs their ability to communicate quickly:

Personal Appearance Enhancement Is the Most Desirable Feature of Contact Lenses That Wearers Report.

The Drawback of Contacts Mentioned by Most People Who Can't Wear Them Is That They Are Difficult to Put In.

More Comfort Is the Most Desired Improvement Suggested by Wearers and Nonwearers of Contact Lenses.

Obviously, the headings contain too much information. Just what should be left out, however, is not easily determined. Much depends on the analysis the writer has performed on

> "As a general rule, you should write headings at each level of the table of contents in the same grammatical form."

equal-level headings are divided consistently using time, place, quantity, factor, or combinations. You want to show consistently such equal-level divisions through parallel headings. For example, if the first major heading is a noun phrase, all other major headings should be noun phrases. If the first second-level heading under a major head is an *-ing* phrase, all second-level headings in this section should be *-ing* phrases. However, authorities also permit varying the form from one level to another level; that is, the second-level heads in one section need to match, but they do not need to match the second-level heads in the other sections, and the third-level heads do not need to match the second-level heads.

The following headings illustrate violations of parallelism:

Programmer Output Is Lagging (sentence).
Increase in Cost of Labor (noun phrase)
Unable to Deliver Necessary Results (decapitated sentence— missing a subject–verb combination at the beginning)

You may correct this violation by making the headings all sentences, all noun phrases, or all decapitated sentences. If you desire all noun phrases, you could construct such headings as these:

Lag in Programmer Output
Increase in Cost of Labor
Inability to Deliver Necessary Results

the material and what he or she determined to be most significant. One analysis, for example, would support these revised headings:

Personal Appearance Most Desirable Feature
Difficulty of Insertion Main Drawback
Comfort Most Desired Improvement

variety of expression In wording headings, as in all other forms of writing, you should use a variety of expressions. Repeating words too frequently makes for monotonous writing, and monotonous writing is not pleasing to the reader. The following outline excerpt illustrates this point:

Oil Production in Texas
Oil Production in Alaska
Oil Production in Louisiana

As a rule, if you make the headings talk well, there is little chance of monotonous repetition. Since your successive sections would probably not be presenting similar or identical information, headings really descriptive of the material they cover would not be likely to use the same words. The headings in the preceding example can be improved simply by making them talk:

Texas Leads in Oil Production.
Alaska Holds Runner-up Position.
Rapidly Gaining Louisiana Ranks Third.

As we say, the same guidelines that make for an informative, logical, and interesting table of contents also apply to the headings for your report.

LO 16 Write reports that are focused, objective, consistent in time viewpoint, smoothly connected, and interesting.

WRITING THE REPORT

When you write your report, you will have already done a good deal of writing. You will have written—and probably rewritten—a problem and purpose statement to guide you through your research. You will have collected written data or recorded your findings in notes, and you will have organized your interpretations of the data into a logical, reader-centered structure. Now it is time to fill in your outline with clearly expressed facts and observations.

When you draft your report, your first priority is to present your information in the right order. You do not need to strive for a perfect draft the first time around. Understand that some pieces will seem to write themselves, while others will be much more difficult. Allow yourself to move along, stitching together the pieces. Once you have a draft to work with, you can perfect it.

Whatever other goals it may achieve, the opening of your report should convey what problem you studied, how you studied it, and (at least generally) what you found out. Why? Because these are the facts that the reader most wants to know when he or she first looks at your report.

Here is a simple introduction that follows this pattern:

In order to find out why sales were down at the Salisbury store, I interviewed the manager, observed the operations, and assessed the environment. A high rate of employee turnover appears to have resulted in a loss of customers, though the deteriorating neighborhood also seems to be a contributing factor.

In a formal report, some brief sections may precede this statement of purpose (for example, facts about the authorization of the study), and there might be extensive front matter (for example, a title page, letter of transmittal, table of contents, and executive summary). What follows the introduction can also vary depending on the size and complexity of the report. For example, it may or may not be appropriate to go into more detail about the research methods and limitations, or to announce specifically how the following sections will be organized. But whatever kind of report you are writing, make sure that the beginning gets across the subject of the report, what kind of data it is based upon, and its likely significance to the reader.

> ## Arguably the most critical parts of your report will be the beginning and ending.

When revising, let the advice in the previous chapters be your guide. As with all the business messages previously discussed, reports should communicate as clearly and quickly as possible. Your readers' time is valuable, and you risk having your report misread or even ignored if your words and formatting do not get your contents across efficiently.

You can help your reader receive the report's message clearly by giving your report some specific qualities of well-written reports. Two critical ingredients are a reader-centered beginning and ending. Such characteristics as objectivity, consistency in time viewpoint, transition, and interest can also enhance the reception of your report. We review these topics in the following pages.

Beginning and Ending

Arguably the most critical parts of your report will be the beginning and ending. In fact, researchers agree that these are the most frequently read parts of a report. Chapter 9 goes into detail about beginnings and endings, but some general advice is in order here.

Your ending will provide a concise statement of the report's main payoff—whether facts, interpretations, or recommendations. In a short report, you may simply summarize your findings with a brief paragraph, since the specific findings will be easy to see in the body of the report. In a longer report, you should make this section a more thorough restatement of your main findings, formatted in an easy-to-digest way. The gist ("so what did you find out?") and significance ("and why should I care?") of your report should come through loud and clear.

Maintaining Objectivity

Good report writing presents facts and interprets them logically. It avoids presenting the writer's biases and attitudes. In other words, it is objective. You can make your report objective by putting aside your prejudices and biases, by approaching the problem with an open mind and looking at all sides of every issue, and by fairly reviewing and interpreting the information you have uncovered. Your role should be much like that of a fair-minded judge presiding over a court of law. You will be

As the next chapter points out, the format and makeup of your report will signal its level of formality. But you will also need to decide how formal your report will be on the stylistic level. Compare the following three versions of the same point:

- The study revealed that 20 percent of the participants were unaware of Jacob's Foods.
- Our study revealed that 20 percent of the participants were unaware of your store.
- We found out that 20 percent of your market had never heard of your store.

Did you notice the decreasing level of formality? What accounts for the differences? Be sure to choose a style that matches the relationship you have with your readers and their preferences. But whatever style you choose, write clearly and readably.

> "You should use personal writing for informal situations and impersonal writing for formal situations."

thorough in your search for the best information and the most reasonable interpretations.

objectivity as a basis for believability
An objective report has an ingredient that is essential to good report writing—believability. Biased writing in artfully deceptive language may at first glance be believable. But if bias is evident at any place in a report, the reader will be suspicious of the entire report. Maintaining objectivity is, therefore, the only sure way to make report writing believable.

the question of impersonal versus personal writing
Recognizing the need for objectivity, the early report writers worked to develop an objective style of writing. Since the source of bias in reports was people, they reasoned that objectivity was best attained by emphasizing facts rather than the people involved in writing and reading reports. They tried to take the human beings out of their report by using an impersonal writing style, that is, writing in the third person without I's, we's, or you's.

In recent years, some writers have questioned impersonal report writing. They argue that personal writing is more forceful and direct than impersonal writing. They point out that writing is more conversational and, therefore, more interesting if it brings both the reader and the writer into the picture. They contend that objectivity is an attitude—not a matter of person—and that a report written in personal style can be just as objective as a report written in impersonal style. These writers argue that impersonal writing frequently leads to an overuse of the passive

voice and a dull writing style. While this last claim may be true, impersonal writing need not be boring. One has only to look at the lively style of writers for newspapers, newsmagazines, and journals.

As in most controversies, the arguments of both sides have merit. In some situations, personal writing is better. In other situations, impersonal writing is better. And in still other situations, either type of writing is good.

Your decision should be based on the facts of each report situation. First, you should consider the expectations of those for whom you are preparing the report. If your reader prefers an impersonal style use it—and vice versa. Then you should consider the formality of the situation. You should use personal writing for informal situations and impersonal writing for formal situations.

Perhaps the distinction between impersonal and personal writing is best made by illustration.

Personal

Having studied the advantages and disadvantages of using coupons, I conclude that your company should not adopt this practice. If you used the coupons, you would have to pay out money for them. You also would have to hire additional employees to take care of the increase in sales volume.

Impersonal

A study of the advantages and disadvantages of using coupons supports the conclusion that the Mills Company should not adopt this practice. The coupons themselves would cost extra money. Also, use of coupons would require additional personnel to take care of the increase in sales volume.

Being Consistent with Time Viewpoint

Presenting information in the right place in time is essential to your report's clarity. Not doing so confuses the reader. Thus, it is important that you maintain a proper time viewpoint.

You have two choices of time viewpoint: past and present. Although some authorities favor one or the other, either viewpoint can produce a good report. The important thing is to be consistent—to select one time viewpoint and stay with it. In other words, you should view all similar information in the report from the same position in time.

If you adopt the past-time viewpoint, you treat the research, the findings, and the writing of the report as past. Thus, you would report the results of a recent survey in past tense: "Twenty-two

In reports, transitions can be words or sentences that show the relationships of succeeding parts. They may appear at the beginning of a part as a way of relating this part to the preceding part. They may appear at the end of a part as a forward look. Or they may appear within a part as words or phrases that help move the flow of information.

Whether you use transitional words or a transitional sentence in a particular place depends on need. If there is a need to relate parts, you should use a transition. Because good, logical organization frequently clarifies the relationships of the parts in a short report, such reports may need only a few transitional words or sentences. Longer and more involved reports, on the other hand, usually require more.

No matter how long the report, you should not use transitions mechanically. You should use them only when they are

> ## "Throughout the report you can improve the connecting network of thought by using sentence transitions wisely."

percent of the managers *favored* a change." You would write a reference to another part of the report this way: "In Part III, this conclusion *was reached*." Your use of the past-time viewpoint would have no effect on references to future happenings. It would be proper to write a sentence like this: "If the current trend continues, 30 percent *will favor* a change by 2011." Prevailing concepts and proven conclusions are also exceptions. You would present them in present tense. For examples, you would write: "Solar energy *is* a major potential source of energy."

Writing in the present-time viewpoint presents as current all information that can logically be assumed to be current at the time of writing. All other information is presented in its proper place in the past or future. Thus, you would report the results of a recent survey in these words: "Twenty-two percent of the managers *favor* a change." You would refer to another part of the text like this: "In Part III, this conclusion *is reached*." In referring to an old survey, you would write: "In 2005 only 12 percent *held* this opinion." And in making a future reference, you would write: "If this trend continues, 30 percent *will hold* this opinion by 2011."

Using Transitions

A well-written report reads as one continuous story. The parts connect smoothly. Much of this smoothness is the result of good, logical organization. However, as with other kinds of documents, transitional techniques also help to connect information.

needed—when leaving them out would produce abruptness or ambiguity regarding the relationship between ideas. Transitions should not appear to be forced. They should blend naturally with the surrounding writing. For example, avoid transitions of this mechanical form: "The last section discussed Topic X. In the next section, Y will be analyzed."

sentence transitions Throughout the report you can improve the connecting network of thought by using sentence transitions wisely. You can use them especially to connect parts of the report. The following example shows how a sentence can explain the relationship between Sections A and B of a report. Note that the first words draw a conclusion for Section B. Then, with smooth tie-in, the next words introduce Section C and relate this part to the report plan. The words in brackets explain the pattern of the thought connections.

[Conclusion of Section B] . . . Thus, the data show only negligible differences in the cost for oil consumption [subject of Section B] for the three models of cars.

[Beginning of Section C] Even though the costs of gasoline [subject of Section A] and oil [subject of Section B] are the more consistent factors of operation expense, the picture is not complete until the costs of repairs and maintenance [subject of Section C] are considered.

In the following examples, succeeding parts are connected by sentences that make a forward-looking reference and thus set

> ## If the writing is to flow smoothly, you will need to connect clause to clause, sentence to sentence, and paragraph to paragraph.

up the next subject. As a result, the shift of subject matter is smooth and logical.

These data show clearly that alternative fuel cars are the most economical. Unquestionably, their operation by gas and hydrogen and their record for low-cost maintenance give them a decided edge over cars fueled by gas only. Before a definite conclusion about their merit is reached, however, one more vital comparison should be made.

The final sentence above clearly introduces the subsequent discussion of an additional comparison. Here is another example of a forecasting sentence:

. . . At first glance the data appear convincing, but a closer observation reveals a number of discrepancies.

The reader knows to expect a discussion of the discrepancies next.

Placing topic sentences at key points of emphasis is another way of using sentences to link the various parts of the report. Usually the topic sentence is best placed at the paragraph beginning. Note in the following example how topic sentences maintain the flow of thought by emphasizing key information.

The Acura accelerates faster than the other two brands, both on a level road and on a 9 percent grade. According to a test conducted by Consumer Reports, Acura reaches a speed of 60 miles per hour in 13.2 seconds. To reach the same speed, Toyota requires 13.6 seconds, and Volkswagen requires 14.4 seconds. On a 9 percent grade, Acura reaches the 60-miles-per-hour speed in 29.4 seconds, and Toyota reaches it in 43.3 seconds. Volkswagen is unable to reach this speed.

Because it carries more weight on its rear wheels than the others, Acura has the best traction of the three. Traction, which means a minimum of sliding on wet or icy roads, is important to safe driving, particularly during the cold, wet winter months. Since traction is directly related to the weight carried by the rear wheels, a comparison of these weights should give some measure of the safety of the three cars. According to data released by the Automobile Bureau of Standards, Acura carries 47 percent of its weight on its rear wheels. Nissan and Toyota carry 44 and 42 percent, respectively.

transitional words Although the most important transition problems concern connection between the major parts of the report, transitions are needed between the lesser parts. If the writing is to flow smoothly, you will need to connect clause to clause, sentence to sentence, and paragraph to paragraph. Transitional words and phrases generally serve to make such connections.

Numerous transitional words are available. The following list shows such words and how you can use them. With a little imagination to supply the context, you can easily see how these words relate ideas. For better understanding, the words are grouped by the relationships they show between what comes before and what follows.

Relationship	Word Examples
Listing or enumeration of subjects	In addition First, second, and so on Besides Moreover
Contrast	On the contrary In spite of On the other hand In contrast However
Likeness	In a like manner Likewise Similarly
Cause–result	Thus Because of Therefore Consequently For this reason
Explanation or elaboration	For example To illustrate For instance Also Too

Maintaining Interest

Like any other form of writing, report writing should be interesting. Actually, interest is as important as the facts of the report, for communication is not likely to occur without interest. Readers cannot help missing parts of the message if their interest is allowed to stray. Interest in the content is not enough to ensure communication. The writing itself must be interesting. If you have ever tried to read dull writing in studying for an examination, you know the truth of this statement.

Perhaps writing interestingly is an art. But if so, it is an art you can develop by working at it. To develop this ability, you need to avoid the rubber-stamp jargon so often used in business and instead work to make your words build concrete pictures. You need to cultivate a feeling for the rhythmic flow of words and sentences. You need to remember that behind every fact and figure there is life—people doing things, machines operating, a commodity being marketed. A technique of good report writing is to bring that life to the surface by using concrete words and active-voice verbs as much as possible. You also should work to achieve interest by not using more words than are necessary.

You can, however, overdo efforts to make report writing interesting. Such is the case whenever your reader's attention is attracted to how something has been said rather than to what has been said. Effective report writing simply presents information in a clear, concise, and interesting manner. Perhaps the purpose and definition of report-writing style are best summarized in this way: Report-writing style is at its best when the readers are prompted to say "Here are some interesting facts" rather than "Here is some beautiful writing."

LO 17   Prepare reports collaboratively.

WRITING COLLABORATIVELY

In your business career, you are likely to participate in collaborative writing projects. That is, you will work on a report with others. Group involvement in report preparation is becoming increasingly significant for a number of reasons. For one, the specialized knowledge of different people can improve the quality of the work. For another, the combined talents of the members are likely to produce a document better than any one of the members could produce alone. A third reason is that dividing the work can reduce the time needed for the project. And fourth, new software tools allow groups to collaborate from different places.

Determining the Group Makeup

As a beginning step, the membership of the group should be determined. The availability and competencies of the people in the work situation involved are likely to be the major considerations. At a minimum, the group will consist of two. The maximum will depend on the number actually needed to do the project. As a practical matter, however, a maximum of five is a good rule since larger groups tend to lose efficiency. More important than size, however, is the need to include all major areas of specialization involved in the work to be done.

In most business situations the highest ranking administrator in the group serves as leader. In groups made up of equals, a leader usually is appointed or elected. When no leader is so designated, the group works together informally. In such cases, however, an informal leader usually emerges. Especially with group writing projects, it is a good idea to have one person in charge of overseeing the entire process.

Planning for Effective Participation

The group's work should be conducted much the way a meeting should be conducted. As described in Chapter 10, leaders and members of meetings have clear roles and duties. Leaders must plan the sessions and follow the plan. They must move the work along. They must control the discussion, limiting those who talk too much and encouraging input from those who are reluctant to participate. Group members should actively participate, taking care not to monopolize. They should be both cooperative and courteous in their work with the group.

In some organizations where teamwork is common, the ground rules may be understood. Ideally, the group will generate its own ground rules to which all members agree. Some groups may even draw up a contract that each member signs as a way to get the group work off to a good start and avoid problems later.

All too often, groups experience results that vary from these patterns. Although a discussion of group development and processes is beyond the scope of this book, you might want to consult one of the many references on the subject.[5] Group members should recognize that effective groups do not just happen. They have

unique characteristics and processes that are planned for and managed explicitly.

Frequency of Collaboration

1%

- Constantly: 42%
- Occasionally: 40%
- Rarely: 18%

Source: Adapted with special permission from *BusinessWeek*, April 2008.

Choosing the Means of Collaboration

Not that many years ago, groups needed numerous face-to-face meetings in order to get their work done. Today there are many other venues for group interactions. Your group should put careful thought into the choice of media that will enable effective collaboration while taking into account members' time constraints, distance from each other, and technological preferences.

If possible, you should have at least two face-to-face meetings—one at the start of the project and another near the end (for example, when doing the final revisions). But the bulk of the collaborating may take place by email, discussion board, blogs, or online collaborative authoring tools such as Google Docs or wikis. You might even use a real-time meeting application or Skype to converse with each other. Whatever tools you use, it is important that you choose them consciously and create any ground rules that will apply to their use.

Researching and Writing the Collaborative Report

Whatever number of meetings is scheduled, the following activities typically occur, usually in the sequence shown. As you review them, it should be apparent that because of the differences in report projects, these activities vary in their implementation.

make a project plan The group should prepare a timeline that clearly states or shows the deadline for each task. Each task should be structured to meet the project's goals.

determine the purpose As in all report projects, the participants must determine just what the report must do. Thus, the group should follow the preliminary steps of determining the problem and purpose of the project as discussed previously. They also need to develop a coherent, shared sense of the report's intended readers and their needs.

identify the factors The group next determines what is needed to achieve the purpose. This step involves determining the factors of the problem, as described earlier in the chapter. An advantage of collaboration is that

Some reports written in business are produced in collaboration with others. Although you will do some work individually, you can expect to plan, organize, and revise the report as a group.

technology in brief

Comment and Review Tools Help Track Others' Changes to Your Document

Comment and reviewing tools help people work together on documents asynchronously. When others review content and edit your document digitally, the commenting tool allows them to express opinions and concerns while the tracking tool makes their editing changes clearly visible. In fact the tools allow you to accept or reject their suggestions individually or en masse.

In the example shown here, the reviewer clicked on the Review tab to reveal commenting and reviewing tools. Using this tool on a tablet PC enables the reviewer to choose from a variety of input methods—keyboard, digital ink, or voice. The tracking system allows reviews to use a variety of colors so others can easily determine whom the changes belong to. The commenting tool inserts identifying information, too. If a reviewer had entered a voice comment in the example below, the user would have simply clicked on the speaker icon to listen to the comment.

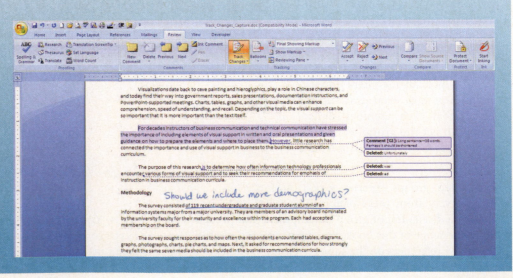

several minds are available for the critical thinking that is so necessary for identifying the factors of the problem.

gather the needed information Before the group can begin writing the report, it must get the information needed. This activity could involve conducting any of the types of research writing mentioned earlier. In some cases, however, group work begins after the information has already been assembled, thus eliminating this step.

interpret the information Determining the meaning of the information gathered is the next logical step for the group. In this step, the participants apply the findings to the problem, thereby selecting the information to be used in the report. In applying the findings to the problem, they also give meaning to the facts collected. The facts do not speak for themselves. Rather, group participants must think through the facts, apply the facts to the problem, derive logical meaning from the facts, and see them from the readers' points of view. Interpretations are only as good as the thinking of the people in the group.

organize the material Just as in any other report-writing project, the group next organizes the material selected for presentation. They will base the report's structure on the time, place, quantity, factor, or other relationships in the data.

plan the writing requirements A next logical step is planning the makeup of the report. In this step the formality of the situation and the audience involved determine the decision. In addition, matters of writing such as tone, style, and formality are addressed. The need for coherence, time, consistency, and interesting writing should be kept in mind.

assign parts to be written After the planning has been done, the group next turns its attention to the writing. The usual practice is to assign each person a part of the report.

write parts assigned Following comes a period of individual work. Each participant writes his or her part. Each will apply the ideas in Chapter 4 about word selection, sentence design, and paragraph construction to writing the assigned parts.

revise collaboratively The group meets and reviews each person's contribution and the full report. This should be a give-and-take session with each person actively participating. It requires that every person give keen attention to the work of each participant, making constructive suggestions wherever appropriate. It requires courteous but meaningful criticisms. It also requires that the participants be open minded, remembering that the goal is to construct the best possible document. In no case should the group merely give automatic approval to the work submitted. In cases of controversy, the majority views of the group should prevail.

edit the final draft After the group has done its work, one member usually is assigned the task of editing the final draft. This gives the document consistency. In addition, the editor serves as a final proofreader. The editor should be the most competent writer in the group. However, since the document reflects on all members, their timely participation in the final proofreading should be encouraged.

If all the work has been done with care and diligence, this final draft should be a report better than anyone in the group could have prepared alone. Those who study groups use the word *synergistic* to refer to groups that function this way. The final report is better than the sum of the individual parts. ∎

Get Online

mhhe.com/FlatleyM2e

for study materials including quizzes and Internet resources.

writing
short reports

With a general understanding of what reports do, how to research them, and how to write them, you are ready to consider the many varieties of reports. We focus in this chapter on the shorter forms—the reports that enable much of any organization's work.

While we describe several common categories of short reports, we do not cover every conceivable type. This would not be possible given the hundreds or even thousands of different kinds of reports that companies produce. The specific requirements for any report you will write will come from the specific situation in which you'll be writing it.

But the guidelines in this and the preceding chapter can help you meet any report-writing challenge. Just remember to learn all you can about your readers, their needs, and their expectations. If possible, find a report like the one you're about to write. Then use your good business-writing judgment to design an attractive, easy-to-read report that delivers exactly what your readers need. ■

LEARNING OBJECTIVES

LO1 Explain the makeup of reports relative to length and formality.

LO2 Discuss four major differences involved in writing short and long reports.

LO3 Choose an appropriate form for short reports.

LO4 Adapt the procedures for writing short reports to routine operational, progress, problem-solving, and audit reports as well as minutes of meetings.

workplace scenario

Preparing Short Reports

Assume again the position of assistant to the president of Technisoft and the report-writing work necessary in this position. Most of the time, your assignments concern routine, everyday problems: human resource policies, administrative procedures, work flow, and the like. Following what appears to be established company practice, you write the reports on these problems in simple email form.

Occasionally, however, you have a more involved assignment. Last week, for example, you investigated a union accusation that the company showed favoritism to the nonunion workers on certain production jobs. Because your report on this very formal investigation was written for the benefit of ranking company administrators as well as union leaders, you used a more formal style and format.

Then there was the report you helped prepare for the board of directors last fall. That report summarized pressing needs for capital improvements. A number of executives contributed to this project, but you were the coordinator. Because the report was important and was written for the board, you made it as formal as possible.

Clearly, reports vary widely. This chapter will help you determine your reports' makeup, style, form, and contents. It will then focus on the short reports that are likely to figure in your business-writing future.

> [The longer the problem and the more formal the situation, the more elaborate the report is likely to be.]

LO 1 Explain the makeup of reports relative to length and formality.

AN OVERVIEW OF REPORT COMPONENTS

As you prepare to write any report, you will need to decide on its makeup. Will it be a simple email? Will it be a long, complex, and formal report? Or will it fall between these extremes?

Your decisions will be based on the needs of your situation. Those needs are related to report length and the formality of the situation. The longer the problem and the more formal the situation, the more elaborate the report is likely to be. The shorter the problem and the more informal the situation, the less elaborate the report is likely to be. Adjusting the report's makeup to its length and formality helps meet the reader's needs in each situation.

To help you understand your choices, we first explain how to decide which components to use for a given report. We then briefly review the purpose and contents of each of these components.

The Report Classification Plan

The diagram in Exhibit 9.1 can help you construct reports that fit your specific need. At the top of the "stairway" are the most formal reports. Such reports have a number of pages that come before the text material, just as this book has pages that come before the first chapter. These pages serve useful purposes, but they also dress up the report. Typically, these *prefatory pages,* as they are called, are included when the problem situation is formal and the report is long. The exact makeup of the prefatory pages may vary, but the most common arrangement includes these parts: title fly, title page, transmittal message, table of contents, and executive summary. Flyleaves (blank pages at the beginning and end that protect the report) also may be included.

As the need for formality decreases and the problem becomes smaller, the makeup of the report changes. Although the changes that occur are far from standardized, they follow a general order. First, the title fly drops out. This page contains only the report title, which also appears on the next page. Since the title fly is used only for reasons of formality, it is the first component to go.

On the next level of formality, the executive summary and the transmittal message are combined. When this stage is reached, the report problem is short enough to be summarized in a short space. As shown in Exhibit 9.1, the report at this stage has three prefatory parts: title page, table of contents, and combination transmittal message and executive summary.

At the fourth step, the table of contents drops out. Another step down, as formality and length requirements continue to decrease,

"ALTHOUGH CONSTRUCTING TITLE PAGES IS EASY, COMPOSING THE TITLE IS NOT."

the combined transmittal message and executive summary drops out. Thus, the report commonly called the *short report* now has only a title page and the report text. The title page remains to the last because it serves as a useful cover page. In addition, it contains the most important identifying information. The short report is a popular form in business.

Below the short-report form is a form that reinstates the transmittal message and summary and presents the entire report as a letter—thus, the *letter report*. And finally, for short problems of more informality, the *email* or *memo* form is used.

This is a general analysis of report change; it does not cover every situation. Most reports, however, will fit within the framework of the diagram. Knowledge of the basic relationship of formality and length to report makeup should help you understand and plan reports.

▼ **EXHIBIT 9.1** Progression of Change in Report Makeup as Formality Requirements and Length Decrease

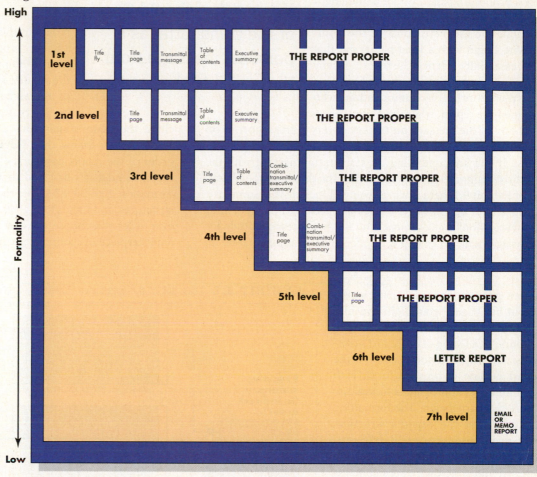

The Report Components

To be able to decide which parts of a long, formal report to include in your reports, you need a basic understanding of each part. This section briefly describes the different report components represented in Exhibit 9.1.

title pages The first two pages of a long, formal report—the *title fly* and *title page*—contain identification information. The title fly contains only the report title. It is included simply to give a report the most formal appearance. The title page, as illustrated on page 258 and in the sample formal report online, is more informative. It typically contains the title, identification of the writer and reader, and the date.

Although constructing title pages is easy, composing the title is not. In fact, on a per-word basis, the title requires more time than any other part of the report. A good title fits the report like a glove, efficiently and precisely covering the contents. For completeness of coverage, consider building your title around the five Ws: *who, what, where, when,* and *why.* Sometimes *how* may be important as well. You may not need to use all the Ws, but they can help you check the completeness of your title. Remember that a good title is concise as well as complete, so be careful not to make your title so long that it is hard to understand. A subtitle can help you be both concise and complete, as in this example: "Employee Morale at Florida Human Resource Offices: Results from a 2011 Survey."

transmittal message As the label implies, the *transmittal message* is a message that transmits the report. In formal situations, it usually takes letter form. In less formal situations, the report can be transmitted orally or by email. Whatever the case, you should think of the transmittal as a personal message from the writer to the reader, with much the same contents you would use if you were handing the report over in a face-to-face meeting with the recipient. Except in cases of extreme formality, you should use personal pronouns (*you, I, we*) and conversational language.

The sample transmittal letters on page 186 (for a proposal), page 259 (for a midlength report), and online (for a long report) illustrate the usual structure for this component. Begin with a brief paragraph that says, essentially, "Here is the report." Briefly identify the report's contents and purpose and, if appropriate, its authorization (who assigned the report, when, and why). Focus the body of the message on the key points of the report or on facts about the report that could be useful for your readers to know. If you are combining the transmittal message with the executive summary, as represented by the third and fourth levels of Exhibit 9.1, here is where you will include that summary. At the end of the message, you should provide a pleasant and/ or forward-looking comment. You might express gratitude for the assignment, for example, or offer to do additional research.

> "You should think of the transmittal as a personal message from the writer to the reader."

be self-explanatory; that is, readers shouldn't have to read other parts of the report in order to make sense of the summary. As pointed out previously, whether the executive summary is one of the prefatory parts (as illustrated in the sample report online) or part of the report proper (as in the sample proposal on p. 187) will depend on how long and how formal the report is.

You construct the executive summary by reducing the parts of the report in order and in proportion. You should clearly identify the topic, purpose, and origin of the report; state at least briefly what kind of research was conducted; present the key facts, findings, and analysis; and include the main conclusions and recommendations. While some writers follow this order, which usually matches the order of the report contents, others put the conclusions and recommendations first and then continue with the other information. Exhibit 9.2 shows the difference between these two structures, and Exhibit 9.3 gives contrasting examples. Whichever order you choose, the executive summary will need to be a masterpiece of economical writing.

table of contents If your short report goes much over 1,500 words (about five pages), you might consider including a brief *table of contents*. This, of course, is a listing of the report's contents. As Chapter 8 points out, it is the report outline in finished form, with page numbers and/or links to indicate where the parts begin. The formatting should reflect the report's structure, with main headings clearly differentiated from subheadings. The section titles should state each part's contents clearly and match the report's headings exactly. The table of contents may also include a list of visuals (or, if long, this list can stand alone). If a separate table of contents would be too formal, you can just list the topics that your report will cover in its introductory section.

executive summary The *executive summary* (also called *synopsis, abstract, précis,* or *digest*) is the report in miniature. For some readers it serves as a preview to the report, but for others—such as busy executives who may not have time to read the whole report—it's the only part of the report they will read. Because of this latter group of readers, the summary should

▼ **EXHIBIT 9.2** Diagram of the Executive Summary in Indirect and Direct Order

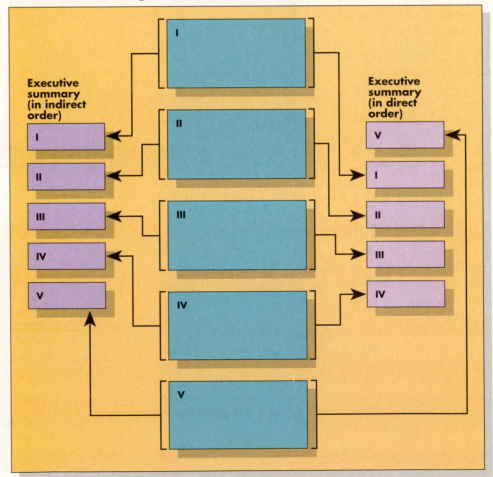

▼ **EXHIBIT 9.3** Example of an Executive Summary in Direct and Indirect Order

[Direct]

EXECUTIVE SUMMARY

To enhance the performance of Nokia's salespeople, this report recommends adding the following topics to Nokia's sales training program:

- Negative effects of idle time
- Projection of integrity
- Use of moderate persuasion
- Value of product knowledge

Supporting these recommendations are the findings and conclusions drawn from a five-day observational study of 20 productive and 20 underperforming salespeople. The study also included an exit interview and a test of the salesperson's product knowledge.

The data show that the productive salespeople used their time more effectively than did the underperforming salespeople. Compared with the latter, the productive salespeople spent less time being idle (28% vs. 53%). They also spent more time in contact with prospects (31.3% vs. 19.8%) and more time developing prospects (10.4% vs. 4.4%).

Observations of sales presentations revealed that productive salespeople displayed higher integrity, used pressure more reasonably, and knew the product better than underperforming salespeople. Of the 20 productive salespeople, 16 displayed images of moderately high integrity (Group II). Underperforming group members ranged widely, with 7 in Group III (questionable) and 5 each in Group II (moderately high integrity) and Group IV (deceitful). Most (15) of the productive salespeople used moderate pressure, whereas the underperforming salespeople tended toward extremes (10 high pressure, 7 low pressure). On the product knowledge test, 17 of the productive salespeople scored excellent and 3 fair. In the other group, 5 scored excellent, 6 fair, and 9 inadequate.

[Indirect]

EXECUTIVE SUMMARY

Midwestern Research associates was contracted to study the performance of Nokia's salespeople. A team of two researchers observed 20 productive and 20 underperforming salespeople over five working days. The study also included an exit interview and a test of the salesperson's product knowledge.

The data show that the productive salespeople used their time more effectively than did the underperforming salespeople. Compared with the latter, the productive salespeople spent less time in idleness (28% vs. 53%). They also spent more time in contact with prospects (31.3% vs. 19.8%) and more time developing prospects (10.4% vs. 4.4%).

Observations of sales presentations revealed that productive salespeople displayed higher integrity, used pressure more reasonably, and knew the product better than underperforming salespeople. Of the 20 productive salespeople, 16 displayed images of moderately high integrity (Group II). Members of the underperforming group ranged widely, with 7 in Group III (questionable) and 5 each in Group II (moderately high integrity) and Group IV (deceitful). Most (15) of the productive salespeople used moderate pressure, whereas the underperforming salespeople tended toward extremes (10 high pressure, 7 low pressure). On the product knowledge test, 17 of the productive salespeople scored excellent and 3 fair. In the other group, 5 scored excellent, 6 fair, and 9 inadequate.

On the basis of these findings, this report recommends adding the following topics to Nokia's sales training program:

- Negative effects of idle time
- Projection of integrity
- Use of moderate persuasion
- Value of product knowledge

It may be desirable to include other report components not discussed here—for example, a copy of the message that authorized the report, various appendices containing supplementary material, a glossary, or a bibliography. These have not been considered in Exhibit 9.1 or this discussion because their inclusion depends on the information needs of the reader, not on the report's length and formality. As with any writing task, you will need to decide what parts to provide given the facts of the situation and your readers' preferences.

LO 2 Discuss four major differences involved in writing short and long reports.

CHARACTERISTICS OF SHORTER REPORTS

The shorter report forms (those at the bottom of the stairway) are by far the most common in business. These are the everyday working reports—those used for the routine information

reporting that is vital to an organization's communication. Because these reports are so common, we cover them in detail here. For advice on writing long, formal reports, consult this book's online resources.

Little Need for Introductory Information

Most of the shorter, more informal reports require little or no introductory material. These reports typically concern day-to-day problems. Their lives are short; that is, they are not likely to be kept on file very long. They are intended for only a few readers, and these readers understand their context and purpose.

This is not to say that all shorter reports have no need for introductory material. Some do need it. In general, however, the need is likely to be small.

Determining what introductory material is needed is simply a matter of answering one question: What does my reader need to know before reading the information in this report? In very

> ## " Because the shorter reports usually solve routine problems, they are likely to be written in the direct order. "

short reports, an incidental reference to the problem, authorization of the investigation, or the like provides sufficient introduction. In extreme cases, however, you may need a detailed introduction comparable to that of the more formal reports. Consult the online chapter on the long report to see what a more elaborate introduction might include.

Reports need no introductory material if their very nature explains their purpose. This holds true for personnel actions. It also holds true for weekly sales reports, inventory reports, and some progress reports.

Predominance of the Direct Order

Because the shorter reports usually solve routine problems, they are likely to be written in the direct order. By *direct order* we mean that the report begins with its most important information—usually the conclusion and perhaps a recommendation. Business writers use this order because they know that their readers' main concern is to get the information needed to make a decision. So they present this information right away.

The form that the direct order takes in longer reports is somewhat different. The main findings will be somewhere up front—either in the letter of transmittal, executive

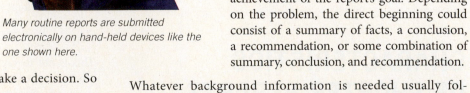

Many routine reports are submitted electronically on hand-held devices like the one shown here.

summary, or both—but the report itself may be organized indirectly. The introduction will present the topic and purpose of the report, but the actual findings may not come out until the body sections, and their most succinct statement will usually appear in the conclusions or recommendations section.

As one moves down the staircase toward the more informal and shorter reports, however, the need for the direct order in the report itself increases. At the bottom of the staircase, the direct order is more the rule than the exception.

Because order is so vital a part of constructing the shorter reports, it is important to understand the difference between the direct arrangement and the indirect arrangement. To make it clear, we will go through each, step by step.

The direct arrangement presents right away the most important part of the report. This is the answer—the achievement of the report's goal. Depending on the problem, the direct beginning could consist of a summary of facts, a conclusion, a recommendation, or some combination of summary, conclusion, and recommendation.

Whatever background information is needed usually follows the direct opening. As noted previously, sometimes little or none is needed in everyday, routine reports. Next come the report findings, organized logically (as described in Chapter 8).

City planners have to write proposals and reports that make sense to both experts and ordinary citizens. Consider incorporating these 10 recommendations from a San Francisco-based planner into your proposals and reports:

1. **Summarize.** Most people don't have time to read a long plan. Write a clear executive summary, and make it a stand-alone document that can be reproduced and distributed separately.

2. **Hit the facts.** Consider writing a one- or two-page fact sheet or flier for your plan or project for such secondary audiences as reporters and others who just want the key details.

3. **Unclutter.** Move lengthy supplementary information into appendixes.

4. **Break it up.** Put such information as definitions, examples, and lists into margin notes, textboxes, or sidebars.

5. **Add on.** If some readers might want additional information, tell them where to find it.

6. **Help navigate.** Use "signposting" tools—such as a table of contents, section previews, and section-specific headers and footers—to help readers find what they need and know where they are in your document.

7. **Add headings.** Break up the text visually with informative headings and subheadings—and use form and placement rather than numbering to indicate the different levels.

8. **Don't overdo acronyms.** Spell out acronyms the first time you use them, and consider including them in a glossary, along with technical terms.

9. **Experiment.** Perhaps black and white text in portrait orientation on 8 ½ × 11-inch paper is not the most effective format to use. Consider adding color, using landscape orientation, and incorporating other kinds of visual interest.

10. **Why not video?** Or other kinds of electronic media? If you will be delivering your document electronically, consider including dynamic content for interest and persuasiveness.

Source: Niko Letunic, "Beyond Plain English," *Planning* 73.9 (2007): 40–44, *ProQuest*, Web, 15 May 2010.

"This has so many different fonts in it, I thought it was a ransom note."

Source: Reprinted with permission of CartoonStock.com, www.cartoonstock.com

> "Deciding whether to use the direct order is best based on your readers' likely response to the report.

Illustrating this arrangement is the following report on a personnel problem.

Clifford A. Knudson, administrative assistant in the accounting department, should be fired. This conclusion has been reached after a thorough investigation brought about by numerous incidents during the past two months. . . .

The recommended action is supported by this information from his work record for the past two months:

- He has been late for work seven times.
- He has been absent without acceptable excuse for seven days.
- Twice he reported for work in a drunken and disorderly condition.
  [And so on to the report's ending].

In contrast, the indirect arrangement begins with whatever introductory material is needed to prepare the reader for the report. Then comes the presentation of facts, with analyses when needed. Next comes the part that accomplishes the goal of the report. If the goal is to present information, this part summarizes the information. If the goal is to reach a conclusion, this part reviews the analyses and draws a conclusion from them. And if the goal is to recommend an action, this part reviews the analyses, draws a conclusion, and, on the basis of the conclusion, makes a recommendation.

Using the personnel problem from the last example, the indirect arrangement would appear like this:

Numerous incidents during the past two months appear to justify an investigation of the work record of Clifford A. Knudson, administrative assistant in the accounting department.

> # MOST SHORT-REPORT SITUATIONS . . . ARE LIKELY TO JUSTIFY THE PERSONAL STYLE BECAUSE OF THEIR RELATIVELY ROUTINE NATURE.

The investigation of his work record for the past two months reveals these points:

- He has been late for work seven times.
- He has been absent without acceptable excuse for seven days.
- Twice he reported for work in a drunken and disorderly condition. [And so on, to the conclusion that Knudson should be fired].

Deciding whether to use the direct order is best based on a consideration of your readers' likely response to the report. If your readers need the report conclusion or recommendation as a basis for an action that they must take, directness will speed their effort by enabling them to quickly receive the most important information. If they have confidence in your work, they may choose not to read beyond this point and to proceed with the action that the report supports. Should they desire to question any part of the report, however, the material is there for their inspection.

On the other hand, if there is reason to believe that it would be better for your readers to arrive at the conclusion or recommendation only after a logical review of the analysis, you should organize your report in the indirect order. This arrangement is especially preferable when you will be recommending something that you know your readers will not favor or want to hear. Presenting the supporting data before the

recommendation will get them ready to accept your solution to the report problem.

More Personal Writing Style

The writing in shorter reports tends to be more personal than in long reports. That is, the shorter reports are likely to use the personal pronouns *I, we,* and *you* rather than only the third person.

Several factors account for this tendency toward personal writing in shorter reports. In the first place, short-report situations usually involve personal relationships. Such reports tend to be from and to people who know each other and who normally address each other informally when they meet. In addition, shorter reports are apt to involve personal investigations and to represent the observations, evaluations, and analyses of their writers. Finally, shorter reports tend to deal with day-to-day, routine problems. These problems are by their very nature informal. It is logical to report them informally, and personal writing tends to produce this informal effect.

As explained in Chapter 8, your decision about whether to write a report in personal or impersonal style should be based on the situation. You should consider the expectations of those who will receive the report. If they expect formality, you should write impersonally. If they expect informality, you should write personally. If you do not know their preferences, you should consider the formality of the situation. Convention favors impersonal writing for the most formal situations. Like the direct and indirect order, the question of personal versus impersonal style involves the matter of relating to the reader in ways that he or she prefers.

Most short-report situations, however, are likely to justify the personal style because of their relatively routine nature.

Less Need for a Structured Coherence Plan

A long, formal report usually needs what we call a "structured coherence plan"—a network of introductions, conclusions, and transitions that guide the reader through the report. Creating such a plan means giving the overall report an overview and a conclusion, providing the same for the individual

Though missing certain components of long, formal reports, short reports require many of the same analytical and organizational skills used to develop longer reports.

technology in brief

Templates Help Writers Format Reports

Templates for word processors help report writers format reports attractively and consistently. Once a template is selected, report writers can concentrate on the report message and let the software create a professional-looking document.

These templates contain margin settings, font type and size for headings and text, and even graphic layouts. Most are designed to help the writer present a report that communicates its message with a professional look. Although standard templates can be used, some companies design their own templates to give their reports consistent and distinct images.

Templates readily set up both short and long reports. In addition to the installed templates, you can find more on the Web. Here you see some templates installed in Microsoft's Word 2007 and one of the templates open in Word.

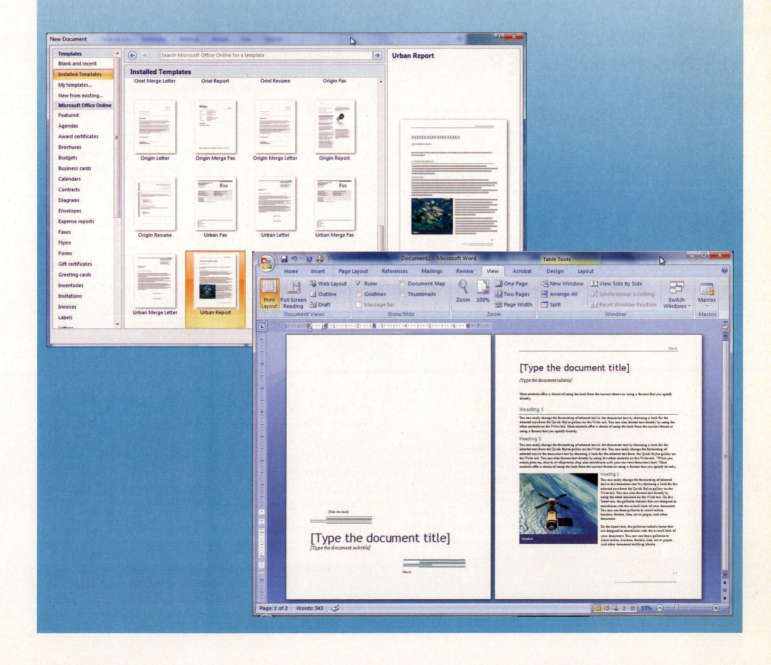

sections, and devising transitions that bridge each section to the next. Such devices enable the reader to know at every point where he or she is in the report and how the current section is related to the overall goal of the report. The online material on the formal report explains further how to write these coherence helpers.

Short reports, because they are short, generally do not need an elaborate coherence plan. Readers will not need many reminders of what they just read or previews of what they're about to read. The report introduction (which should contain an overview), clear headings, and brief transitional devices (such as "Second," "next," and quick references to previous points) will usually be sufficient to keep readers on track.

LO 3   Choose an appropriate form for short reports.

FORMS OF SHORTER REPORTS

As noted earlier, the shorter report forms are by far the most numerous and important in business. In fact, the three forms represented by the bottom three steps of the stairway in Exhibit 9.1 make up the bulk of written reports. Here we describe the particular traits of each.

emphasizing conclusions and recommendations. Such a beginning serves much the same function as the executive summary of a longer, more formal report.

After the summary comes whatever introductory material is needed. Sometimes none is needed. Usually, however, a single paragraph covers the facts of authorization and a brief statement of the problem and its scope. After the introductory words come the findings, analyzed and applied to the problem. From all this comes a conclusion and, if needed, a recommendation. These last two elements—conclusions and recommendations—should be restated or summarized at the end even though they also appear in the beginning summary. Omitting them would end the report too abruptly and stop it before it reached its logical goal.

The mechanics of constructing the short report are much the same as the mechanics of constructing the more formal, longer types. The short report uses the same form of title page and page layout. Like the longer reports, it uses headings. But because of the short report's brevity, the headings rarely go beyond the two-division level. In fact, one level of division is most common. Like any other report, the short report uses visuals, an appendix, and a bibliography when these are needed.

Letter Reports

The second of the more common shorter report forms is the letter report—that is, a report in letter form. Letter reports are used primarily to present information to persons outside

> "Letter reports are used primarily to present information to persons outside the organization, especially when the information is to be sent by mail or fax."

The Short Report

One of the more popular of the less formal report forms is the short report. Representing the fifth step in the formality stairway (Exhibit 9.1), this report consists of only a title page and text. Its popularity may be explained by the middle-ground impression of formality that it conveys. Including the most important prefatory part gives the report at least some appearance of formality. And it does this without the tedious work of preparing the other prefatory pages. The short report is ideally suited for the short but somewhat formal problem.

Like most of the less formal report forms, the short report may be organized in either the direct or indirect order, but the direct order is far more common. As illustrated by Exhibit 9.2, this plan begins with a quick summary of the report, including and

the organization, especially when the information is to be sent by mail or fax. For example, a company's written evaluation of its experience with a particular product may be presented in letter form and sent to the person who requested it. An outside consultant may deliver analyses and recommendations in letter form. Or the officer of an organization may report certain information to the membership in a letter.

Typically, the length of letter reports is three or four pages or less, but they may be longer or shorter.

As a general rule, letter reports are written personally, using *I, you,* and *we* references (see the case illustration on pages 251–252). Exceptions exist, of course, such as letter reports for very important readers—for example, a company's board of directors. Otherwise, the writing style recommended for letter

This direct-order letter report compares two hotels for a meeting site. Organized by the criteria used to evaluate the choices, it interprets the pertinent information and reaches a decision. The personal style is appropriate.

INTERNATIONAL COMMUNICATION ASSOCIATION

314 N Capitol St. NW • Washington, DC 20001 • 202.624.2411
www.icahg.org

October 26, 2012

Professor Helen Toohey
Board of Directors
International Communication Association
Thunderbird American Graduate School of International Management
15249 N. 59th Ave.
Glendale, AZ 85306-6000

Dear Professor Toohey:

Subject: Recommendation of Convention Hotel for the 2013 Meeting

The Hyatt Hotel is my recommendation for the International Communication Association meeting next October. The Hyatt has significant advantages over the Marriott, the other potential site for the meeting.

> *Direct order emphasizes the decision.*

First, the Hyatt has a definite downtown location advantage, and this is important to convention goers and their spouses. Second, accommodations, including meeting rooms, are adequate in both places, although the Marriott's rooms are more modern. Third, Hyatt room costs are approximately 15 percent lower than those at the Marriott. The Hyatt, however, would charge $500 for a room for the opening session. Although both hotels are adequate, because of location and cost advantages the Hyatt appears to be the better choice from the members' viewpoint.

> *Preview describes the structure of the upcoming information.*

Origin and Plan of the Investigation

In investigating these two hotels, as was my charge from you at our October 7 board meeting, I collected information on what I believed to be the three major factors of consideration in the problem. First is location. Second is adequacy of accommodations. And third is cost. The following findings and evaluations form the basis of my recommendation.

> *Bases of comparison (factors) permit hotels (units) to be compared logically.*

The Hyatt's Favorable Downtown Location

The older of the two hotels, the Hyatt is located in the heart of the downtown business district. Thus it is convenient to the area's major mall as well as the other downtown shops. The Marriott, on the other hand, is approximately nine blocks from the major shopping area. Located in the periphery of the business and residential area, it provides little location advantage for those wanting to shop. It does, however, have shops within its walls that provide for virtually all of the guests' normal needs. Because many members will bring spouses, however, the downtown location does give the Hyatt an advantage.

> *Short sentences and transitional words increase readability and move ideas forward.*

Board of Directors   -2-   October 26, 2012

Adequate Accommodations at Both Hotels

Both hotels can guarantee the 600 rooms we will require. Because the Marriott is newer (built in 2008), its rooms are more modern and, therefore, more appealing. The 19-year-old Hyatt, however, is well preserved and comfortable. Its rooms are all in good condition, and the equipment is up to date.

The Marriott has 11 small meeting rooms and the Hyatt has 13. All are adequate for our purposes. Both hotels can provide the 10 we need. For our opening session, the Hyatt would make available its Capri Ballroom, which can easily seat our membership. It would also serve as the site of our presidential luncheon. The assembly facilities at the Marriott appear to be somewhat crowded, although the management assures me that their largest meeting room can hold 600. Pillars in the room, however, would make some seats undesirable. In spite of the limitations mentioned, both hotels appear to have adequate facilities for our meeting.

Lower Costs at the Hyatt

Both the Hyatt and the Marriott would provide nine rooms for meetings on a complimentary basis. Both would provide complimentary suites for our president and our executive director. The Hyatt, however, would charge $500 for use of the room for the opening session. The Marriott would provide this room without charge.

Convention rates at the Hyatt are $169 for singles, $179 for double-bedded rooms, and $229 for suites. Comparable rates at the Marriott are $189, $199, and $350. Thus, the savings at the Hyatt would be approximately 15 percent per member.

Cost of the dinner selected would be $35 per person, including gratuities, at the Hyatt. The Marriott would meet this price if we would guarantee 600 plates. Otherwise, they would charge $38. Considering all of these figures, the total cost picture at the Hyatt is the more favorable one.

In conclusion, while both hotels would meet our needs, the significant location and cost advantages of the Hyatt make it the more desirable site for next year's conference.

Sincerely,

Willard K Mitchell

Willard K. Mitchell
Executive Secretary

reports is much the same as that recommended for any other reports. Certainly, clear and meaningful expression is a requirement for all reports.

Letter reports may be in either the direct or the indirect order. If such a report is to be mailed, there is some justification for using the indirect order. Because such reports arrive unannounced, it is logical to begin with a reminder of what they are, how they originated, and other helpful background information. A letter report written to the membership of an organization, for example, might appropriately begin as follows:

As authorized by your board of directors last January 6, this report reviews member expenditures for travel.

If a letter report begins in the direct order, a subject line is appropriate. The subject line consists of identifying words appearing at the top of the letter, usually right after the salutation. Although subject lines may be formed in many ways, one acceptable version begins with the word *Subject* and follows it with words that identify the situation. As the following example illustrates, this identifying device helps prepare readers for the opening paragraph.

Subject: Travel Expenditures of Association Members, Authorized by Board of Directors, January 2012

Association members are spending 11 percent more on travel this year than they did the year before. Current plans call for a 10 percent increase for next year.

Regardless of which type of beginning is used, the organizational plans for letter reports correspond to those of longer, more formal types. Thus, the indirect-order letter report follows its introduction with a logical presentation and analysis of the information gathered. From this presentation, it develops a conclusion or recommendation, or both, in the end. The direct-order letter report follows the initial summary-conclusion-recommendation

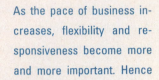
> ## Some email and memo reports rival the longer forms in formality.

section with whatever introduction is appropriate. For example, the direct beginning illustrated previously could be followed with these introductory sentences:

These are the primary findings of a study authorized by your board of directors last January. Because they concern information vital to all of us in the Association, they are presented here for your confidential use.

Following such an introduction, the report would present the supporting facts and their analyses. The writer would systematically build the case supporting the opening comment. With either the direct or indirect order, a letter report may close with whatever friendly, goodwill comment fits the occasion.

Email and Memo Reports

As we noted in Chapter 2, email is a heavily used form of written communication in business. It has largely eclipsed memoranda, but memos are still written, especially in cases where computers aren't easily accessible or the writer prefers to deliver a print message. Both email and memos can be used for internal written reports—that is, for reports—written by and to people in an organization.

Because email and memos are primarily communication between people who know each other, they are usually informal. Many are hurried, casual messages. Some, however, are formal, especially reports directed to readers high in the administration of the organization. In fact, some email and memo reports rival the longer forms in formality. Like the longer forms, they may use headings to facilitate reading and visuals to support the text.

Because they are largely internal, email and memo reports tend to be problem-solving reports. They are intended to help improve operations, lay the groundwork for an innovation,

Guess Row Study

Introduction

Producers are becoming increasingly interested in using GPS-based guidance systems as either an enhancement to or in replacement of mechanical markers in planting operations. Recently, a study was conducted to assess the accuracy of mechanical markers for planting operations, and compare this to manual GPS guidance and GreenStar™ AutoTrac. While the pass-to-pass accuracy of the StarFire receiver has been determined to be +/- 4 inches by the University of Illinois, the measurements taken in this study are more indicative of what producers are achieving in the field.

The guess row is the distance between the outside rows of two side-by-side passes made in the field (Figure 1). If the planter is set up to plant 30-inch rows, the perfect guess row width would be 30-inches. Significant guess row variability causes difficulty in using mismatched row equipment (i.e. 16 row planter harvested with a 12 row corn head). In addition, wide guess rows may allow weed escapes that decrease yields.

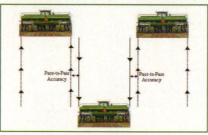

Figure 1: Pass to pass accuracy

Methods

Servi-Tech, a crop consulting company offering services primarily in Kansas, Nebraska, and Iowa, measured the guess row width on a number of fields in these three states. Twenty consecutive guess row measurements were taken in each field. The data presented in this discussion are from corn and soybean fields planted in 30-inch rows only. The distribution of fields is shown in Table 1.

Table 1 Distribution of Fields Measured

	Mechanical Markers	Manual GPS Guidance	AutoTrac	All Data
Number of Fields Measured	70	9	19	98

Note: all planting using AutoTrac was done with JD8000T tractors.

In addition to guess row width and guidance type, additional information was recorded for each field, including:

- Crop
- Tillage system
- Field topography
- Tractor and planter model
- Planter width
- Approximate planting speed
- Time of day planted

After preliminary analysis of the data, it was determined that in some fields consistent planter draft to one direction (often caused by improper set up) resulted in guess row variability over and above that attributable to the guidance system used. In order to remove these fields from the analysis, odd and even passes were analyzed and 35 fields were removed.

Results

While the average guess row width for all marker systems was similar (Figure 2), both the manual GPS

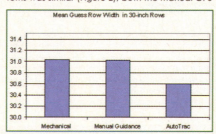

Figure 2: Mean Guess Row Width for all guidance systems

guidance and AutoTrac systems exhibited much less variability than that of mechanical markers (Figure 3; Table 2). Range in guess row width for manual GPS guidance and AutoTrac was nearly half that of mechanical marker systems. The standard deviation for manual GPS guidance and AutoTrac planted guess rows was 2.1 inches compared to 3.3 inches for the mechanical marker planted fields.

Conclusions

Guess row width in fields planted with GPS based guidance systems was less variable than those planted with mechanical marker systems. On average, GPS based guidance systems were as accurate as those fields planted with mechanical marker systems. The test

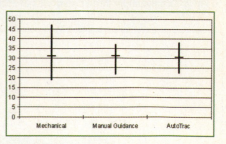

Figure 3: Mean Guess Row Width and Range

data showed many row crop planters were not set up properly (unit spacing or marker arm mis-adjustment), causing them to pull one direction consistently or resulting in varied pass-to pass 'guess row' width. Experienced operators may compensate for this automatically when using mechanical marker systems, so proper planter setup is more important with automatic steering systems.

While the guess row widths for both the manual GPS guidance system and AutoTrac were similar, AutoTrac would be expected to deliver this accuracy over a wide range of conditions consistently. Manual GPS guidance system accuracy depends on how well the operator can follow the steering cues. As time progresses, the operator may become fatigued, resulting in a reduced accuracy. This is not a factor with GreenStar AutoTrac.

Table 2

	All Data	Mechanical	Manual Guidance	AutoTrac
Maximum	50	47	37	38
Minimum	19	19	22	22.5
Mean	31.3	31.0	31.0	30.6
Range	31	28	15	15.5
Standard Deviation	3.4	3.3	2.1	2.1
Coefficient of Variation	0.11	0.11	0.07	0.07

The bottom line is that GreenStar AutoTrac was found to be capable of delivering the same to slightly better accuracy than producers achieve using mechanical markers in the fields used for the study. Coupled with the fact that AutoTrac users will be less fatigued at the end of the day, GreenStar AutoTrac may be able to help your operation during one of the most important times of the growing season, planting. For more information about GreenStar Parallel Tracking or AutoTrac, visit your local John Deere dealer.

Source: Deere & Company, *Growing Innovations*, Winter 2002: 3, Web, 16 June 2010. Reprinted with permission.

---

solve a problem, or otherwise assist decision makers in the organization.

Written Reports in Other Forms

While many written reports in business will take the form of short reports, letter reports, or email reports, they can take a variety of other forms as well. The report featured in

Exhibit 9.4 appeared in an online newsletter by the John Deere company. It uses objectively gathered and reported evidence to persuade readers of the value of a John Deere product. Reports can also appear in pamphlets, white papers, and other publications, and they are often uploaded to the Web as stand-alone documents in pdf format. You can apply your report-writing knowledge to all these forms and more. Just be sure to choose the appropriate form for your readers and purpose.

A Progress Report in Email Form

This email report summarizes a sales manager's progress in opening a new district. It begins with the highlights—all a busy reader may need to know. Organized by three categories of activity, the factual information follows. The writer–reader relationship justifies a personal style.

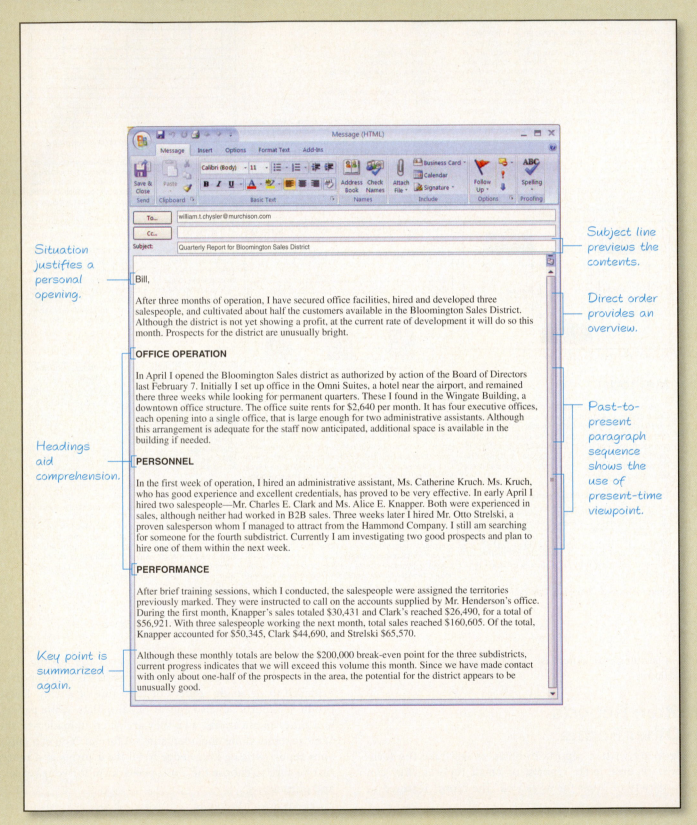

Situation justifies a personal opening.

Headings aid comprehension.

Key point is summarized again.

Subject line previews the contents.

Direct order provides an overview.

Past-to-present paragraph sequence shows the use of present-time viewpoint.

To... william.t.chysler@murchison.com

Cc...

Subject: Quarterly Report for Bloomington Sales District

Bill,

After three months of operation, I have secured office facilities, hired and developed three salespeople, and cultivated about half the customers available in the Bloomington Sales District. Although the district is not yet showing a profit, at the current rate of development it will do so this month. Prospects for the district are unusually bright.

OFFICE OPERATION

In April I opened the Bloomington Sales district as authorized by action of the Board of Directors last February 7. Initially I set up office in the Omni Suites, a hotel near the airport, and remained there three weeks while looking for permanent quarters. These I found in the Wingate Building, a downtown office structure. The office suite rents for $2,640 per month. It has four executive offices, each opening into a single office, that is large enough for two administrative assistants. Although this arrangement is adequate for the staff now anticipated, additional space is available in the building if needed.

PERSONNEL

In the first week of operation, I hired an administrative assistant, Ms. Catherine Kruch. Ms. Kruch, who has good experience and excellent credentials, has proved to be very effective. In early April I hired two salespeople—Mr. Charles E. Clark and Ms. Alice E. Knapper. Both were experienced in sales, although neither had worked in B2B sales. Three weeks later I hired Mr. Otto Strelski, a proven salesperson whom I managed to attract from the Hammond Company. I still am searching for someone for the fourth subdistrict. Currently I am investigating two good prospects and plan to hire one of them within the next week.

PERFORMANCE

After brief training sessions, which I conducted, the salespeople were assigned the territories previously marked. They were instructed to call on the accounts supplied by Mr. Henderson's office. During the first month, Knapper's sales totaled $30,431 and Clark's reached $26,490, for a total of $56,921. With three salespeople working the next month, total sales reached $160,605. Of the total, Knapper accounted for $50,345, Clark $44,690, and Strelski $65,570.

Although these monthly totals are below the $200,000 break-even point for the three subdistricts, current progress indicates that we will exceed this volume this month. Since we have made contact with only about one-half of the prospects in the area, the potential for the district appears to be unusually good.

LO 4 Adapt the procedures for writing short reports to routine operational, progress, problem-solving, and audit reports as well as minutes of meetings.

TYPES OF SHORT REPORTS

Because reports are written for many different purposes in many different companies, the variety of short reports is infinite. But several common types have developed on the basis of needs and situations that many companies share. Here we discuss five of these types: routine operational, progress, problem-solving, and audit reports, and minutes for meetings.

Even these types will have particular requirements based on where you are working. Always study your company's ways of reporting before contributing a report yourself.

Routine Operational Reports

The majority of the reports written within companies are routine reports that keep supervisors, managers, and team members informed about the company's operations. These can be daily, weekly, monthly, or quarterly reports on the work of each department or even each employee. They can relate production data, information on visits to customers, issues that have arisen, or any kind of information that others in the organization need on a routine basis.

Whatever the form, the routine operational report should convey clearly and quickly what readers most need and want to know about the time period in question. It is also an opportunity for you, the writer, to showcase your ability to gather needed information on deadline.

When using standardized forms for periodic reports, you should consider developing a template macro or merge document with your word processing application. A macro would fill in all the standard parts for you, pausing to let you fill in the variable information. A template merge document would prompt you for the variables first, merging them with the primary document later. However standardized the process, you will still need to be careful to gather accurate information and state it clearly.

Progress Reports

You can think of an internal progress report as a routine operational report except that it tends to be submitted on an as-needed basis and, as its name implies, it focuses on progress toward a specific goal. If you are working on a project for an external client, you may also need to submit progress reports to show that your work is on track. For example, a fund-raising organization might prepare weekly summaries of its efforts to achieve its goal. Or a building contractor might prepare a report on progress toward completing a building for a customer. Typically, the contents of these reports concern progress made, but they also may include such related topics as problems encountered or anticipated and projections of future progress.

> "The majority of the reports written within companies are routine reports that keep supervisors, managers, and team members informed about the company's operations."

The form and contents of these reports will vary from company to company and manager to manager. Many will be submitted on predesigned forms. Others may not use forms but will follow a prescribed format. Still others will be shaped by the writer's own judgment about what to include and how to present it. The nature and culture of the organization can heavily influence the forms taken by these reports.

For example, one innovative format for weekly reporting is the 5-15 report.[1] The name comes from the fact that it is intended to be read in 5 and written in 15 minutes. It is intended to inform bosses of main events from the past and also enable employees to share their opinions and accomplishments. Clearly, this format would work best in an organization where employees have nonroutinized jobs and the management values the employees' opinions.

Progress reports follow no set form. They can be quite formal, as when a contractor building a large office building reports to the company for whom the offices are being built. Or they can be very informal, as in the case of a worker reporting by email to his or her supervisor on the progress of a task being performed. Some progress reports are quite routine and structured, sometimes involving filling in blanks on forms devised for the purpose. Most, however, are informal, narrative reports, as illustrated by the example in on page 256.

As with most reports, you have some choice about the tone to use when presenting your information. With progress reports, you want to emphasize the positive if possible. The overall message should be "I (or we) have made progress." The best way to convey this message confidently, of course, is to be sure that

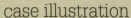

case illustration
A Midlength Recommendation Report of Midlevel Formality

This report, with its title page and combined letter of transmittal and executive summary, would fall on the fourth level of Exhibit 9.1. It is organized indirectly in order to prepare the reader for the students' recommendations. The authors are careful to base their recommendations only on their research and their expertise as students, not on knowledge or authority that only a grocery store expert would have.

Increasing Student Patronage at Kirby's Grocery

Title makes the topic and purpose of the report clear.

April 28, 2012

Prepared for:

Mr. Claude Douglas, Owner
Kirby's Grocery
38 Lance Avenue
Crestview, IN 45771

Page uses an attractive but simple template.

Prepared by:

Kirsten Brantley, Business Communication Student
College of Business
P. O. Box 236
Metropolitan University
Crestview, IN 45770-0236

METROPOLITAN UNIVERSITY

College of Business, P. O. Box 236, Crestview, IN 45770-0236
Phone: (421)555-5555, Fax: (421)555-5566, Web: business.mu.edu

May 28, 2012

Mr. Claude Douglas
Kirby's Grocery
319 Lance Avenue
Crestview, IN 45771

Dear Mr. Douglas:

As you requested, our Business Communication class conducted a study to determine ways to increase Metropolitan University students' awareness of Kirby's Grocery and attract more students to your store. This report presents the results.

Identifies the project and "hands over" the report.

To gather our information, we first interviewed assistant manager Bradley Vostick, who leads the store's marketing efforts. To get a veteran customer's perspective, we also interviewed our professor, Beth Rawson, a long-time Kirby's customer. Next we researched MU campus events, publications, transportation issues, demographics, and the Lance Avenue area surrounding Kirby's. Finally, the class did walkthroughs of Kirby's to gain firsthand reactions to the store as well as quantified data in the form of an exit survey on overall reactions to Kirby's.

We found that Kirby's is part of a niche market that offers a wide variety in a small space, much like the surrounding Lance Avenue area. Given these findings, we recommend the following:

Combines letter of transmittal and executive summary.

- Targeting health-conscious, older MU students who enjoy shopping.
- Using Internet-based media to reach these potential customers.
- Focusing on your strengths to make these shoppers aware of the experience that is Kirby's Grocery.

Thank you for allowing us the opportunity to do this real-world project. We enjoyed learning about your store and hope that our research will bring many more MU students to Kirby's Grocery.

Ends with goodwill comments.

Sincerely,

Kirsten Brantley

Kirsten Brantley
For Professor Beth Rawson's Business Communication Class

Increasing Student Patronage at Kirby's Grocery

Introduction

Objective of the study

Kirby's Grocery is a full-service neighborhood grocery store in the vicinity of Metropolitan University. With its appealing range of products and proximity to the university, its potential to attract student customers is great. Yet according to a survey conducted by Professor Beth Rawson's Fall 2011 Business Communication class, only one in three MU students has ever shopped at Kirby's. As a follow-up to this study, our Business Communication class conducted research to determine how Kirby's might attract more MU student shoppers. This report presents our results and recommendations.

Opening summarizes the problem and purpose.

Research methods

The research for this study was conducted in three phases:

- Phase One: As preparation for the observational part of the study, the class gathered supplemental information about a variety of topics related to Kirby's. It was carried out by groups of three to four students, with each group focusing on one of seven particular "beats." These beats included MU campus events and publications, MU's demographic information, and interviews with Kirby's customers and Bradley Vostick of Kirby's.

- Phase Two: This was the main phase of our research. For this phase, 13 pairs of students visited Kirby's during the week of March 7–14, 2012, to gather observational data. Each pair consisted of an observer, who made oral comments about any and all aspects of the store, and a recorder, who recorded these observations. On average, each pair spent approximately 40 minutes in the store, and each pair was required to make a small purchase. At the end of their visits, the observers all completed exit surveys to quantify their overall reactions to Kirby's and to provide some demographic information about themselves.

Detailed description of research builds confidence in the validity of the findings.

- Phase Three: Given our findings, we gathered information to develop our recommendations for marketing Kirby's to MU students.

The following sections describe the study participants, present the observational data, and offer our recommendations.

Preview adds to the report's coherence.

Demographics of the Participants

Sentence previews table.

While our observer number of 13 was very small in comparison to the entire MU population of 33,000, it was actually a fairly representative sample in terms of student diversity, gender, and age. The following table shows how these observers compared to the general MU population.

Lone table in nonacademic report does not need to be numbered.

Report includes a special section to further support the validity of the findings.

Demographics of Store Observers		
	Study Participants	**MU Population**
Diversity	77% (11) European-American, 23% (2) African-American	71.5% European-American, 12% African-American
	77% (11) US citizens	83% US citizens
Gender	47% (6) female, 54% (7) male	54.2% female, 45.8% male
Average Age	24	23

Paragraphs interpret and elaborate on the table.

Compared to the MU population, our sample of 13 was relatively diverse. In addition to including two African-American participants, it included two non-US participants, one from Russia and one from Sweden.

The gender ratios were also relatively close. The MU population is 54.2 percent female to 45.8 percent male. Again, our observers came very close to this ratio, with 47 percent female and 54 percent male.

The average age for full-time students at Metropolitan University is 23. The average age of our observers was 24. This included a student who is 41 years old, but even without this outlier, our group closely represented the average MU student in terms of age.

In addition, all students in our class (26) were juniors and seniors at MU, and most were business students with some background in marketing. Through class discussion, we were able to bring our collective perspective as MU students to bear on our observations.

Qualitative Findings

Section preview adds coherence.

This section presents the qualitative results from our observational research, broken down into two categories: perceived strengths and perceived weaknesses.

2

 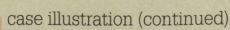

Perceived Areas of Strength

Three main positive reactions came out of this research:

- Students were impressed with the wide product variety.
- Students were happy to see organic and health food products.
- Kirby's employees provided excellent service to their customers.

Section starts with a helpful summary.

Product variety was seen as the strongest asset of Kirby's. Of the 13 observation surveys, 11 mentioned the large variety of products offered by Kirby's as a positive aspect of the store. Overall, the consensus was that the selection offered by Kirby's in such a small space was impressive. This was especially apparent in the beer aisle, which received the most praise of any section in Kirby's for a selection that rivals that of specialty stores.

Organic and health food products also received a large positive reaction, being mentioned by almost two-thirds of the observers. While health may not be the main concern of the stereotypical college student, it is certainly appealing to older students. Since the average age of an MU student is 23, it is likely that Kirby's organic and health food selection can also be a strong selling point for getting more students into the store.

Paragraphs present and interpret data.

Customer service was the third most mentioned positive aspect of Kirby's. During observations, employees at Kirby's were consistently cheerful and helpful. The long-time customer we interviewed, Professor Rawson, cited Kirby's excellent customer service as one of the reasons she continues to shop there. She commented that the employees of Kirby's care more about their customers' shopping experiences than employees of other stores, and the data compiled by the class supported this claim.

Not only were students asked if they needed help, but they also observed that employees knew their customers, which makes the customer feel more like family than just another person wanting groceries. When observers made their small purchases, they noted that they were treated in the same friendly manner as customers who were checking out with filled carts.

Perceived Areas of Weakness

Two main negative reactions came out of this research:

- Students observed a number of dirty shelves and floors.
- The placement of some products was confusing.

List provides another helpful summary.

About half of the observers made note of areas of Kirby's that seemed to need a good cleaning, with specific remarks about stained floor tiles, produce on the floor

3

that hadn't been swept up, and dusty shelves. This was a significant negative for several student shoppers, as dirty floors and shelves don't shed the kindest light on the products for sale, especially when compared to the seeming sterility of larger grocery stores like Kroger's and Biggs.

But the largest negative reaction to Kirby's concerned the random-seeming placement of a variety of products. Examples included cakes next to whole turkeys, freezers next to greeting cards, and hot peppers next to candies. This confused student shoppers because the placement of some of these products did not fall in line with the aisle signs. While Kirby's is a smaller grocery store and is certainly impacted by the limits of space, the class as a whole felt that more could be done to eliminate the appearance of a random product layout.

Paragraphs add more helpful data and interpretation.

Quantitative Findings

The following figure contains the composite results of the 13 exit surveys. Students were asked to rate their Kirby's experience on a variety of topics on a scale of one to five, with one being the worst and five being the best. The observers took the survey immediately after completing their walkthroughs of the store.

Paragraph introduces the figure.

Lone figure in a nonacademic report does not need to be numbered.

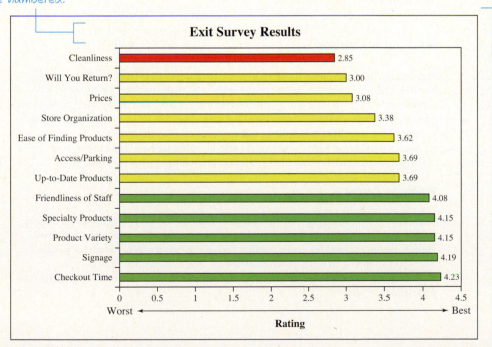

Visual, textual, and numerical elements work together to present specific findings clearly.

4

These results simply quantify what was discovered in the qualitative phase of the observation. Checkout time, friendliness, variety, and specialty products were the highest scorers, while cleanliness received the lowest rating. Still, Kirby's scored above average in all categories, which is an important positive result.

Along these lines, the "Will You Return?" score is encouraging. Though it may seem negative when compared to the other reactions, a score of 3.00 is actually above average. This means that with only one trip through Kirby's, there is a better than average chance that students will return to purchase groceries.

Paragraphs help the reader interpret the findings.

Prices ranked just above "Will You Return?" at 3.08. Again, its comparative rating is low, but it is still above average. Price is an important consideration for student shoppers, and Kirby's has a tough time competing with prices offered by the nearby Kroger store, its main competitor. Even given these two facts, though, observers felt that Kirby's had slightly better than average prices, which is another important positive result.

Interesting to note are the scores for Signage, Ease of Finding Products, and Store Organization. Signage was rated high at 4.19, while Ease of Finding Products was rated lower (3.62), and Store Organization even lower (3.38). These numbers correlate with the student shopper reactions. While Kirby's has excellent signs, some of the aisles are difficult to find because of displays blocking them, and the placement of certain products adjacent to other unrelated products only increases this confusion.

Recommendations

Paragraph summarizes main impression and leads into recommendations.

From our compiled data on Kirby's Grocery, we learned that Kirby's is not a large, faceless grocery chain that slashes prices in order to make up for poor customer service and variety. Rather, Kirby's is a niche-market store that offers wide variety and excellent service for a decent price. Yet only about a third of the MU population is aware of its excellent variety and customer service. The following recommendations for Kirby's aim to increase its customer base through targeted awareness-raising advertising that focuses on promoting the store's uniqueness.

Whom to Target

Since Kirby's is something of a niche-market store, it will only truly appeal to a niche market of MU students. Kirby's should focus on attracting those shoppers who want variety, healthy selections, and a familiar feel. Kirby's is a grocery store for people who want shopping to be an experience, not an errand. It can therefore be especially appealing to the more mature, somewhat alternative segment of the MU population.

5

How to Reach Them

While Kirby's has been using the MU Coupon Book for campus ads and participating in campus events such as Welcome Week, the store's marketing efforts do not take advantage of a key fact about modern students: they are heavy users of Internet-based social-networking sites. A 2008 study found that over 85 percent of college students use Facebook, where they spend over six hours per week and which they visit over six times per day (Ana M. Martinez Aleman and Katherine Link Wartman, *Online Social Networking on Campus*). A 2009 study estimated that Facebook had over 20 million users in the 18-to-25-age range (Justin Smith, *InsideFacebook.com*). Such sites thus represent a huge opportunity for Kirby's to reach its student market.

You can take advantage of these sites in two main ways: creating a profile page and advertising.

Creating a Free Online Profile

Kirby's currently has an attractive website, but it is unlikely to receive many student visitors. Free social-networking websites such as Facebook (*www.facebook.com*) and MySpace (*www.myspace.com*) can help you build a student fan base and generate a buzz about your store. These sites require only that one register in order to create and post a "profile" page. A company can feature its major selling points, photos, directions, customer testimonials, special promotions, a link to its website, and other material on its profile page, which these sites' templates makes relatively easy to do.

Once the page is posted, users can learn about your site using the search engine. If they like what they see and want to be kept updated about special offerings, they can click a link to include Kirby's in their network. This will place your logo and name on their own profile pages, where all their friends will see it and perhaps consider becoming "fans" of Kirby's themselves. In this way, your store can take advantage of "viral marketing."

Using Paid Advertising

It is also possible to advertise on social-networking websites. For example, with Facebook, the most popular site among college students, you can use an easy-to-complete template to design a brief advertisement. You can then target the ad to the Facebook users you want to reach—for example, those between the ages of 18 and 25 in the MU area. When those users visit their Facebook pages, they will see your ad displayed in the right-hand Ad Space.

The cost for these ads varies depending on whether you choose to pay per view (how many times users see your ad) or per click (how many times users click on your ad to go visit your website or profile), as well as on what other advertisers targeting the same market are offering to pay. The current minimum cost per click is $.01; the current minimum cost per 1,000 views is $.02, though these low "bids" will not be accepted if other businesses are competing for the same space with the same users. Facebook's "Ads: Campaign Cost and Budgeting" page can help you plan your campaign given whom you want to reach and what you are willing to spend each day.

6

Shows knowledge of the store's current efforts.

Recent research supports claim.

Briefly citing sources in the text is acceptable in an informal report.

Links make it easy to go learn more.

Paragraphs adapt research to reader's needs.

What to Say

Kirby's advertisements need to focus on promoting the store's variety and uniqueness to the MU student body. It has to separate itself from the idea that it is simply another grocery store and emphasize that it encompasses a wide variety in a small space, just like the eclectic Lance Avenue area in which it is located.

Promotions for students should focus on its wide beer selection (perhaps mentioning the exact number of domestic and imported brands offered), on its organic and health food selection, and on its unique products such as sushi and fresh peanut butter. These advertisements will not appeal to the entire MU student body, but it will make the students who are likely to value Kirby's strengths aware of these and give them a desirable, convenient alternative to shopping at a giant superstore.

Paragraphs use main findings to suggest a marketing strategy.

Conclusion

We found that Kirby's Grocery offers a shopping experience that simply cannot be found at larger grocery stores. The variety and customer service are top notch, and this makes a trip to Kirby's an experience rather than an errand (perhaps this could be a slogan?). By taking advantage of the large-scale marketing opportunities offered by the Internet, Kirby's can raise awareness of its many positive qualities among the MU student body well beyond what it currently achieves with its current outreach efforts. This strategy is also appealing because it can greatly increase Kirby's visibility at no to very little cost.

Ending wraps up the report in a positive way.

7

you or your team has in fact made some progress on the issue at hand.

Problem-Solving Reports

Many short reports are *problem-solving reports*. These reports help decision makers figure out what to do any time a problem arises within an organization—which is often. For example, a piece of equipment may have broken down, causing mayhem on the production line. Or employees may have gotten hurt on the job. Or, less dramatically, a company procedure may have become outdated, or a client company may want to know why it's losing money. If we define *problem* as an issue facing the company, we could include many other scenarios as well—for example, whether or not a company should adopt flextime scheduling or what location it should choose for a new store.

recommendations. They may want only good data and careful analysis so that they can formulate a course of action themselves. Whether you are preparing an internal or external report, it is important to understand how far your readers want you to go toward proposing solutions.

You have some latitude when deciding how direct to make your opening in a problem-solving report. If you believe that your readers will be open to any reasonable findings or recommendations, you should state those up front. If you think your conclusions will be unexpected or your readers will be skeptical, you should still state your report's purpose and topic clearly at the beginning but save the conclusions and recommendations until the end, after leading your readers through the details. Exhibit 9.5, a pattern for a problem-solving report used by the U.S. military, follows this more indirect route. As

> [When writing a problem-solving report, especially one that makes recommendations, you need to show that your study was thorough and your reasoning sound.]

Whatever the context, the writer of a problem-solving report needs to gather facts about the problem or issue, define it clearly, research solutions, and, if appropriate, recommend a course of action.

Like progress reports, problem-solving reports can be internal or external. Internal problem-solving reports are usually assigned, but sometimes employees may need to write unsolicited problem-solving reports—for example, if they must recommend that a subordinate be fired or if they feel that a change in procedures is necessary. External problem-solving reports are most often written by consulting companies for their clients. In these cases, the report is the main product that the client is paying for.

A type of problem-solving report that deserves special attention is a *feasibility study*. For these reports, writers study several courses of action and then propose the most feasible, desirable one. For instance, you might be asked to compare service providers for data backup and recommend the one that suits the company's needs and budget best. Or you might investigate what type of onsite childcare center, if any, is feasible for your organization. Sometimes feasibility studies are not full-blown problem-solving reports. They may offer detailed analysis but stop short of making a recommendation. The analysis they provide nevertheless helps decision makers decide what to do.

In fact, many short reports that help solve company problems may not be complete problem-solving reports. Decision makers who assign research reports may not want

always, try to find out which method of organization your readers prefer.

While they usually propose action, problem-solving reports are not true persuasive messages. Because they have either been assigned or fall within an employee's assigned duties, the writer already has a willing reader. Furthermore, the writer has no obvious personal stake in the outcome the way he or she does with a persuasive message. However, when writing a problem-solving report, especially one that makes recommendations, you do need to show that your study was thorough and your reasoning sound. The decision makers may not choose to follow your advice, but your work, if it is carefully performed, still helps them decide what to do and reflects positively on you.

Audit Reports

A specialized type of report is the audit report. This type is written to hold an organization accountable to certain standards that they are required to meet. While audit reports can assess an organization's finances, operations, or compliance with the terms of a contract, and while they can be written by internal or external auditors, the most common type of audit report is that written by an accounting firm to verify the truthfulness of a company's financial reports. These reports are short and standardized. You can find such reports in almost any corporate annual report. But accounting firms are also contracted to write longer, less standardized reports that help the company assess its financial health and adopt better

> # IF YOU ARE AN ACCOUNTANT WORKING FOR AN INDEPENDENT ACCOUNTING FIRM, YOU MAY WELL FIND YOURSELF INVOLVED IN WRITING . . . AUDIT REPORTS.

▼ **EXHIBIT 9.5** Military Form for an Indirect Problem-Solving Report

---

DEPARTMENT OF THE AIR FORCE
HEADQUARTERS UNITED STATES AIR FORCE
WASHINGTON, DC 20330

REPLY TO
ATTN OF   AFODC/Colonel Jones

SUBJECT   Staff Study Report

TO:

PROBLEM

1. --
--.

FACTORS BEARING ON THE PROBLEM

  2. Facts.

    a.--
--.

    b---
--------------------.

  3. Assumptions.

  4. Criteria.

  5. Definitions.

DISCUSSION

  6. --.

  7. --.

  8. --.

CONCLUSION

  9. --.

ACTION RECOMMENDED

  10. ---.

  11. --------------------------------.

JOHN J. JONES, Colonel, USAF   2 Atch
Deputy Chief of Staff, Operations 1. -----------------------
                                 2. -----------------------

---

financial scandals of Enron, WorldCom, and other publicly traded companies. To restore and maintain investor confidence in companies' financial reports, Sarbanes-Oxley requires companies to have not only their financial records but also their financial reporting practices audited by external parties. As an employee, you may find yourself having to write reports related to this kind of audit. If you are an accountant working for an independent accounting firm, you may well find yourself involved in writing such audit reports.

Meeting Minutes

Many short reports in business, especially internal ones, do not recommend or even analyze. Instead, they describe. Trip reports, incident reports, and other descriptive reports are meant to provide a written record of something that happened. Whatever their type and specific purpose, they all share the need to be well organized, easy to read, and factual. Perhaps the most common of these reports is minutes for meetings.

© 2009 Ted Goff

"I suggest we take a look at the floating, glowing incident report first."

accounting practices. Long-form audit reports vary greatly in their makeup, but, like other reports, they tend to include an executive summary followed by an introduction, methodology and standards used, findings, discussion, and conclusions or recommendations.

As Chapter 8 notes, the Sarbanes-Oxley Act of 2002 has had an enormous impact on financial record keeping and reporting. This new set of federal regulations was prompted by the

Minutes of the Policy Committee
Semiannual Meeting
November 21, 2011, 9:30–11:30 A.M., Conference Room A

Present: Megan Adami (chair), D'Marie Simon, DeAnne Overholt, Michelle Lum, Joel Zwanziger, Rebecca Shuster, Jeff Merrill, Donna Wingler, Chris Woods, Tim Lebold (corporate attorney, guest).

Absent: Joan Marian, Jeff Horen (excused), Leonna Plummer (excused)

Complete preliminary information provides a good record.

Minutes

Minutes from the May 5, 2011, meeting were read and approved.

Announcements

Chris Woods invited the committee to a reception for Milton Chen, director in our Asia region. It'll be held in the executive dining room at 3:00 P.M. tomorrow. Chris reminded us that Asia is ahead of the United States in its use of wireless technology. He suggested that perhaps we can get some idea of good policies to implement now.

Section headings help readers retrieve information.

Old Business—Email Policy

Joel Zwanziger reported the results of his survey on the proposed new email policy. While only 16 percent of the employees strongly favored the policy, the remaining 84 percent were not opposed. The committee approved a January 1, 2012, implementation subject to its distribution to all employees before the Christmas break.

Web Surfing Policy

D'Marie Simon reported on the preliminary findings of other companies in the industry. Most have informal guides but no official policies. The guidelines generally are that all surfing must be related to the job and that personal surfing should be done on breaks. The committee discussed the issue at length. It approved a policy that reflects the current general guidelines.

Discussions are summarized and actions taken are included.

Temp Policy

Tim Lebold presented the legal steps we need to take to get our old and new temporary employees to sign a nondisclosure agreement prior to working here as we've been discussing in relation to a new temp policy. The committee directed Tim to begin the process so that the policy could be put in force as soon as possible.

New Business—Resolution

Michelle Lum proposed that a resolution of thanks be added to the record recognizing Megan for her terrific attention to detail as well her clear focus on keeping the committee abreast of policy issues. It was unanimously approved.

Resolutions often include descriptive language.

Next Meeting

The next meeting of the committee will be May 3, 2012, from 9:30–11:30 A.M. in Conference Room A.

Adjournment

Closing completes the information.

The meeting was adjourned at 11:25 A.M.

Respectfully submitted,

Megan Adami
Megan Adami

Signing signifies the minutes are official records.

Minutes provide a written record of a group's activities and decisions, a history that includes announcements, reports, significant discussions, and decisions. Minutes might report who will do what and when, but they are primarily a summary that reports the gist of what happened, not a verbatim transcript. Minutes include only objective data; their writer carefully avoids using descriptive adjectives such as *brilliant, intelligent,* and *reasonable.* However, if the group passes a resolution that specific wording be officially recorded, a writer would then include it. Accurate minutes are important because they can have some legal significance as to whether decisions are binding.

The physical form is typically a memo or email, but the layout varies among organizations. Basically, it should enable the reader to easily focus on the content as well as easily retrieve it. Some writers find that numbering items in the minutes to agree with the numbering of a meeting's agenda helps in retrieving and reviewing specific discussions. Subheads are often useful, especially if they are bold, italicized, or colored to make them stand out. Most important, minutes should provide an adequate record.

The case illustration on page 269 shows typical minutes. The following preliminary, body, and closing items may be included.

Preliminary Items

- Name of the group.
- Name of the document.
- Type of meeting (monthly, emergency, special).
- Place, date, and time called to order.
- Names of those attending including guests (used to determine if a quorum is present).
- Names of those absent and reasons for absence.

Body Items

- Approval of the minutes of the previous meeting.
- Meeting announcements.
- Old business—Reports on matters previously presented.
- New business—Reports on matters presented to the group.

Closing Items

- Place and time of the next meeting.
- Notation of the meeting's ending time.
- Name and signature of the person responsible for preparing the minutes.

When you are responsible for preparing the minutes of a meeting, you can take several steps to make the task easier. First, get an agenda in advance. Use it to complete as much of the preliminary information as possible, including the names of those expected to attend. If someone is not present, you can easily move that person's name to the absentee list. You might even set up a table in advance with the following column headings to encourage you to take complete notes.

Topic	Summary of Discussion	Action/Resolution

Bear in mind that meeting minutes, while they look objective, almost always have political implications. Because minutes are the only tangible record of what happened, meeting

Playing possum doesn't work anymore, Stephmeyer! I want that report by 5 P.M. or else!

participants will want their contributions included and cast in a positive light. Since you cannot record every comment made, you will need to decide which ones to include, whether or not to credit a particular speaker, how to capture the group's reaction, and so forth. Use your good judgment when translating a rich oral event into a written summary.

You can consult the online chapter on long reports to see how to adapt this chapter's guidelines for short reports to longer, more formal reports. As you might expect, these too will be shaped by your goals and by the readers' needs and expectations. ■

Get Online

mhhe.com/FlatleyM2e

for study materials including quizzes and Internet resources.

communicating **orally**

LEARNING OBJECTIVES

LO1 Discuss talking and its key elements.

LO2 Explain the challenges of listening and how to overcome them.

LO3 Describe good phone and voice mail techniques.

LO4 Explain the techniques for conducting and participating in meetings.

LO5 Select and organize a subject for effective formal presentations to a specific audience.

LO6 Identify and select appropriate presentation methods.

LO7 Describe how audience and self-analysis contribute to formal presentations.

LO8 Explain the use of voice and physical aspects such as posture, walking, facial expression, and gestures in effective oral communication.

LO9 Plan for visuals to support presentations.

LO10 Work effectively with a group in preparing and making a team presentation.

LO11 Define virtual presentations and differentiate between them and face-to-face presentations.

As you know, your work will involve oral as well as written communication. The written communication will probably be more challenging, but the oral communication will take up more of your time. In fact, you are likely to spend more time in oral communication than in any other work activity. ■

workplace scenario

Communicating Orally on the Job

Your job as assistant director in the Public Relations Department at BioGen Tech, Inc., seems somewhat different from what you expected. It makes full use of your specialized college training, as you expected; but it also involves duties for which you did not train because you did not expect them. Most of these duties seem to involve some form of oral communication. In fact, you probably spend more of your work time talking and listening than performing any other activity.

To illustrate, take today's activities. Early this morning, you discussed a morale problem with some of your supervisors. You don't think they understood what you said. After that, you conducted a meeting of the special committee to plan the department's annual picnic. As chairperson, you ran the meeting. It was a disaster, you felt—everybody talking at once, interrupting, arguing. It was a wonder that the committee made any progress. It seemed that everybody wanted to talk but nobody wanted to listen.

In the afternoon, you had other job duties involving oral communication. After you returned from lunch, you must have had a phone conversation every 20 minutes or so. You felt comfortable with most of these calls, but you thought some of the callers needed a lesson or two in phone etiquette. Also, using voice input, you dictated a few messages and emails between phone calls.

Last week's activities were similar. Your boss asked you to fill in as a speaker at an awards dinner where your firm presented scholarships to business students. You also had to present an oral report to BioGen's executive committee on a survey that your department had conducted to determine local opinions about a dispute between BioGen and its union. You did your best, but you felt uneasy about what you were doing.

Such assignments are becoming more and more a part of your work as you move up the administrative ladder at BioGen. You must try to do them better, since your future promotions are at stake. The following review of oral communications should help you in this effort.

Much of the oral communication that goes on in business is the informal, person-to-person communication that occurs whenever people get together. Obviously, we all have experience with this form of communication, and most of us do it reasonably well. But all of us can improve our informal talking and listening with practice.

> **As a first step in improving your talking ability, think for a moment about the qualities you like in a good talker—one with whom you would enjoy talking in ordinary conversation.**

In addition, other more formal oral communication take place in business. Sometimes businesspeople conduct and participate in committee meetings, call one another on the phone, and even dictate their messages and reports. And frequently, they are called upon to make formal presentations: speeches, lectures, or oral reports. All these kinds of oral communication are a part of the work that businesspeople do.

This chapter reviews the range of oral communication activities from simple talking to meetings to formal presentations in order to give you an understanding of the types of oral communication situations you will encounter in business.

CONVERSING INFORMALLY

Conversing effectively involves two basic activities—talking and listening. While rather simple tasks for most, a conscious effort to polish these activities can improve one's conversational skills. Since conversations are so prevalent in most

business jobs, having good conversation skills will be a valuable asset.

LO 1 Discuss talking and its key elements.

Talking Informally

While most of us do a reasonably good job of informal talking, most of us could stand to improve. To improve our talking ability, we need to be aware of its nature and qualities. We need to assess our abilities. Then we need to work to overcome our shortcomings.

As a first step in improving your talking ability, think for a moment about the qualities you like in a good talker—one with whom you would enjoy talking in ordinary conversation. Then think about the opposite—the worst conversationalist you can imagine. If you will get these two images in mind, you can form a good picture of the characteristics of good talking. This mental picture likely includes good voice quality, excellence in

The Conference Board, along with Corporate Voices for Working Families, the Partnership for 21st Century Skills, and the Society for Human Resource Management, asked several executives to indicate the skills they felt were very important for new graduates to have in the workplace. The top five skills were oral communications (95.4%); teamwork/collaboration (94.4%); professionalism/work ethic (93.8%); written communications (93.1%); and critical thinking/problem solving (92.1%).

The executives were also asked to rate graduates' skills in these areas as "excellent" or "deficient." Interestingly, when rating four-year graduates, 46.3 percent of the respondents gave an "excellent" rating to graduates' skills in information technology application (which was 11th on the executives' list of important skills, with 81.0%), but only 24.8 percent gave an "excellent" rating to graduates' oral communication skills (first on the list). Written communication, writing in English, and leadership skills appeared on the "deficient" list.

The results of this study encourage us to keep working to improve our communication skills. This chapter and several others in this book provide many useful strategies and tips for doing so.

Source: *Are They Really Ready To Work? Employers' Perspectives on the Basic Knowledge and Applied Skills of New Entrants to the 21st Century U.S. Workforce, The Conference Board,* The Conference Board Inc., 2006, Web, 4 June 2010.

When talking with others informally, you should accord them the courtesy you expect of them.

talking style, accuracy of word choice, and adaptation to the listener. As these elements control the overall quality of oral expression, we will now review them.

elements of good talking

The techniques of good talking use four basic elements: (1) voice quality, (2) style, (3) word choice, and (4) adaptation.

Voice quality Good voice quality is central to good talking. By voice quality we mean the vocal sounds one hears when another speaks. Primarily voice quality refers to the pitch and resonance of the sounds made though speed and volume also affect the listener's experience. Voices vary widely from the unpleasant to the melodious, but we can each work for improvement.

Perhaps the best way of improving voice quality is to consider your own experiences. You know the effect of talking that is too fast or too slow. You know the effect of a monotone voice. You know the effect of a high-pitched voice, a guttural voice, a melodious voice. With this knowledge in mind, you should analyze your own voice, perhaps with the assistance of a recorder. Listen carefully to yourself. Fit what you hear into impressions you have gained from your life experiences. Then do what you can to improve. It will take conscious effort.

Style Talking style refers to how the three parts of voice quality—pitch, speed, and volume—blend together. It is the unique way these parts combine that gives personality to one's oral expression.

From the self-analysis described in our review of voice quality, you also should have a good idea of your talking style. What is the image your talking projects? Does it project sincerity? Patience? Enthusiasm? Is it polished? Smooth? Rough? Dull? After your honest assessment, you should be able to determine how you want to improve your style deficiencies.

Word choice A third quality of talking is word choice. Of course, word choice is related to one's vocabulary. The larger the vocabulary, the more choices one has. Even so, you should keep in mind the need for the listener to understand the words you choose. In addition, the words you choose should be appropriate. They should suit the situation whether formal, informal, serious, or light. And they should respect the listener's knowledge of the subject matter—that is, they should not talk down to or above the listener.

Adaptation Adaptation is the fourth quality of good talking. It is an extension of our discussion in the paragraphs above. Adaptation means fitting the message to the intended listener. Primarily this means fitting the words to the listener's interests and capacity to understand. But it also can include voice and style. To illustrate, the voice, style, and words in an oral message aimed at a sales team would be different from the same message aimed at the technology support staff. Similarly, these qualities might vary in messages delivered in different cultures as well as in different social situations.

courtesy in talking
We all know talkers who drown out others with their loud voices, who butt in while others are talking, or who attempt to dominate others in conversation. They are universally disliked. Good talkers encourage others to make their voices heard. They practice courtesy in their conversations.

This emphasis on courtesy does not suggest that you should be submissive in your conversations—that you should not be assertive in pressing your points. It means that you should accord others the courtesy that you expect of them.

LO 2 Explain the challenges of listening and how to overcome them.

Listening

Listening is an important facet of conversing, and it is also an area in which businesspeople need help. Evidence shows that weakness on the receiving side (listening) can cause many problems.

the nature of listening
When listening is mentioned, we think primarily of the act of sensing sounds. In human communication, of course, the sounds are mainly spoken words. Viewed from a communication standpoint, however, the listening process involves the addition of interpreting and remembering.

> " Viewed from a communication standpoint, the listening process involves not only sensing sounds but also the addition of interpreting and remembering. "

Improve your listening skills by listening actively and focusing your attention on the speaker.

Sensing How well we sense the words around us is determined by two factors. One factor is our ability to sense sounds—how well our ears can pick them up. As you know, we do not all hear equally well, although hearing devices can reduce our differences in this respect.

The other factor is our attentiveness to listening. More specifically, this is our mental concentration—our will to listen. Our mental concentration on the communication symbols that our senses can detect varies from moment to moment. It can range from almost totally blocking out those symbols to concentrating on them very intensely. From your own experience, you can recall moments when you were oblivious to the words spoken around you and moments when you listened with all the intensity you could muster. Most of the time, your listening fell somewhere between these extremes.

Interpreting From your study of the business communication process in Chapter 1, you know that interpretation enables you to give meanings to the symbols you sense. This activity will be influenced by the unique contents of your mind: your knowledge, emotions, beliefs,

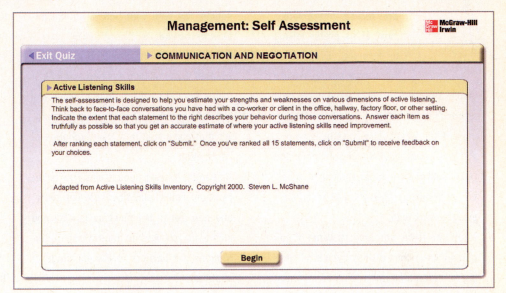

Communication in brief

Self-Assessment of Listening Practices Can Help You Identify Areas Needing Improvement

One of the easiest ways to improve one's listening skills is to identify areas that need improvement or polish. This site shown here has a short and easy quiz that not only immediately reports a score, but it also interprets the score so one knows where to put the extra effort to get the best results. You can find it at <http://www.mhhe.com/business/management/buildyourmanagementsskills/updated_flash/topic13b/quiz.html>.

Management: Self Assessment

McGraw-Hill Irwin

◄ Exit Quiz   ► COMMUNICATION AND NEGOTIATION

▶ **Active Listening Skills**

The self-assessment is designed to help you estimate your strengths and weaknesses on various dimensions of active listening. Think back to face-to-face conversations you have had with a co-worker or client in the office, hallway, factory floor, or other setting. Indicate the extent that each statement to the right describes your behavior during those conversations. Answer each item as truthfully as possible so that you get an accurate estimate of where your active listening skills need improvement.

After ranking each statement, click on "Submit." Once you've ranked all 15 statements, click on "Submit" to receive feedback on your choices.

Adapted from Active Listening Skills Inventory, Copyright 2000. Steven L. McShane

Begin

---

biases, experiences, and expectations. It will also be influenced by your cultural, organizational, and professional contexts. Thus you may sometimes give messages meanings different from the meanings that others give them, especially if you do not take into account the speaker's unique frame of reference.

Remembering Remembering what we hear is the third activity involved in listening. Unfortunately, we retain little of what we hear. We remember many of the comments we hear in casual conversation for only a short time—perhaps for only a few minutes or hours. Some we forget almost as we hear them. According to authorities, we even quickly forget most of the message in formal oral communications (such as speeches), remembering only a fourth after two days.

improving your listening ability
Improving your listening is largely a matter of mental conditioning—of concentrating on the activity of sensing. You have to want to improve it, since listening is a willful act. If you are like most of us, you are often tempted not to listen or you just find it easier not to listen. We human beings tend to avoid work, and listening may be work.

After you have decided that you want to listen better, you must make an effort to pay attention. This will involve discipline and practice. You must force yourself to be alert, to pay attention to the words spoken.

Voice input systems allow writers to concentrate on word choice and message composition, freeing them from typing and spelling concerns. But careful proofreading is still essential, especially for easily confused words and sound-alikes.

Active listening is one technique individuals can use successfully. It involves focusing on what is being said and reserving judgment. Other components include sitting forward and acknowledging with "um-hm" and nodding. Back-channeling is a variation of this technique that groups can use. An audience

1. *Stop talking.* Unfortunately, most of us prefer talking to listening. Even when we are not talking, we are inclined to concentrate on what to say next rather than on listening to others. So you must stop talking before you can listen.

2. *Put the talker at ease.* If you make the talker feel at ease, he or she will do a better job of talking. Then you will have better input to work with.

3. *Show the talker you want to listen.* If you can convince the talker that you are listening to understand rather than oppose, you will help create a climate for information exchange. You should look and act interested. Doing things like reading, looking at your watch, and looking away distracts the talker.

4. *Remove distractions.* The things you do also can distract the talker. So don't doodle, tap with your pencil, shuffle papers, or the like.

5. *Empathize with the talker.* If you place yourself in the talker's position and look at things from the talker's point of view, you will help create a climate of understanding that can result in a true exchange of information.

6. *Be patient.* You will need to allow the talker plenty of time. Remember that not everyone can get to the point as quickly and clearly as you. And do not interrupt. Interruptions are barriers to the exchange of information.

7. *Hold your temper.* From our knowledge of the workings of our minds, we know that anger impedes communication. Angry people build walls between each other. They harden their positions and block their minds to the words of others.

8. *Go easy on argument and criticism.* Argument and criticism tend to put the talker on the defensive. He or she then tends to "clam up" or get angry. Thus, even if you win the argument, you lose. Rarely does either party benefit from argument and criticism.

9. *Ask questions.* By frequently asking questions, you display an open mind and show that you are listening. And you assist the talker in developing his or her message and in improving the correctness of meaning.

10. *Stop talking!* The last commandment is to stop talking. It was also the first. All the other commandments depend on it.

Source: To some anonymous author goes a debt of gratitude for these classic and often-quoted comments about listening.

---

can leverage technologies such as chatting, texting, and tweeting to comment on presentations in real time, which helps them keep a sharp focus on what is being said. Whatever technique you choose, improvement requires hard work.

In addition to working on the improvement of your sensing, you should work on the accuracy of your interpreting. To do this, you will need to think in terms of what words mean to the speakers who use them rather than what the dictionary says they mean or what they mean in your mind. You must try to think as the speaker thinks—judging the speaker's words by the speaker's knowledge, experiences, viewpoints, and situations. Like improving your sensing, improving your ability to hear what is being said requires conscious effort.

Remembering what you hear also requires conscious effort. Certainly, there are limits to what the mind can retain, but authorities agree that few of us come close to them. By taking care to hear what is said and by working to make your interpreting process give more accurate meanings to the words you hear, you add strength to the messages you receive. The result should be improved retention.

From the preceding review it should be clear that to improve your listening ability, you must set your mind to the task. Poor listening habits are ingrained in our makeup. We can alter these habits only through conscious effort.

LO 3 Describe good phone and voice mail techniques.

Using the Phone

Most of us have had long experience in using the phone and may feel that we have little to learn about it. No doubt, some of us have excellent phone skills. But you have only to call a few randomly selected businesses to learn that not everyone who talks on the phone is proficient in its use. You will get some gruff, cold greetings, and you will be subjected to a variety of discourtesies. And you will find instances of inefficient use of time (which, of course, is costly). This is not to say that the problem is major, as most progressive businesses are aware of the need for good phone habits. But poor phone techniques are found often enough to justify reviewing the subject of phone use in a business communication textbook.

professional voice quality In reviewing good phone techniques, keep in mind that a phone conversation is a relatively lean medium of communication. Usually only voices are heard. Impressions are received only from the words and the quality of the voices. Thus, when speaking by phone, it is extremely important that you work to make your voice sound pleasant and friendly.

One often-suggested way of improving your phone voice is to talk as if you were face to face with the other person—even smiling and gesturing as you talk if this helps you be more natural. In addition, you would do well to put into practice the suggestions given earlier in this chapter concerning the use of the voice in talking (voice quality, variation in pitch, and speed). Perhaps the best instructional device for this problem is to record one of your phone conversations. Then judge for yourself how you come across and what you need to do to improve.

courtesy If you have worked in business for any length of time, you have probably experienced most of the common phone discourtesies. You probably know that most of them

Whether in or out of the office, those using mobile phones should practice the same voice quality and courtesies as on land lines.

If you are not certain with whom you should talk, explain the purpose of your call:

"This is Payton Kubicek of Easy Menu Planning. We have a question about your service warranty. May I talk with the proper executive about it?"

When an assistant or someone else who is screening calls answers the phone, the recommended procedure is first to identify the company or office and then to make an offer of assistance:

"Lenaghan Insurance Company. How may I help you?"
"Ms. Reyes's office. May I help you?"

When a call goes directly into the office of the executive, the procedure is much the same, except that the executive identifies herself or himself:

"Seaton Realty. Dave Seaton speaking. May I help you?"

When an assistant answers for an executive (the usual case), special care should be taken not to offend the caller. Following a question like "Who is calling?" by "I am sorry, but Mr. Gordon is not in" leaves the impression that Gordon may be in but does not want to talk with this particular

> ❝ One often-suggested way of improving your phone voice is to talk as if you were face to face with the other person— even smiling and gesturing as you talk if this helps you be more natural. ❞

are not intended as discourtesies but result from ignorance or unconcern. The following review should help you avoid them and incorporate business etiquette into your phone conversations.

The recommended procedure when you are calling is to introduce yourself immediately and then to ask for the person with whom you want to talk:

"This is Payton Kubicek of Easy Menu Planning. May I speak with Ms. Ashley Murillo?"

caller. A better procedure would be to state directly "Mr. Gordon is not in right now. May I ask him to return your call?" Or perhaps "May I tell him who called?" or "Can someone else help you?" could be substituted for the latter sentence.

Especially irritating to callers is being put on hold for unreasonable periods of time. If the person being called is on another line or involved in some other activity, it may be desirable to place the caller on hold or ask if the caller would like to leave a message. But good business etiquette dictates that the choice

> ## IF YOU WANT THE LISTENER TO RETURN YOUR CALL, STATE THAT PRECISELY, INCLUDING WHEN YOU CAN BE REACHED. SLOWLY GIVE THE NUMBER WHERE YOUR CALL CAN BE RETURNED.

should be the caller's. If the hold continues for a period longer than anticipated, the assistant should check back with the caller periodically showing concern and offering assistance. Equally irritating is the practice of having an assistant place a call for an executive and then put the person called on hold until the executive is free to talk. Although it may be efficient to use assistants for such work, as a matter of courtesy and etiquette the executive should be ready to talk the moment the call goes through.

Assistants to busy executives often screen incoming calls. In doing so, they should courteously ask the purpose of the calls. The response might prompt the assistant to refer the caller to a more appropriate person in the company. It also might reveal that the executive has no interest in the subject of the call, in which case the assistant should courteously yet clearly explain this to the caller. If the executive is busy at the moment, the assistant should explain this and either suggest a more appropriate time for a call or promise a callback by the executive. But in no case should the assistant promise a callback that will not be made. Such a breach of etiquette would likely destroy any goodwill between the caller and the company.

effective phone procedures At the beginning of a phone conversation that you have initiated, it is good practice to state the purpose of the call. Then you should cover systematically all the points involved. For really important calls, you should plan your call, even to the point of making notes of the points to cover. Then you should follow your notes to make certain you cover them all.

Courteous procedure is much the same in a phone conversation as in a face-to-face conversation. You listen when the other person is talking. You refrain from interrupting. You avoid dominating the conversation. And perhaps most important of all, you cover your message quickly, saving time (and money) for all concerned.

effective voice mail techniques Often when the person you are calling is not available, you will be able to leave a voice message in a voice mailbox. Not only does this save you the time involved in calling back the person you are trying to reach, but it also allows you to leave a more detailed message than you might leave with an assistant. However, you need to be prepared for this to be sure your message is both complete and concise.

You begin the message nearly the same way you would a phone call. Be as courteous as you would on the phone and speak as clearly and distinctly as you can. Tell the listener in a natural way your name and affiliation. Begin with an overview of the message and continue with details. If you want the listener to take action, call for it at the end. If you want the listener to return your call, state that precisely, including when you can be reached. Slowly give the number where your call can be returned. Close with a brief goodwill message. For example, as a program coordinator for a professional training organization, you might leave this message in the voice mailbox of one of your participants:

> **This is Stanelle Clare from Metroplex Development Institute. I'm calling to remind Ms. Melanie Wilson about the Chief Executive Round Table (CERT) meeting next week (Wednesday, July 20) at the Crescent Hotel in Dallas. Dr. Stevens of the Masley Optimal Wellness Center will present the program on Executive Health in the 21st Century. We will begin with breakfast at 7:30 AM and conclude with lunch at noon. Some of the CERT members will play golf in the afternoon at Dallas Country Club. If Ms. Wilson would like to join them, I will be glad to make a tee time for her. She can contact me at 940-240-1003 before 5:00 PM this Friday. We look forward to our Chief Executive Round Table meeting next Wednesday. Thank you.**

Using Voice Input

Improvements in both quality and ease of use of voice recognition programs are giving dictation a comeback. By combining these with some simple techniques, writers can use voice to become more productive by dictating documents.

gather the facts Your first logical step in dictating is to get all the information you need for the message. This step involves such activities as getting past correspondence from files, consulting with other employees, and ascertaining company policy. Unless you get all the information you need, you will be unable to work without interruption.

plan the message With the facts of the case before you, you next plan the message. You may prefer to do this step in your mind or to jot down a few notes or an outline. Whatever your preference, your goal in this step is to decide what your message will be and how you will present it. In this step, you apply the procedures covered in our earlier review of message and report writing.

technology in brief

Voice Input Saves Writers Time

Dictating messages and reports is probably one of the most underutilized input methods for writers today. However, speech recognition technology has been improved to allow continuous speech and short setup periods with little training. Additionally, it works with most standard word processing, presentation, and email applications on desktop PCs to smartphones to tablets. It is inexpensive compared to the value it offers writers. Not only does such technology spell correctly, it can quickly learn specialized vocabularies. And it is generally faster for most people than writing by hand or keying information because most people can speak 140 to 160 words per minute. Although proofreading dictated documents is a bit different because it involves looking for homophones (words that sound alike) rather than misspelled or misused words, most applications offer users the ability to play back the dictation, which will help writers catch other errors.

make the words flow Your next step is to begin dictating the message. Simple as this step appears, you are likely to have problems with it. Thinking out loud even to the computer frightens most of us at first. The result is likely to be slow and awkward dictation.

Overcoming this problem requires self-discipline and practice. You should force yourself to concentrate and to make the words flow. Your goal should be to get the words out—to talk through the message. You need not be too concerned about producing a polished work on the first effort. You will probably need to revise, perhaps several times. After you have forced your way through several messages, your need to revise will decrease and the speed and quality of your dictation will improve.

1. Turn off the ringer in meetings and other places where it would be disruptive.
2. Do not use the cell phone at social gatherings.
3. Do not place the phone on the table while eating.
4. Avoid talking whenever it will annoy others. Usually this means when within earshot of others.
5. Avoid discussing personal or confidential matters when others can hear you.
6. Do not talk in an excessively loud voice.
7. Preferably call from a quiet place, away from other people.
8. If you must talk while around people, be conscious of them. Don't hold up lines, obstruct the movements of others, or make any other problems for those around you.
9. Avoid using the phone while driving (the law in many states).

speak clearly Because your dictation must be heard clearly by your system, you should speak as distinctly as you can. Even small improvements in accuracy—say from 95 percent to 99 percent—will have big payoffs in the time it takes you to complete documents.

give paragraphing, punctuation, and other instructions as needed How much of the paragraphing, spelling, punctuation, and other mechanics you dictate depends on how well trained your system is. The more often you use the software, the more it knows your dictation style and the fewer instructions it will need. If you take care to spell out words your system doesn't know, it will train your system and serve you better.

LO 4 Explain the techniques for conducting and participating in meetings.

An effective meeting leader uses participants' time effectively through careful planning and control.

Conducting and Participating in Meetings

Although meetings are often criticized as a waste of time, they are a dominant part of the workplace today. One estimate is that new hires will spend 25 percent of their time in meetings while middle managers spend 50 percent and top executives spend 75 percent giving and listening to presentations.[1]

Your role in a meeting will be to contribute to its effectiveness whether as a leader or a participant. Of course, the leader's role is the primary one, but good participation is also vital. The following paragraphs review the techniques of performing well in these roles.

techniques of conducting meetings How you conduct a meeting depends on the formality of the occasion. Meetings of such groups as formal committees, boards of directors, and professional organizations usually follow generally accepted rules of conduct called *parliamentary procedure*. These very specific rules are too detailed for review here. When you are involved in a formal meeting, you would do well to study one of the many books covering parliamentary procedure before the meeting. For less formal meetings, you can depart somewhat from parliamentary procedure and those techniques. But you should keep in mind that every meeting has goals and time limits that such departures should never hinder you from reaching.

Plan the meeting A key to conducting a successful meeting is to plan it thoroughly. That is, you develop an agenda by selecting the items that need to be covered to achieve the goals of the meeting. Then arrange these items in the most logical order. Items that explain or lead to other items should come before the items they explain or lead to. After preparing the agenda, make it available to those who will attend if the meeting is formal. For informal meetings, you may find keeping the agenda in mind satisfactory.

Follow the agenda You should follow the plan for the meeting item by item. In most meetings the discussion tends to stray

technology in brief

Collaborative Tools Support Virtual Meetings

Virtual meetings are becoming common in small and large businesses alike. No longer do businesses need sophisticated teleconferencing equipment to work together from different locations. A typical desktop or laptop with an Internet connection will work nicely. And soon you'll be able to participate from a tablet or a 4Gsmartphone, too. With the proper system configuration, meeting participants can both see and hear others as well as see and work with various software applications.

Businesses are using this technology with their employees, their suppliers, and their customers. Some of the uses include training, sales presentations, review meetings, product demonstrations, and much more—sometimes even just-in-time meetings. All uses help the businesspeople do their jobs while saving both time and travel costs.

One such meeting tool is GoToMeeting, a web-based application that has won awards for its technology. Because the technology is scalable, meeting size can vary widely. And its cost and ease of use make it readily available to large and small businesses alike.

and new items tend to come up. As leader, you should keep the discussion on track. If new items come up during the meeting, you can take them up at the end—or perhaps postpone them to a future meeting.

Move the discussion along As leader, you should control the agenda. When one item has been covered, bring up the next item. When the discussion moves off subject, move it back on subject. In general, do what is needed to proceed through the items efficiently. But you should not cut off discussion before all the important points have been made. Thus, you will have to use your good judgment. Your goal is to permit complete discussion on the one hand and to avoid repetition, excessive details, and useless comments on the other.

Control those who talk too much Keeping certain people from talking too much is likely to be one of your harder tasks. A few people usually tend to dominate the discussion. Your task

as leader is to control them. Of course, you want the meeting to be democratic, so you will need to let these people talk as long as they are contributing to the goals of the meeting. However, when they begin to stray, duplicate, or bring in useless matter, you should step in. You can do this tactfully and with all the decorum of business etiquette by asking for other viewpoints or by summarizing the discussion and moving on to the next topic.

Encourage participation from those who talk too little Just as some people talk too much, some talk too little. In business groups, those who say little are often in positions lower than those of other group members. Your job as leader is to encourage these people to participate by asking them for their viewpoints and by showing respect for the comments they make.

Control time When your meeting time is limited, you need to determine in advance how much time will be needed to cover each item. Then, at the appropriate times, you should end

Meeting participants should contribute to a meeting when their expertise would help and give others a chance to contribute, too.

Participate The purpose of meetings is to get the input of everybody concerned. Thus, you should participate. Your participation, however, should be meaningful. You should talk only when you have something to contribute, and you should talk whenever you have something to contribute. Additionally, you will often be taking notes and sometimes minutes for the record (see the example on the book's website). Practice professional etiquette as you work courteously and cooperatively with others in the group.

Do not talk too much As you participate in the meeting, be aware that other people are attending. You should speak whenever you have something to say, but do not get carried away. As in all matters of etiquette, always respect the rights of others. As you speak, ask yourself whether what you are saying really contributes to the discussion. Not only is the meeting costing you time, but it is costing other people's time and salaries as well as the opportunity costs of other work they might be doing.

[**You may find it helpful to announce the time goals at the beginning of the meeting and to remind the group members of the time status during the meeting.**]

discussion of the items. You may find it helpful to announce the time goals at the beginning of the meeting and to remind the group members of the time status during the meeting.

Summarize at appropriate places After a key item has been discussed, you should summarize what the group has covered and concluded. If a group decision is needed, the group's vote will be the conclusion. In any event, you should formally conclude each point and then move on to the next one. At the end of the meeting, you can summarize the progress made. You also should summarize whenever a review will help the group members understand their accomplishments. For some formal meetings, minutes kept by a secretary provide this summary.

techniques for participating in a meeting From the preceding discussion of the techniques that a leader should use, you know something about the basic guidelines that a participant should follow. The following review emphasizes them.

Follow the agenda When an agenda exists, you should follow it. Specifically, you should not bring up items not on the agenda or comment on such items if others bring them up. When there is no agenda, you should stay within the general limits of the goal for the meeting.

Cooperate A meeting by its very nature requires cooperation from all the participants. So keep this in mind as you participate. Respect the leader and his or her efforts to make progress. Respect the other participants, and work with them in every practical way.

Be courteous Perhaps being courteous is a part of being cooperative. In any event, you should be courteous to the other group members. Specifically, you should respect their rights and opinions, and you should permit them to speak.

LO 5 Select and organize a subject for effective formal presentations to a specific audience.

MAKING FORMAL PRESENTATIONS

The most difficult kind of oral communication for many people is a formal presentation. However, those who give them effectively are more likely to get resources, promotions, and influence.[2] Most of us do not feel comfortable speaking before others. We can become more comfortable and be better public speakers by learning what good speaking techniques are and then putting those techniques into practice.

Selection of the Topic

Your first step in formal speechmaking is to determine the topic of your presentation. In some cases, you will be assigned a topic, usually one within your area of specialization. In fact, when you are asked to make a speech on a specified topic, it is likely to be because of your knowledge of the topic. In some cases, your choice of topic will be determined by the purpose of your assignment, as when you are asked to welcome a group or introduce a speaker.

If you are not assigned a topic, then you must find one on your own. In your search for a suitable topic, you should be guided by three basic factors. The first is your background and knowledge. Any topic you select should be one with which you are comfortable—one within your areas of proficiency. The second basic factor is the interests of your audience. Selecting a topic that your audience can appreciate and understand is vital to the success of your speech. The third basic factor is the occasion of the speech. Is the occasion a meeting commemorating a historic event? A monthly meeting of an executives' club? An annual meeting of a hairstylists' association? Whatever topic you select should fit the occasion. A speech about Japanese management practices might be quite appropriate for the members of the executives' club but not for the hairstylists. Your selection should be justified by all three factors.

Pepper . . . and Salt
THE WALL STREET JOURNAL

ENGLEMAN.

"Instead of a story, can mommy practice the presentation she has to give tomorrow?"

audience; "gentlemen" fits an all-male audience; and "my fellow Rotarians" fits an audience of Rotary Club members. Some speakers eliminate the greeting and begin with the speech, especially in more informal and technical presentations.

introduction The introduction of a presentation has much the same goal as the introduction of a written report: to prepare the listeners (or readers) to receive the message. But it usually has the additional goal of arousing interest. Unless you can arouse interest at the beginning, your presentation is likely to

> ## "The techniques of arousing interest are limited only by the imagination."

Preparation of the Presentation

After you have decided what to talk about, you should gather the information you need for your speech. This step may involve searching through your mind for experiences or ideas, conducting research in a library or in company files, gathering information online, or consulting people in your own company or other companies. In short, you do whatever is necessary to get the information you need.

When you have that information, you are ready to begin organizing your speech. Although variations are sometimes appropriate, you should usually follow the time-honored order of a speech: *introduction, body, conclusion.* This is the order described in the following paragraphs.

Although not really a part of the speech, the first words usually spoken are the greeting. Your greeting, of course, should fit the audience. "Ladies and gentlemen" is appropriate for a mixed

fail. The situation is somewhat like that of the sales message. At least some of the people with whom you want to communicate are not likely to be interested in receiving your message. As you will recall from your study of listening, it is easy for a speaker to lose the audience's attention. To prove the point, ask yourself how many times your mind has drifted away from the speaker's words when you have been part of an audience. There is no question about it: You, the speaker, will have to work to gain and hold the attention of your audience.

The techniques of arousing interest are limited only by the imagination. One possibility is a human-interest story, for storytelling has strong appeal. For example, a speaker presenting a message about the opportunities available to people with original ideas might open this way: "Nearly 150 years ago, an immigrant boy of 17 walked the streets of our town. He had no food, no money, no belongings except the shabby clothes he wore. He had only a strong will to work—and an idea."

Communication in brief

Making Presentations More Social

Engaging your audience through carefully planned interactivity not only enhances your presentation but also helps create a conversation with the audience. Chuck Dietrich, CEO of SlideRocket, gives five tips for connecting with your audience before, during, and after your presentation.

1. **Create Anticipation.** Employ social media your audience is likely to use, such as online community tools, to hone the subject. Solicit their feedback and network with key contacts.

2. **Create a Social-Friendly Presentation.** While creating a media-rich presentation is one way to hold an audience's attention, including live data, RSS feeds, and other streaming information lets you use "smart" data to support your key ideas. Also, catchy phrases and summary statements of key ideas that can be tweeted is a good way to increase retention. And creating and displaying a hashtag encourages effective use of the back channel, which can both enrich a presentation with additional comments and serve as a way to review the key ideas.

3. **Use Interactive Polling.** Eliciting your audience's opinions and knowledge through polling tools helps you keep them involved and gives you much better feedback that you can use in the presentation. It helps you know where they are when you start, move through your content, and finish.

4. **Use the Back Channel Wisely.** Inviting your audience to comment on your presentation while you are delivering it is risky, especially if the commenting gets out of control. It is important that you see the comments, but not necessarily important that the audience does. However, you should acknowledge them. If the number of participants is large, you may want to have an assistant filter them and select the ones that are important and representative of them to answer them at designated times during the presentation.

5. **Keep the Conversation Going after You've Left the Podium.** Continuing the tweeting, sharing helpful links, and conversing on a community site are ways to stay connected.

While these strategies may feel a little scary at first, you'll find that presenting to an engaged audience can be both easier and more stimulating for you as well as your audience. And it gets easier as you learn to manage the tools, time, and tasks.

Source: Adapted from "Five Tips for Making Your Presentations More Social," by Chuck Dietrich, Mashable.com, April 29, 2010. Reprinted with permission of Chuck Dietrich.

Humor, another possibility, is probably the most widely used technique. To illustrate, an investment broker might begin a presentation on investment strategy as follows: "What you want me to give you today is some 'tried and trusted' advice on how to make money in the stock market. This reminds me of the proverbial 'tried and trusted' bank teller. He was trusted; and when they caught him, he was tried." Humor works best and is safest when it is closely related to the subject of your presentation.

Other effective ways for gaining attention at the opening are using quotations and questions. By quoting someone the audience would know and view as credible, you build interest in your topic. You also can ask questions. One kind of question is the rhetorical question—the one everyone answers the same, such as "Who wants to be freed of burdensome financial responsibilities?" Another kind of question gives you background information on how much to talk about different aspects of your subject. With this kind of question, you must follow through by basing your presentation on the response. If you had asked "How many of you have IRAs?" and nearly everyone put a hand up, you wouldn't want to talk about the importance of IRAs. You could skip that part of your presentation, spending more time on another aspect, such as managing one's IRA effectively.

Yet another possibility is the startling statement or statistic that presents facts and ideas to rivet people's attention. Illustrating this possibility is the beginning of a speech to an audience of retailers on a plan to reduce shoplifting: "Last year, right here in our city, in your stores, shoplifters stole over $3.5 million of your merchandise! And most of you did nothing about it."

In addition to arousing interest, your opening should lead into the theme of your speech. In other words, it should set up your message as the examples above do.

Following the attention-gaining opening, it is appropriate to tell your audience the subject (theme) for your speech. In fact, in cases where your audience already has an interest in what you have to say, you can begin here and skip the attention-gaining opening. Presentations of technical topics to technical audiences typically begin this way. A presenter on computer security might say, "We're here today to discuss strategies to stay ahead of the threat to the security of business data." Whether you lead into a statement of your topic or begin with it, that statement should be clear and complete.

Because of the nature of your subject, you may find it undesirable to reveal a position early. In such cases, you may prefer to move into your subject indirectly—to build up your case before revealing your position. This inductive pattern may be especially desirable when your goal is to persuade—when you need to move the viewpoints of your audience from one to another. But in most business-related presentations you should make a direct statement of your theme early in the speech.

body Organizing the body of your presentation is much like organizing the body of a report. You take the whole and divide it into comparable parts. Then you take those parts and divide them. You continue to divide as far as it is practical to do so. In presentations, however, you are more likely to use factors rather than time, place, or quantity as the basis of division because in most speeches your presentation

Good speakers project their personal qualities—confidence, sincerity, friendliness, enthusiasm, and interest.

> ## Extemporaneous presentations generally sound natural to the listeners, yet they are (or should be) the product of careful planning and practice.

is likely to be built around issues and questions that are subtopics of the subject. Even so, time, place, and quantity subdivisions are possibilities.

You need to emphasize the transitions between the divisions because, unlike the reader who can see them, the listener may miss them if they are not stressed adequately. Without clear transitions, you may be talking about one point and your listener may still be back on your previous point.

conclusion Like most reports, the presentation usually ends by drawing a conclusion. Here you bring all that you have presented to a head and achieve whatever goal the speech has. You should consider including these three elements in your close: (1) a restatement of the subject, (2) a summary of the key points developed in the presentation, and (3) a statement of the conclusion (or main message). Bringing the talk to a climactic close—that is, making the conclusion the high point of the presentation—is usually effective. Present the concluding message in strong language—in words that gain attention and will be remembered. In addition to concluding with a summary, you can give an appropriate quote, use humor, and call for action. The following close of a presentation comparing Japanese and American management techniques illustrates this point: "These facts make my conclusion clear. We are not Japanese.

We do not have the Japanese culture. Most Japanese management methods have not worked—cannot work—will not work in our society."

LO 6 Identify and select appropriate presentation methods.

Selection of the Presentation Method

With the presentation organized, you are ready to prepare it. At this time, you need to decide on your method of presentation—that is, whether to present extemporaneously, to memorize it, or to read it.

presenting extemporaneously Extemporaneous presentation is by far the most popular and effective method. With this method, you first thoroughly prepare your presentation, as outlined above. Then you prepare notes and present from them. You usually rehearse, making sure you have all the parts clearly in mind, but you make no attempt to memorize. Extemporaneous presentations generally sound natural to the listeners, yet they are (or should be) the product of careful planning and practice.

memorizing The most difficult method is memorizing. If you are like most people, you find it hard to memorize a long succession of words. And when you do memorize, you are likely to memorize words rather than meanings. Thus, when you make the speech, if you miss a word or two, you become confused—and so does your speech. You even may become panic-stricken.

Probably few of the speakers who use this method memorize the entire speech. Instead, they memorize key passages and use notes to help them through the presentation. A delivery of this kind is a cross between an extemporaneous and a memorized presentation.

reading The third presentation method is reading. Unfortunately, most of us tend to read aloud in a dull monotone. We also miss punctuation marks, fumble over words, lose our place, and so on. Of course, many speakers overcome these problems, and with effort you can, too. One effective way is to practice with a recorder and listen to yourself. Then you can be your own judge of what you must do to improve your delivery. You would be wise not to read speeches until you have mastered this presentation method. In most settings, it is a breach of etiquette

to read. Your audience is likely to be insulted, and reading is unlikely to be as well received as an extemporaneous delivery. However, when you are in a position where you will be quoted widely, such as President of the United States or the CEO of a major company, reading from a carefully prepared speech is recommended. Many top executives today use teleprompters when delivering read speeches, and many of these appear well done, especially with practice.

LO 7 Describe how audience and self-analysis contribute to formal presentations.

Audience Analysis and Self-Analysis

One requirement of good presenting is to know your audience. You should study your audience both before and during the presentation.

preliminary analysis Analyzing your audience before the presentation requires that you size it up—that you search for audience characteristics that could affect how you should present your speech.

technology in brief

Presentation Delivery Tools Help You Convey Your Message Effectively

Delivery tools can help you to do a better job of preparing and delivering oral presentations. One tool within PowerPoint, Presenters View, should help you plan, practice, and deliver good presentations. You can see its major tools in the screenshot here.

As your audience sees only the slide, you are seeing the presenter's view. You see the current slide being projected and its slide notes. Additionally, you see the title of the upcoming slide as well as the elapsed time since the beginning of the presentation. Furthermore, along the right column are several buttons that allow you to start or end the show on one click, black out the screen to bring the attention back to

you, and perform other actions. As the presenter, you have the flexibility to skip slides or change the ordering on the fly. The slider bar at the bottom enables you easily to pull up slides during question-and-answer sessions as well.

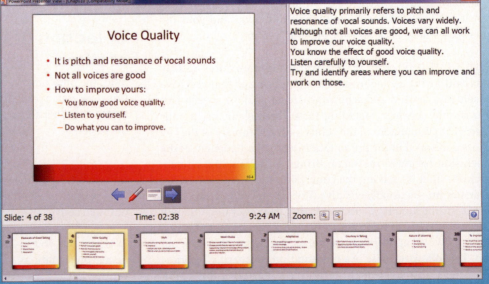

For example, the size of your audience is likely to influence how formal or informal your presentation should be. As a rule, large audiences require more formality. Personal characteristics of your audience, such as age, gender, education, experience, and knowledge of the subject matter, also should influence how you make your speech—affecting the words, illustrations, and level of detail you use. Like writing, presentations should be adapted to the audience. And the more you know about the audience, the better you will adapt your presentation to them.

analysis during the presentation

Your audience analysis should continue as you make the speech. *Feedback* is information about how your listeners are receiving your words. Armed with this information, you can adjust your presentation to improve the communication result.

Your eyes and ears will give you feedback information. For example, facial expressions will tell you how your listeners are reacting to your message. Smiles, blank stares, and movements will give you an indication of whether they understand, agree with, or accept it. You can detect from sounds coming (or not coming) from them whether they are listening. If questions are in order, you can learn directly how your message is coming across. In general, you can learn much from your audience by being alert; and what you learn can help you make a better speech.

self-analysis

A preliminary to good presentations is to analyze yourself as a speaker. In oral presentations you, the speaker, are a very real part of the message. The members of your audience take in not only the words you communicate but also what they see in you. And what they see in you can significantly affect the meanings that develop in their minds. Thus, you should carefully evaluate your personal effect on your message. You should do whatever you can to detect and overcome your shortcomings and to sharpen your strengths.

The following summary of characteristics that should help you as a speaker may prove useful, but you probably already know what they are. To some extent, the problem is recognizing whether you lack these characteristics. To a greater extent, it is doing something about acquiring them. The following review should help you pinpoint and deal with any problem areas.

Confidence A primary characteristic of effective oral reporting is confidence—your confidence in yourself and the confidence of your audience in you. The two are complementary, for your confidence in yourself tends to produce an image that

Successful oral presentations to large audiences are the result of thorough preparation.

> "You should carefully evaluate your personal effect on your message."

gives your audience confidence in you; and your audience's confidence in you can give you a sense of security that increases your confidence in yourself.

Typically, you earn your audience's confidence over periods of association. But there are things you can do to project an image that builds confidence. For example, preparing your presentation diligently and practicing it thoroughly gives you confidence in yourself. That confidence leads to more effective communication, which increases your listeners' confidence in you.

Another confidence-building technique is an appropriate physical appearance. Unfair and illogical as it may seem, certain types of dress and hairstyles create strong images in people's minds, ranging from highly favorable to highly unfavorable. You should work to develop the physical appearance that projects an image in which that audience can have confidence.

Yet another confidence-building technique is simply to talk in strong, clear tones. Such tones do much to project an image of confidence. Although most people can do little to change their natural voice, they can use sufficient volume.

Sincerity Your listeners are quick to detect insincerity. And if they detect it in you, they are likely to give little weight to what you say. On the other hand, sincerity is valuable to conviction, especially if the audience has confidence in your ability. The

> ## WITH A LITTLE SELF-ANALYSIS AND A LITTLE MIRROR WATCHING AS YOU PRACTICE SPEAKING, YOU CAN FIND WAYS OF IMPROVING YOUR PROJECTION OF FRIENDLINESS. "

way to project an image of sincerity is clear and simple: You must *be* sincere. Pretense of sincerity is rarely successful.

Thoroughness Generally, a thorough presentation is better received than a scanty or hurried presentation. Thorough coverage gives the impression that time and care have been taken, and this tends to make the presentation believable. But thoroughness can be overdone. Too much detail can drown your listeners in a sea of information. The secret is to leave out unimportant information. This, of course, requires good judgment. You must ask yourself just what your listeners need to know and what they do not need to know. Striking such a balance is the secret to achieving integrity in your presentation.

Friendliness A speaker who projects an image of friendliness has a significant advantage in communicating. People simply like friendly people, and they are generally receptive to what such people say. Like sincerity, friendliness is hard to feign and must be honest to be effective. Most people are genuinely friendly. Some, however, are just not able to project a genuinely friendly image. With a little self-analysis and a little mirror watching as you practice speaking, you can find ways of improving your projection of friendliness.

These are but a few of the characteristics that should assist you as a speaker. There are others: *interest, enthusiasm, originality, flexibility,* and so on. But the ones discussed are the most significant and the ones that most speakers need to work on. Through self-analysis and dedicated effort, you can improve your speaking ability.

LO 8 Explain the use of voice and physical aspects such as posture, walking, facial expression, and gestures in effective oral communication.

Effective Delivery Techniques

Audiences rate the effectiveness of presentations on what they see and hear. How a presenter uses his or her environment and voice contributes to the success of one's presentation. A discussion of the factors that affect appearance and voice are discussed here.

appearance and physical actions As your listeners hear your words, they are looking at you. What they see is a part of the message and can affect the success of your presentation. What they see, of course, is you and what surrounds you. In your efforts to improve the effects of your oral presentations, you should understand the communication effects of what your listeners see.

The communication environment Much of what your audience sees is the physical things that surround you as you speak: the stage, lighting, background, and so on. These things tend to create a general impression. Although not visual, outside noises have a related influence. For the best communication results, the factors in your communication environment should contribute to your message, not detract from it. Your own experience as a listener will tell you what factors are important.

Personal appearance Your personal appearance is a part of the message your audience receives. Of course, you have to accept the physical traits you have, but most of us do not need to be at a disadvantage in appearance. All that is necessary is to use what you have appropriately. Specifically, you should dress in a manner appropriate for the audience and the occasion. Be clean and well groomed. Use physical movements and facial expressions to your advantage.

Posture Posture is likely to be the most obvious of the things that your audience sees in you. Even listeners not close enough to detect facial expressions and eye movements can see the general form of the body.

You probably think that no one needs to tell you about good posture. You know it when you see it. The trouble is that you are not likely to see it in yourself. One solution is to have others tell you whether your posture needs improvement. Another is to practice speaking before a mirror or watch yourself on video.

In your efforts to improve your posture, keep in mind what must go on within your body to form a good posture. Your body weight must be distributed in a way consistent with the impression you want to make. You should keep your body erect without appearing stiff and comfortable without appearing limp. You should maintain a poised, alert, and communicative bearing. And you should do all this naturally. The great danger with posture is an artificial appearance.

Walking Your audience also forms an impression from the way you walk before it. A strong, sure walk to the speaker's position conveys an impression of confidence. Hesitant, awkward steps convey the opposite impression. Walking during the presentation can be good or bad, depending on how you do it. Some speakers use steps forward and to the side to emphasize points. Too much walking, however, attracts attention and detracts from the message. You would be wise to walk only when you are reasonably sure that this will have the effect you want. You would not want to walk away from a microphone.

Facial expression Probably the most apparent and communicative physical movements are facial expressions. The problem, however, is that you may unconsciously use facial expressions that convey unintended meanings. For example, if a frightened speaker tightens the jaw unconsciously and begins to grin, the effect may be an ambiguous image that detracts from the entire communication effort. A smile, a grimace, and a puzzled frown all convey clear messages. Of course, you should choose those expressions that best convey your intended meaning.

Eye contact is important. The eyes, which have long been considered "mirrors of the soul," provide most listeners with information about the presenter's sincerity, goodwill, and flexibility. Some listeners tend to

Effective presenters use friendly facial expressions and direct eye contact to connect with members of their audience.

[**Even though gestures have various meanings, they are strong, natural helps to speaking.**]

shun presenters who do not look at them. On the other hand, discriminate eye contact tends to show that you have a genuine interest in your audience.

Gestures Like posture, gestures contribute to the message you communicate. Just what they contribute, however, depends on the context. A clenched fist, for example, certainly adds emphasis to a strong point. But it also can be used to show defiance, make a threat, or signify respect for a cause. And so it is with other gestures.

Even though gestures have various meanings, they are strong, natural helps to speaking. It appears natural, for example, to emphasize a plea with palms up and to show disagreement with palms down. Raising first one hand and then the other reinforces a division of points. Slicing the air with the hand shows several divisions. Although such gestures are generally clear, we do not all use them in exactly the same way.

In summary, it should be clear that physical movements can help your speaking. Just which physical movements you should use depends on you and the situation. The appropriateness of physical movements is related to personality, physical makeup, and the size and nature of the audience. A presenter appearing

before a formal group should generally use relatively few physical movements. A presenter appearing before an informal group should use more. Which physical movements you should use on a given occasion is a matter for your best judgment.

use of voice Good voice is an obvious requirement of good speaking. Like physical movements, the voice should not hinder the listener's concentration on the message. More specifically, it should not detract attention from the message. Voices that cause such difficulties generally fall into these areas of fault: (1) lack of pitch variation, (2) lack of variation in speed, (3) lack of vocal emphasis, and (4) unpleasant voice quality.

Lack of pitch variation Speakers who talk in monotones are not likely to hold the interest of their listeners for long. Since most voices are capable of wide variations in pitch, the problem usually can be corrected. The failure to vary pitch generally is a matter of habit—of voice patterns developed over years of talking without being aware of their effect.

Lack of variation in speaking speed Determining how fast to talk is important. As a general rule, you should present the easy parts of your message at a fairly fast rate and the hard parts

Some Gesture Differences across Cultures

Gestures	U.S. Meanings	Other Meanings
	Victory	When it's presented backward in Australia and the United Kingdom, it's equivalent to the middle finger gesture in the United States.
	Good luck. Used by students at the U of Texas, Texas A & M, and the University of South Florida to cheer for their teams.	In Spain, Portugal, and Italy, it is interpreted as a sexual insult.
	Success	In Bangladesh, Iran, and West Africa, it's a rude gesture. In Egypt, it means perfect or very good.
	OK	In Japan, the o sign means money. On the Autoban drivers use this gesture to call one a jerk.
	Yes	The vertical head wobble so common here means "yes" and not "no." In India, the head wobble means No.
	Come here	In India, this gesture is considered rude. The comparable Indian gesture is with the palm facing down and moving like you're doing the "dog paddle."

and the parts you want to emphasize at a slower rate. The reason for varying the speed of presentation should be apparent: it is more interesting. A slow presentation of easy information is irritating; hard information presented fast may be difficult to understand.

A problem related to the pace of speaking is the incorrect use of pauses. Properly used, pauses emphasize upcoming subject matter and are an effective means of gaining attention. But frequent pauses for no reason are irritating and break the listeners' concentration. Pauses become even more irritating when the speaker fills them in with distracting nonwords such as *uh, like, you know,* and *OK.*

Lack of vocal emphasis A secret of good speaking is to give words their proper emphasis by varying the manner of speaking. You can do this by (1) varying the pitch of your voice, (2) varying the pace of your presentation, and (3) varying the volume of your voice. As the first two techniques have already been discussed, only the use of voice volume requires comment here.

You must talk loudly enough for your entire audience to hear you, but not too loudly. Thus, the loudness—voice volume—for a large audience should be greater than that for a small audience. Regardless of audience size, however, variety in voice volume is good for interest and emphasis. It produces contrast, which is one way of emphasizing the subject matter. Some speakers incorrectly believe that the only way to show emphasis is to get louder and louder. But you can also show emphasis by going from loud to soft. The contrast with what has gone on earlier provides the emphasis. Again, variety is the key to making the voice more effective.

Unpleasant voice quality It is a hard fact of communication that some voices are more pleasant than others. Fortunately, most voices are reasonably pleasant. But some are raspy, nasal, or unpleasant in another way. Although intensive training often can improve such voices, some speakers must live with them. But concentrating on variations in pitch, speed of delivery, and volume can make even the most unpleasant voice acceptable.

Improvement through self-analysis and imitation You can overcome any of the foregoing voice faults through self-analysis. In this day of audio and video recorders, it is easy to hear and see yourself talk. Since you know good speaking when you hear it, you should be able to improve your vocal presentation. One of the best ways to improve your presentation skills is through watching others. Watch your instructors, your peers, television artists, professional speakers, and anyone else who gives you an opportunity. Today you can even watch top corporate executives on webcasts and video presentations. Analyze these speakers to determine what works for them and what does not. Imitate those good techniques that you think would help you and avoid the bad ones. Take advantage of any opportunity you have to practice speaking.

> "Properly used, pauses emphasize upcoming subject matter and are an effective means of gaining attention."

technology in brief

Phone Apps Can Help Control a Presentation

Phone apps can be used as a remote presentation tool that helps a presenter control the AV. Using one saves you from carrying around and installing extra hardware and it's always as readily available as your phone. The iPhone app you see here, Stage Hand, is a great tool for those using Keynote. It lets the presenter control the slides, time the presentation, and even view slide notes right on the phone.

Communication in brief

Make Your Last Slide Work

Whether you use 10 or 110 slides, the powerful impact of the last one demands your special attention. As you can see here in these last slides from slideshows on SlideShare.net, their authors seem to have different ideas of what works in their settings. One author simply signals the presentation is over, another uses it to open the Q & A session, some use it for branding, and some use it to emphasize the key ideas they want their audience to remember.

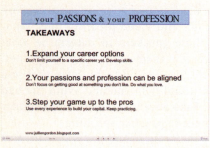

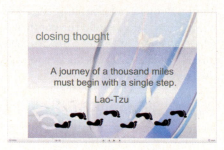

In oral presentations, appropriately handled visuals can be effective in communicating messages clearly.

LO 9 Plan for visuals to support presentations.

Use of Visuals

The spoken word is severely limited in communicating. Sound is here briefly and then gone. A listener who misses the vocal message may not have a chance to hear it again. Because of this limitation, presentations often need strong visual support: slides with talking points, charts, tables, photos, video, and the like. Since visuals may be as vital to the success of a presentation as the words themselves, they should be an integral part of the planning process.

proper use of design Effective visuals are drawn from the message. They fit the one speech and the one audience.

In selecting visuals, you should search through your presentation for topics that appear vague or confusing. Whenever a visual of some kind will help eliminate vagueness or confusion, you should use it. You should use visuals to simplify complex information and improve cohesiveness, as well as to emphasize or add interest. Visuals are truly a part of your message, and you should look at them as such.

After deciding that a topic deserves visual help, you determine what form that help should take. That is, should the visual be a bulleted list, an outline, a chart, a diagram, a picture, or what? You should select your visuals primarily on the basis of their ability to communicate content. Simple and obvious as this suggestion may appear, people violate it all too often. They select visuals more for appearance and dramatic effect than for communication effect.[3]

types to consider
Because no one type of visual is best for all occasions, you should have a flexible attitude toward visuals. You should know the strengths and weaknesses of each type, and you should know how to use each type effectively.

In selecting visuals, you should keep in mind the available types. You will mainly consider the various types of graphics—the text-based charts and tables, data-generated graphs, and pictures—discussed in Chapter 3. Each of these types has its strengths and

weaknesses and can be displayed in various ways, generally classified as nonprojected or projected. Nonprojected techniques include such media as posters, flip charts, models, and handouts; projected techniques include slides, transparencies, and computer projections.

audience size, cost, and ease of preparation considerations
Your choice of visuals also should be influenced by the audience size and formality, the cost of preparing and using the media (visuals), and the ease and time of preparation. Exhibit 10.1 illustrates how the different media fare on these dimensions, helping guide you to the best choice for your particular needs.

handling of visuals
Visuals usually carry key parts of the message. Thus, they are points of emphasis in your presentation. You blend them in with your words to communicate the message. How you do this is to some extent an individual matter but you should keep in mind the following list of dos and don'ts.

- Make certain that everyone in the audience can see the visuals. Too many or too-light lines on a chart, for example, can be hard to see. An illustration that is too small can be meaningless to people far from the speaker. Even fonts must be selected and sized for visibility.

Digital Visual Presenters (also called document cameras) give speakers the flexibility to show a wide variety of objects from an antique map to three-dimensional objects to videos.

[**After deciding that a topic deserves visual help, you determine what form that help should take.**]

▼ **EXHIBIT 10.1** Selection Guide for Media Choice

	Media	Image Quality	Audience Size	Cost	Ease of Preparation
Nonprojected	Poster	Very good	Small	$$	Medium
	Flip chart	Good	Small	$	Short
	Presentation board	Good	Small	$	Short
	Real object or model	Very good	Small	$–$$$$	Short to long
	Chalkboard or whiteboard	Fair	Medium	$	None
	Photos	Very good	Medium	$$	Short to medium
	Handouts	Excellent	Large	$–$$	Short to long
Projected	35mm slides	Very good	Large	$	Medium
	Overhead transparencies	Very good	Medium	$	Short
	Document cameras, visual presenters, digital presenters	Very good	Medium	None	None
	TVs/VCRs	Excellent	Medium to large	$–$$$$	Short to long
	Computer projection (PC and Web-based apps)	Very good	Medium to large	None	Short to long

- Explain the visual if there is any likelihood that it will be misunderstood.

- Organize the visuals as a part of the presentation. Fit them into the presentation plan.

- Emphasize the visuals. Point to them with physical action and words. Use laser presenter tools and slide animations to emphasize. Most presentation applications and tablet PCs let you annotate slides easily.

- Talk to the audience—not to the visuals. Look at the visuals only when the audience should look at them. When you want the audience to look at you, you can regain attention by covering the visual or making the screen in PowerPoint white or black (toggle the W or B keys).

- Avoid blocking the listeners' views of the visuals. Make certain that the listeners' views are not blocked by lecterns, pillars, and chairs. Take care not to stand in anyone's line of vision.

use of the presentation application While there are dozens of PC- and Web-based presentation applications available, PowerPoint currently is the one most widely used in the workplace. Web-based apps such as SlideRocket, Google Docs, Acrobat Presentations, and most others will usually both import and export in PowerPoint format, making it a defacto standard. Therefore, the primary issue around presentation applications is not which one to use but whether or not to use them at all.

Prominent Ivy League professors and high-ranking military officers have called PowerPoint corrupt and banned its use. It has been blamed for everything from shuttle accidents to numbing and dumbing down its audience; however, its use prevails because it can be an effective tool when used appropriately and in appropriate contexts.

These applications are best when used to supplement a speaker's presentation, not replace it. They should be used to help an audience understand the speaker's ideas faster and more accurately than words alone could do. However, some speakers use them in a teleprompter-like manner, reading wordy text from slides. Others use them to entertain in ways that distract the audience rather than aid in understanding or retention. This misuse has led to much of the current consternation.

However, by focusing on helping your audience and serving their purposes, you can use these applications as effective communication tools. With careful planning of the content and using the technology to convey the ideas as a visual story, you can enhance your ability to communicate them.

In Chapter 3 you learned about designing effective presentations by considering layout, art, type, and color elements. These elements can help the readability and comprehension of your message. Layout, whether original or template-based, is important but so are the same concepts you've learned for organizing, wording, and summarizing documents. Descriptive titles and labels are equally as important here as they are in messages

> By focusing on helping your audience and serving their purposes, you can use these applications as effective communication tools.

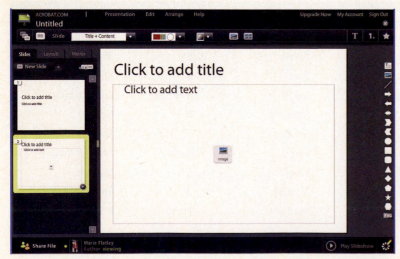

Some new Web-based presentation tools such as SlideRocket, Google Presentations, and Adobe Presenter allow teams to collaborate easily on their presentations.

and reports. Art and photos can be inserted, pasted, and created in these applications to help a speaker communicate the message better. Type as you learned earlier is critical in readability—its size, font, and style, all convey messages. The size of type is governed by the speaking environment; basically, it should be easily readable from all parts of the room. Color is important in background, text, charts, and other visual selection.

Other features of these applications such as animation, transitions, and media integration have their place, too. There is a plethora of online tutorials, videos, ebooks, Webcasts, and print books that can teach you how to exploit these features in ways that contribute to improving the ability to communicate the message.[4]

Using the technology effectively along with having backup plans will also reflect on you as an amateur or a professional. Audiences generally don't like speakers who read from the screens, especially ones who turn their backs to the audience. Equally important is proper pacing. A speaker tuned in to both the content difficulty and to the audience will be able to adjust the pace to fit the situation. In addition to displaying good timing, a speaker can look polished by using navigation shortcuts as needed. In PowerPoint 2010, these navigation shortcuts can be brought up with F1 during a presentation if needed, but it's usually best to know them—at least the ones you find most useful.

Finally, a good presenter uses the closing slide effectively. Ideally, ending with the key idea or concept is best. This is the statement you want the audience to give when someone asks them what you spoke about. Sometimes it's referred to as an elevator statement, but it's a short, concise summary statement of your presentation. By ending with it on your final slide, you give your audience an important assist in remembering it later.

COPYRIGHT JOHN S. PRITCHETT

LO 10 Work effectively with a group in preparing and making a team presentation.

Team Presentations

Another type of presentation you may be asked to give is a group or team presentation. To give this type of presentation, you will need to use all you have learned about giving individual presentations. We will mention other ideas you should consider in your team presentation.

First, you will need to take special care to plan the presentation—to determine the sequence of the presentation as well as the content of each team member's part. You also will need to select carefully supporting examples to build continuity from one part of the presentation to the next.

Groups should plan for the physical aspects of the presentation, too. You should coordinate the type of delivery, use of notes, visuals, and styles and colors of attire to present a good image of competence and professionalism. And you should plan transitions so that the team will appear coordinated.

Another presentation aspect—physical staging—is important as well. Team members should know where to sit or stand, how visuals will be handled, how to change or adjust microphones, and how to enter and leave the speaking area.

Attention to the close of the presentation is especially strategic. Teams need to decide who will present the close and what will be said. If a summary is used, the member who presents it should attribute key points to appropriate team members. If there is to be a question-and-answer session, the team should plan how to conduct it. For example, will one member take the questions and direct them to a specific

> " *In all of their extra planning activities, teams should not overlook the need to plan for rehearsal time.* "

team member? Or will the audience be permitted to ask questions to specific members? Some type of final note of appreciation or thanks needs to be planned with all the team nodding in agreement or acknowledging the final comment in some way.

In all of their extra planning activities, teams should not overlook the need to plan for rehearsal time. Teams should consider practicing the presentation in its entirety several times as a group before the actual presentation. During these rehearsals, individual members should critique thoroughly each other's contributions, offering specific ways to improve. After first rehearsal sessions, outsiders (nonteam members) might be asked to view the team's presentation and critique the group. Moreover, the team might consider recording the presentation so that all members can evaluate it. In addition to a more effective presentation, the team can enjoy the by-products of group cohesion and *esprit de corps*. Successful teams know the value of rehearsing and will build such activity into their presentation planning schedules.

These points may appear obvious, but careful attention to them will result in a polished, coordinated team presentation.

LO 11 Define virtual presentations and differentiate between them and face-to-face presentations.

It is a good idea to rehearse a team presentation with some colleagues before delivering it to an important audience.

Understanding the nature of this technology, the differences between virtual and face-to-face presentations, and some techniques to use with it will become more important as its use in business grows.

a definition of virtual presentations A virtual presentation is one usually delivered from a desktop over the Internet to an audience located anywhere in the world where there is Internet access. While it could be delivered with both audio and video components, so the audience could see and hear the presenter, about 80 percent of today's users view PowerPoint slides on the Internet and listen over a phone or VOIP connection. Usually no other special hardware or costly software is needed. These presentations can also be recorded, allowing audiences to view them at different times as well at different places.

Virtual presentations are being used in businesses in many of the same ways face-to-face presentations are used—to inform and to persuade. They can improve productivity by giving even remote employees up-to-date information and training, avoiding down time for travel and reducing travel costs. They can allow sales people to reach broader audiences as well as highly targeted specialized audiences worldwide.

> [Virtual presentations are being used in businesses in many of the same ways face-to-face presentations are used—to inform and to persuade.]

Virtual Presentations

One relatively new venue for oral presentations is the virtual or online venue (also called webcasts, webinars, or eseminars). While videoconferencing has been around for years, several factors seem to be driving the use of this technology now. Some of these factors are negative—high costs of travel in both dollars and time and widely dispersed business operations. But positives are at work as well, including both better technology and high speed networks. With better hardware and more widely accessible connections to the Internet, several companies have developed easy-to-use, Web-based applications. WebEx, once the defacto standard in this area, now has competitors in such products as Citrix's GoToMeeting, Microsoft's Live Meeting, Adobe Connect, Raindance, and more. And the affordable costs make this technology attractive to both large and small businesses for presentations to both large and small audiences.

differences between face-to-face and virtual presentations The major difference between face-to-face and virtual presentations is that the dynamics have changed— the speaker cannot see the audience and sometimes the audience cannot see the speaker. Some argue that being able to see the presenter is not critical, and the technology has given us some tools to help the speaker get feedback from the audience. In Exhibit 10.2, you can see some of the tools available to the viewer using Cisco's WebEx. Each viewer can configure the screen to his or her preference. For this particular meeting the presenter turned on the video feed of himself, which many viewers appreciate. The list of participants shows the people present and gives their sign-on names. It has a button just below the list that allows participants to raise their hands to let the speaker know they have a question or to give feedback to a question the speaker might ask. The tool also includes a chat box for real-time questions and answers. Obviously, the

▼ **EXHIBIT 10.2** Cisco's WebEx has Several Tools that can enhance the interaction between the speaker and audience.

Source: This screenshot has been reproduced by McGraw-Hill with the permission of Cisco Systems Inc. and/or its affiliated entities. © Cisco Systems, Inc. and/or its affiliated entities. All rights reserved. Cisco WebEx and Meeting Center are trademarks or registered trademarks of Cisco Systems, Inc. and/or its affiliated entities.

speaker cannot present and type answers to questions at the same time, so this feature is usually handled by an assistant or copresenter. And the predominant window here is the slide being discussed. Viewers often run this window at full screen size, toggling back to the other tools as needed. Presenters can also poll the audience during a presentation and display the results immediately.

To deliver a virtual presentation effectively, a presenter needs to do some preliminary, delivery, and closing activities. First is to choose a user-friendly, simple technology. Then send out announcements of the presentation along with a note encouraging the audience to pretest their systems before the designated start time for the presentation. If needed, you might want to arrange to have a technical person on hand to troubleshoot, anticipating that some will have trouble connecting, others will fall behind, and occasionally your time will expire. With a technical person on hand, these typical problems can be resolved quickly. Also, you'll need to arrange ahead of time for an assistant if you need one. And you need to create something for early arrivers to view in the first 5 to 10 minutes before you start. This could be an announcement, news of an upcoming presentation, information about your products and services, or even a countdown clock. You will also want to tell participants where additional information is available, including your slides, a recording of the presentation, and other business links.

The delivery of your presentation will be much like that for other presentations, except you will be doing it from your desktop and may use a headphone. You may want to use the highlighter or an animation effects tool in PowerPoint to help you emphasize key points that you would otherwise physically point to in a face-to-face presentation. You will want to plan breaks where you will poll or quiz the audience or handle questions

that have come in through the back channel or chat tool. If you use the presenter's view in PowerPoint, you can set the timer to help you do this at regular intervals as well as gauge the timing through the questions and feedback.

In the closing, you will want to allow time to evaluate the success of your presentation as well as to handle questions and answers. Watching your time is critical because some systems will drop you if you exceed your requested time.

Overall, presenting virtually requires the same keys to success as other presentations—careful planning, attentive delivery, and practice. ■

Get Online

mhhe.com/FlatleyM2e

for study materials including quizzes and Internet resources.

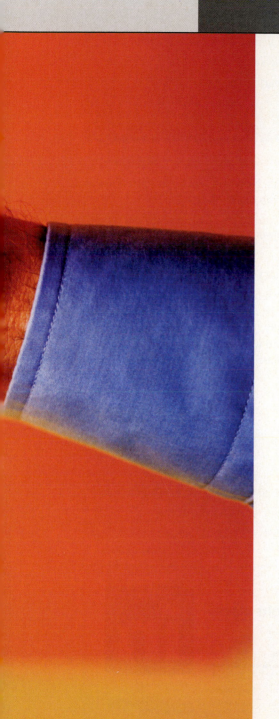

communicating in the job search

O f all the things you do in life, few are more important than getting a job. Whether it involves your first job or one further down your career path, job seeking is directly related to your success and your happiness. It is vital that you conduct the job search properly—that you prepare wisely and carefully and proceed diligently. The following review of job-search strategies should help you succeed. ▪

workplace scenario

Conducting the Job-Search Process

Introduce yourself to this chapter by assuming a role similar to one you are now playing. You are Jason Andrews, a student at Olympia University. In a few months, you will complete your studies for work in marketing.

You believe that it is time to begin seeking the job for which those studies have been preparing you. But how do you do this? Where do you look? What does the search involve? How should you present yourself

for the best results? The answers to these and related questions are reviewed in the following pages.

CONDUCTING PRELIMINARY ACTIVITIES IN THE JOB SEARCH

As you have made friends and acquaintances in your life, you have already begun some of the preliminaries of building a network of contacts. And when you decided to major in business, you were likely beginning to think about some work you might like to do one day. Furthermore, as you and your friends found summer jobs, part-time jobs, and internships, you discovered some ways to find employers. Now you will learn some ways to enhance these preliminary job search skills.

LO 1 Develop and use a network of contacts in your job search.

Building a Network of Contacts

You can begin the job search long before you are ready to find employment. In fact, you can do it now by building a network of contacts. More specifically, you can build relationships with people who can help you find work when you need it. Such people include classmates, professors, and businesspeople.

technology in brief

Trusted Professional Networking Can Become a Powerful Tool

One of the most widely known professional networking tools is LinkedIn. A reason often mentioned for its recent growth surge is the trust it has enabled between the people connected. This screen shows the Learning Center where you see how to connect with others, help in searching for a job or for employees, and get answers from trusted others on business questions you pose.

There is no cost for its basic service, but you can upgrade to enable the advanced features. In addition to the easy-to-use dashboard you get when signing in, those you invite to link to you enter and maintain their own data.

One of its best features is the recommendation tag where job seekers can ask

others to recommend them. Those recommending could be anyone who can attest to

your strengths—your professors or former bosses or even lifetime friends.

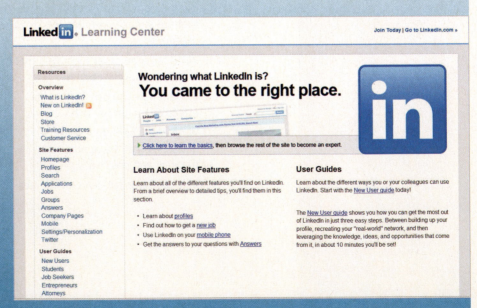

At present, your classmates are not likely to be holding positions in which they make or influence hiring decisions. But in the future, when you may want to make a career change, they may hold such positions. Right now, some of them may know people who can help you. The wider your circle of friends and acquaintances, the more likely you are to make employment contacts.

Knowing your professors and making sure that they know you also can lead to employment contacts. Because professors often consult for business, they may know key executives and be able to help you contact them. Professors sometimes hear of position openings, and in such cases they can refer you to the hiring executives. Demonstrating your work ethic and your ability in the classroom is probably the best way to get your professors to know you and help you. Take advantage of opportunities to meet your professors outside the classroom, especially the professors in your major field.

virtually any activity that provides contacts with business leaders can be mutually beneficial, both now and in the future.

LO 2 Assemble and evaluate information that will help you select a job.

Identifying Appropriate Jobs

To find the right job, you need to investigate both internal and external factors. The best fit occurs when you have carefully looked at yourself: your education, personal qualities, experience, and any special qualifications. However, to be realistic, these internal qualities need to be analyzed in light of the external factors. Some of these factors may include the current and projected job market, economic needs, location preferences, and family needs.

> "To find the right job, you need to investigate both internal and external factors.

Obviously, meeting key business executives also can lead to employment contacts. You may already know some through family and friends. But broadening your relationships among businesspeople would be helpful. You can do this in various ways, especially through college professional groups such as the Association for Information Technology Professionals, Delta Sigma Pi, and the Society for the Advancement of Management. By taking an active role in the organizations in your field of study, especially by working on program committees and by becoming an officer, you can get to know the executives who serve as guest speakers. You also might meet businesspeople online. If you share a particular interest on a blog or twitter feed or are known as one who contributes valuable tweets and comments to others' blogs, you may get some good job leads there.

If your school offers internships, you can make good career contacts through them. But you should find the one that is best for you, one that offers you the best training for your career objective. And by all means, do not regard an internship as just a job. Regard it as a foundation step in your career plan. The experience you gain and the contacts you make in an internship might lead to your first career position. In fact, if you perform well, your internship could turn into full-time employment.

In addition to these more common ways of making contacts, you can use some less common ones. By working in community organizations such as charities, community improvement groups, and fund-raising groups, you can meet community leaders. By attending meetings of professional associations you can meet the leaders in your field. In fact, participation in

analyzing yourself When you are ready to search for a job, you should begin the effort by analyzing yourself. In a sense, you should look at yourself much as you would look at a product or service that is for sale. After all, when you seek employment, you are really selling your ability to work—to do things for an employer. A job is more than something that brings you money. It is something that gives equal benefits to both parties—you and your employer. Thus, you should think about the qualities you have that enable you to be an accountable and productive worker that an employer needs. This self-analysis should cover the following categories.

© Randy Glasbergen.
www.glasbergen.com

"I néver know whére to put thé funny thing ovér thé léttér é whén I'm writing my résumé."

Source: Copyright © Randy Glasbergen. Reprinted with permission.

education The analysis might well begin with education. Perhaps you have already selected your career area such as accounting, economics, finance, information systems, international business, management, or marketing. If you have, your task is simplified, for your specialized curriculum has prepared you for your goal. Even so, you may be able to note special points—for example, electives that have given you special skills or that show something special about you, such as psychology courses that have improved your human-relations skills, communication courses that have improved your writing and speaking skills, or foreign language courses that have prepared you for international assignments.

If you have pursued a more general curriculum, such as general business or liberal arts, you will need to look at your studies closely to see what they have prepared you to do. Perhaps you will find an emphasis on computers, written communication, human relations, or foreign languages—all of which are sorely needed by some businesses. Or perhaps you will conclude that

willingness to work, your personality, your experience. Or perhaps you can explain, for example, by noting that while working your way through school may have limited your academic performance, it gave you valuable business qualities such as initiative, collaboration, and risk-taking.

personal qualities Your self-analysis also should cover your personal qualities. Employers often use personality tests such as the Myers-Briggs to screen new hires, and you can take them online as well as at most campus career centers. Qualities that relate to working with people are especially important. Qualities that show leadership or teamwork ability are also important. And if you express yourself well in writing or speaking, note this, for good communication skills are valuable in most jobs.

Of course, you may not be the best judge of your personal qualities, for we do not always see ourselves as others see us. You may need to check with friends to see whether they agree with your assessments. You also may need to check your record for

> In analyzing your education, you should look at the quality of your record—grades, projects, honors, and special recognitions.

your training has given you a strong general base from which to learn specific business skills.

In analyzing your education, you should look at the quality of your record—grades, projects, honors, and special recognitions. If your record is good, you can emphasize it. But what if your work was mediocre? As we will point out later, you will need to shift the emphasis to your stronger sales points—your

evidence supporting your assessments. For example, organization membership and participation in community activities are evidence of people and teamwork skills. Holding office in an organization is evidence of leadership ability. Participation on a debate team, college bowl, or collegiate business policy team is evidence of communication skills.

work experience If you have work experience, you should analyze it. Work experience in your major deserves emphasis. In fact, such work experience becomes more and more important as you move along in your career. Work experience not related to the job you seek also can tell something important about you—even if the work was part-time. Part-time work can show willingness and determination, especially if you have done it to finance your education. And almost any work experience can help develop your skills in dealing with people and taking responsibility.

special qualifications Your self-analysis also should include special qualifications that might be valuable to an employer. The ability to speak a foreign language can be very helpful for certain business environments. Athletic participation, hobbies, and interests also may be helpful. To illustrate, athletic experience might be helpful for work for a sporting goods distributor, a hobby of automobile mechanics might be helpful for work with an automotive service company, and an interest in music might be helpful for work with a piano manufacturer or an online music Web site. An interest in or skills with computers would be valuable across a broad range of businesses.

Career fairs and job boards are good places to look for announcements of job openings.

> ## ACCORDING TO SOME EMPLOYMENT REPORTS, PERSONAL CONTACTS ARE THE LEADING MEANS OF FINDING EMPLOYEES.

You also might take an interest inventory such as the Strong Interest Inventory or a personality profiler such as Type Focus. These tests help match your interests and personality to those of others successful in their careers. Most college counseling and career services make these tests available to their students, and some are available online. Getting good help in interpreting the results is critical to providing you with valuable information.

registrants containing school records, résumés, and recommendations for review by prospective employers. Most have directories listing the major companies with contact names and addresses. And most provide interviewing opportunities. Campus career services often hold career fairs. They are an excellent place to find employers who are looking for new graduates as well as to gather information about the kinds of jobs different

analyzing outside factors After you have analyzed yourself, you need to combine this information with the work needs of business and other external influences. Your goal in this process is to give realistic direction to your search for employment. Where is the kind of work you are seeking available? Are you willing to move? Is such a move compatible with others in your life—your partner, your children, your parents? Does the location meet with your lifestyle needs? Although the availability of work may drive the answer to some of these questions, you should answer them as well as you can on the basis of what you know now and then conduct your job search accordingly. Finding just the right job should be one of your most important goals.

LO 3 Identify the sources that will lead you to an employer.

Finding Your Employer

You can use a number of sources in your search for an employer with whom you will begin or continue your career. Your choice of sources will probably be influenced by the stage of your career.

career services If you are just beginning your career, one good possibility is the career services at your school. Most large schools have career services, and these attract employers who are looking for suitable applicants. Many offer excellent job-search counseling and maintain databases on

Apps abound to help job searchers find job announcements, create documents, and manage the job search process.

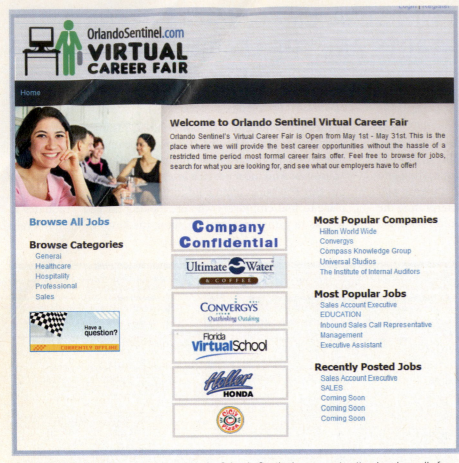

Virtual job fairs like this one sponsored by the *Orlando Sentinel* are easy to attend and usually free to the job candidates.

employment opportunities for many kinds of work. Many are limited, however, in the opportunities they provide for new college graduates. Classified ads are good sources for experienced workers who are seeking to improve their positions, and they are especially good sources for people who are conducting a major search for high-level positions. However, they are only a partial list of jobs available.

online sources In addition to finding opportunities in classifieds, you also will find them in online databases. Monster.com, for example, lists jobs available throughout the country, with new opportunities posted regularly. Many companies even post job openings on the their own Web sites, some with areas dedicated to new college graduates.

If you are working now, you may want to check the company's intranet or portal for positions there, too. And professional associations often maintain job databanks. Furthermore, you could use blogs and social networking sites to post queries about job openings that readers might have information about. At Twitjobsearch.com, a job search engine for Twitter, you can see Twitter postings for jobs around the world. All these online systems are sources for job opportunities. See the textbook Web site for links to many useful Web sites.

companies offer. By attending them early, you often find out about internships and summer jobs and gather ideas for selecting courses that might give you a competitive advantage when you do begin your career search.

network of personal contacts As has been noted, the personal contacts you make can be extremely helpful in your job search. In fact, according to some employment reports, personal contacts are the leading means of finding employees. Obviously, personal contacts are more likely to be a source of employment opportunities later in your career—when you may need to change jobs. Acquaintances may provide job leads outside those known to your friends. Social networking sites such as LinkedIn and JigSaw help people connect.

classified advertisements Help-wanted advertisements in newspapers and professional journals, whether online or in print, provide good sources of

personal search agents In addition to searching online sources, you can request that job notices be sent to you automatically by Web sites. These sites use tools called personal search agents or job agents. Using a filter based on a confidential profile you complete for the site, these tools find jobs that match your profile and send you job alerts via email and/or text messages about these jobs.

Starting with a very precise or narrow profile first is wise. You can always modify your profile to something broader later if you find the number or nature of the job leads isn't what you expected. If you learn of a job listing that interests you for a company recruiting at your school, you should ask the recruiter about it. Not only will it show the employer you have done your homework, but it will also show that you have a sincere interest in working for the company.

Web résumés To make yourself more visible to potential employers, you may want to consider posting your résumé to the Web. Some employers actively search for new employees on university Web sites. Posting a Web page résumé is not difficult. Today's word processors let you save your

> " To make yourself more visible to potential employers, you may want to consider posting your résumé to the Web. "

documents in hypertext markup language (HTML), creating a basic Web page for you. Additionally, easy-to-use Web page building and generating tools are available on the Web to help novices create Web résumés. Once posted, it is a good idea to link your Web page to your major department or to a business student club, allowing more potential employers to find your résumé. With a little extra effort, you can create a Web page that greatly expands on the printed résumé. You will want to put your Web page address on your printed résumé as well as cross-reference your online Web pages to each other.

employment agencies Companies that specialize in finding jobs for employees can be useful. Of course, such companies charge for their services. The employer sometimes pays the charges, usually if qualified applicants are scarce. Executive search consultants (headhunters) are commonly used to place experienced people in executive positions. Employment agencies also can help job seekers gain temporary employment.

Temping can lead to permanent employment with a good fit. It allows the worker to get a feel for the company and the company to observe the worker before making a job commitment.

prospecting Some job seekers approach prospective employers directly, either by personal visit, mail, or email. Personal visits are effective if the company has an employment office or if a personal contact can set up a visit. Mail contacts typically include a résumé and a cover letter. An email contact can include a variety of documents and be sent in various forms. The construction of these messages is covered later in the chapter.

PREPARING THE APPLICATION DOCUMENTS

After your search has uncovered a job possibility, you pursue it. How you pursue it depends on the circumstances of the case. When it is convenient and appropriate to do so, you make contact in person. It is convenient when the distance is not great, and it is appropriate when the employer has invited such a contact. When a personal visit is not convenient and appropriate, you apply online or by mail, fax, or email.

Whether or not you apply in person, you are likely to use some written material. If you apply in person, probably you will take a résumé with you to leave as a record of your qualifications. If you do not apply in person, of course, the application is completely in writing. Typically, it consists of a résumé, a cover message, and a reference sheet. At some point in your employment efforts, you are likely to use each of these documents.

Video résumés are one tool job candidates are using today. Companies like Workblast, Optimal Resume, Resumebook.tv, Britelab.com, and others are making it easy, even bringing them to college campuses at times.

technology in brief

Web Page Résumés Can Work for You

Posting a Web page profile is another way of showcasing yourself and your communication skills. Not only can you add much more detail than on a print résumé, but you can also use colorful photos, videos, and sounds. You can show examples of real projects, documents, and presentations you have created as well as demonstrate your skills and creativity. A Web page résumé can range from a simple one you create by completing an online form, to the mailable one you see on page 319, to a sophisticated one, like the one you see here, that uses a full range of media and interaction.

Today several Web-based tools are available for creating multimedia résumés. You can find links to some of these on the text Web site. The one you see here is available at VisualCV.com. You can present your résumé along with video, graphics highlighting accomplishments, and samples of your work—both your writing and your presentations. The tool not only helps you create a

personalized look for your site but is also an easy way to do so. And it provides an excellent place for you to update it as you gain more skills and accomplishments. Be sure to remember to include the URL of your

Web résumé on both your print résumé as well as LinkedIn and other appropriate social network sites. You might even want to print it on business cards that you give out to prospective employers.

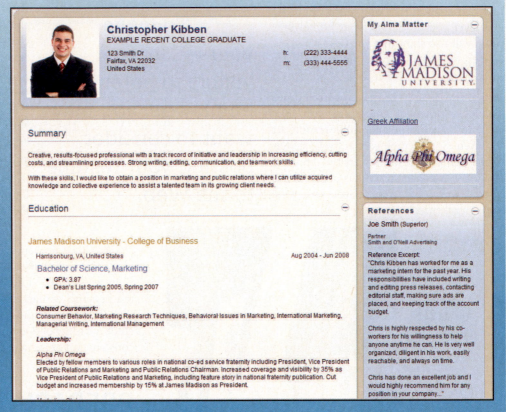

Preparing these documents is much like preparing a sales document—both types involve selling. You are selling a product or services—your ability to do work. The résumé and reference sheet are much like the supporting material that accompanies the sales message. The cover message is much like the sales message. These similarities should become obvious to you as you read the following pages.

As in preparing a sales campaign, you begin work on a written application for a job by studying what you are selling, and what you are selling is you. Then you study the work. Studying yourself involves taking personal inventory—the self-analysis discussed earlier in the chapter. You should begin by listing all the information about you that you

believe an employer would want to know. Studying the work means learning as much as you can about the company—its plans, its policies, its operations. You can study the company's Web site, read its annual report and other publications, find any recent news articles about the company, and consult a variety of business databases. (See Chapter 8 for a more detailed list of resources for company information.) You can also learn the requirements of the work the company wants done. Today, campus career centers and student organizations often invite employers to give information sessions. Reading about various careers in the *Opportunity Outlook Handbook* at <http://www.bls.gov/oco/> will tell you about the nature of the work as well as salary range and

workplace scenario

Writing Résumés and Applications

In your role as Jason Andrews, you consider yourself well qualified for a position in marketing. You know the field from both personal experience and classroom study. You grew up in a middle-class neighborhood. From an early age, you worked at a variety of jobs, the most important of which was a job as a pollster. You were a restaurant host and a food server for two years. Your college studies were especially designed to prepare you for work in marketing. You studied Olympia University's curriculum in marketing, and you carefully chose the electives that would give you the best possible preparation for this work. As evidenced by your grades, your preparation was good.

Now it is time to begin your job search. Over the past weeks you followed good procedures in looking for employment (as reviewed in the preceding pages). Unfortunately, you had no success with the recruiters who visited your campus. Now you will send written applications to a select group of companies that you think might use a person with your knowledge and skills. You have obtained the names of the executives you should contact at these companies. You will send them the application documents—résumé and cover message. The following discussion shows you how to prepare these documents for best results, both in print and digital form.

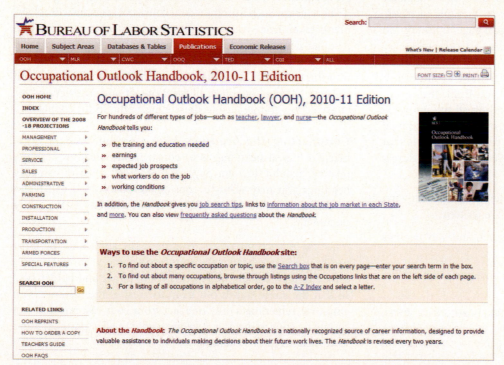

The *Occupational Outlook Handbook* is one of the best resources for finding out about a wide variety of jobs, including needed education, expected earnings, job activities and conditions, and more.

vita, curriculum vita, qualifications brief, or *data sheet*), or a cover message, résumé, and reference sheet? The résumé is a summary of background facts in list form. You will probably select the combination of cover message and résumé, for this arrangement is likely to do the best job. Still, some people prefer to use the cover message alone. When you send a print cover message, it usually contains substantial detail, for it must do the whole sales job. When you send a digital message, it can be adapted to the channel chosen. You will include the reference sheet when asked or when it supports your case.

LO 4 Compile print and digital résumés that are strong, complete, and organized.

demand. Sometimes you can get this information through personal investigation. More often, you will have to develop it through logical thinking.

With this preliminary information assembled, you are ready to plan the application. First, you need to decide just what your application will consist of. Will it be just a cover message, a cover message and a résumé (also called a

Constructing the Résumé

After you have decided to use the résumé, you must decide whether to use a print or a digital format. The traditional print format is used in face-to-face interviews where you know it will be used exclusively there. If you have reason to believe the company will store your résumé digitally, you should use a scannable print format. Constructing these forms is similar, but they differ in some very important ways.

A digital format, on the other hand, is used when sending your application document by email or submitting or posting it via the Web. Depending on the capabilities of the recipient's system and any forms an employer may specify, the documents can range from a low-end ASCII or text form to midrange attached files, to high-end, full-featured Web pages. In both the print and digital formats, you set up the documents to present your credentials in the most favorable way.

After deciding what your format will be, you construct the parts. In selecting these parts you not only choose how to present them, but you also tailor the content and order to the specific job you are applying for. While the print résumé you will use now when just coming out of school will generally be one page long, after you've worked several years it may grow to a couple of pages. However, the digital version has no physical page limitation, so you should include all that is relevant to the particular job.

traditional print résumé
You will want to include in the résumé all background information you think the reader should have about you. This means including all the information that a cover letter reviews plus supporting and incidental details. Designed for quick reading, the résumé lists facts that have been arranged for the best possible appearance. Rarely does it use sentences.

The arrangements of résumés differ widely, but the following procedures generally describe how most are written:

- Construct a heading for the entire résumé and subheadings for the parts.

- Include other vital information such as objectives and contact information.

- Logically arrange information on education (institutions, dates, degrees, major field); information on employment (dates, places, firms, and accomplishments); personal details (memberships, interests, achievements, and the like—but not religion, race, and gender); and special information derived from other information (achievements, qualifications, capabilities).

- Arrange the data for best eye appeal, making the résumé balanced—not crowded and not strung out.

- Add a reference sheet as needed.

Selecting the background facts Your first step in preparing the résumé is to review the background facts you have assembled about yourself and then to select the facts you think will help your reader evaluate you. You should include all the information covered in the accompanying cover message, for this is the most important information. In addition, you should include significant supporting details not covered in the accompanying cover message.

Arranging the facts into groups After selecting the facts you want to include, you should sort them into logical groups. Many grouping arrangements are possible. The most conventional is the three-part grouping of *Education, Experience,* and *Skills* or *Interests.* Another possibility is a grouping by job functions or skills, such as *Selling, Communicating,* and *Managing.* You may be able to work out other logical groups.

You also can derive additional groups from the four conventional groups mentioned above. For example, you can have a group of *Achievements.* Such a group would consist of special accomplishments taken from your experience and education information. Another possibility is to have a group consisting of information highlighting your major *Qualifications.* Here you would include information drawn from the areas of experience, education, and skills or personal qualities. Illustrations of and instructions for constructing groups such as these appear later in the chapter.

Constructing the headings With your information organized, a logical next step is to construct the headings for the résumé. Exhibit 11.1 on page 311 provides a list of category headings you may want to consider. Probably you will begin by constructing the main head—the one that covers the entire document.

Since the main topic of any résumé is the applicant, the most widely used main head is the applicant's name. It should be presented clearly; usually this means using larger and bolder type so that the name stands out from the rest of the résumé. If an employer remembers only one fact from your résumé, that fact should be your name. It can be presented in all caps or caps and lowercase, as in this example:

Terrence P. Lenaghan

The next level of headings might be *Objective, Education, Experience,* and *Skills.* These headings can be placed to the left or centered above the text that follows.

A variation on these topic headings is the talking head. This form uses words that tell the nature of what follows. For example, instead of the topic head, *Education,* a talking head might read *Specialized Training in Accounting* or *Computer Skills Acquired.* Obviously, these heads add to the information covered. They help the reader interpret the facts that follow.

Academic Achievements	Computer Knowledge	International Travel	References
Academic History	Computer Languages	Internship Experience	Related Course Work
Academic Honors	Computer Proficiencies	Internship(s)	Related Experience
Academic Training	Computer Systems	Job History	Relevant Course Work
Accomplishments	Computer Skills	Languages	Research Experience
Activities	Consulting Experience	Leadership Roles	Seminars
Additional Professional Training	Cooperative Education Experience	License(s)	Skill(s) Summary
Additional Experience	Cooperative Education	Major Accomplishments	Skills and Attributes
Additional Training	Course Highlights	Management Experience	Skills and Qualifications
Affiliations	Course Work Included	Memberships	Special Awards and Recognitions
Appointments	Courses of Interest	Memberships and Activities	Special Training
Areas of Expertise	Credentials	Military Experience	Special Awards
Associations	Degree(s)	Military Service	Special Abilities
Athletic Involvement	Designations	Military Training	Special Skills
Awards	Dissertation	Objective	Special Interests
Awards and Distinctions	Education	Occupational History	Special Projects or Studies
Background and Interests	Education Highlights	Other Skills	Special Licenses and Awards
Business Experience	Education and Training	Other Experience	Special Courses
Career Goal	Educational Background	Overseas Experience	Strengths
Career Highlights	Employment	Overseas Employment	Student Teaching
Career History	Employment Objective	Planning & Problem Solving	Student Teaching Experience
Career Objective	Employment History	Portfolio	Study Abroad
Career Profile	Exhibitions and Awards	Position Objective	Summary
Career Related Fieldwork	Experience(s)	Practicum Experience	Summary of Experience
Career Related Workshops	Experience Highlights	Professional Objective	Summary of Qualifications
Career Related Training	Extracurricular Involvement	Professional Affiliations	Teaching Experience
Career Related Experience	Field Placement	Professional Affiliations & Awards	Teaching and Coaching Experience
Career Skills and Experience	Foreign Language	Professional Employment	Teaching and Related Experience
Career Summary	Graduate School	Professional Experience	Thesis
Certificate(s)	Graduate School Employment	Professional Leadership	Travel Abroad
Certifications	Graduate School Activities	Professional Memberships	Travel Experience
Classroom Experience	Hardware/Software	Professional Organizations	Volunteer Experience
Coaching Experience	Highlights of Qualifications	Professional Qualifications	Work Experience
Coaching Skills	Honors, Activities, & Organizations	Professional Seminars	Work History
College Activities	Honors	Professional Summary	Workshops and Seminars
Communication Experience	Honors and Awards	Publications	
Community Involvement	International Experience	Published Works	
Computer Background		Qualifications	
Computer Experience			

Source: College of Business, *The Job Campaign Workbook* (Eau Claire, WI: University of Wisconsin–Eau Claire, 2009) 17, *Student Professional Development Programs,* Web, 3 June 2009.

As you can see from the illustrations in the chapter, the headings are distinguished from the other information in the résumé by both placement (left, centered) and form (the use of different sizes, styles, and color of type). The main head should appear to be the most important of all (larger and heavier). Headings for the groups of information should appear to be more important than the information under them. Choose heading forms carefully, making sure they are neither so heavy and large that they offend

A survey of over 600 hiring managers revealed some of the major reasons applicants are rejected. Here are some of them along with a solution.

Problem	Explanation	Solution
Lying	Employers reported they are on the lookout for the significant increase in lies or exaggerated claims made in people's résumés.	Don't Lie.
No apparent accomplishments	Employers reported that many people's résumés are just dull job descriptions. Candidates do not list any kind of results achieved on the job.	Use specific facts noting demonstrated skills and past accomplishments achieved.
Lengthy résumé	Surveyed managers reported that résumés only get a 15-second review. Often only the first page is read.	Write a concise one-page résumé noting top achievements. Highlight only the relevant recent information related to doing the targeted job. Use action words to create more powerful sentences.
Spelling mistakes and use of microtype	A top complaint with every manager and HR person in the survey was spelling mistakes. Employers felt typographical errors reflected the poor quality of work they can expect from you. Reducing the font size to cram more into a résumé often results in making it harder to read, and many employers noted that they simply skip reading the ones with very small type.	Proofread! Use a 12-point font and a nice layout that is easily read.
No cover letter	Surveyed employers stated cover letters are very influential and can snag an interview by themselves. They repeatedly noted that it is a BIG MISTAKE to use no cover letter at all.	Take the time to create a targeted letter addressing the specific employer's needs.

Source: Robin Ryan, "Résumé Mistakes Can Cost You the Job," *Career Counselor Articles*, 8 Oct. 2008: <http://www.robinryan.com/articles/mistakes/>.

---

nor so light and small that they show no distinctions. Your goal is to choose forms that are pleasing to the eye and properly show the relative importance of the information.

Sometimes those looking for jobs are tempted to use readily available templates. While this shortcut might initially speed up the creation of the résumé, it does have a few serious disadvantages. Primarily, it makes one look very similar to other applicants using the same template, and most recruiters recognize templates at a glance as a shortcut. Also, most templates are not optimized for recent college graduates when they bury the education section near the end. You are usually best served either by creating your own unique résumé or by thoroughly customizing a template to fit you and the job for which you are applying.

> The main head should appear to be the most important of all (larger and heavier).

Including contact information Your address, phone number, and email address are the most likely means of contacting you. Most authorities recommend that you display them prominently somewhere in the résumé. You also may want to display your Web page addresses. The most common location for displaying contact information is at the top, under your name.

When it is likely that your address or phone number will change before the job search ends, you may want to include two addresses and numbers: one current and the other permanent. If you are a student, for example, your address at the time of applying for a job may change before the employer decides to contact you. Therefore, you may want to consider using the voice mail on your cell phone or an Internet-based voice

> ## "ONE STRATEGY IS TO CHOOSE VERBS THAT DESCRIBE BOTH THE WORK YOU WANT TO DO AS WELL AS THE WORK YOU HAVE DONE, MAKING IT EASIER FOR THE READER TO SEE HOW YOU HAVE TRANSFERABLE SKILLS."

message service (such as Google Voice) so that you can receive your messages wherever you go.

The purpose of making the contact information prominent and inclusive has been to make it easy for the employer to reach you. However, recently, in the interest of privacy, some schools have begun advising their students to include only their names, phone numbers, and an innocuous email address created specifically for job searches. For business use, a professional email address is always preferable to an informal one such as surferchick@gmail.com. However, you will likely still need to include complete information on application forms provided by employers.

Including a statement of objective Although not a category of background information, a statement of your objective is appropriate in the résumé. Headings such as *Career Objective, Job Objective,* or just *Objective* usually appear at the beginning.

Not all authorities agree on the value of including the objective, however. Recommending that they be omitted from today's résumés, some authorities suggest that the résumé should concentrate instead on skills, experience, and credentials. They argue that the objective includes only obvious information that is clearly suggested by the remainder of the résumé. Moreover, they point out that an objective limits the applicant to a single position and eliminates consideration for other jobs that may be available.

Those favoring the use of a statement of objective reason that it helps the recruiter see quickly where the applicant might fit into the company. Since this argument appears to have greater support, at least for the moment, you should probably include the objective. When your career goal is unclear, you may use broad, general terms. And when you are considering a variety of employment possibilities, you may want to have different versions of your résumé for each possibility.

Primarily, your statement of objective should describe the work you seek. When you know the exact job title of a position you want at the targeted company, use it.

> Objective: Marketing Research Intern

Another technique includes using words that convey a long-term interest in the targeted company, as in this example. However, using this form may limit you if the company does not have the career path you specify.

> Objective: Sales Representative for McGraw-Hill leading to sales management.

Also, wording the objective to point out your major strengths can be very effective. It also can help set up the organization of the résumé.

> Objective: To apply three years of successful ecommerce accounting experience at a small startup to a larger company with a need for careful attention to transaction management and analysis.

Presenting the information The information you present under each heading will depend on your good judgment. You should list all the facts that you think are relevant. You will want to include enough information to enable the reader to judge your ability to do the work you seek.

Your coverage of work experience should identify completely the jobs you have held. Minimum coverage would include dates, places, firms, and responsibilities. If the work was part-time or volunteer, you should say so without demeaning the skills you developed on the job. In describing your duties, you should select words that highlight what you did, especially the parts of this experience that qualify you for the work you seek. Such a description will reflect your practice of good business ethics. For example, in describing a job as credit manager, you could write "Credit Analyst for Macy's Inc., St. Petersburg, Florida, 2007–10." But it would be more meaningful to give this fuller description: "Credit Analyst for Macy's Inc., St. Petersburg, Florida, 2007–10, supervising a staff of seven in processing credit applications and communications."

If your performance on a job shows your ability to do the work you seek, you should consider emphasizing your accomplishments in your job description. For example, an experienced marketer might write this description: "Marketing Specialist for Colgate-Palmolive, 2007–2010. Served in advisory role to company management. Developed marketing plan that increased profits 14 percent in two years." Or a successful advertising account executive might write this description: "Phillips-Ramsey Inc., San Diego, 2007–10. As account executive, developed successful campaigns for nine accounts and led development team in increasing agency volume 18 percent."

As you can see from the previous examples, the use of action verbs strengthens job descriptions. Verbs are the strongest of all words. If you choose them well, they will do much to sell your ability to do work. One strategy is to choose verbs that describe both the work you want to do as well as the work you have done, making it easier for the reader to see how you have transferable skills. A list of the more widely used action verbs appears in Exhibit 11.2.

The underlined words are especially good for pointing out <u>accomplishments</u>.

Clerical/Detail Skills

approved
arranged
catalogued
checked
classified
collected
compiled
confirmed
copied
detected
dissected
executed
generated
<u>implemented</u>
inspected
monitored
operated
organized
prepared
processed
purchased
recorded
retrieved
scheduled
screened
specified
systematized
tabulated
validated

Communication Skills

addressed
arbitrated
arranged
articulated
authored
collaborated
composed
<u>convinced</u>
corresponded
<u>developed</u>
directed
drafted
edited
enlisted

formulated
influenced
interpreted
lectured
mediated
moderated
negotiated
persuaded
presented
promoted
publicized
reconciled
recruited
reported
spoke
translated
wrote

Creative Skills

acted
built
conceived
conceptualized
created
customized
designed
<u>developed</u>
devised
directed
established
fabricated
fashioned
<u>founded</u>
illustrated
<u>initiated</u>
instituted
integrated
<u>introduced</u>
<u>invented</u>
<u>originated</u>
performed
planned
<u>revitalized</u>
shaped

Financial Skills

administered
allocated

analyzed
appraised
audited
balanced
budgeted
calculated
computed
consolidated
converted
<u>developed</u>
dispensed (financial)
forecast
managed
marketed
planned
projected
researched

Helping Skills

advised
assessed
assisted
challenged
clarified
coached
counseled
demonstrated
diagnosed
educated
<u>expedited</u>
facilitated
guided
motivated
referred
rehabilitated
represented

Management Skills

accomplished
addressed
administered
allocated
analyzed
anticipated
approved
assigned
<u>attained</u>
chaired

completed
conserved
consolidated
contracted
controlled
coordinated
critiqued
decided
defined
delegated
delivered
developed
directed
evaluated
executed
guided
hired
<u>implemented</u>
<u>improved</u>
<u>increased</u>
initiated
led
organized
oversaw
planned
prioritized
produced
recommended
reviewed
scheduled
<u>strengthened</u>
supervised

Research Skills

analyzed
clarified
collected
compiled
conducted
critiqued
detected
diagnosed
discovered
evaluated
examined
experimented
extracted

gathered
identified
inspected
interpreted
interviewed
investigated
organized
reviewed
sampled
summarized
surveyed
systematized

Teamwork/ Interpersonal Skills

clarified
collaborated
coordinated
facilitated
harmonized
negotiated
networked

Technical Skills

accessed
assembled
built
calculated
charted
computed
configured
designed
devised
diagnosed
<u>engineered</u>
fabricated
installed
maintained
operated
<u>overhauled</u>
performed troubleshooting
programmed
remodeled
repaired
retrieved
solved
<u>upgraded</u>

Training/Supervision Skills

adapted
advised
assembled
clarified
coached
communicated
conducted
coordinated
demonstrated
demystified
<u>developed</u>
enabled
encouraged
evaluated
explained
facilitated
guided
informed
instructed
lectured
<u>persuaded</u>
set goals
stimulated
<u>trained</u>
tutored

More Accomplishment Verbs

<u>achieved</u>
<u>acquired</u>
<u>earned</u>
<u>eliminated</u> (waste)
<u>expanded</u>
<u>founded</u>
<u>improved</u>
<u>pioneered</u>
<u>reduced</u> (losses)
<u>resolved</u> (problems)
<u>restored</u>
<u>revamped</u>
<u>solved</u>
<u>spearheaded</u>
<u>transformed</u>

Source: From *Damn Good Resume Guide: A Crash Course in Resume Writing* by Yana Parker, copyright © 1989, 1996, 2002 by Yana Parker. Used by permission of Ten Speed Press, an imprint of the Crown Publishing Group, a division of Random House, Inc.

Because your education is likely to be your strongest selling point for your first job after college, you will probably cover it in some detail. However, unless it adds something unique, you usually do not include your high school education once you have finished a college degree. Similarly, you also minimize the emphasis on all your education as you gain experience. At a minimum, your coverage of education should include institutions, dates, degrees, and areas of study. For some jobs, you may want to list and even describe specific courses, especially if you have little other information to present or if your coursework has uniquely prepared you for those jobs. If your grade-point average (GPA) is good, you may want to include it. Remember, for your résumé, you can compute your GPA in a way that works best for you as long as you label it accurately. For example, you may want to select just those courses in your major, labeling it Major GPA. Or if your last few years were your best ones, you may want to present your GPA for just that period. In any case, include GPA when it works favorably for you.

What personal information to list is a matter for your best judgment. In fact, the trend appears to be toward eliminating such information. If you do include personal information, you should probably omit race, religion, gender, age, and marital status because current laws prohibit hiring based on them. But

activities is evidence of experience and interest in working with people. Hobbies and athletic participation tell of your balance of interests. Such information can be quite useful to some employers, especially when personal qualities are important to the work involved.

Authorities disagree on whether to list references on the résumé. Some think that references should not be contacted until negotiations are further along. Others think that references should be listed because some employers want to check them early in the screening process. In a recent study by the Society for Human Resource Management 2,500 human resource professionals said that 96 percent of their companies always check references.[1] Therefore, including them on the résumé would make it easier for the company to proceed through the background check process. Clearly, both views have substantial support. You will have to make the choice based on your best knowledge of the situation.

When you do list someone as a reference, good business etiquette requires that you ask for permission first. Although you will use only those who can speak highly of you, sometimes asking for your reference's permission beforehand helps that person prepare better. And, of course, it saves you from unexpected

> ## "Remember, for your résumé, you can compute your GPA in a way that works best for you as long as you label it accurately."

not everyone agrees on this matter. Some authorities believe that at least some of these items should be included. They argue that the law only prohibits employers from considering such information in hiring—that it does not prohibit applicants from presenting the information. They reason that if such information helps you, you should use it. The illustrations shown in this chapter support both viewpoints.

Personal information that is generally appropriate includes all items that tell about your personal qualities. Information on your organization memberships, civic involvement, and social

embarrassment such as a reference not remembering you, being out of town, or, worse yet, not having anything to say.

A commonly used tool is a separate reference sheet. When you use it, you close the résumé with a statement indicating references are available. Later, when the reader wants to check references, you give her or him this sheet. The type size and style of the main heading of this sheet should match that used in your résumé. It may say something like "References for [your name]." Below this heading is a listing of your references, beginning with the strongest one. In addition to solving the

reference dilemma, use of this separate reference sheet allows you to change both the references and their order for each job. A sample reference sheet is shown on page 320.

Sometimes you may have good reason not to list references, as when you are employed and want to keep the job search secret. If you choose not to list them, you should explain their absence. You can do this in the accompanying cover message, or you can do it on the résumé by following the heading "References" with an explanation, such as "Will be furnished on request."

How many and what kinds of references to include will depend on your background. If you have an employment record, you should include one for every major job you have held—at least for recent years. You should include references related to the work you seek. If you base your application heavily on your education or your personal qualities, or both, you should include references who can vouch for these areas: professors, clergy, community leaders, and the like. Your goal is to list those people who can verify the points on which your appeal for the job is based. At a minimum, you should list three references. Five is a good maximum.

Your list of references should include accurate contact information along with appropriate job titles. Employers need to be able

developed one skill on one job and another skill on another job, this organizational plan groups related skills together. It is particularly good for those who have had many jobs, for those who have taken nontraditional career paths, and for those who are changing fields. Creating this kind of résumé takes much work and careful analysis of both jobs and skills to show the reader that you are a good match for the position. If you use a functional résumé, be sure that readers can see from the other sections—such as employment and education—where you likely developed the skills that you are emphasizing. Enabling your readers to make these connections lends credibility to your claims to have such skills.

An *accomplishments/achievements* layout (on page 327) presents a picture of you as a competent worker. It puts hard numbers and precise facts behind your skills and traits. Refer to Exhibit 11.2 for some good verb choices to use in describing accomplishments. Here is an example illustrating this arrangement in describing work done at a particular company:

> Successfully managed the Austin store for two years in a period of high unemployment with these results:
> - Reduced employee absentism 55 percent.
> - Increased profits 17 percent.
> - Grew sales volume 10 percent.

[After you have identified the information you want to include on your résumé, you will want to organize or group items to present yourself in the best possible light.]

to easily contact the references. Useful are phone numbers and email addresses as well as mailing addresses. Be sure to verify the accuracy and preferences of your references. Job titles (officer, manager, president, supervisor) are helpful because they show what the references are able to tell about you. It is appropriate to include forms of address: Mr., Mrs., Ms., Dr., and so on.

Organizing for strength After you have identified the information you want to include on your résumé, you will want to organize or group items to present yourself in the best possible light. Three strategies for organizing this information are the *reverse chronological approach,* the *functional* or *skills approach,* and the *accomplishments/achievements* or *highlights approach.*

The *reverse chronological* organizational layout (on page 321) presents your education and work experience from the most recent to oldest. It emphasizes the order and time frame in which you have participated in these activities. It is particularly good for those who have progressed in an orderly and timely fashion through school and work.

A *functional* or *skills* layout (on page 326) organizes around three to five areas particularly important to the job you want. Rather than forcing an employer to determine that you

Information covered under a *Highlights* or *Summary* heading may include key points from the three conventional information groups: education, experience, and personal qualities. Typically, this layout emphasizes the applicant's most impressive background facts that pertain to the work sought, as in this example:

> *Highlights*
> - ***Experienced:*** three years of practical work as programmer/analyst in designing and developing financial databases for the banking industry.
> - ***Highly trained:*** B.S. degree with honors in management information systems.
> - ***Self-motivated:*** proven record of successful completion of three online courses.

Although such items will overlap others in the résumé, using them in a separate group emphasizes strengths while showing where they were obtained. See an example of an accomplishments layout on page 327.

Writing impersonally and consistently Because the résumé is a listing of information, you should write without personal pronouns (no *I*'s, *we*'s, *you*'s). You should also write all equal-level headings and the parts under each heading in the same (parallel) grammatical form. For example, if one major

" THE ATTRACTIVENESS OF YOUR RÉSUMÉ WILL SAY AS MUCH ABOUT YOU AS THE WORDS. "

heading in the résumé is a noun phrase, all the other major headings should be noun phrases. The following four headings illustrate the point. All but the third (an adjective form) are noun phrases. The error can be corrected by making the third a noun phrase, as in the examples to the right:

Not Parallel	Parallel
Specialized study	Specialized study
Experience in promotion work	Experience in promotion work
Personal and physical	Personal and physical qualities
Qualified references	Qualified references

The following items illustrate grammatical inconsistency in the parts of a group:

Have good health

Active in sports

Ambitious

Inspection of these items shows that they do not fit the same understood words. The understood word for the first item is *I* and for the second and third, the understood words are *I am*. Any changes that make all three items fit the same understood words would correct the error.

Making the form attractive The attractiveness of your print résumé will say as much about you as the words. The appearance of the information that the reader sees plays a part in forming his or her judgment. While using a template is one solution, it will make you look like many other applicants. A layout designed with your reader and your unique data in mind will probably do a better job for you. Not only will your résumé have a distinctive appearance, but the design should sell you more effectively than one where you must fit your data to the design. A sloppy, poorly designed presentation, on the other hand, may even ruin your chances of getting the job. Thus, you have no choice but to give your résumé and your cover message an attractive physical arrangement.

Designing the résumé for eye appeal is no routine matter. There is no one best arrangement, but a good procedure is to approach the task as a graphic designer would. Your objective is to design an arrangement of type and space that appeals to the eye. You would do well to use the following general advice for arranging the résumé.

Margins look better if at least an inch of space is left at the top and bottom of the page and on the left and right sides of the page. Your listing of items by rows and columns appears best if the items are short and if they can be set up in two uncrowded columns, one on the left side of the page and one on the right side. Longer items of information are more appropriately set up in lines extending

across the page. In any event, you would do well to avoid long and narrow columns of data with large sections of wasted space on either side. Arrangements that give a heavy crowded effect also offend the eye. Extra spacing between subdivisions and indented patterns for subparts are especially pleasing to the eye.

While layout is important in showing your ability to organize and good spacing increases readability, other design considerations such as font and paper selection affect attractiveness almost as much. Commercial designers say that type size for headings should be at least 14 points and for body text, 10 to 12 points. They also recommend using fewer than four font styles on a page. Some word processing applications have a "shrink to fit" feature that allows the user to fit information on one page. It will automatically adjust font sizes to fit the page. Be sure the resulting type size is both appropriate and readable.

Another factor affecting the appearance of your application documents is the paper you select. The paper should be appropriate for the job you seek. In business, erring on the conservative side is usually better; you do not want to be eliminated from consideration simply because the reader did not like the quality or color of the paper. The most traditional choice is white, 100 percent cotton, 20- to 28-lb. paper. Of course, reasonable variations can be appropriate.

Contrasting bad and good examples The résumés on pages 318–319 are at opposing ends of the quality scale.

Shortcomings in the first example (on page 318) are obvious. First, the form is not pleasing to the eye. The weight of the type is heavy on the left side of the page. Failure to indent wrapped lines makes reading difficult.

This résumé also contains numerous errors in wording. Information headings are not parallel in grammatical form. All are in topic form except the first one. The items listed under *Personal* are not parallel either. Throughout, the résumé coverage is scant, leaving out many of the details needed to present the best impression of the applicant. Under *Experience*, little is said about specific tasks and skills in each job; and under *Education*, high school work is listed needlessly. The references are incomplete, omitting street addresses, job titles, and more.

The next résumé (on page 319) appears better at first glance, and it gets even better as you read it. It is attractively arranged. The information is neither crowded nor strung out. The balance is good. Its content is also superior to that of the other example. Additional words show the quality of Mr. Andrews's work experience and education, and they emphasize points that make him suited for the work he seeks. This résumé excludes trivial personal information and has only the facts that tell something

Incompleteness and Bad Arrangement in a Traditional Print Résumé

This résumé presents Jason Andrews ineffectively (see "Workplace Scenario" for "Résumés and Applications"). It is scant and poorly arranged.

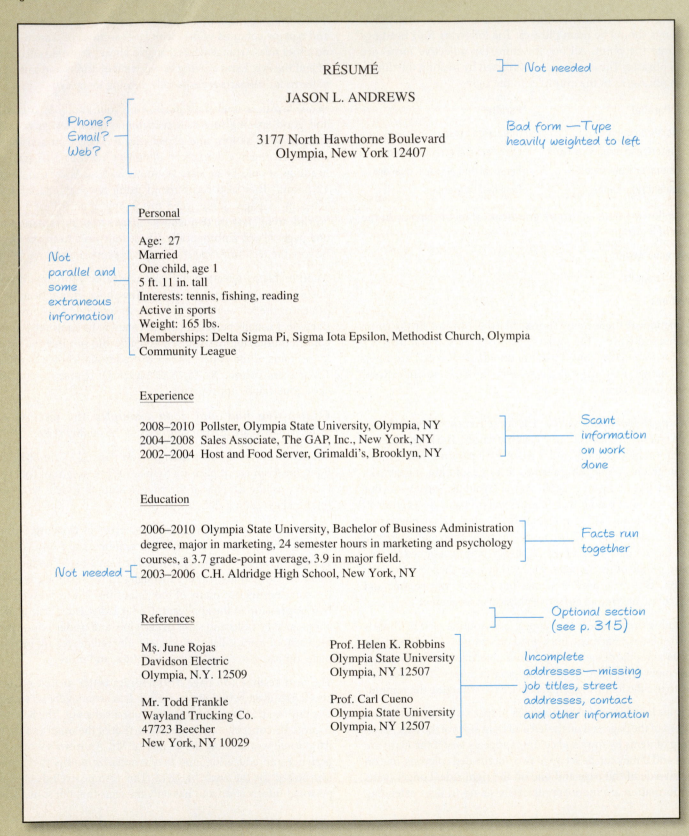

RÉSUMÉ — *Not needed*

JASON L. ANDREWS

Phone? Email? Web? —

3177 North Hawthorne Boulevard
Olympia, New York 12407

Bad form — Type heavily weighted to left

Personal

Not parallel and some extraneous information —

Age: 27
Married
One child, age 1
5 ft. 11 in. tall
Interests: tennis, fishing, reading
Active in sports
Weight: 165 lbs.
Memberships: Delta Sigma Pi, Sigma Iota Epsilon, Methodist Church, Olympia Community League

Experience

2008–2010 Pollster, Olympia State University, Olympia, NY
2004–2008 Sales Associate, The GAP, Inc., New York, NY
2002–2004 Host and Food Server, Grimaldi's, Brooklyn, NY

Scant information on work done

Education

2006–2010 Olympia State University, Bachelor of Business Administration degree, major in marketing, 24 semester hours in marketing and psychology courses, a 3.7 grade-point average, 3.9 in major field.

Facts run together

Not needed — 2003–2006 C.H. Aldridge High School, New York, NY

References

Optional section (see p. 315)

Ms. June Rojas
Davidson Electric
Olympia, N.Y. 12509

Prof. Helen K. Robbins
Olympia State University
Olympia, NY 12507

Mr. Todd Frankle
Wayland Trucking Co.
47723 Beecher
New York, NY 10029

Prof. Carl Cueno
Olympia State University
Olympia, NY 12507

Incomplete addresses—missing job titles, street addresses, contact and other information

Thoroughness and Good Arrangement in a Traditional Print Résumé

This complete, **reverse chronologically organized** résumé presents Jason Andrews's case effectively (see "Workplace Scenario" for "Résumés and Applications").

Jason L. Andrews

3177 North Hawthorne Boulevard
Olympia, NY 12407-3278
914.967.3117 (Voice/Message)
jandrews@gmail.com

Presents contact data clearly

Objective

A position in marketing that will lead to work as a marketing manager for an ebusiness.

Education

Bachelor of Business Administration
Olympia State University—May 2011
GPA: 3.7/4.0

Major: Marketing
Minor: Psychology
Dean's List

Emphasizes education by position

Highlights most relevant courses and subjects

Related Coursework:

- Strategic Marketing
- Marketing Research
- Marketing Communications & Promotion
- Global Marketing

- Interpersonal Communication
- Statistical Analysis
- Consumer and Buyer Behavior
- Social Psychology

☐ Research Projects: Cultural Influence on Purchasing, Customer Brand Preference, and Motivating Subordinates with Effective Performance Appraisals.

Experience

Intern-Pollster, Olympia State University, Olympia, NY, May 2011–present
- Survey over 20 students and alumni weekly over the phone and in person
- Compile statistical data and present reports to the Chancellor's Council
- Supervise a team of ten undergraduate pollsters
- Exceeded university goals by 5% last year for the number of surveys completed

Emphasizes positions; de-emphasizes dates

Action verbs portray an image of a hard worker with good interpersonal skills

Sales Associate, The Gap, Inc., New York, NY, Jan. 2009–April 2011
- Was named top store sales associate four of eight quarters
- Created merchandise displays
- Trained new sales associates

Host and Food Server, Grimaldi's, Brooklyn, NY, Aug. 2007–Dec. 2008
- Provided exceptional customer service
- Worked well as part of a team to seat and serve customers quickly and efficiently

Activities

Includes only most relevant information

Delta Sigma Pi (professional); Sigma Iota Epsilon (honorary), treasurer and president, Board of Stewards for church; League of Olympia, served as registration leader, tennis, blogging, reading, and jogging

Thoroughness and Good Arrangement for a Reference Sheet

This reference sheet presents Jason Andrews's references completely.

Jason L. Andrews
3177 North Hawthorne Boulevard
Olympia, NY 12407-3278
914.967.3117 (Voice/ Message)
jandrews@gmail.com

Heading format matches résumé

Ms. June Rojas, Polling Supervisor
Olympia State University
7114 East 71st Street
Olympia, NY 12509-4572
Phone: 518.342.1171
Fax: 518.342.1200
Email: June.Rojas@osu.edu

Mr. Todd E. Frankle, Store Manager
The Gap, Inc.
Lincoln Square
New York, NY 10023-0007
Phone: 212.466.9101
Fax: 212.468.9100
Email: tfrankle@gap.com

Professor Helen K. Robbins
Department of Marketing
Olympia State University
Olympia, NY 12507-0182
Phone: 518.392.6673
Fax: 518.392.3675
Email: Helen.Robbins@osu.edu

Professor Carol A. Cueno
Department of Psychology
Olympia State University
Olympia, NY 12507-0234
Phone: 518.392.0723
Fax: 518.392.7542
Email: Carol.Cueno@osu.edu

Complete information and balanced arrangement

Traditional Print Résumé Organized in Reverse Chronological Format

Large size emphasizes name

Manny Konedeng
5602 Montezuma Road • Apartment 413 • San Diego • California • 92115
Phone: (619) 578-8508 • Email: mkonedeng@gmail.com

Includes complete contact information

OBJECTIVE

A financial analyst internship with a broker-dealer where both analytical and interpersonal communication skills and knowledge are valued

Uses descriptive statement with two highly important qualities

EDUCATION

Bachelor of Science Degree in Business Administration, May 2010, San Diego State University, Finance Major

Expands and emphasizes strongest points through precise detail

Dean's List
Current GPA: 3.32/4.00
Accomplishments:
- Published in *Fast Company Magazine* and the *San Diego Union Tribune*
- Won Greek Scholarship
- Finished in top five in mathematics competition

Related Courses:
- Business Communication, A
- Investments, A
- Tax Planning, A–
- Estate Planning, A
- Risk Management, A
- Business Law, B+

Computer Skills:
- Microsoft Office—Excel, Word, PowerPoint, and Access
- Web-based Applications—Surveymonkey, Blogger, GoToMeeting, Twitter
- Research Tools—SPSS, Internet Explorer, Google Advanced Search

WORK EXPERIENCE

Sales and Front Desk, Powerhouse Gym, Modesto, CA 95355   Summer 2009
- Sold memberships and facilitated tours for the fitness center
- Listened to, analyzed, and answered customers' inquires
- Accounted for membership payments and constructed sales reports
- Trained new employees to understand company procedures and safety policies

Emphasizes position held rather than place or date

Relay Operator, MCI, Riverbank, CA 95367   Summers 2007 & 2008
- Assisted over 100 callers daily who were deaf, hard of hearing, or speech disabled to place calls
- Exceeded the required data input of 60 wpm with accuracy
- Multitasked with typing and listening to phone conversations
- Was offered a promotion as a Lead Operator

Uses descriptive action verbs

Co-founder and owner, Fo Sho Entertainment, Modesto, CA 95355   2006
- Led promotions for musical events in the Central Valley
- Managed and hosted live concerts
- Created and wrote proposals to work with local businesses
- Collaborated with team members to design advertisements

UNIVERSITY INVOLVEMENT

Communications Tutor, San Diego State University, San Diego, CA 92182   Spring 2010
- Critiqued and evaluated the written work for a business communication course
- Set up and maintained blog for business communication research

Includes items that will set him apart from other applicants

Recruitment Chairman, Kappa Alpha Order Fraternity, San Diego, CA 92115   Fall 2009
- Supervised the selection process for chapter membership
- Individually raised nearly $1,000 for chapter finances
- Organized recruitment events with business sponsors, radio stations, and special guests

REFERENCES

Will gladly furnish personal and professional references on request

Provides closure and says someone will speak for him

case illustration

Multimedia Résumé Using a Web-Based App, Visual CV, with Customized Form and Content

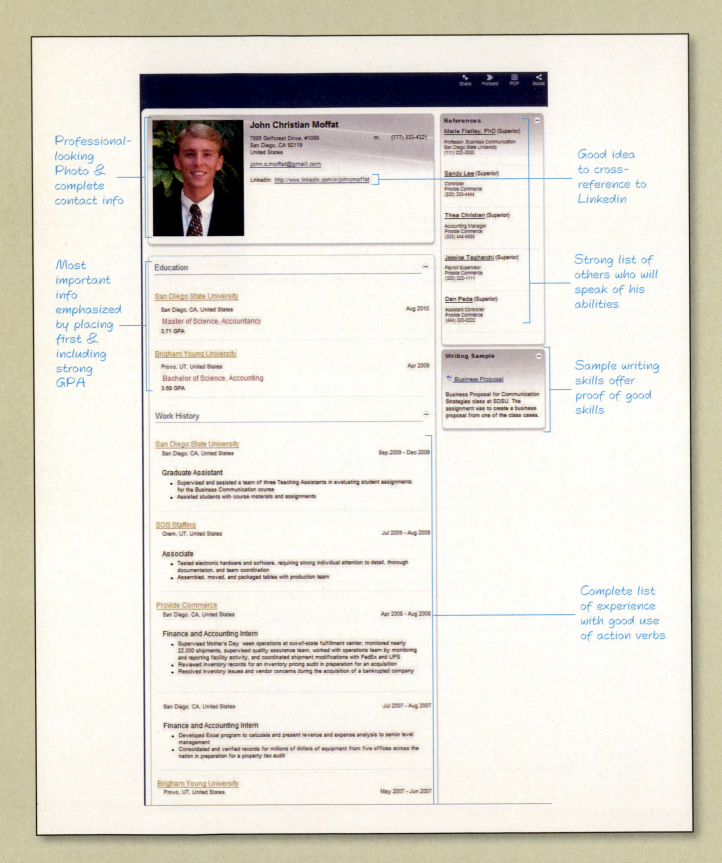

Professional-looking Photo & complete contact info

Most important info emphasized by placing first & including strong GPA

Good idea to cross-reference to Linkedin

Strong list of others who will speak of his abilities

Sample writing skills offer proof of good skills

Complete list of experience with good use of action verbs

John Christian Moffat

7895 Golfcrest Drive, #1089
San Diego, CA 92119
United States

m: (777) 333-4321

john.c.moffat@gmail.com

LinkedIn: http://www.linkedin.com/in/johnomoffat

References

Marie Flatley, PhD (Superior)
Professor, Business Communication
San Diego State University
(111) 222-3333

Sandy Lee (Superior)
Controller
Provide Commerce
(222) 333-4444

Thea Christian (Superior)
Accounting Manager
Provide Commerce
(333) 444-5555

Jessica Tagharchi (Superior)
Payroll Supervisor
Provide Commerce
(333) 222-1111

Dan Peda (Superior)
Assistant Controller
Provide Commerce
(444) 333-2222

Writing Sample

Business Proposal

Business Proposal for Communication
Strategies class at SDSU. The
assignment was to create a business
proposal from one of the class cases.

Education

San Diego State University

San Diego, CA, United States   Aug 2010

Master of Science, Accountancy
3.71 GPA

Brigham Young University

Provo, UT, United States   Apr 2009

Bachelor of Science, Accounting
3.68 GPA

Work History

San Diego State University
San Diego, CA, United States   Sep 2009 - Dec 2009

Graduate Assistant
- Supervised and assisted a team of three Teaching Assistants in evaluating student assignments for the Business Communication course
- Assisted students with course materials and assignments

SOS Staffing
Orem, UT, United States   Jul 2009 - Aug 2009

Associate
- Tested electronic hardware and software, requiring strong individual attention to detail, thorough documentation, and team coordination
- Assembled, moved, and packaged tables with production team

Provide Commerce
San Diego, CA, United States   Apr 2008 - Aug 2008

Finance and Accounting Intern
- Supervised Mother's Day week operations at out-of-state fulfillment center; monitored nearly 22,000 shipments, supervised quality assurance team, worked with operations team by monitoring and reporting facility activity, and coordinated shipment modifications with FedEx and UPS
- Reviewed inventory records for an inventory pricing audit in preparation for an acquisition
- Resolved inventory issues and vendor concerns during the acquisition of a bankrupted company

San Diego, CA, United States   Jul 2007 - Aug 2007

Finance and Accounting Intern
- Developed Excel program to calculate and present revenue and expense analysis to senior level management
- Consolidated and verified records for millions of dollars of equipment from five offices across the nation in preparation for a property tax audit

Brigham Young University
Provo, UT, United States   May 2007 - Jun 2007

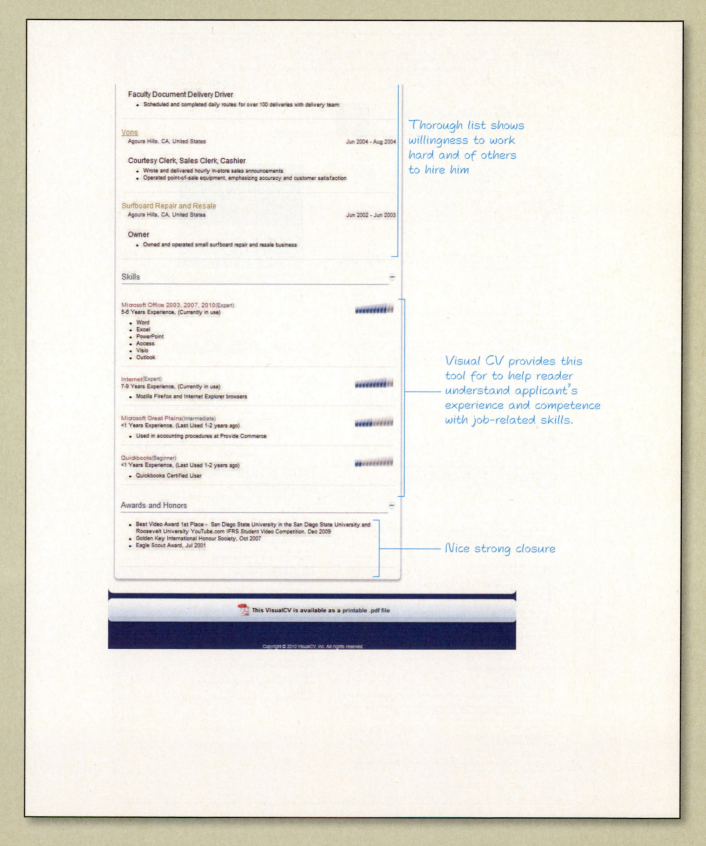

Faculty Document Delivery Driver
- Scheduled and completed daily routes for over 100 deliveries with delivery team

Thorough list shows willingness to work hard and of others to hire him

Vons
Agoura Hills, CA, United States   Jun 2004 - Aug 2004

Courtesy Clerk, Sales Clerk, Cashier
- Wrote and delivered hourly in-store sales announcements
- Operated point-of-sale equipment, emphasizing accuracy and customer satisfaction

Surfboard Repair and Resale
Agoura Hills, CA, United States   Jun 2002 - Jun 2003

Owner
- Owned and operated small surfboard repair and resale business

Skills

Microsoft Office 2003, 2007, 2010 (Expert)
5-6 Years Experience, (Currently in use)
- Word
- Excel
- PowerPoint
- Access
- Visio
- Outlook

Internet (Expert)
7-9 Years Experience, (Currently in use)
- Mozilla Firefox and Internet Explorer browsers

Visual CV provides this tool for to help reader understand applicant's experience and competence with job-related skills.

Microsoft Great Plains (Intermediate)
<1 Years Experience, (Last Used 1-2 years ago)
- Used in accounting procedures at Provide Commerce

Quickbooks (Beginner)
<1 Years Experience, (Last Used 1-2 years ago)
- Quickbooks Certified User

Awards and Honors

- Best Video Award 1st Place - San Diego State University in the San Diego State University and Roosevelt University YouTube.com IFRS Student Video Competition, Dec 2009
- Golden Key International Honour Society, Oct 2007
- Eagle Scout Award, Jul 2001

Nice strong closure

This VisualCV is available as a printable .pdf file

LinkedIn Full Profile Integrating References and Recommendations with Skills and Experience

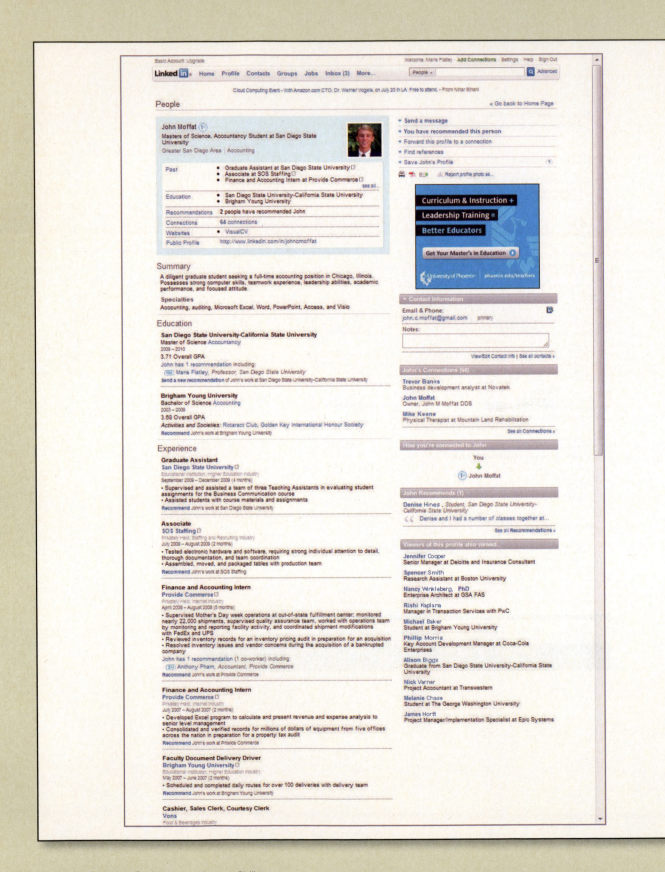

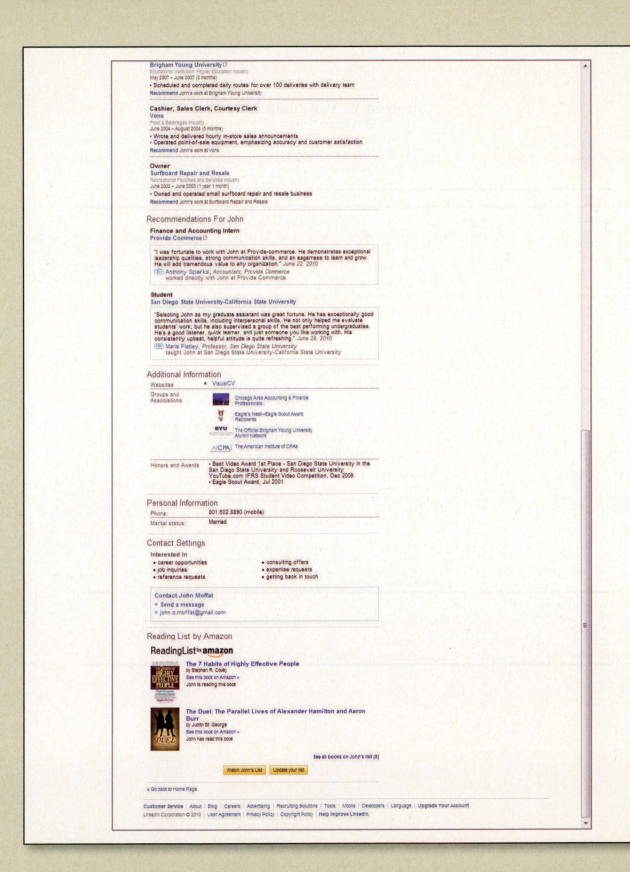

Traditional Print Résumé Using the Functional Organization for the Skills Section

Carolynn W. Workman
12271 69th Terrace North
Seminole, FL 33772
727.399.2569 (Voice/Message)
cworkman@comcast.net

Emphasizes tight organization through use of horizontal ruled lines

Objective	An accounting position with a CPA firm

Education

Emphasizes degree and GPA through placement

Bachelor of Science: University of South Florida, December 2010
Major: Business Administration
Emphasis: Accounting
GPA: 3.42 with Honors

Uses internal bullets to increase readability

Accounting-Related Course Work:
Financial Accounting ❖ Cost Accounting and Control ❖ Accounting Information Systems ❖ Auditing ❖ Concepts of Federal Income Taxation ❖ Financial Policy ❖ Communications for Business and Professions

Activities:
Vice-President of Finance, Beta Alpha Psi
Editor, Student Newsletter for Beta Alpha Psi
Member, Golden Key National Honors Society

Emphasizes key skills relevant to objective

Skills
Computer

- ▶ Assisted in installation of small business computerized accounting system using QuickBooks Pro.
- ▶ Prepared tax returns for individuals in the VITA program using specialty tax software.
- ▶ Mastered Excel, designing data input forms, analyzing and interpreting results of most functions, generating graphs, and creating and using macros.

Accounting

- ▶ Experienced with financial statements and general ledger.
- ▶ Reconciled accounts for center serving over 1300 clients.
- ▶ Experienced in preparing income, gift, and estate tax returns.
- ▶ Processed expense reports for twenty professional staff.
- ▶ Experienced in using Great Plains and Solomon IV.

Varies use of action verbs

Business Communication

- ▶ Conducted client interviews and researched tax issues.
- ▶ Communicated both in written and verbal form with clients.
- ▶ Delivered several individual and team presentations on business cases, projects, and reports to business students.

Work History
Administrative Assistant

Office of Student Disability Services, University of South Florida Tampa, FL. Spring 2010.

Tax Assistant

Rosemary Lenaghan, Certified Public Accountant. Seminole, FL 2009.

References available upon request

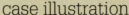

Traditional Print Résumé Using Highlights of Qualifications and Accomplishments Sections

Diana W. Chan

2411 27th Street
Moline, IL 61265
309.764.0017 (Mobile)
dwc@gmail.com

JOB TARGET	TRAINER/TRANSLATOR for a large, worldwide industrial company

HIGHLIGHTS OF QUALIFICATIONS

Emphasizes those qualifications most relevant to position sought

- Experienced in creating and delivering multimedia PowerPoint presentations.
- Enthusiastic team member/leader whose participation brings out the best in others.
- Proficient in analytical ability.
- Skilled in gathering and interpreting data.
- Bilingual—English/Spanish.

EDUCATION

Presents the most important items here

DEGREE	B.S. English—June 2010—Western Illinois University
EMPHASIS	Education MAJOR GPA—3.87/4.00
HONORS	Dean's List, four semesters
Chevron Scholarship, Fall 2009
MEMBER	Mortar Board, Women's Golf Team

EMPLOYMENT

Identifies most significant places of work and de-emphasizes less important work

DEERE & COMPANY, INC.   CONGRESSMAN BILL FOSTER
Student Intern, Summer 2009   Volunteer in Computer Services, Fall 2008

Several years' experience in the restaurant business including supervisory positions.

ACCOMPLISHMENTS

Presents only selected accomplishments from various work and volunteer experience that relate to position sought

- ► Trained executives to create effective cross-cultural presentations.
- ► Developed online training program for executive use of GoToMeeting.
- ► Designed and developed a database to keep track of financial donations.
- ► Coded new screens and reports; debugged and revised screen forms for easier data entry.
- ► Provided computer support to virtual volunteers on election committee.

REFERENCES

Optional—provides positive closure

Will gladly furnish personal and professional references on request.

about Andrews's personal qualities. Complete contact information permits the reader to contact the references easily. Job titles tell how each is qualified to evaluate the subject.

scannable print résumé

Although paper résumés are not obsolete, a more recent addition to the job-search process is the scannable résumé. This résumé bridges the print-to-digital gap. It is simply one that can be scanned into a database and retrieved when a position is being filled. Since the objective is getting your résumé reviewed in order to be interviewed, you should use the following strategies to improve your chances that the computer will retrieve it.

Include keywords One strategy, using keywords, is often recommended for use with both digital scanning and online profiles. These keywords are usually nouns or concrete words that describe skills and accomplishments precisely. Instead of listing a course in comparative programming, you would list the precise languages compared, such as PHP, C++, and Java. Instead of saying you would like a job in information systems, you would name specific job titles such as systems analyst, network specialist, or application specialist. Using industry-specific terminology is highly recommended.

Some ways to identify the keywords in your field are by reading job announcements, listening to recruiters, and listening to your professors. Start building a list of words you find used repeatedly. From this list, choose those words most appropriate for the kind of work you want to do. Amplify your use of abbreviations, acronyms, and jargon appropriate to the work you want to do. In the early days of preparing scannable résumés, some experts recommended using a separate keyword section at the beginning of the résumé, loading it with all the relevant terms. Reportedly this technique improved the odds of the résumé being retrieved. If this helps you ensure that your résumé includes all the appropriate terms, you might still use it. However, today most résumé writers are well aware of the importance of using keywords and consciously work to integrate them into their résumés. This is especially true of those who use the hybrid résumés to cover both the face-to-face and scanning purposes in one document.

Choose words carefully Unlike the traditional résumé, the scannable résumé is strengthened not by the use of action verbs but rather by the use of nouns. Informal studies have shown that those retrieving résumés from such databases tend to use precise nouns.

For the hybrid résumé, one you use in both face-to-face and scanning situations, you can combine the use of precise nouns with strong action verbs. The nouns will help ensure that the résumé gets pulled from the database, and the verbs help the face-to-face recruiter see the link to the kind of work you want to do.

Present the information Since you want your résumé to be read accurately, you will use a font most scanners can read without problem. Some of these fonts include Helvetica, Arial, Calibri, Cambria, Garamond, and Times Roman. Most scanners can easily handle fonts between 10 and 14 points. Although many handle bold, when in doubt use all caps for emphasis rather than bold. Also, because italics often confuse scanners, avoid them. Underlining is best left out as well. It creates trouble with descending letters such as g or y when the line cuts through the letter. In fact, you should use all lines sparingly. Also, avoid graphics and shading wherever possible; they just confuse the software. Use white paper to maximize the contrast, and always print in the portrait mode. The résumé on pages 330 and 331 is a scannable résumé employing these guidelines.

Today companies accept résumés by mail, fax, and email as well as online. In fact, some estimate that over 80 percent of recruiters use the online site LinkedIn.[2] Be sure to choose the channel that serves you best. If a company asks for résumés by fax and email, it may prefer to capture them electronically. Others still prefer to see an applicant's ability to organize and lay out a printed page. Some employers give the option to the sender. Obviously, when speed gives you a competitive advantage, you'll choose the fax, email, or online options. However, you do lose some control over the quality of the document. If you elect to print and send a scannable résumé, it is best not to fold it. Just mail it in a 9×12 envelope. For a little extra cost, you will help ensure that your résumé gets scanned accurately rather than wondering if your keywords were on a fold that a scanner might have had difficulty reading.

digital résumé

Transmitting a digital résumé involves making decisions about the receiver's preferences and capabilities for receiving them as well as leveraging the technology to present you in the best possible light. These documents range from low-end plain text files, to formatted word processor files, to full-blown multimedia documents and Web pages.

While much of the content of a digital résumé is similar to that of the print résumé, two important changes should be made. The first is to delete all contact information except your email address. Not only can you lose control over the distribution of the document since digital files can be passed along easily and quickly, but your information could be added to databases and sold. Many experts recommend setting up a Web-based email account that you use solely for your job search. Second, you should date the résumé. That way when an unscrupulous recruiter pulls it from a database and presents it to your boss two years later, you will be able to explain that you are truly happy working there and that the résumé is clearly dated before you went to work for your employer. These content changes should be made to all forms of the digital résumé.

The low-end digital résumé is usually a document saved as a plain (unformatted) ASCII or text file. You will use it when an employer requests that form. Sometimes you will send it as an attached file and other times you will place it inside your email. Since you can create it in your word processor and run a spell checker on it, you will probably want to cut and paste from it when you are completing online applications. It is also a good idea to test it out by sending it to yourself and viewing it with as many different email programs as you can. Then you will know if you need to shorten lines, add spacing, or make other changes to improve its readability.

To help ensure readability, you may want to send your résumé as a formatted attached file. Of course, you would only send it this way when you know the receiver welcomes getting résumés this way. You have a couple of choices of file format with attached files. You could send it in a standard word processing file format, one that is widely read by a variety of programs. Or you could send it in RTF (rich text format), PDF (portable document file), or XPS (XML Paper Specification) format. All these formats attempt to preserve the layout of your document. You also can help by using standard fonts most readers are likely to have installed or by embedding your font, so that the receiver's view is the one you intended.

The multimedia format can be a dramatic extension of the print résumé. Not only can you add links, color, and graphics, but you can also add sound, animation, and even video. If your receiver is like many others today, he or she is likely able to receive HTM files within the email program. You could use the email as a cover message with a link to a Web page profile (an example is shown on page 322), or you could put the HTM résumé file inside the email. An HTM file allows you to display links to supporting files as well as include color, graphics, photos, and so on in your résumé. If used effectively, it could enhance your

> ❝ **To help ensure readability, you may want to send your résumé as a formatted attached file.** ❞

strengths and showcase your knowledge, creativity, and skills.

Since length is not the issue it is with the print résumé, the digital résumé should include all the detail needed to support your case. You also should take care to use the terms and keywords on which the document is likely to be searched, including nouns, buzzwords, jargon, and even acronyms commonly used in the field. You want your résumé retrieved when an appropriate position is available.

LO 5   Write targeted cover messages that skillfully sell your abilities.

Writing the Cover Message

You should begin work on the cover message by fitting the facts from your background to the work you seek and arranging those facts in a logical order. Then you present them in much the same way that a sales writer would present the features of a product or service, carefully managing the appeal. Wherever possible, you adapt the points you make to the reader's needs. Like those of sales messages, the organizational plans of cover messages vary depending on whether the print or digital channel is chosen.

print cover letters   Cover letters come in two types: solicited (invited) and unsolicited (prospecting). As their names suggest, a solicited letter is written in response to an actual job opening, and unsolicited letter is written when you don't know whether a job exists but would like to investigate the possibility

Companies often describe themselves and the jobs on their Web sites.

Digital ASCII/Text Résumé for Use with Online Databases and Requests from Employers

Notice how the writer has expanded the length through some added text when no longer confined to one physical page.

Manny Konedeng
5602 Montezuma Road
Apartment 413
San Diego, California 92115
Phone: (619) 578-8058
Email: mkonedeng@yahoo.com

Avoids italics and underlines yet is arranged for both scanner and human readability

OBJECTIVE

A financial analyst internship with a broker-dealer where both analytical and interpersonal communication skills and knowledge are
valued

Uses all caps and spacing for enhanced human readability

EDUCATION

Bachelor of Science Degree in Business Administration, May 2010
San Diego State University, Finance Major

Deanís List
Current GPA: 3.32/4.00

Related Courses

Business Communication A
Investments A
Tax planning A-
Estate Planning A
Risk Management A
Business Law B+

All items are on one line and tabs avoided for improved comprehension

Computer Skills

Microsoft Office: Excel, Word, PowerPoint, Access
Web-based Applications: Surveymonkey, Blogger, GoToMeeting, Twitter
Research Tools: SPSS, Internet Explorer

Accomplishments

Published in Fast Company Magazine and the San Diego Union Tribune
Won Greek scholarship
Finished in top five mathematics competition

WORK EXPERIENCE

Powerhouse Gym, Sales and Front Desk, Summer 2009 Modesto,
CA 95355

Integrates precise nouns and industry-specific jargon as keywords

Sold memberships and facilitated tours for the fitness center
Listened to, analyzed, and answered customers inquires
Accounted for membership payments and constructed sales reports
Trained new employees to understand company procedures and safety
policies

MCI, Relay Operator, Summer 2007 & 2008, Riverbank, CA 95367

Assisted over 100 callers daily who were deaf, hard of hearing, or
speech disabled to place calls
Exceeded the required data input of 60wpm with accuracy
Multitasked with typing and listening to phone conversations
Was Offered a promotion as a Lead Operator

Fo Sho Entertainment, Co-founder and Owner, Modesto, CA 95355

Led promotions for musical events in the Central Valley
Managed and hosted live concerts
Created and wrote proposals to work with local businesses
Collaborated with team members to design advertisements

UNIVERSITY EXPERIENCE

Information Decision Systems, Communications Tutor, Spring 2010,
San Diego, CA 92182
Critiqued and evaluated the written work for a business communica-
tion course
Set up and maintained blog for business communication research

Kappa Alpha Order Fraternity, Recruitment Chairman, Fall 2009,
San Diego, CA 92115

Supervised the selection process for chapter membership
Individually raised nearly $1,000 for chapter finances
Organized recruitment events with business sponsors, radio
stations, and special guests

Avoids graphics and extra lines

ACTIVITIES AND SERVICE

Campus Leadership

Recruitment Chairman, Kappa Alpha Order Fraternity
Supervised all new member recruitment
Coordinated fundraisers for chapter finances
Organized recruitment events with business sponsors, radio
stations, and special guests
Advocated Freshmen Summer Orientation and Greek life

Correspondent for External Chapter Affairs, Kappa Alpha Order
Fraternity

Communicated with chapter alumni and National Office to fulfill
chapter obligations

Upsilon Class Treasurer, Kappa Alpha Order Fraternity

Managed chapter budgets and expenditures

Several Interfraternity Council Roles

Member, Fraternity Men against Negative Environments and Rape
Situations
Co-chairman, Greek Week Fundraiser
Candidate, IFC Treasurer

Professional and Community Service

Member, Finance & Investment Society
Presenter, Peer Health Education
Marshal, SDSU New Student & Family Convocation
Sponsor, Muscular Dystrophy national philanthropy
Sponsor, Service for Sight philanthropy
Sponsor, Victims of Domestic Violence philanthropy
Sponsor, Camp Able philanthropy
Associated Students Good Neighbor Program volunteer
Volunteer, Designated Driver Association
Volunteer, Beach Recovery Project

Adds other relevant information since there is no physical page limit

REFERENCES

Available upon request

Uses black on white contrast for improved scanning accuracy

of employment with a company. Generally, a cover letter is organized according to the following plan:

• An introduction that gets the reader's attention and provides just a brief summary of why you are interested or qualified, or it previews the information in the body of the letter. If you are writing a solicited letter, you will also mention where you learned of the position.

• A body that matches your qualifications to the reader's needs. You should also use good sales strategy, especially the you-viewpoint and positive language.

• A conclusion that requests action such as an interview and provides contact information that makes a response easy.

Case Illustrations on pages 338–341 provide examples of effective cover letters.

Gaining attention in the opening As in sales writing, the opening of the cover message has two requirements: It must gain attention and it must set up the review of information that follows.

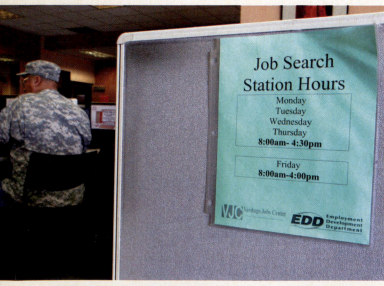

Career services is a good place to look for company information and announcements of job openings.

Gaining attention is especially important in prospecting messages. Such letters are likely to reach busy executives who have many things to do other than read cover messages. Unless the writing gains favorable attention right away, the executives probably will not read them. Even invited messages must gain attention because they will compete with other invited messages. Invited messages that stand out favorably from the beginning have a competitive advantage.

As the cover message is a creative effort, you should use your imagination in writing the opening. But the work you seek should guide your imagination. Take, for example, work that requires an outgoing personality and a vivid imagination such as sales or public relations. In such cases, you would do well to show these qualities in your opening words. At the opposite extreme is work of a conservative nature, such as accounting or banking. Openings in such cases should normally be more restrained.

In choosing the best opening for your case, you should consider whether you are writing a prospecting or an invited message. If the message has been invited, your opening words should begin qualifying you for the work to be done. They also should refer incidentally to the invitation, as in this example:

> Will an honors graduate in accounting with experience in tax accounting qualify for the work you listed in today's *Times*?

In addition to fitting the work sought, your opening words should set up the review of qualifications. The preceding example meets this requirement well. It structures the review of qualifications around two areas: education and experience.

You can gain attention in the opening in many ways. One way is to use a topic that shows understanding of the reader's operation or of the work to be done. Employers are likely to be impressed by applicants who have made the effort to learn something about the company, as in this example:

> Now that Taggart, Inc., has expanded operations to Central America, can you use a broadly trained international business major who knows the language and culture of the region?

Communication in brief

Developing a Professional Portfolio

Imagine yourself in an interview. The interviewer says, "This position requires you to use PowerPoint extensively. How are your presentation and PowerPoint skills?" What do you say? Of course you say your skills are excellent. And so does everyone else who interviews.

One way you can set yourself apart from other applicants is to take a professional portfolio to an interview to demonstrate your qualifications. A portfolio may contain a title page, your résumé, references list, cover letter, a transcript, a program description, copies of licenses and certifications, work samples, letters of recommendation, personal mission statements—whatever creates your best professional image. All you need to do is put your documents in sheet protectors in a professional looking three-ring binder for easy editing and updating and create tab dividers for the sections of the portfolio, and you're on your way. One note of advice, though: Protect your information by including a confidentiality statement; removing any student ID numbers, SSN numbers, or other private information from your documents; and using copies rather than originals of any licenses or certificates.

Source: "Portfolios," *University of Wisconsin–Eau Claire Career Services*, University of Wisconsin–Eau Claire, 9 Mar. 2008, Web, 5 June 2009.

> " In addition to fitting the work sought, your opening words should set up the review of qualifications. "

Another way is to make a statement or ask a question that focuses attention on a need of the reader that the writer seeks to fill. The following opening illustrates this approach:

> How would you like to hire a University of South Florida business major to fill in for your vacationing summer employees?

If you seek more conservative work, you should use less imaginative openings. For example, a message answering an advertisement for a beginning accountant might open with this sentence:

> Because of my specialized training in accounting at State University and my practical experience in cost-based accounting, I believe I have the qualifications you described in your *Journal* advertisement.

Sometimes one learns of a job possibility through a company employee. Mentioning the employee's name can gain attention, as in this opening sentence:

> At the suggestion of Mr. Michael McLaughlin of your staff, I am sending the following summary of my qualifications for work as your loan supervisor.

Many other possibilities exist. In the final analysis, you will have to use what you think will be best for the one case. But you should avoid the overworked beginnings that were popular a generation or two ago such as "This is to apply for . . ." and "Please consider this my application for . . ." Although the direct application these words make may be effective in some cases (as when answering an advertisement), the words are timeworn and dull.

Selecting content Following the opening, you should present the information about your qualifications for the work. Begin this task by reviewing the job requirements. Then select the facts about you that qualify you for the job.

If your application has been invited, you may learn about the job requirements from the source of the invitation. If you are answering an advertisement, study it for the employer's requirements. If you are following up an interview, review the interview for information about job requirements. If you are prospecting, your research and your logical analysis should guide you.

In any event, you are likely to present facts from three background areas: education, experience, and skills and/or personal details. You also may include a fourth—references. But references are not exactly background information. If you include references, they will probably go on a separate reference sheet.

Which facts to include and how much to emphasize each should depend on the job and on your background. Most of the jobs you will seek as a new college graduate will have strong educational requirements. Thus, you should stress your education. When you apply for work after you have accumulated experience, you will probably need to stress experience. As the years go by, experience becomes more and more important—education, less and less important. Your personal characteristics are of some importance for some jobs, especially jobs that involve working with people.

If a résumé accompanies the cover message, your message may rely on it too much. Remember that the message does the selling and the résumé summarizes the significant details. Thus, the message should contain the major points around which you build your case, and the résumé should include these points plus supporting details. As the two are parts of a team effort, somewhere in the message you should refer the reader to the résumé.

Organizing for persuasion You will want to present the information about yourself in the order that is best for you. In general, the plan you select is likely to follow one of three general orders. The most common order is a logical grouping of the information, such as education, experience, and skills and/or personal details. A second possibility is a time order. For example, you could present the information to show a year-by-year preparation for the work. A third possibility is an order based on the job requirements. For example, selling, communicating, and managing might be the requirements listed in an advertised job.

Merely presenting facts does not ensure conviction. You also will need to present the facts in words that make the most of your assets. You could say, for example, that you "held a position" as sales manager; but it is much more convincing to say that you "supervised a sales force of 14." Likewise, you do more for yourself by writing that you "earned a degree in business administration" than by writing that you "spent four years in college." And it is more effective to say that you "learned tax accounting" than to say that you "took a course in tax accounting."

You also can help your case by presenting your facts in reader-viewpoint language wherever this is practical. More specifically, you should work to interpret the facts based on their meaning for your reader and for the work to be done. For example, you could present a cold recital like this one:

> I am 21 years old and have an interest in mechanical operations and processes. Last summer I worked in the production department of a container plant.

Or you could interpret the facts, fitting them to the one job:

> The interest I have held in things mechanical over most of my 21 years would help me fit into one of your technical manufacturing operations. And last summer's experience in the production department of PrintSafe Marking Company is evidence that I can and will work hard.

Since you will be writing about yourself, you may find it difficult to avoid overusing I-references. But you should try. An overuse of *I*'s sounds egotistical and places too much attention on the often repeated word. Some *I*'s, however, should be used. The message is personal. Stripping it of all I-references would rob it of its personal warmth. Thus, you should carefully manage the number of I-references. You want neither too many nor too few.

Overall, you are putting your best foot forward, not only as a prospective employee but also as a person. Carefully shaping the character you are projecting is arguably just as important to the success of your cover message as using convincing logic.

Driving for action in the close The presentation of your qualifications should lead logically to the action that the close proposes. You should drive for whatever action is appropriate in your case. It could be a request for an interview, an invitation to engage in further communication (perhaps to answer the reader's questions), or an invitation to contact references. Rarely would you want to ask for the job in a first message. You are concerned mainly with opening the door to further negotiations.

Your action words should be clear and direct. As in the sales message, the request for action may be made more effective if it is followed by words recalling a benefit that the reader will get from taking the action. The following closes illustrate this technique, although some may think the second may be overly aggressive in some circumstances:

> The highlights of my education and experience show that I have been preparing for a career in human resources. May I now discuss beginning this career with you? You can reach me at 727-921-4113 or by email at owensmith@att.com to talk about how I can help in your human resource work.

> I am very much interested in discussing with you how my skills will contribute to your company's mission. If I do not hear from you by Friday, April 22, I'll call on Monday to arrange a time for a mutually convenient meeting.

Contrasting cover messages Illustrating bad and good techniques, the following two cover messages present the qualifications of Jason L. Andrews, the job seeker described in the workplace scenario at the beginning of the chapter.

The first message (page 336) follows few of the suggestions given in the preceding pages.

It begins with an old-style opening. The first words stating that this is an application are obvious and of little interest. The following presentation of qualifications is a matter-of-fact,

technology in brief

Websites Offer Valuable Interview Advice

The Web is a rich resource for help with interviewing. Your school's career center may have a Web site with interview schedules. Sites such as Monster.com and many of the other online job database sites offer tips on all aspects of interviewing. You can get ideas for questions to ask interviewers, techniques for staying calm, and methods of handling the telephone screening interview. They even include practice interactive virtual interviews with immediate feedback on your answers to questions as well as suggestions and strategies for handling difficult questions. The Monster site includes a planner listing a host of good common-sense tips from polishing your shoes to keeping an interview folder to keeping track of all written and verbal communication. Using these sites to help you prepare for interviews not only will help you feel more confident and interview more effectively, but also can help you evaluate the company as well.

[**The presentation of your qualifications should lead logically to the action that the close proposes.**]

uninterpreted review of information. Little you-viewpoint is evident. In fact, most of the message emphasizes the writer (note the *I*'s), who comes across as bored and selfish. The information presented is scant. The closing action is little more than an I-viewpoint statement of the writer's availability.

The better message (page 337) begins with an interesting question that sets the stage for the following presentation. The review of experience is interpreted by showing how the experience would help in performing the job sought. The review of education is similarly covered. Notice how the interpretations show that the writer knows what the job requires. Notice also that reader-viewpoint is stressed throughout. Even so, a moderate use of *I*'s gives the letter a personal quality and the details show the writer to be a thoughtful, engaged person. The closing request for action is a clear, direct, and courteous question. The final words recall a main appeal of the letter.

You can see several examples of cover letters on pages 338–341. The letters include both solicited and prospecting letters as well as those targeted to specific jobs and those that are more general.

email cover messages An email cover message can take different forms depending on the document file format it introduces. Like other email messages, it needs a clear subject line; like print cover messages, it needs a formal salutation and closing. And its purpose is still to highlight your qualifications for the particular job you are applying for. While it could be identical to one you might create for print, most readers prefer shorter documents onscreen. The primary job of the email cover message is to identify the job, highlight the applicant's strengths, and invite the reader to review the résumé.

Notice how the solicited cover message below quickly gains the reader's attention in the opening, highlights the skills in the body, and calls for action in the close.

To: Kate Troy <kate_troy@thankyoutoo.com>
From: Megan Adami <mmadami@msn.com>
Date: October 1, 2008
Subject: Web Design Intern Position

Dear Ms. Troy:

Yesterday my advisor here at Brown University, Dr. Payton Kubicek, suggested that I contact you about the summer intern position in Web design you recently announced.

At Brown I have taken courses that have given me a good understanding of both the design aspects as well as the marketing functions that a good Web site needs. Additionally, several of my course projects involved working with successful Web-based businesses, analyzing the strengths and weaknesses of their business models.

I would enjoy applying some of these skills in a successful site targeted at the high-end retail customers that Thankyoutoo.com attracts. You will see from my Web page profile at http://www.meganadami.com/ that my design skills complement those on your company's website, allowing me to contribute almost immediately. Please let me know as soon as possible when we can talk further about this summer position.

Sincerely,

Megan Adami
mmadami@gmail.com

LO 6   Explain how you can participate effectively in an interview.

HANDLING THE INTERVIEW

Your initial contact with a prospective employer can be by mail, email, phone, or a personal (face-to-face) visit. Even if you contact the employer by mail, a successful application will eventually involve a personal visit—or an *interview,* as we will call it.

> "The primary job of the email cover message is to identify the job, highlight the applicant's strengths, and invite the reader to review the résumé."

This cover message is dull and poorly written.

Dear Mr. Stark:

This is to apply for a position in marketing with your company.

At present, I am completing my studies in marketing at Olympia State University and will graduate with a Bachelor of Business Administration degree with an emphasis in marketing this May. I have taken all the courses in marketing available to me as well as other helpful courses such as statistics, organizational psychology, and ecommerce.

I have had good working experience as a host and food server, sales associate, and pollster. Please see details on the enclosed résumé. I believe that I am well qualified for a position in marketing and am considering working for a company of your size and description.

Because I must make a decision on my career soon, I request that you write me soon. For your information, I will be available for an interview on March 17 and 18.

Sincerely,

Sometimes, before inviting candidates to a formal interview session, recruiters use phone interviews for preliminary screening. It helps them save time by narrowing the number of applicants to invite to face-to-face interviews and save money by minimizing the costs associated with travel, meals, and overnight expenses.

You can prepare for the phone interview questions as you would a face-to-face interview. However, you can have some of your thoughts written down in front of you. You'll also want to be sure to turn off call waiting so your call isn't interrupted and to take it on a phone with an adequately charged battery. Also, try to take the call in a quiet environment and be prepared to take notes. Be sure to thank the interviewer and to follow it up with a thank-you note, which is covered later in this chapter.

Much of the preceding parts of this chapter concerned the mail contact. Now our interest centers on the interview. In a sense, the interview is the key to the success of the application—the "final examination," so to speak. You should carefully prepare for the interview, as the job may be lost or won in it. The following review of employment interview highlights should help you understand how to deal with the interview in your job search. You will find additional information about interviewing in the resource links on the textbook website.

This better cover message follows textbook instructions.

Dear Mr. Stark:

Is there a place in your marketing department for someone who is well trained in the field and can talk easily and competently with clients? My background, experience, and education have given me these special qualifications.

All my life I have lived and worked with a wide variety of people. I was raised by working parents in a poor section of New York City. While in high school, I worked mornings and evenings in New York's garment district, primarily as a host and food server. For two years, between high school and college, I worked full time as a pollster for Olympia State University. Throughout my four years of college, I worked half time as a sales associate for Old Navy. From these experiences, I have learned to understand marketing. I speak marketing's language and listen carefully to people.

My studies at Olympia State University were specially planned to prepare me for a career in marketing. I studied courses in advertising, marketing research, and integrated marketing communication. In addition, I studied a wide assortment of supporting subjects: economics, business communication, information systems, psychology, interpersonal communication, and operations management. My studies have given me the foundation to learn an even more challenging practical side of marketing work. I plan to begin working in June after I receive the Bachelor of Business Administration degree with honors (3.7 grade point average on a basis of 4.0).

These brief facts and the information in my résumé describe my diligent efforts to prepare for a position in marketing. May I talk with you about beginning that position? You can reach me at 914.967.3117 to arrange an interview to talk about how I could help in your marketing department.

Sincerely,

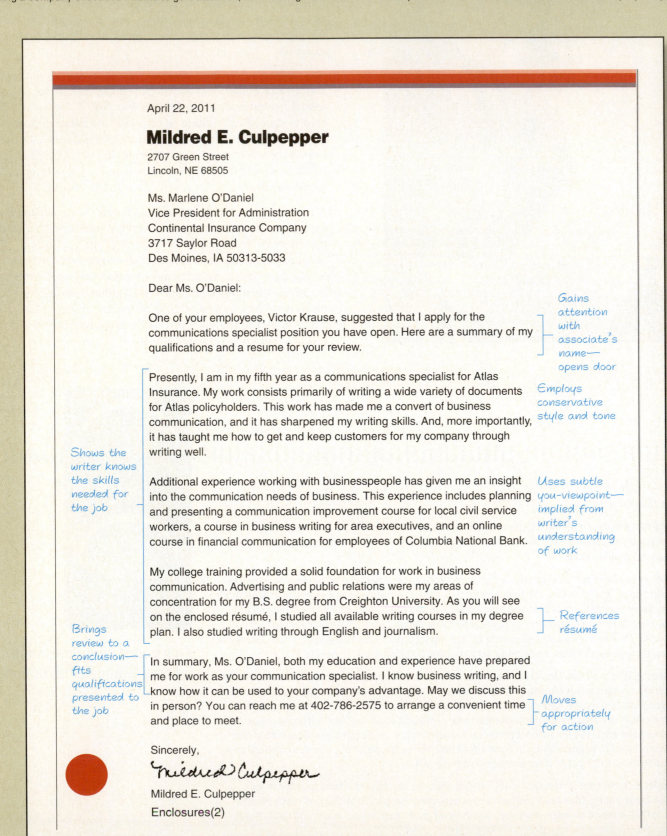

April 22, 2011

Mildred E. Culpepper
2707 Green Street
Lincoln, NE 68505

Ms. Marlene O'Daniel
Vice President for Administration
Continental Insurance Company
3717 Saylor Road
Des Moines, IA 50313-5033

Dear Ms. O'Daniel:

One of your employees, Victor Krause, suggested that I apply for the communications specialist position you have open. Here are a summary of my qualifications and a resume for your review.

Gains attention with associate's name—opens door

Presently, I am in my fifth year as a communications specialist for Atlas Insurance. My work consists primarily of writing a wide variety of documents for Atlas policyholders. This work has made me a convert of business communication, and it has sharpened my writing skills. And, more importantly, it has taught me how to get and keep customers for my company through writing well.

Employs conservative style and tone

Shows the writer knows the skills needed for the job

Additional experience working with businesspeople has given me an insight into the communication needs of business. This experience includes planning and presenting a communication improvement course for local civil service workers, a course in business writing for area executives, and an online course in financial communication for employees of Columbia National Bank.

Uses subtle you-viewpoint—implied from writer's understanding of work

My college training provided a solid foundation for work in business communication. Advertising and public relations were my areas of concentration for my B.S. degree from Creighton University. As you will see on the enclosed résumé, I studied all available writing courses in my degree plan. I also studied writing through English and journalism.

References résumé

Brings review to a conclusion—fits qualifications presented to the job

In summary, Ms. O'Daniel, both my education and experience have prepared me for work as your communication specialist. I know business writing, and I know how it can be used to your company's advantage. May we discuss this in person? You can reach me at 402-786-2575 to arrange a convenient time and place to meet.

Moves appropriately for action

Sincerely,

Mildred Culpepper

Mildred E. Culpepper

Enclosures(2)

A Cover Letter Responding to an Advertisement

Three job requirements listed in an advertisement determined the plan used in this letter. Not only does it include interest and good organization, but it also shows good form with Word 2010's installed Median template.

4407 Sunland Avenue
Phoenix, AZ 85040-9321

July 8, 2011

Ms. Anita O. Alderson, Manager
Tompkins-Oderson Agency, Inc.
3901 Tampico Avenue
Los Angeles, CA 90032-1614

Dear Ms. Alderson:

Uses reader's words for good attention gainer

Sound background in advertising … well trained … works well with others….

Demonstrates ability to write advertising copy through writing style used

These key words in your July 6 advertisement in the *Times* describe the person you want, and I believe I am that person.

Shows clearly what the writer can do on the job through interpretation

I have gained experience in every area of retail advertising while working for the *Lancer*, our college newspaper. I sold advertising, planned layouts, and wrote copy. During the last two summers, I gained firsthand experience working in the advertising department of Wunder & Son. I wrote a lot of copy, some of which I am enclosing for your inspection; you will find numerous other examples on my blog at <http://janekbits.blogspot.com>. This experience clearly will help me contribute to the work in your office.

Shows strong determination through good interpretation

In my major, I studied marketing with a specialization in advertising and integrated marketing communications. My honor grades show that I worked hard, especially on a project using a variety of media raising money for schools in Louisiana, Texas, Mississippi, and Florida's oil spill damaged areas. Understanding the importance of being able to get along well with people, I actively participated in Sigma Chi (social fraternity), the Race for the Cure (breast cancer), and Alpha Kappa Psi (honorary business fraternity). From the experience gained in these associations, I am confident that I can fit in well at Tompkins-Oderson.

Provides good evidence of social skills

Leads smoothly to action

As you can see from this description and the enclosed résumé, I am well qualified for your position in advertising. You can email me at janek@hotmail.com or call and text message me at 602-713-2199 to arrange a convenient time to talk about my joining your team.

Uses a clear and strong drive

Sincerely,

Michael S. Janek

Michael S. Janek

enclosures

A Prospecting Cover Letter

Straightforward prospecting letter targeted and sent as an attached file to a particular receiver. It uses the Origin template from Word 2007.

Jimmy I. Goetz
12712 Sanchez Drive
San Bernadino, CA 92405
Phone: 714-399-2569

Mr. Conrad W. Butler
Office Manager
Darden, Inc.
14326 Butterfield Road
San Francisco, CA 94129

Dear Mr. Butler:

Gains attention with question   Can Darden, Inc., use a hardworking Grossmont College business administration major who wants a career in today's technology-intensive office? My experience, education, and personal qualities qualify me well for this work.   *Sets up rest of letter tightly*

Justifies job search   My five years of work experience (see attached résumé) have taught me the major aspects of office work. For the past two years I have been in charge of payroll at Gynes Manufacturing Company. As the administrator of payroll, I have had to handle all types of office operations, including records management and general communication. Although I am happy at this job, it does not offer the career opportunity I see at Darden.   *Brings out highlights with review of experience*

Complementing my work experience are my studies at Grossmont College. In addition to studying the prescribed courses in my major field of business office technology, I selected electives in Dreamweaver, QuickBooks, and professional speaking to help me in my career objective. And I believe I have succeeded. In spite of full-time employment through most of my time in college, I was awarded the Associate of Arts degree last May with a 3.3 grade point average (4.0 basis). But most important of all, I learned from my studies how office work should be done efficiently.   *Interprets positively*

Sets up action and uses adaptation in concluding statement   In addition, I have the personal qualities that would enable me to fit smoothly into your organization. I like people, and through experience I have learned how to work with them as both a team player and a leader.

I am well prepared for work in office administration, Mr. Butler. May I meet with you to talk about working for Darden? Please call me at 714-399-2569 or email me at jgoetz@gmail.com to arrange an interview.   *Requests action clearly and appropriately*

Sincerely,

Jimmy I. Goetz

Jimmy I. Goetz

April 9, 2011

Written by a recent college graduate seeking her first job, this letter was prepared for use with a number of different types of companies. It's shown on Word 2010's installed Apothecary template.

MARY A. SUNDERLAND

5/17/2011

5 Nicks Landing
Poquoson, VA 23662

Mr. Nevil S. Shannon
Director of Human Resources
Snowdon industries, Inc.
1103 Bosewell Circle
Baltimore, MD 21202

Dear Mr. Shannon:

Effective attention-getting question

Good organization plan set-up

Will you please review my qualifications for work in your management trainee program? My education, work attitude, and personal skills qualify me for this program.

Good interpretation of education

My education for administration consists primarily of four years of business administration study at State University. The Bachelor of Business Administration degree I will receive in June has given me a broad foundation of business knowledge. As a general business major, I studied all the functional fields (management, marketing, information systems, finance, accounting) as well as the other core business subjects (communications, statistics, law, economics, ethics, production, and human resources). I have the knowledge base that will enable me to be productive now. And I can build upon this base through practical experience.

Skillfully handles lack of experience

Individually adapted

As I am seeking my first full-time job, I must use means other than work experience to prove my work attitude. My grade point record at State is evidence that I took my studies seriously and that I worked hard. My 3.8 overall average (4.0 basis) placed me in the top 10 percent of the graduating class. I also worked diligently in student associations. My efforts were recognized by the special assignments and leadership roles you see listed in the enclosed résumé. I assure you that I would bring these work habits with me to Snowdon Industries.

Good use of fact to back up personal qualities

Throughout college, I devoted time to the development of my personal skills. As an active member of the student chapter of the Society for the Advancement of Management, I served as treasurer and program chairperson. I participated in intramural golf and volleyball. And I was an active worker in the Young Republicans, serving as publicity chairperson for three years. All this experience has helped me to have the balance you seek in your administrative trainees.

Good ending message

Clear request for action — flows logically from preceding presentation

These highlights and the additional evidence presented in the enclosed résumé present my case for a career in management. May I have an interview to continue my presentation? You can reach me at 301.594.6942 or marymahoney@yahoo.com. I could be in your office at your convenience to talk about working for Snowdon.

Sincerely,

Mary A. Sunderland

Mary A. Sunderland
Enclosure

Investigating the Company

Before arriving for an interview, you should learn what you can about the company: its products or services, its personnel, its business practices, its current activities, its management. Such knowledge will help you talk knowingly with the interviewer. And perhaps more important, the interviewer is likely to be impressed by the fact that you took the time to investigate the company. That effort might even give you a competitive advantage.

Making a Good Appearance

How you look to the interviewer is a part of your message. Thus, you should work to present just the right image. Interviewers differ to some extent on what that image is, but you would be wise to present a conservative appearance. This means avoiding faddish, offbeat styles, preferring the conservative, conventional business colors such as black, brown, navy, and gray. Remember that the interviewer wants to know whether you fit into the role you are seeking. You should appear to look like you want the job.

Some may argue that such an insistence on conformity in dress and grooming infringes on one's personal freedom. Perhaps it does. We will even concede that employers should not force such biases on you. But you will have to be realistic if you want a successful career. If the people who can determine your future have fixed views on matters of dress and grooming, it is good business sense to respect those views.

Anticipating Questions and Preparing Answers

You should be able to anticipate some of the questions the interviewer will ask. Questions about your education (courses, grades, honors, and such) are usually asked. So are questions about work experience, interests, career goals, location preferences, and activities in organizations. You should prepare answers to these questions in advance. Your answers will then be thorough and correct, and your words will display poise and confidence. Your preparation will also reflect your interest.

In addition to general questions, interviewers often ask more complicated ones. Some of these are designed to test you—to learn your views, your interests, and your ability to deal with difficult problems. Others seek more specific information about your ability to handle the job in question. Although such questions are difficult to anticipate, you should be aware that they are likely to be asked.

Sometimes interviewers will throw in tough or illegal questions to test your poise. These are naturally stressful, but being prepared for these kinds of questions will keep you cool and collected.

The job interview is the final examination of the application process. Appropriate grooming and relaxed, yet enthusiastic behavior are helpful to the applicant's success.

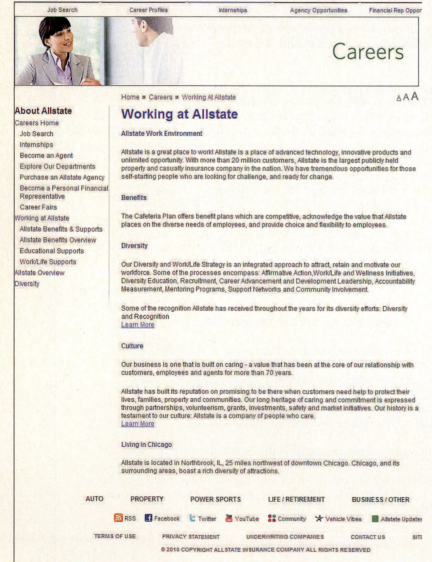

Typical Interview Questions

What can you do for us?

Would you be willing to relocate? To travel?

Do you prefer to work with people or alone?

How well has your performance in the classroom prepared you for this job?

What do you expect to be doing in 10 years? In 20 years?

What income goals do you have for those years (10 and 20 years ahead)?

Why should I rank you above the others I am interviewing?

Why did you choose _____ for your career?

How do you feel about working overtime? Nights? Weekends?

Did you do the best work you are capable of in college?

Is your college record a good measure of how you will perform on the job?

What are the qualities of the ideal boss?

What have you done that shows leadership potential? Teamwork potential?

What are your beginning salary expectations?

"You walk the walk and talk the talk. We need someone who can also blog the blog!"

If you get through these types of questions, some brainteasers or puzzles may be thrown your way. Microsoft often gets credit for starting this trend because the company used it extensively in attempting to hire only the best and brightest employees. Other companies soon followed, often creating their own versions of some of these questions or creating some tougher ones of their own. Many of these questions do not have a right answer; rather, they are designed to elicit an applicant's thinking, logic, and creativity skills. In answering them, be sure that you reason aloud rather than sitting there silently so that you can show you are thinking. Feel free to make assumptions as well as to supply needed information. Giving a good answer the interviewer has not heard before is often a good strategy.

Tough and Illegal Interview Questions

What is your greatest weakness?

With hindsight, how could you have improved your progress?

What kind of decisions are most difficult for you?

What is the worst thing you have heard about this company?

See this pen I'm holding? Sell it to me.

Tell me about a time when you put your foot in your mouth.

What kinds of people do you find it difficult to deal with?

What religion do you practice?

How old are you?

Are you married?

Do you plan to have children?

Martin Yate, *Knock 'em Dead* 2010
(Avon, MA: Adams Media Corp., 2010) 153–252.

Brainteaser or Puzzle Interview Questions

Why are manhole covers round?

Why do mirrors reverse right and left instead of up and down?

How many piano tuners are there in the world?

How many times a day do a clock's hands overlap?

Design a spice rack for a blind person.

Why are beer cans tapered at the top and bottom?

You have eight coins, and one of them is lighter than the others. Find the light coin in two weighings of a pan balance.

William Poundstone, *How Would You Move Mount Fuji?: Microsoft's Cult of the Puzzle: How the World's Smartest Companies Select the Most Creative Thinkers* (Boston, MA: Little, Brown and Company, 2003) 80–86, 118–20.

Recently, the behavioral interview style has become popular with campus recruiters. Rather than just determining your qualifications for the job, interviewers are attempting to verify if you can do the work. They ask questions about current situations because how you behave now is likely to transfer to similar situations in another job.

should be brought to the interviewer's attention. So she asked, "Do you attach any importance to business plans written as class projects in your evaluation?" The anticipated affirmative answer allowed her to show her successful project. For another example, a student who wanted to bring out his knowledge of the prospective employer's operations did so with this question: "Will your company's expansion in the Bakersfield area create new job opportunities there?" How many questions of this sort you should ask will depend on your need to supplement your interviewer's questioning. You might also want to ask questions to determine if the company is a good fit for you such as "How would you describe the work environment?" Your goal should be to make certain that both the interviewer and you get all the information you consider important.

> # Sending a brief thank-you message by letter, email, or phone is an appropriate follow-up step.

For more practice preparing for questions, check the resource links on the textbook Web site.

Putting Yourself at Ease

Perhaps it is easier to say than to do, but you should be at ease throughout the interview. Remember that you are being inspected and that the interviewer should see a calm and collected person. How to appear calm and collected is not easy to explain. Certainly, it involves talking in a clear and strong voice. It also involves controlling your facial expressions and body movements. Developing such controls requires self-discipline—working at it.

You may find it helpful to convince yourself that the stress experienced during an interview is normal. Or you may find it helpful to look at the situation realistically—as merely a conversation between two human beings. Other approaches may work better for you. Use whatever approaches work. Your goal is to control your emotions so that you present the best possible appearance to the interviewer.

Helping to Control the Dialogue

Just answering the questions asked is often not enough. Not only are you being evaluated, but you are evaluating others as well. The questions you ask and the comments you play off them should bring up what you want the interviewer to know about you. Your self-analysis revealed the strong points in your background. Now you should make certain that those points come out in the interview.

How to bring up points about you that the interviewer does not ask is a matter for your imagination. For example, a student seeking a job in advertising believed that a certain class project

LO 7 Write application follow-up messages that are appropriate, friendly, and positive.

FOLLOWING UP AND ENDING THE APPLICATION

The interview is only an early step in the application process. A variety of other steps can follow. Sending a brief thank-you message by letter, email, or phone is an appropriate follow-up step. It not only shows courtesy but also it can give you an advantage because some of your competitors will not do it. If you do not hear from the prospective employer within a reasonable time, it is appropriate to inquire by phone, email, or letter about the status of your application. You should certainly do this if you are under a time limit on another employer's offer. The application process may end with no offer (frequently with no notification at all—a most discourteous way of handling applicants), with a rejection notice, or with an offer. How to handle these situations is reviewed in the following paragraphs.

Writing Follow-up Messages

a thank-you message After an interview it is courteous to write a thank-you message, whether or not you are interested in the job. If you are interested, the message can help your case. It singles you out from the competition and shows your interest in the job.

Such messages are usually short. They begin with an expression of gratitude. They say something about the interview, the job, or such. They take care of any additional business (such

as submitting information requested during the interview). And they end on a goodwill note—perhaps a hopeful look to the next step in the negotiations. The following message does these things:

Dear Mr. Tesone:

Thank you for talking with me yesterday. You were most helpful, and you did a good job of selling me on Sony Corporation of America.

As you requested, I have enclosed samples of the financial analysis I developed as a class project. If you need anything more, please let me know.

I look forward to the possibility of discussing employment with you soon.

Sincerely,

a follow-up to an application When a prospective employer is late in responding or you receive another offer with a time deadline, you may need to write a follow-up message. Employers are often just slow, but sometimes they lose

the application. Whatever the explanation, a follow-up message may help to produce action.

Such a message is a form of routine inquiry. As a reason for writing, it can use the need to make a job decision or some other good explanation. The following message is an example:

Dear Ms. Yang:

Because the time is approaching when I must make a job decision, will you please tell me the status of my application with you?

You may recall that you interviewed me in your office November 7. You wrote me November 12 indicating that I was among those you had selected for further consideration.

SAIC remains one of the organizations I would like to consider in making my career decision. I will very much appreciate hearing from you by December 3.

Sincerely,

a job acceptance Job acceptances in writing are merely favorable response messages with an extra amount of goodwill. Because the message should begin directly, a yes answer in the beginning is appropriate. The remainder of the message should contain a confirmation of the starting date and place and comments about the work, the company, the interview—whatever you would say if you were face to face with the reader. The message need not be long. This one does the job well:

Dear Ms. Garcia:

Yes, I accept your offer of employment. After my first interview with you, I was convinced that Allison-Caldwell was the organization for me. It is good to know that you think I am right for Allison-Caldwell.

Following your instructions, I will be in your Tampa headquarters on May 28 at 8:30 am ready to work for you.

Sincerely,

a message refusing a job

Messages refusing a job offer follow the indirect refusal pattern. One good technique is to begin with a friendly comment—perhaps something about past relations with the company. Next, explain and present the refusal in clear yet positive words. Then end with a more friendly comment. This example illustrates the plan:

Dear Mr. Chen:

Meeting you and the other people at Northern was a genuine pleasure. Thank you for sharing so much information and for the generous job offer that followed.

In considering the offer, I reflected on the many topics we discussed, particularly on the opportunity to work abroad. While I have accepted an offer with a firm that has extensive opportunities along these lines, I was very impressed with all I learned about Northern.

I appreciate the time and the courteous treatment you gave me.

Sincerely,

a resignation

At some point in your career you are likely to resign from one job to take another. When this happens, probably you will inform your employer of your resignation orally. But when you find it more practical or comfortable, you may choose to resign in writing. In some cases, you may do it both ways. As a matter of policy, some companies require a written resignation even after an oral resignation has been made. Or you may prefer to give a written resignation following your oral announcement of it.

Your resignation should be as positive as the circumstances permit. Even if your work experiences have not been pleasant, you will be wise to depart without a final display of anger. As an anonymous philosopher once explained, "When you write a resignation in anger, you write the best letter you will ever regret."

The indirect order is usually the best strategy for negative messages like a resignation. But many are written in the direct

> After an interview it is courteous to write a thank-you message, whether or not you are interested in the job.

order. They present the resignation right away, following it with expressions of gratitude, favorable comments about past working experiences, and the like. Either approach is acceptable. Even so, you would do well to use the indirect order, for it is more likely to build the goodwill and favorable thinking you want to leave behind you.

The example below shows the indirect order, which is well known to you. It begins with a positive point—one that sets up the negative message. The negative message follows, clearly yet positively stated. The ending returns to positive words chosen to build goodwill and fit the case.

Dear Ms. Shuster:

Working as your assistant for the past five years has been a genuinely rewarding experience. Under your direction I have grown as an administrator. And I know you have given me a practical education in retailing.

As you may recall from our past discussions, I have been pursuing the same career goals that you held early in your career. So you will understand why I am now resigning to accept a store

> ## NEARLY AS IMPORTANT AS KEEPING YOUR RÉSUMÉ UPDATED IS KEEPING UP ON YOUR PROFESSIONAL READING.

management position with Lawson's in Belle River. I would like my employment to end on the 31st, but I could stay a week or two longer if needed to help train my replacement.

I leave with only good memories of you and the other people with whom I worked. Thanks to all of you for a valuable contribution to my career.

Sincerely,

LO 8 Maintain your job-search activities.

Continuing Job-Search Activities

Some authorities recommend continuing your job search two weeks into a new job. It provides insurance if you should discover the new job isn't what you expected. In any case, continuously keeping your finger on the pulse of the job market is a good idea. Not only does it provide you with information about changes occurring in your field, but it also keeps you alert to better job opportunities as soon as they are announced.

maintaining your résumé While many people intend to keep their résumés up to date, they just do not make it a priority. Some others make it easy by updating as changes occur. And a few update their résumés at regularly designated times such as a birthday, New Year's Day, or even the anniversary of their employment. No matter what works best for you, updating your résumé as you gain new accomplishments and skills is important. Otherwise, you will be surprised to find how easily you can lose track of important details.

reading job ads/professional journals Nearly as important as keeping your résumé updated is keeping up on your professional reading. Most trade or professional journals have job notices or boards you should check regularly. These ads give you insight into what skills are in demand, perhaps helping you choose assignments where you get the opportunity to develop new skills. Staying up to date in your field can be stimulating; it can provide both challenges and opportunities. ■

Get Online

mhhe.com/FlatleyM2e

for study materials including quizzes and Internet resources.

endnotes

CHAPTER 1

1. Chuck Martin, *Tough Management: The 7 Winning Ways to Make Tough Decisions Easier, Deliver the Numbers, and Grow the Business in Good Times and Bad* (New York: McGraw-Hill, 2005): 1, print.

2. Lindsey Gerdes, "The Best Places to Launch a Career," *Bloomberg BusinessWeek*, Bloomberg L. P., 14 Sept. 2009, Web, 4 Mar. 2010.

3. National Association of Colleges and Employers (NACE), "Employers Cite Qualities, Attributes of 'Perfect' Job Candidate," *NACE*, National Association of Colleges and Employers, 29 Jan. 2009, Web, 3 Mar. 2010.

4. Ronald Alsop, "Business Schools: The Recruiters' Picks (a Special Report)," *The Wall Street Journal* 17 Sept. 2007, Eastern ed.: R3, print.

5. Ping Lin, Debra Grace, Sudha Krishnan, and Jeanette Gilsdorf, "Failure to Communicate," *The CPA Journal* 80.1 (2010): 63–66; *ProQuest*, Web, 4 Mar. 2010.

6. "Study Offers Insights on Effective Communication from the Perspective of Employees," *Towers Perrin Monitor*, Towers Perrin HR Services, 7 Jan. 2005, Web, 3 Mar. 2010.

7. "The Challenge Facing Workers in the Future," *HR Focus* Aug. 1999: 6 ff, print.

8. Lynn A. Karoly and Constantijn W. A. Panis, *The 21st Century at Work: Forces Shaping the Future Workforce and Workplace in the United States* (Santa Monica, CA: RAND Corporation, 2004); *RAND Corporation,* Web, 4 Mar. 2010.

9. Karoly and Panis xiv.

10. See Aneel Karnani, "The Case Against Corporate Social Responsibility," *WSJ.com*, Dow Jones & Company, Inc., 23 Aug. 2010, Web, 4 Sept. 2010.

11. Geoffrey B. Sprinkle and Laureen A. Maines, "The Benefits and Costs of Corporate Social Responsibility," *BusinessHorizons* 53.5 (2010): 445–453, *OhioLINK Electronic Journal Center*, Web, 4 Sept. 2010; "Generation G: That Would Be G for 'Generosity,' not G for 'Greed,':" *trendwatching.com*, trendwatching.com, Feb. 2009, Web, 4 Sept. 2010.

12. See Edgar H. Schein, *Organizational Culture and Leadership,* 3rd ed. (San Francisco: Jossey-Bass, 2004), which reviews the literature and offers a current perspective.

13. For discussions of problem solving, see John R. Hayes, *The Complete Problem Solver*, 2nd ed. (Hillsdale, NJ: Lawrence Erlbaum, 1989); Janet E. Davidson and Robert J. Sternberg, eds., *The Psychology of Problem Solving* (Cambridge, UK: Cambridge University Press, 2003); Rosemary J. Stevenson, *Language, Thought, and Representation* (Chichester, UK: John Wiley, 1993); and Arthur B. VanGundy, *Techniques of Structured Problem Solving* (New York: Van Nostrand Reinhold, 1988).

14. See Dorothy A. Winsor, *Writing Power: Communication in an Engineering Center* (Albany: SUNY Press, 2003).

CHAPTER 2

1. Paula Wasley, "Tests Aren't Best Way to Evaluate Graduates' Skills, Business Leaders Say in Survey," *Chronicle of Higher Education*, The Chronicle, Jan. 2008, Web, 23 Jan. 2008.

2. Robert H. Lengel and Richard L. Daft, "The Selection of Communication Media as an Executive Skill," *The Academy of Management Executive* 2.3 (1988): 226, print.

3. Bob Rosner, "How to Keep Your Privacy in the Workplace," *Working Wounded*, ABC News.com, 13 July 2007, Web, 16 Mar. 2010.

4. Heidi Schultz, *The Elements of Electronic Communication* (Boston: Allyn and Bacon, 2000) 43–47, print.

5. Sheryl Lindsell-Roberts, *135 Tips on Email and Instant Messages: Plus Blogs, Chatrooms, and Texting* (Boston: Houghton Mifflin Harcourt, 2008) 18, print.

6. Janis Fisher Chan, *E-Mail: A Write It Well Guide—How to Write and Manage E-Mail in the Workplace.* (Oakland, CA: Write It Well, 2008) 198, print.

7. Vera Terminella and Marcia G. Reed, *Email: Communicate Effectively* (Upper Saddle River, NJ: Pearson Education, 2003) 13, print.

8. Teddy Wayne, "Drilling Down: Social Networks Eclipse Email," *The New York Times*, The New York Times Company, 18 May 2009, Web, 21 May 2009.

9. Jake Swearingen, "Four Ways Social Networking Can Build Business," *bnet.com*, CBS Interactive, 2009, Web, 8 May 2009.

10. Jackie Ford, "Why Employers Should Reconsider Facebook Fishing," *MarketWatch.com, The Wall Street Journal* Digital Network, 11 Feb. 2009, Web, 8 May 2009.

CHAPTER 3

1. Stephen Few, *Now You See It: Simple Visualization Techniques for Quantitative Analysis*, Oakland, CA: Analytic Press, 2009, 1, print.

2. Sabrina Bresciani and Martin J. Eppler, "The Benefits of Synchronous Collaborative Information Visualization: Evidence from an Experimental Evaluation," *IEEE Transactions on Visualization and Computer Graphics* 15.6 (2009): 1073–1080, print.

3. Anne Bamford, *The Visual Literacy White Paper (Adobe.com)*, 2003, Web, 12 April 2010.

4. Jane E. Miller, "Implementing 'Generalization, Example, Exceptions (GEE),'" *The Chicago Guide to Writing about Numbers: The Effective Presentation of Quantitative Information* (Chicago: The University of Chicago Press, 2004): 265, print.

5. For an excellent expanded discussion and more examples of errors in charts and graphs, see Bill "MrExcel" Jelen, "Knowing When Someone is Lying to You with a Chart," *Charts and Graphs for Microsoft Office Excel 2007* (Indianapolis, IN: Que Publishing, 2007).

6. "Average Annual Full-time Undergraduate Resident Tuition & Fees," *Minnesota Office of Higher Education*, 2010, Web, 12 April 2010.

7. "US Internet Population Diversifies," eMarketer, 9 April 2010, Web, April 2010.

8. Dyan Machan, "Business By Avatar," *Smart Money*, April 2010, 36, print.

9. "B2B Sales Pros Turn to LinkedIn," *eMarketer Digital Intelligence*, 9 April 2010, Web, 12 April 2010.

10. George I. Long, "Employer-provided 'Quality-of-life' Benefits for Workers in Private Industry," Compensation and Working Conditions, Bureau of Labor Statistics, 24 October 2007, Web 10 August 2009.

11. *The Wall Street Journal*, February 8, 2010.

12. *The Wall Street Journal*, April 9, 2009.

13. Theophilus B. A. Addo, "The Effects of Dimensionality in Computer Graphics," *Journal of Business Communication* 31 (1994): 253, print.

14. "B2B Sales Pros Turn to LinkedIn," *eMarketer Digital Intelligence*, 15 April 2010, Web, 15 April 2010.

15. Adapted from "Million Dollar Club," *Wall Street Journal*, March 18, 2009, p. A1, print.

16. Justin Smith, "December Data on Facebook's US Growth by Age and Gender: Beyond 100 Million," 04 January 2010, Web, April 16, 2010.

17. Jon Gibs, "Is Social Media Impacting How Much We Email?, *Nielsenwire*, 09 September 28, 2009, Web, 17 April 2010.

18. Adapted from "The Argument for and Against Oil Abundance," *Bloomberg Businessweek*, 18 January 2010, 48, Print.

19. Adapted from "The Globalization of White Collar Work: The Facts and Fallout of Next-Generation Offshoring," Booz & Company/Duke University Offshoring Network, 2006, Web 20 August 2009.

20. Deere & Co., *Yahoo! Finance*, Web, 27 July 2010.

21. Ships Map, *MarineTraffic.com*, Web, 8 Feb 2010.

22. Carl Bialik, "Justice—Wait for It—on the Checkout Line," *Wall Street Journal*, 19 August 09, Web, 17 April 2010.

23. Bill Hill, Microsoft Project Manager, video interview, 29 May 2006.

CHAPTER 7

1. Rich Gray, "Spamitize Your Inbox," *Smart Computing in Plain English 8.7* (2000): 66, *Smart Computing*, Web, 16 Apr. 2010.

2. "Effective E-Mail: The Seven Golden Rules You Know (But May Forget to Follow)," *eMarketer*, eMarketer, 10 Mar. 2006, Web, 16 Apr. 2010.

3. See Helen Rothschild Ewald and Roberta Vann, "'You're a Guranteed Winner': Composing 'You' in a Consumer Culture," *Journal of Business Communication* 40 (2003): 98–117, print.

4. Charles A. Hill, "The Psychology of Rhetorical Images," *Defining Visual Rhetorics*, ed. Charles A. Hill and Marguerite Helmers (Mahwah, NJ: Lawrence Erlbaum, 2004) 30–38, print.

5. Jim Sterne and Anthony Priore, *Email Marketing: Using Email to Reach Your Target Audience and Build Customer Relationships* (New York: John Wiley & Sons, 2000) 143, print.

6. For further information, visit the Federal Trade Commission website at <www.flc.gov/spam/>.

7. Nick Usborne, as quoted in Sterne and Priore, *Email Marketing* 151.

8. Alan Weiss, *How to Write a Proposal That's Accepted Every Time,* expanded 2nd ed. (Peterborough, NH: Kennedy Information, Inc., 2003) 13, print.

9. "What a Private Sector Company Can Learn From Government Proposals," *CapturePlanning.com*, CapturePlanning.com, 2007, Web, 16 Apr. 2010.

CHAPTER 8

1. Leah Graham and Panagiotis Takis Metaxas, "'Course It's True; I Saw It on the Internet!': Critical Thinking in the Internet Era," *Communications of the ACM* 46.5 (2003): 73, print.

2. William G. Zikmund et al., *Business Research Methods*, 8th ed. (Mason, OH: South-Western, 2009) 398, print.

3. Zikmund, 395.

4. Equivalent interval techniques (developed by L. L. Thurstone), scalogram analysis (developed by Louis Guttman), and the semantic differential (developed by C. E. Osgood, G. J. Suci, and P. H. Tannenbaum) are more complex techniques.

5. Two especially good resources are Allan R. Cohen and Stephen L. Fink, *Effective Behavior in Organizations*, 7th ed. (New York: McGraw-Hill/Irwin, 2002) and Gerald L. Wilson, *Groups in Context: Leadership and Participation in Small Groups*, 6th ed. (New York: McGraw-Hill, 2001).

CHAPTER 9

1. See Joyce Wycoff, "5–15 Reports: Communication for Dispersed Organizations," *InnovationNetwork.biz*, InnovationNetwork 2001, Web, 20 May 2010, and Pat Croce, "Catching the 5:15—A Simple Reporting System Can Help You Keep Tabs on Your Business," *CNNMoney.com*, Cable News Network, 1 Mar. 2004, Web, 20 May 2010.

CHAPTER 10

1. Nick Souter, *Persuasive Presentations: How to Get the Response You Need* (New York: Sterling Publishing, 2007), print.

2. Kennard T. Wing, "Simple Secrets of Power Presenters," *Strategic Finance* 90.12 (2009): 21–23, *Business Source Premier*, EBSCO, Web, 24 May 2010.

3. For a revealing review on the strengths and weaknesses of slideware, see "Learning to Love PowerPoint" by David Byrne and "Power Corrupts. PowerPoint Corrupts. Absolutely." by Edward R. Tufte, both in *Wired,* September 2003.

4. Two excellent sources for more in-depth detail on using presentation applications are Nancy Duarte's *Slide:ology. The Art and Science of Creating Great Presentations*, (O'Reilly: Canada) 2008, and Rick Altman's *Why PowerPoint Presentations Still Suck & How You Can Make Them Even Better*, (Harvest Books: Pleaston, CA) 2nd ed., 2009.

CHAPTER 11

1. Cheryl Soltis, "Eagle-Eyed Employers Scour Résumé for Little White Lies," *The Wall Street Journal*, 21 March 2006: B7, print.

2. Elizabeth Garone, "Job Hunting Under the Boss's Nose," *The Wall Street Journal*, 22 June 2010: D4, print.

credits

CHAPTER 1

Page 2: © Ryan McVay/Getty Images; 8: © From www.corpwatch.org; 8: © GRANTLAND® Copyright Grantland Enterprises, www.grantland.net; 9: © From John Deere website; 11: © Saxpix.com/age fotostock; 12: © Creatas/JupiterImage.

CHAPTER 2

Page 20: © Stockbyte/Getty Images; 27: © Image Source/PunchStock; 28: © STOCK4B-RoyaltyFree/Image Source; 30: Courtesy of Verizon Wireless Multimedia Library; 31: © http://www.sangreat.net/free-cartoons/; 34: © Bloomberg via Getty Images; 35: © Reprinted with permission of Artizans; 36: © Copyright © 2010 Dell Inc. All Rights Reserved. Reprinted with permission.

CHAPTER 3

Page 38: © fStop/Getty Images; 45: © The McGraw-Hill Companies, Inc./John Flournoy, photographer; 46: © "Reprinted with permission of Smart Money, Dyan Machan, "Business By Avatar," April 2010, p. 36. Copyright © 2010 Dow Jones & Company, Inc. All Rights Reserved Worldwide."; 53: From MarineTraffic.com, 28 February 2010. Reprinted with permission; 55: © Tony Watson/Alamy; 56: © Reprinted with permission of Zeke Smith, © 2003; 57: © Reprinted with permission by David Carpenter.

CHAPTER 4

Page 64: © Tetra Images/Corbis; 72: © amana images inc./Alamy; 74: © GRANTLAND® Copyright Grantland Enterprises, www.grantland.net; 75: © Digital Visions/Getty Images; 76: © Huntstock/Getty Images; 77: © Image Source/Alamy; 78: © Freudenthal Verhagen/Getty Images; 79: © Jon Parker Lee/Alamy; 82: © Chris Garrett/Getty Images; 86: © Rich Reid/Getty Images; 89: Courtesy of Stephanie Crown; 90: © Photodisc/Getty Images; 90: © Katheryn Lemieux, King Features Syndicate; 91: © Masterfile Royalty Free; 92: © Copyright © Randy Glasbergen. Reprinted with permission.

CHAPTER 5

Page 94: © Ingram Publishing/SuperStock; 97: © Stockbyte/Punchstock Images; 98: © Biddiboo/Getty Images; 101: © Alexander Walter/Getty; 102: © From The Wall Street Journal, permission Cartoon Features Syndicate; 109: © Purestock/Getty Images; 119: © Blend Images/Alamy.

CHAPTER 6

Page 126: © Ingram Publishing/SuperStock; 130: © L. Clarke/Corbis; 134: © Toru Hanai/Reuters/Landov; 135: Courtesy of Stephanie Crown; 136: © Scott Linnett/San Diego Union Tribune; 137: © Bob Jacobson/Corbis; 139: © Ted Goff, www.tedgoff.com. Reprinted with permission; 143: © D. Hurst/Alamy; 149: © Ted Goff, www.tedgoff.com. Reprinted with permission.

CHAPTER 7

Page 150: © Photodisc/Getty Images; 152: © JupiterImages/Brand X/Alamy; 153 top: © Michael Kelley/Getty Images; 153 bottom: © Ralph Henning/Alamy; 154: © Kuttig - Travel/Alamy; 155: © Image Source/Corbis; 157 top: © Newmann/Corbis; 157 bottom: © Digital Visions/Getty Images; 161: © Red Chopsticks/Getty Images; 162: © Jim Whitmer; 163: © Frank Herholdt/Getty Images; 164 top: © moodboard/Alamy; 164 bottom: © Milk Processors of America/AP Images; 166, 167: Courtesy of Marie Flatley; 168: © RubberBall/Alamy; 181 left: © Photodisc/age footstock; 181 right: © Jonathan Fredin/AP Images; 184: © moodboard/Alamy; 192: © VEER Mark Adams/Getty Images; 193: © Ted Goff, www.tedgoff.com. Reprinted with permission.

CHAPTER 8

Page 194: © Janis Christie/Getty Images; 199: © Digital Vision/Getty Images; 201: © LWA-Dann Tardif/Corbis; 201: © Copyright 2010 LexisNexis, a division of Reed Elsevier Inc. All Rights Reserved. LexisNexis and the Knowledge Burst logo are registered trademarks of Reed Elsevier Properties Inc. and are used with the permission of LexisNexis; 207: From © www.hoovers.com; 210: © Copyright © InfoSpace, Inc. Reprinted with permission; 211: © Copyright © InfoSpace, Inc. Reprinted with permission; 213: © Alta Vista Search page; 217: © Digital Vision/Alamy; 225: © Keith Brofsky/Getty Images; 225: © Reprinted with permission; 238: © Stockbyte/Getty Images.

CHAPTER 9

Page 240: © Janis Christie/Getty Images; 246: © Left Lane Productions/Corbis; 247: © Reprinted with permission of CartoonStock.com, www.cartoonstock.com; 248: © Comstock/JupiterImages; 251: © From Lesikar's Business Communication: Connecting in a Digital World 12E by Kathryn Rentz, Marie E. Flatley and Paula Lentz 12E, pp. 350-358. Reproduced with permission of The McGraw-Hill Companies, Inc; 253: © Reprinted with permission of eMarketer; 268: © 2009 Ted Goff, www.tedgoff.com. Reprinted with permission; 270: © Tribune Media Services, Inc. All Rights Reserved. Reprinted with permission.

CHAPTER 10

Page 272: © Digital Vision; 275: © Digital Vision/Getty Images; 276: © Blend Images/Jose Luis Pelaez Inc/Getty Images; 277: © John A. Rizzo/Digital Vision/Getty Images; 279: © Ron Levine/Digital Vision/Getty Images; 281: © ZITS © 2001 ZITS Partnership, King Features Syndicate; 282: © BananaStock/Jupiterimages; 283: © Courtesy of GoToMeeting, a Citrix Online Service; 284: © Ron Chapple Stock/Alamy; 285: © From The Wall Street Journal, permission Cartoon Features Syndicate; 286: Reprinted with permission of Chick Dietrich; 287: © Triangle Images/Digital Vision/Getty Images; 289: © Ryan McVay/Getty Images; 291: © Eric Andras/Photoalto/Getty Images; 294: © Andres Rodriguez/Alamy; 295: Courtesy of ELMO USA CORP; 297: © Cartoon by John S. Pritchett. Reprinted with permission; 298: © Digital Vision/Getty Images; 299: © This screenshot has been reproduced by McGraw-Hill with the permission of Cisco Systems Inc. and/or its affiliated entities. © Cisco Systems, Inc. and/or its affiliated entities. All rights reserved. Cisco WebEx and Meeting Center are trademarks or registered trademarks of Cisco Systems, Inc. and/or its affiliated entities.

CHAPTER 11

Page 300: © Spike Mafford/Getty Images; 303: © Copyright © Randy Glasbergen. Reprinted with permission; 304: © Jeff Greenberg/The Image Works; 306A: Used with permission of the Orlando Sentinel; 306B: TwitJobSearch.com is a product of WorkDigital Ltd. Reprinted with permission; 307: © Patagonik Works/Getty Images; 308: Reprinted with permission of Visual VC, Inc. 315: © 2009 Anne Gibbons, King Features Syndicate; 322: Reprinted with permission of Visual VC, Inc. 332: Bloomberg via Getty Images; 337: © Yuri Arcurs/Alamy; 342: © Digital Vision; 343: © Tribune Media Services, Inc. All Rights Reserved. Reprinted with permission; 345: © Tetra Images/Getty Images; 346: Courtesy of Marie Flatley.

"Get Online" photos (all chapters): © BLOOM Image/Getty Images

SUPPLEMENTARY CHAPTER B

Page B-6: © From QuickAndDirtyTips.com, Copyright © 2010, reprinted by permission of St. Martin's Griffin, an imprint of St. Martin's Press, LLC.

SUPPLEMENTARY CHAPTER C

Page C-3: © From www.xe.com; C-3: © Reprinted with permission of Luuk Van Waes.